WALKING IN AUSTRIA

by
Kev Reynolds

2 POLICE SQUARE, MILNTHORPE, CUMBRIA LA7 7PY
www.cicerone.co.uk

MOUNTAIN SAFETY

All mountain activities have their dangers, and the routes described in this book are no exception. Anyone who walks or climbs in the Alps should recognise this fact and take responsibility for themselves and their companions along the way. While the author and publisher have made every effort to ensure that the information contained herein was correct when the guide went to press, they cannot accept responsibility for any loss, injury or inconvenience sustained by any person using this book.

International Mountain Distress Signal
(To be used in emergency only)
Six blasts on a whistle (and flashes with a torch after dark) spaced evenly for one minute, followed by a minute's pause. Repeat until an answer is received. The response is three signals per minute followed by a minute's pause.

The following signals are used to communicate with a helicopter – in an emergency only:

Help required:
raise both arms
above head to
form a 'V'

Help not required:
raise one arm above
head, extend other
arm downward

Note i: *mountain rescue can be very expensive – be adequately insured*
Note ii: *mountain rescue is free to members of the Austrian Alpine Club (see Appendix A)*

Emergency telephone number: 140 (mountain rescue)

ABOUT THE AUTHOR

Kev Reynolds first led mountain holidays in Austria in 1967, since when he has returned to walk, trek and climb there on numerous occasions. A freelance author and photojournalist, he has written and illustrated brochures on walking in Austria for the Austrian National Tourist Office, produced publicity material for local tourist authorities there, and organised walking holidays for travel companies in several Austrian provinces. A member of the Alpine Club, Austrian Alpine Club, and the Outdoor Writers and Photographers Guild, Kev was the first honorary member of the British Association of International Mountain Leaders (BAIML). He is author of more than 40 books, including guides to the Alps, Pyrenees and Himalaya, and several on walking in southern England. In 2013 Cicerone published a collection of short stories and anecdotes gathered from Kev's 50-year mountain career, with the title *A Walk in the Clouds*. When not trekking or climbing in one of the world's great ranges, he lives among what he calls 'the Kentish Alps' and during the winter months travels throughout Britain to share his enthusiasm for the high places in a variety of lectures. Check him out on www.kevreynolds.co.uk.

Alpine titles by the same author, published by Cicerone Press:

100 Hut Walks in the Alps

Alpine Pass Route

Alpine Points of View

Central Switzerland

Chamonix to Zermatt

Ecrins National Park

The Bernese Alps

The Swiss Alps

Tour of Mont Blanc

Tour of the Jungfrau Region

Tour of the Oisans: The GR54

Tour of the Vanoise

Trekking in the Alps

Trekking in the Silvretta and Rätikon Alps (forthcoming)

Walking in the Alps

Walking in the Valais

Walking in Ticino

Walks in the Engadine

© Kev Reynolds 2009
First edition 2009
ISBN-13: 978 1 85284 538 4
Reprinted 2011 and 2014 (with updates)
Printed in China on behalf of Latitude Press Ltd.
A catalogue record for this book is available from the British Library.
All photographs are by the author.

For mountain lovers everywhere.

ACKNOWLEDGEMENTS

In four decades of enjoyment of the Austrian Alps I have benefited from the kindness, generosity and hospitality of countless people. In particular I have Marian Telsnig (one-time Press Officer at the ANTO) to thank for giving me many opportunities to explore her mountains and introduce them to others. Subsequent staff of the ANTO (too many to mention by name) have also been extremely helpful, as were Elke Basler at the Carinthia Tourist Office, and Horst Kaschnig, mountain guide in Bad Eisenkappel, who showed me around the Karawanken range. The late Cecil Davies, author of the first Cicerone guide to Austria, was always generous with information and advice, whilst officials at the YHA, Inghams and Thomson Holidays enabled me at various times to earn money in Austria by doing what I love most. It was a pleasure and a privilege to lead literally scores of walkers on routes in these mountains, and I gained much from them all. To Alan Henson, Dave Horley, Grazyna Tlaczala and Lise Winther, my thanks for update information. As ever, I'm in awe of the Cicerone team in Milnthorpe who have managed to create this guide-book from my skeleton manuscript with their skills and talents – my thanks too for their continued friendship, which counts for much. And lastly, for all the days and trails, huts, camps and cols we've shared in mountains around the world, my love and gratitude for my wife makes this her book as much as it is mine.

Advice to Readers

While every effort is made by our authors to ensure the accuracy of guidebooks as they go to print, changes can occur during the lifetime of an edition. If we know of any, there will be an Updates tab on this book's page on the Cicerone website (www.cicerone.co.uk), so please check before planning your trip. We also advise that you check information about such things as transport, accommodation and shops locally. Even rights of way can be altered over time. We are always grateful for information about any discrepancies between a guidebook and the facts on the ground, sent by email to info@cicerone.co.uk or by post to Cicerone, 2 Police Square, Milnthorpe LA7 7PY, United Kingdom.

Front cover: Crossing the Keesbach below the Plauener Hut (Route 32)

CONTENTS

Map Key 9
Overview Map 10

INTRODUCTION
Austria's Alps 13
Mountain Flowers 19
Wildlife 22
Getting There 24
Transport within Austria 26
Accommodation 27
The Austrian Alpine Club 31
The Routes 32
Equipment 37
Recommended Maps 38
Using this Guide 39

1 RÄTIKON ALPS
Introduction 43
Route 1   Douglass Hut – Lünersee Circuit – Douglass Hut 49
Route 2   Douglass Hut – Totalp Hut – Lünersee Alm – Douglass Hut 50
Route 3   Douglass Hut – Schesaplana 52
Route 4   Douglass Hut – Cavelljoch – Douglass Hut 53
Route 5   Rätikon Höhenweg Nord 55
Route 6   Tschagguns – Lindauer Hut 61
Route 7   Tilisuna Hut – Sulzfluh 63

2 SILVRETTA ALPS
Introduction 67
Route 8   Gaschurn – Tübinger Hut 73
Route 9   Tübinger Hut – Hochmaderer Joch – Bielerhöhe 74
Route 10   Bielerhöhe – Saarbrucker Hut 77
Route 11   Wiesbadener Hut – Litzner Sattel – Saarbrucker Hut 79
Route 12   Bielerhöhe – Wiesbadener Hut – Radsattel – Bielerhöhe 80
Route 13   Galtür – Jamtal Hut 85
Route 14   Hut to Hut across the Silvretta Alps 89

3 ÖTZTAL ALPS
Introduction 92
Route 15   Hut to Hut across the Ötztal Alps 103

Walks in the Ötztal
Route 16   Obergurgl – Schönwies Hut – Rotmoostal 111
Route 17   Obergurgl) – Schönwies Hut) – Langtalereck Hut 114
Route 18   Langtalereck Hut – Hochwilde Haus 116

4 STUBAI ALPS
Introduction 121

Walks in the Sulztal
Route 19   Circular Walk from Gries-im-Sulztal..................... 131
Route 20   Gries-im-Sulztal – Winnebachsee Hut 132
Route 21   Gries-im-Sulztal – Sulztalalm – Amberger Hut 134
Route 22   Hut to Hut in the northwest Stubai Alps 139

Walks in the Stubaital
Route 23   Neder – Pinnisalm – Innsbrucker Hut..................... 143
Route 24   Ranalt – Nürnberger Hut 147
Route 25   Nürnberger Hut – Niederl – Grünausee 148
Route 26   Oberiss – Franz Senn Hut 151
Route 27   Franz Senn Hut – Rinnensee......................... 152
Route 28   The Stubaier Höhenweg............................ 155

5 ZILLERTAL ALPS
Introduction 161
Route 29   Ramsau – Laberg – Mayrhofen 169
Route 30   Mayrhofen – Finkenberg – Mayrhofen 170
Route 31   Mayrhofen – Niedermoor – Penkenalm 173
Route 32   Zillergrund Reservoir – Plauener Hut 175
Route 33   Madseit – Höllenstein Hut – Lanersbach.................. 178
Route 34   Breitlahner – Berliner Hut.......................... 181
Route 35   Schlegeis Reservoir – Pfitscher-Joch-Haus 185

Hut to Hut in the Zillertal Alps
Route 36   The Berliner Höhenweg 187
Route 37   The Zillertal Höhenweg 191

6 KITZBÜHELER ALPS
Introduction 194

Walks from Söll and Ellmau
Route 38   Söll – Scheffau 203
Route 39   Ellmau – Hochsöll 206
Route 40   Ellmau – Panoramaweg – Rahnhartalm – Ellmau.............. 208

Walks from Westendorf and Brixen
Route 41   Westendorf – Brixen – Westendorf 210
Route 42   Westendorf – Nachsöllberg – Einködlscharte – Westendorf........ 214
Route 43   Westendorf – Brechhornhaus – Talkaser 217

Route 44 Westendorf – Gampenkogel – Talkaser 219
Route 45 Westendorf – Einködlscharte – Brixenbachgraben Valley – Brixen. . . . 220
Route 46 Brixen – Hochbrixen – Söll 222

Walks from Kitzbühel
Route 47 Kitzbühel – Schwarzkogel 225
Route 48 Hechenmoos – Bochumer Hut 228
Route 49 Hechenmoos – Tristkogel – Saaljoch –
          Bochumer Hut – Hechenmoos 230

Walks from Saalbach and Hinterglemm
Route 50 Saalbach – Hinterglemm – Lindlingalm 234
Route 51 Mitterlengau – Tristkogel – Hochtorsee 239
Route 52 Saalbach – Spielberghaus – Burgeralm 241
Route 53 Saalbach – Spielberghaus – Kleberkopf. 243
Route 54 Saalbach – Barnkogel – Spielberghorn – Saalbach 245
Route 55 Saalbach – Geierkogel – Viehhofen. 248
Route 56 Saalbach – Klinglertörl– Zell am See. 250

Walks from Zell Am See
Route 57 Zell am See – Thumersbach– Zell am See. 255
Route 58 Zell am See – Viehhofen. 258
Route 59 Zell am See – Maurerkogel – Rohrertörl – Schmittenhöhe. 260

7 KAISERGEBIRGE
Introduction 263
Route 60 Kufstein – Hinterbärenbad – Hans-Berger-Haus 269
Route 61 Kufstein – Vorderkaiserfelden Hut. 273
Route 62 Vorderkaiserfelden Hut – Pyramidenspitze 274
Route 63 Kufstein – Vorderkaiserfelden Hut – Stripsenjochhaus. 275
Route 64 Stripsenjochhaus – Steinerne Rinne – Ellmauer Tor – Grutten Hut. . . . 278
Route 65 Söll – Hintersteiner See – Söll. 281
Route 66 Scheffau – Wilder-Kaiser-Steig – Riedl Hut – Ellmau 285
Route 67 Ellmau – Gaudeamus Hut – Grutten Hut – Riedl Hut – Ellmau 288
Route 68 The Wilder-Kaiser-Steig. 291
Route 69 Griesenau – Griesner Alm. 294
Route 70 Griesenau – Stripsenjochhaus. 297
Route 71 Griesner Alm – Stripsenkopf – Feldberg – Griesner Alm 298
Route 72 A Tour of the Wilder Kaiser. 300

8 DACHSTEINGEBIRGE
Introduction 302

Walks from Filzmoos
Route 73 Filzmoos – Hofpürgl Hut – Sulzenhals – Sulzenalm – Filzmoos 308
Route 74 Filzmoos – Sulzenalm – Filzmoos 312
Route 75 The Gosaukamm Circuit. 314

Walks from the Bachlalm

Route 76   Bachlalm – Tor – Dachstein-Südwand Hut – Bachlalm 317
Route 77   Bachlalm – Sulzenhals – Rötelstein 321
Route 78   Bachlalm – Sulzenhals – Hofpürgl Hut – Filzmoos 322

Walks from Ramsau Am Dachstein

Route 79   Vorderer Gosausee – Hintere Seealm 326
Route 80   Steeg-Gosau – Hallstatt – Steeg-Gosau 327

9 HOHE TAUERN

Introduction 330

Walks from Badgastein

Route 81   Badgastein – Palfnersee – Badgastein 343
Route 82   Badgastein – Graukogel – Reedsee – Badgastein. 345
Route 83   Badgastein – Böckstein – Badgastein 348
Route 84   Badgastein – Oberer Bockhartsee – Sportgastein. 351

Walks from Kaprun

Route 85   Kaprun – Krefelder Hut. 356
Route 86   Krefelder Hut – Salzburger Hut – Kaprun 358
Route 87   Kaprun – Scharfer Grat 360
Route 88   Kaprun – Heinrich-Schwaiger-Haus 362
Route 89   Kaprun – Austriaweg. 363
Route 90   Hut to Hut across the Glockner Group 365

Walks from Matrei in Osttirol

Route 91   Matreier Tauernhaus – Innergschlöss 372
Route 92   Innergschlöss – Ochsnerwaldweg – Innergschlöss 375

The Virgental

Route 93   Ströden – Essener-Rostocker Hut 377
Route 94   The Venediger Höhenweg 379

THE TAUERNTAL

Route 95   Europa Panoramaweg Goldried – Kals-Matreier-Törlhaus –
            Kalser Höhe – Goldried 384
Route 96   Matrei – Sudetendeutsche Hut(2656m) – Matrei. 387

Walks from Kals Am Grossglockner

Route 97   Kals – Stüdl Hut 390
Route 98   Kals – Glorer Hut – Lucknerhaus 393

10 KARAWANKEN

Introduction 398
Route 99   Bärental – Klagenfurter Hut 403
Route 100   Klagenfurter Hut – Bielschitza 406
Route 101   Schaidasattel – Hochobir 409

Appendix A	Useful Addresses	412
Appendix B	Bibliography	413
Appendix C	Menu Items	415
Appendix D	German–English Glossary	417
Appendix E	Index of Routes	420

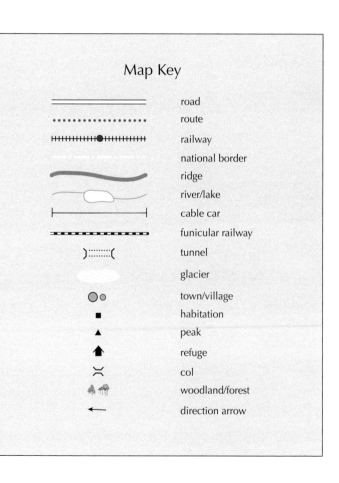

Map Key

	road
	route
	railway
	national border
	ridge
	river/lake
	cable car
	funicular railway
	tunnel
	glacier
	town/village
	habitation
	peak
	refuge
	col
	woodland/forest
	direction arrow

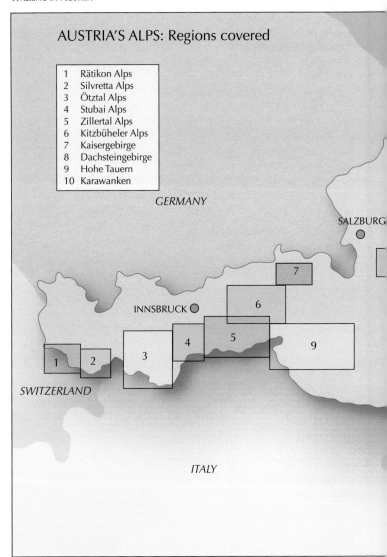

AUSTRIA'S ALPS: Regions covered

1 Rätikon Alps
2 Silvretta Alps
3 Ötztal Alps
4 Stubai Alps
5 Zillertal Alps
6 Kitzbüheler Alps
7 Kaisergebirge
8 Dachsteingebirge
9 Hohe Tauern
10 Karawanken

GERMANY

SALZBURG

INNSBRUCK

SWITZERLAND

ITALY

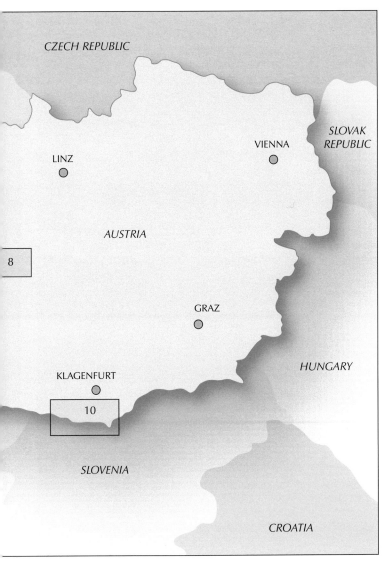

From the Fuldaer Höhenweg walkers gain a direct view of the Taschachferner (Ötztal Alps, Route 15)

INTRODUCTION

At four o'clock on a June morning in 1967 I gazed breathless with wonder as the sun rose out of a distant valley, and flooded its glow across a sea of mountains whose snowfields and glaciers turned pink with the new day. My companions\and I had spent the night with neither tent nor sleeping bag for comfort on a summit modest in altitude but generous in outlook, and greeted the dawn with smiles of delight. Then we descended as fast as we could. As we did we won a second sunrise, then another, and another, racing for pre-dawn shadows while the sun hastened to spread its goodness over all the Eastern Alps.

I was young then, leading walking groups in Austria's mountains, and loving every moment, every trail, every summit, valley, lake and meadow starred with flowers. Loving the pure alpine air, the cleanliness of the villages, the punctuality of bus and train, the certainty of a waymarked path, the smiles of each hut warden amused by my poor attempts to speak German. Loving life.

Forty years on I no longer race to beat the sunrise. Instead, I linger, sprawl on an *alm* pasture and dream. A *klettersteig* can still set my pulse racing, and trails continue to seduce me into wonderland, but now I take my time to get there. I'll sit for ages and listen to the birds, a stream, or the brush-strokes of the wind against a rock. But the sight of chamois or marmot thrills me even more than it did four decades ago, while a pass is as good as a summit, a mattress in a hut as welcome as any hotel bed, a night under a blanket of stars as enriching as ever.

Austria's Alps still draw me back, and repay every visit a thousandfold.

AUSTRIA'S ALPS

With more than 40,000km of well-maintained, waymarked footpaths; with countless attractive villages, hospitable hotels, inns and restaurants, pristine campsites, the world's finest chain of mountain huts, an integrated public transport system, and breathtaking scenic variety, Austria must surely count as one of Europe's most walker-friendly countries.

It's a country of great diversity, whose mountains range from gentle grass-covered 'hills' of around 2000m, to rugged limestone spires and turrets erupting from a fan of scree, or snow-draped, glacier-clad peaks whose reflections are cast in crystal-clear lakes. In their valleys some of the continent's loveliest villages are hung about with flowers in summer. On mid-height hillsides centuries-old timber haybarns and stone-built chalets squat among the pastures; these are the *alms* which add an historic dimension to the landscape. Elsewhere, heavy-eaved farmhouses double as restaurants; some provide accommodation in a rustic setting, and complement the hundreds of mountain huts built in remote locations, virtually every one of which exploits a viewpoint of bewitching beauty.

The Leoganger Steinberge, seen from the Spielberghorn (Kitzbüheler Alps, Route 54)

The Eastern Alps of Austria extend from west to east in two distinct but roughly parallel chains of around 400km each, before subsiding in the wooded hills of the Wienerwald. The chain which carries the German border is known as the *Mittelgebirge* (the rocky Northern Limestone Alps), while its southern and higher counterpart, the *Hochgebirge*, is distinguished by such snow-draped and glacier-clad groups as the Silvretta, Ötztal, Stubai and Zillertal Alps. In the heart of the country Austria's highest mountain, the elegant Grossglockner, reaches 3798m and casts its benediction over the surrounding valleys.

This is a guide to ten mountain districts stretching eastward from the Rätikon Alps on the borders of Liechtenstein and Switzerland, to the little-known Karawanken, shared with Slovenia, in the sunny province of Carinthia. Each district has its own distinctive appeal, with fine scenery, plenty of accommodation, and numerous walking opportunities. There'll be something to suit every taste and all degrees of commitment. And you'll no doubt be left wanting more.

Rätikon Alps

In Vorarlberg, Austria's westernmost province, the Rätikon Alps spread along the borders of Liechtenstein and Switzerland on the southwest side of the Montafon valley. These are limestone mountains, ragged and rugged, with a choice of valleys flowing from them down to the Montafon trench, from which access is most easily gained. The highest summit is that of the 2965m Schesaplana, a walker's peak at the head of the Brandnertal, whose main resort village, Brand, is on a bus route from the railway station at Bludenz. Schruns, Tschagguns and Gargellen also make useful valley bases, but with several well-situated mountain huts built in the high country below attention-grabbing peaks, some of the best walks either start from particular huts or make tours from one hut to another.

Silvretta Alps

At the 2354m Plasseggenpass limestone gives way to crystalline rock, which continues into and throughout the Silvretta Alps, and takes the *Hochgebirge* and the border with Switzerland further east. The Silvretta mountains have their fair share of glaciers and snowfields, and elegant peaks such as Piz Buin and the Dreiländerspitze. More huts offer accommodation for walkers and climbers in remote locations, and some of the finest walks cross cols leading from one valley to another. Access is from both the Montafon and Paznaun valleys, the two linked by the Silvretta Hochalpenstrasse which crosses the 2036m Bielerhöhe, overlooking an attractive dammed lake.

The main resorts are St Gallenkirch and Gaschurn in the Montafon valley, and Galtür and Ischgl in Paznaun, while accommodation can also be found at the Bielerhöhe itself.

Ötztal Alps

An impressive district of 3000m mountains, whose highest summit is the 3772m Wildspitze, the Ötztal Alps contain the largest number of glaciers in the Eastern Alps. Rising east and south of the Inn river, the massif spreads over the border into Italy, but from its glacial heartland, three major valley systems drain northward to the Inn: the Kaunertal, Pitztal and the valley from which it takes its name, the Ötztal, with the neighbouring Stubai Alps immediately to the east of that. The latter valley is fed by the Ventertal and, its upper tributary, the Gurglertal, famed for the winter and summer resort of Obergurgl which, at

The 2965m summit of Schesaplana (Rätikon Alps, Route 3)

1927m, is Tyrol's highest parish. Other resort villages worth considering for a walking holiday are Sölden, Längenfeld, Mandarfen, Plangeross and Feichten.

Stubai Alps

This complex district, like its neighbours to east and west, has a glacial core and some very fine valleys worth exploring, most of which are easily accessible from Innsbruck. Although primarily a crystalline range, the limestone Kalkkogel, flanking the lower Stubaital, is a Dolomite lookalike across whose southern flank one of Austria's finest hut tours picks its way towards its close. Numerous huts located at the head of tributary valleys make obvious destinations for walks, while the Stubaier Höhenweg links no less than eight of them in an understandably popular circuit. Of the many resort villages, both Längenfeld and Sölden lie in the Ötztal, Kühtai and Gries im Sellrain give access from the north, while Neustift is the best developed for exploring the mountains above the Stubaital.

Zillertal Alps

East of the Brenner Pass the Zillertal Alps are known as much for their skiing potential as for their summer walking possibilities, especially around Mayrhofen, with the nearby slopes of the Tuxertal being developed with ski tows and cableways. The Zillertal itself pushes deep into the mountains, with a choice of tributaries cutting off herring-bone fashion from it. As with the Stubai Alps most, if not all, of these tributaries have mountain huts at their head from which both climbing and walking routes can be enjoyed. With a covering of either snow or ice, the massif's highest summits capture the imagination and make a photogenic backdrop to a wonderland of walks. Of the valley bases, perhaps the best are those that lie in a line along the Zillertal: Zell am Ziller, Mayrhofen and Finkenberg.

Kitzbüheler Alps

All the previously mentioned groups spill across international borders, but the Kitzbüheler Alps lie 'inland' so to speak, and have no frontiers. North of the Zillertal Alps and the Venediger group, these are grass-covered mountains of modest proportions. But on them will be found some of Austria's best routes for the walker of moderate ability and ambition. A wealth of trails strike across hillsides and over summits with long views north to the limestone ranges, south to the crystalline border mountains, or southeast to snowy giants of the Hohe Tauern. Söll, Scheffau and Ellmau lie in a glorious valley between the grassy Kitzbüheler Alps and the abrupt wall of the Wilder Kaiser. Westendorf and Brixen lie in a parallel valley to the south, with Kitzbühel, one of Austria's premier ski resorts and the hub of the range, at its eastern end, while Saalbach and Hinterglemm lie in the Glemmtal easily accessible from the lovely 'Lakes and Mountains' resort of Zell am See, and offer some of the best walking of the whole district.

Kaisergebirge

A small, compact group of limestone mountains of the Mittelgebirge lying north of the Kitzbüheler Alps and

The 3497m Schrankogel dominates the upper Sulztal (Stubai Alps, Route 21)

The extensive south face of the Dachstein (Dachsteingebirge, Route 76)

bordered on the west by the Inn river shortly before it flows into Germany, the Kaisergebirge is divided into two main ridges: the Zahmer, or 'tame' Kaiser, and the Wilder (wild) Kaiser. Between the two lie the charming valleys of the Kaisertal and Kaiserbachtal, with a linking ridge at the Stripsenjoch. The scenery is dramatic, the climbing awesome, the walking first class, with some exciting *klettersteig* (*via ferrata*) routes to consider, and several fine huts too. On the south side of the Wilder Kaiser, Söll, Scheffau, Ellmau and Going make good valley bases. St Johann in Tirol lies to the southeast, while Kufstein on the west has the Kaisertal close by.

Dachsteingebirge

Another limestone group, this is topped by the glacier-clad Hoher Dachstein (2995m), while the outlying crest of the Gosaukamm contrasts the main block of mountains with its finely-shaped

individual turrets, pinnacles and peaks such as the Bischofsmütze giving character to the whole district. The Dachstein lies southeast of Salzburg on the edge of the Salzkammergut lake region, rising above the Hallstätter See and Gosausee, with the Ramsau terrace and Enns valley to the south. Filzmoos and Ramsau are good walking centres for routes on the south side of the mountains, with Hallstatt a romantic lakeside base on the north.

Hohe Tauern

This large area boasts Austria's largest national park, its highest mountain, the Grossglockner, and the spectacular ice-covered Venediger group, the latter rising to the east of the Zillertal Alps. Several distinctive groups make up the Hohe Tauern region, the main crest of which lies south of the Salzach river valley; a great block of mountains breached by three major north-south roads, two of which have tunnels, the third being the famous Grossglockner Hochalpenstrasse. On the northern side, Badgastein and Kaprun are recommended centres, while Matrei in Osttirol and Kals am Grossglockner serve the southern valleys. Tremendous high mountain scenery and exhilarating walks make this an excellent region in which to base a holiday.

Karawanken

Surprisingly little-known to mountain walkers from the UK, the Karawanken is a narrow range of mountains along whose crest runs the Austro–Slovenian border south of Klagenfurt. Carinthia, the province in which the range lies, is noted for its lakes and sunshine, but the Karawanken receives little publicity. However, these sun-bleached limestone mountains of modest altitude (the highest, Hochstuhl, is only 2237m), are both dramatic and accessible, and form a scenic background to walks that lead through woodland and meadow. There are longer, more demanding routes, and much to explore from such unassuming centres as Ferlach and Bad Eisenkappel.

MOUNTAIN FLOWERS

A botanist with remarkable powers of observation was among a group of walkers I was leading in the Alps a few summers ago. When quizzed about the apparent anomaly of a tiny group of plants flowering in a confined site surrounded by an entirely different species, he explained 'there are no accidents in nature; this particular plant grows in this precise location because here and here alone, conditions are perfect for it to flourish. A few centimetres away, and

A cushion of moss campion (Silene acaulis) in the Zillertal Alps

The yellow Turkscap lily

Below (from left): *the spring gentian (*Gentiana verna*); the fringed pink, or ragged dianthus, a lime-loving plant seen in the Karawanken; alpenroses in the Rätikon Alps.*

one or more of those essential conditions may be missing or dominated by others that deny its growth.'

In Austria's Alps, as elsewhere, the range, diversity and distribution of mountain plants is enormous. Grouped by habitat, soil, climate and altitude, they are also limited by competition, by grazing or cultivation. And as we have seen, conditions that favour some plants on a given site may be absent elsewhere. Those conditions may not be obvious except to the trained botanist, but happily it is not essential to have a botanical background to enjoy the wealth of alpine flowers that add so much to a mountain walking holiday, for there will always be surprises.

Many of the best-known alpines such as gentians, anemones, soldanellas and primulas flower early in the lower valleys shortly after winter's snow has melted – on occasion as the snow melts, with exposed islands of turf bursting into flower in the midst of a mottled snowfield. But as the snowline recedes up the hillside, these same flowers appear higher up, while those of the lower valleys may have faded or disappeared completely. By the middle of July grazing cattle will have cleared the upper pastures of most of the flowers, but above those pastures rock faces and screes that are inaccessible to domestic animals will give a sometimes startling display of alpines, often luxuriant but slow-growing cushion plants that exploit what may seem to the untrained eye to be an entirely hostile environment.

In the west, in Vorarlberg with its a mix of lime and granite formations, a rich variety of flowers is there to be enjoyed, among the most common being arnica, edelweiss and saxifrage. Adjacent to the Lindauer Hut in the Rätikon Alps there's a noted alpine garden in which visitors can identify specific plants that are likely to be in flower at any given time and place.

In neighbouring Tyrol, a province that claims to be 'nature's own alpine garden', early summer meadows can seem bewitchingly colourful and fragrant. Here too both limestone and crystalline mountains provide a range of habitats and the full gamut of alpine landscapes ranging from green wooded hills to glacier-draped peaks and dolomitic fingers of rock. Each has its own specific flora. In the highest valleys of the Ötztal Alps, for example, the deep blue-violet *Primula glutinosa* is worth noting, as is the pink-flowered creeping azalea *Loiseleuria procumbens* which is known to grow up to 3000m. Also found at a similar altitude on scree or rocky ridges, is the rare Mont Cenis bellfower, *Campanula cenisia*, a dwarf plant with tiny slaty-blue flowers. Among other surprises is a reported sighting of a fringe of martagon lilies (*Lilium martagon*) near the top of a cliff face at around 2235m by the Riffelsee. This plant with its pendulous Turkscap flowers is usually confined to woods or meadows.

The Hohe Tauern rewards botanist, walker and climber in equal measure. Around Austria's highest peak, the Grossglockner, turf dampened by snowmelt produces a mass of *Primula minima*, its colour ranging from blue-mauve to magenta-pink. The wonderfully fragrant *Daphne striata* is also here. A straggling or prostrate bush 15–20cm tall, it has clusters of reddish purple flowers with a ruff of down-pointing leaves at its best in June. Among the gentians to be seen is the common but very lovely spring gentian, *Gentiana verna*, as well as *Gentiana nivalis*, the so-called snow gentian, and the biennial *Gentianella ciliata*, a brilliant blue flower with fringed lobes.

In the Karawanken mountains of Carinthia which spread into Slovenia, many native plants are reminiscent of those found in the Dolomites, which would suggest that strands of dolomitic rock appear in the Carinthian limestone. *Aster bellidiastrum*, a tall perennial that resembles a large common daisy has taken on a rosy-pink tinge. There are purple coloured aquilegias, and the aptly-named *Schneerose* (Snow rose) hellebore, *Helleborus niger*. Cyclamen grace the pinewoods, lemon-yellow poppies bring colour to white screes and, of course, a great splash of pink or scarlet on the hillsides betrays the presence of the ubiquitous alpenrose almost everywhere.

WILDLIFE

Alpine flowers may be a colourful adornment to the mountains, but the sighting of wildlife can be a highlight of any walk. In the Austrian Alps there should be plenty of opportunities to study birds and animals in their natural environment, but since most of the mammals are notoriously shy, you'll need to walk quietly and remain alert to be rewarded. On some of our trips we've studied ibex on an exposed ridge above the Braunschweiger Hut, had young marmots play round our stationary

boots, watched roe deer watching us, and been impressed by the grace and speed of a small herd of chamois racing across a near-vertical scree. Each of these experiences served to enrich our day and remains imprinted on memory long after.

Ibex (*Steinbock* in German) must count among the most striking to observe in the wild. The male, with its large, knobbly, swept-back curving horns and stub of a beard, is the king of the mountains. It has fairly short legs and a stocky body, but its powerful muscles enable it to spring onto narrow ledges of rock with surprising ease, or race away from danger with an unexpected turn of speed. The female is smaller and less showy than the male. With a grey or coffee-coloured coat and much shorter horns, she spends most of the year away from adult males, and when sighted could be mistaken for a chamois. It is only in the autumn-to-winter mating season that males seek out the females. First, they fight for the right to mate, and then the hills echo to the sound of clashing horns. Some hut wardens spread salt near their huts to entice ibex to graze nearby, and this is often the best way to observe them.

Less stocky than the ibex, the **chamois** (*Gemse*) is distinguished by short, sickle-shaped horns and a white rump. Its thick winter coat moults during May or June, and in summer it takes on a dark reddish-brown colour with a black stripe along the spine, and a white lower jaw. Like the ibex, the chamois is well adapted to the severity of its habitat, and is more resistant to the harsh winter weather than the roe deer, with whom it shares the forests when snow covers its normal high altitude territory. It's a graceful and extremely agile animal, but also a very shy one with a keen sense of smell and acute hearing which makes it difficult to approach undetected. When startled the chamois makes a sharp wheezing snort as warning.

Of all alpine mammals the **marmot** is the most endearing and most often seen. These sociable furry rodents live in colonies below the snowline and can be observed in many regions covered by this book. Growing to the size of a large hare and weighing up to 10kg, the marmot spends from 5–6 months each winter in hibernation, emerging rather lean in springtime, but soon fattening up on the summer grasses. Towards late September, having accumulated a good reserve of fat during the summer, the adults prepare their nests in readiness for winter, with dried grasses scythed with

In the early summer, young marmots may be seen in the alpine meadows

their sharp teeth. The famous warning whistle is emitted from the back of the throat by an alert adult sitting up on its haunches; its main enemies being the **fox** and **eagle**.

Among other mammals that may be seen by chance in these mountains is the carnivorous **stoat** which sometimes attacks young birds in ground-sited nests, but favours **voles** or even young **mountain hares**. In summer its coat is a russet-fawn which changes to white in winter, and it invariably makes its nest beneath a rock or a pile of stones.

Both the dainty **roe deer** and more powerful **red deer** inhabit the wooded areas, of which Austria has so many. Having a nervous disposition and exceptional hearing, neither are easy to catch unawares. The **red squirrel**, on the other hand, can often be detected scampering along a forest path, or scrabbling up a tree, its almost black coat and tufted ears being recognisable features.

Coniferous woods are home to the **nutcracker** who, with a *kre kre kre* alarm call, rivals the jay as policeman of the woods. With large head, strong beak, tawny speckled breast and swooping flight, the nutcracker is adept at breaking open pine cones in order to access the fatty seeds which it hides to feed on in winter. **Capercaillie** and **black grouse** are also present in wooded valleys and the lower mountain slopes.

The **alpine chough** is among the most common of birds to be met on trips into the higher mountain regions. The unmistakable yellow beak and coral-red feet distinguish it from other members of the crow family, and it will often hop around popular summits and vantage

23

The pastoral idyll of the summer Alps

points to gather crumbs left by visiting walkers and climbers.

GETTING THERE

By Air

A number of airports in Austria and neighbouring Germany have regular flights from the UK, although some of the services mentioned below are charters only. All airports listed have good onward train and/or coach connections, and most areas organise local taxi pickup services. Readers are warned, however, that air travel information is especially vulnerable to change, so you are advised to check carefully in advance.

AIRLINE WEBSITES

www.austrianairlines.co.uk
www.britishairways.com
www.easyjet.com
www.flyniki.com
www.lufthansa.com
www.ryanair.com
www.thomsonfly.com

Zürich airport in Switzerland is linked to the main rail network with a number of daily Austria-bound trains, and provides another option worth considering – especially for destinations in western Austria, as the airport is only 120km from Bregenz.

Austria/Germany	UK	Airline
Friedrichshafen (Germany)	London Stansted	Ryanair
Graz	London Stansted	Ryanair
Innsbruck	London Gatwick	British Airways
Klagenfurt	London Stansted	Ryanair
Linz	London Stansted	Ryanair
Munich (Germany)	London Stansted	EasyJet
	Edinburgh	EasyJet
	Bristol	British Airways
	London Heathrow	British Airways
	London City	Lufthansa
	London Heathrow	Lufthansa
	Manchester	Lufthansa
	Birmingham	Lufthansa
Salzburg	London Stansted	Ryanair
	London Gatwick	British Airways
	Manchester	Thomsonfly
	Coventry	Thomsonfly
Vienna	London Heathrow	Austrian Airlines
	London Heathrow	British Airways
	Manchester	British Airways
	London Stansted	Fly Niki

By Rail

Holidaymakers keen to reduce their carbon footprint may wish to consider rail travel. For the majority of Austria's alpine regions, Innsbruck- or Salzburg-bound trains will take care of most needs, with easy access to regional lines that serve the rest of the country.

Travelling from London St Pancras to Paris (Gare du Nord) via Eurostar allows a speedy start to the journey, although changing trains in Paris can be time-consuming. The onward route is through France and Switzerland (Basel and Zürich), then on to Bludenz, Landeck and Innsbruck. Alternatively, consider Eurostar to Brussels, then take the Vienna-bound express through Germany, with the option of changing trains in Munich for Salzburg or Innsbruck.

Since most rail journeys to Austria will involve overnight travel, it's a good idea to book a couchette to ensure greater comfort and the chance of an unbroken night's sleep.

By Car

Driving to Austria from the UK is neither the fastest nor the cheapest travel option – nor is it the most relaxing. But for visitors planning to camp and walk in several different areas, it may be the most practical. Conventional car ferries operate regular services between Harwich and the Hook of Holland; and between Dover and Ostend or Calais, while the Channel Tunnel offers a quicker crossing, with peak-time journeys on Le Shuttle running every 15 minutes.

For destinations in western Austria, possibly the fastest routing is via Brussels, Köln and Stuttgart, while for Salzburg, central and eastern Austria, consider travelling via Brussels, Köln, Frankfurt and Nürnberg.

On arrival at the Austrian border drivers must purchase a *vignette* windscreen sticker which authorises use of the country's *autobahns*. Proof of vehicle ownership (or a letter from the owner giving permission to drive the car) is necessary, as is a driving licence for British or other EU nationals. Non-EU nationals will need an International Driving Licence. A red warning triangle, first aid kit, and 'Green Card' third party insurance cover, are all compulsory.

Note that some of the more spectacular alpine routes are toll roads (the Silvretta and Grossglockner Hochalpenstrassen, for example), and a number of other dramatic pass roads are unsuitable for towing caravans and trailers.

TRANSPORT WITHIN AUSTRIA

Austria has an extensive, integrated public transport system that gives especially good value for the walker. On the whole

Meadows adorned with 'hairy men' form a regular feature in Austria's valleys

The Zillertalbahn between Jenbach and Mayrhofen is one of several private railways useful to walkers

train and connecting bus schedules are dovetailed to minimise waiting times, so a local timetable obtained on arrival at your chosen base ought to be carried along with guidebook and map. Note, however, that in general services are greatly reduced on Sundays and public holidays, and that some of the more remote villages may have just one bus each day.

The rail network operated by Austrian Federal Railways (Österreichische Bundesbahnen (ÖBB) www.oebb.at) serves the majority of towns, and their trains are clean and punctual. The *Regionalzug* service stops at every station and as a consequence is slow, while Eurocity international express (EC), or the Austrian Intercity express (IC) trains are the fastest. There are also several privately operated railways such as the Zillertalbahn (Jenbach to Mayrhofen) and

Graz-Köflacherbahn (Graz to Köflach). Train times are clearly displayed at all stations. For departures study the yellow posters (headed *Abfahrt*), while the white posters give arrival times (*Ankunft*).

The efficient *postbus* service (www.postbus.at), together with the *bahnbus* operated by the ÖBB and departing from railway stations, visits most inhabited valleys not served by train. These are of immense importance, not only to visiting walkers but to outlying communities. Local bus timetables (*Fahrpläne*) are usually fixed to bus stops (*Haltestelle*) or displayed outside post offices. They are also often available from tourist information offices.

ACCOMMODATION

There should be no shortage of accommodation in any of the areas covered by this guide, for with some justification Austria prides itself on its tourist infrastructure, and almost every town and village offers a choice of hotels, *pensionen, gasthöfe, gästehaus* and private rooms (*privatzimmer*) at mostly affordable prices. Enquire at the local tourist office for their accommodation list. Some of the larger resorts also have accommodation boards fitted outside their tourist office, and many have campsites in the vicinity.

Camping

As a general rule, campsites are clean and well-managed, with immaculate washrooms and good showers. Many have laundry facilities, small shops and restaurants attached. Sites are usually open between May and September, with seasonal variations in price.

Hotels

Hotels and *pensionen* are star-graded; one star being the most basic, leading to extravagant five-star luxury. Budget accommodation usually remains in the one- or two-star categories, with a considerable difference in price rising thereafter. But a two-star room will often have modest en-suite facilities and include a standard continental breakfast. Note that a *hotel-garni* provides no meals other than breakfast.

A *pension* is a bed-and-breakfast hotel (also known as *hotel-garni*). Though often fairly small and family-run, when located in towns and cities, *pensionen* may occupy a section of a large apartment block or other building. Most of those in mountain villages tend to be in attractive, traditional houses.

Gasthof and Gästehaus

In practical terms a *gasthof* is a hotel in everything but name, while a *gästehaus* often denotes a small bed-and-breakfast hotel. A *gasthaus*, on the other hand, is a restaurant, although some also offer rooms, in which case look for the words '*mit Unterkunft*'.

Private Rooms

Renting a room in a private house is a favoured holiday option. These *privat zimmer* can vary greatly, with facilities ranging from a basic bedroom with shared bathroom, and breakfast left on a tray outside your room, to hotel-standard accommodation. Most rooms are let on a bed-and-breakfast basis, but it is advisable to check first – tourist offices usually have details. Look for houses displaying the *Zimmer frei* notice.

Mountain Huts

No alpine country has a greater number or variety of mountain huts than Austria, with a network of at least 1000 *hütten* built in the most idyllic of locations. Of these more than half are owned and run by member groups of the Austrian and German Alpine Clubs (*Österreichischer* and *Deutscher Alpenverein* – ÖAV/DAV), the others being either privately owned or belonging to separate organisations. All are listed in what is often termed 'the green book' – *Alpenvereinshütten Band 1: Ostalpen* published by Rother, and available from the Austrian Alpine Club (see below).

Staffed from at least July to the end of September, but often with an open period which extends either side of the high summer period, accommodation

The Bremer Hut, one of more than a thousand built in the Austrian Alps

on offer ranges from large mixed-sex communal dormitories (*matratzenlager*) to two- or four-bedded rooms suitable for couples or families. Sheet sleeping bags are obligatory, so take your own. Separate-sex washrooms with showers are the norm, although some of the older and more remote huts are

HUT CATEGORIES

Huts belonging to either the ÖAV or DAV are divided into three categories which offer discounts of varying amounts on overnight charges (not meals) for *Alpenverein* members – including members of the UK branch of the Austrian Alpine Club (see below).

- *Category I:* These huts are usually situated at least 1hr's walk from mechanised transport or the nearest road, and may have basic facilities. Members have priority in allocation of accommodation, and claim a minimum 50% reduction.

- *Category II:* Located in popular areas, and usually reached by road or cableway, these huts are often open throughout the year. With better facilities and more varied catering than at Category I huts, members have a minimum discount of 30%.

- *Category III:* Primarily used by day-visitors and accessible by mechanised transport (car or cableway). These huts are almost akin to hotels, offering a minimum overnight discount of 10% to *Alpenverein* members.

Walking group near Grieralm in the Tuxertal (Zillertal Alps, Route 33)

still rather basic in their amenities. However, despite the name, most of Austria's huts resemble mountain inns rather than the simple refuges of old. Wardens provide refreshments, snacks, meals and drinks (coffee, tea, hot chocolate, lemonade, beer and wine), with a choice of evening meals sometimes matching in variety the menus of local valley restaurants. (See Appendix C for a translation of menu items.) In ÖAV and DAV huts, the evening menu usually includes a *Bergsteigeressen* (literally, the mountaineer's meal – available only to *Alpenverein* members). Low-cost and high in calories, for the hungry walker prepared to take 'pot luck' the *Bergsteigeressen* offers very good

HUT ETIQUETTE

When arriving at a mountain hut remove boots before entering, place them on a rack in the bootroom, and help yourself to a pair of hut shoes (clogs or slippers) provided. Locate the warden to book bedspace for the night, and make a note of meal times. It is often possible to purchase a litre of boiled water – *Teewasser* - to make tea or coffee for yourself between meals, so carry a supply of teabags and/or instant coffee with you. Make your bed as soon as you have been allocated a room, using your own sheet sleeping bag (sleeping bag liner); blankets and pillows are provided, but keep a torch handy. Lights out (*Hüttenruhe*) is usually 10pm. Before leaving in the morning, make sure you have entered details of your planned route and destination in the visitors' book provided.

value. Since most of the income for self-employed hut wardens is derived from the sale of food and drinks (the overnight fee goes to the club owning the hut), it follows that all users ought to make some purchases. Self-catering facilities are not provided, other than in bivouac huts and winter rooms.

Many walks in this guide choose a mountain hut as their destination, for the majority are not only situated among exciting landscapes, but have refreshments available on arrival. Multi-day hut-to-hut tours, of which several are included in this book, are an Austrian speciality worth tackling.

Package Holidays

Holiday packages providing both accommodation and travel can offer a very useful service at competitive prices for independent walkers looking for a base in specific locations. The following tour operators are among many with packages to various Austrian resorts: Crystal Holidays (www.crystalholidays. co.uk), HF Holidays (www.hfholidays. co.uk), Inghams (www.inghams.co.uk), Inn Travel (www.inntravel.co.uk) and Thomson Lakes and Mountains (www. thomsonlakesandmountains.co.uk). There are, of course, many other UK and Irish tour companies that organise all-inclusive walking holidays in Austria.

THE AUSTRIAN ALPINE CLUB

Founded in Vienna in 1862 the Österreichischer Alpenverein is the world's second oldest mountaineering club (Britain's own Alpine Club began in 1857), with one of the largest memberships. In addition to the provision and maintenance of mountain huts, the

Evening light at the Stripsenjochhaus (Kaisergebirge, Route 63)

club is involved in organising mountain-eering courses, waymarking and main-taining footpaths and the production of maps and guidebooks.

In 1948 a UK section, officially known today as Sektion Britannia, was established to promote and facilitate visits to the Eastern Alps for UK-based enthusiasts. From its current headquar-ters in Dorset, the AAC produces a quarterly newsletter, organises a regu-lar programme of lectures, walks and meets, and supports various alpine hut projects with financial donations, but its main attractions for many members must surely be reduced hut charges and mountaineering insurance. Anyone planning to undertake a mountain walk-ing holiday in Austria is strongly recom-mended to join, for as the late Cecil Davies wrote in *Mountain Walking in Austria* (the predecessor of this guide): 'Apart from the priorities and reductions

Austrian Alpine Club
12a North Street
Wareham, Dorset BH20 4AG
☎ 01929 556 870
e-mail: aac.office@aacuk.org.uk
website: www.aacuk.org.uk

at the huts … if you are an AV-member in an AV hut, you "belong"'.

THE ROUTES

Austria's mountains make an almost per-fect destination for the first-time visitor to the Alps. Though many regions have glaciers, snowfields and abrupt rock walls, on the whole the mountains are not as intimidating as some of their larger neighbours in the Central and South-Western Alps. That is not to sug-gest there's a shortage of dramatic

Summit ridge of the Bielschitza (Karawanken, Route 101)

scenery – far from it! And the routes described in this book have been chosen to make the most of Austria's rich landscape diversity – the lakes, flower meadows, tiny hamlets, huts, and abundant vantage points that can take your breath away with surprise.

With more than 40,000km of paths to choose from, the principal objective of each walk is to enable you to enjoy a day's exercise among some of Europe's best-loved mountains. But to gain the most from a walking holiday in Austria, it is advisable to be reasonably fit before you go, for most routes described here involve considerable uphill effort.

If you've never walked in the Alps before, avoid being too ambitious in your plans for the first few days until you've come to terms with the scale of the terrain. A rough guide in terms of time, distance and height gain and loss is given at the head of each walk description, which should aid the planning of an itinerary.

Grading of walks

The walks fall into three categories, graded 1–3, with the highest grade reserved for the more challenging routes. This grading system is purely subjective, but is offered to provide a rough idea of what to expect. Grade 1 walks are fairly modest and likely to appeal to most active members of the family, while the majority of routes are graded 2–3, largely because of the nature of the landscape which can be pretty challenging. The grading of walks is not an exact science and each category covers a fairly wide spectrum. Inevitably there will be overlaps and

variations and, no doubt, a few anomalies which may be disputed by users, but they are offered in good faith and as a rough guide only.

- **Grade 1:** Suitable for family outings; mostly short distances or walks along gently graded paths or tracks with little height gain.
- **Grade 2:** Moderate walking, usually on clear footpaths with a reasonable amount of height gain. Walkers should be adequately shod and equipped.
- **Grade 3:** More strenuous routes on sometimes rough or unclear paths. Some modest scrambling may be required, or the use of ladders, fixed ropes or cables as support. A 'head for heights' may be called for. On some of these routes there will be passes to cross, screes to tackle, or a minor summit to reach. In short, true alpine walking. There will be steep ascents and descents, some exposed sections, and fairly long distances involved. Walkers attempting these should be 'mountain fit' and well equipped.

Waymarking

Most of the paths adopted by these routes are well maintained, signed and waymarked. These waymarks (invariably red and white bars) may be found on rocks, trees, fenceposts or other immovable wayside objects. Some of the trails are colour coded with additional numbers or letters, and this information will usually be translated onto relevant maps and signposts.

Signposts will be found at significant points (usually major path

Main photo: *Trail signing is good almost everywhere*
Inset photos (top to bottom): *Hut keepers sometimes add direction markers on rocks along the trail; Be warned that route numbers added to waymarks do not always correspond with numbers on maps; Wilder-Kaiser-Steig waymark (Kaisergebirge, Routes 66 and 68); Waymarks below Tör (Dachsteingebirge, Routes 76, 78 and 79)*

Fixed cables on the Jubilaumssteig (Kaisergebirge, Route 64)

junctions) along the way, indicating not only the path's destination, but an estimate of the time it will take to get there with *Std* being an abbreviation of *Stunden* (hours). On occasion you may come upon a sign which says *Nur für Geübte*, which means *only for the experienced* – an indication that the route ahead could be difficult, exposed, or safeguarded with fixed ropes, chains or ladders.

Sections of route marked *Klettersteig* (the German equivalent of Italy's famed *via ferrata*) often involve sustained exposure and a concentration of metal ladders, rungs and fixed ropes. To attempt such routes one needs to have scrambling experience and specialised equipment such as harnesses, slings and karabiners. A few examples of such routes are described in this guide – with adequate advanced warnings given.

Rarely do described routes stray into unpathed terrain, but where they do, cairns and/or additional waymarks often guide the way. In such places it is essential to remain vigilant to avoid becoming lost – especially in poor visibility. If in doubt about the onward route, return to the last point where you were certain of your whereabouts and try again. By consulting the map at regular intervals along the walk, it should be possible to keep abreast of your position and anticipate junctions before you reach them.

For safety's sake never walk alone on remote trails, moraine-bank paths or glaciers. Should you prefer to walk in a

SAFETY CHECKLIST

- Before setting out, check the weather forecast – available from hut keepers, tourist offices and local TV channels – and be aware that all alpine regions are subject to rapidly changing conditions. Throughout the day watch for tell-tale signs and be prepared for the worst by having adequate clothing.

- Study route details beforehand, noting any particular difficulties and the time needed to complete the route. Do not overestimate your abilities, and make sure you can safely reach your destination before nightfall.

- On a full day's walk carry food (and emergency rations such as chocolate or dried fruit), and at least one litre of liquid per person to avoid dehydration.

- Leave details of your planned itinerary and expected time of return with a responsible person. If staying in huts, enter details in the visitors' book provided.

- Be vigilant when crossing wet rocks, scree, snow patches and mountain streams. If your route is safeguarded with fixed ropes or chains, ensure they have not worked loose before using them.

- Do not stray onto glaciers unless you are with experienced companions and have the necessary equipment and knowledge to deal with crevasse rescue. Keep away from icefalls and hanging glaciers.

- Avoid dislodging stones onto others below.

- Never be reluctant to turn back in the face of deteriorating weather or if the route becomes hazardous. In the event of your being unable to reach your expected destination, try to send a message to avoid the rescue services being called out.

- Carry map and compass (and GPS if you have one) – and know how to use them.

- Always carry some first aid equipment, as well as a whistle and torch for use in emergencies.

- Make a note of the International Mountain Distress Signal printed at the front of this book: six blasts on a whistle (and flashes with a torch after dark) spaced evenly for one minute, followed by a minute's silence. Repeat until an answer is received and your position located. The response is three signals followed by a minute's pause.

- Be insured against accidents – rescue and subsequent medical treatment. AAC membership (see above) carries automatic insurance for this. Don't forget to take your European Health Insurance (EHI) card with you to obtain medical treatment on the same terms as native Austrians.

- Finally, please help keep the mountains and their valleys litter-free.

The rock wall of the Kuchelmooskar en route to the Plauener Hut (Zillertal Alps, Route 32)

group but have not made prior arrangements to join an organised walking holiday, a number of tourist authorities arrange day walks with a local guide. Enquire at the tourist office of your nearest resort.

EQUIPMENT

Experienced hillwalkers will no doubt have their own preferences in regard to clothing and equipment, but the following list is offered to newcomers to the Alps. Some items will clearly not be needed if you envisage tackling only valley routes.

Clothing

- Walking boots – must be comfortable, a good fit, have ankle support and plenty of grip in the soles
- Trainers or similar for wear in huts, hotels and villages
- Wind- and water-proof jacket and overtrousers
- Warm hat and sunhat
- Gloves
- Fleece or sweater
- Shirts – 2 or 3 for a fortnight's holiday
- Warm trousers, slacks or breeches – jeans are not recommended (cold when wet and difficult to dry)
- Long woollen socks
- Underwear

Miscellaneous

- Rucksack – with waterproof liner and/or cover
- Sheet sleeping bag (for overnights in huts)
- Bivvy bag – in case of emergencies
- Telescopic umbrella – excellent rain protection, and ideal for spectacle wearers
- Trekking pole(s) – these are highly recommended

37

TICK ALERT

In common with 26 other European countries, Austria is home to the tick, an insect second only to the mosquito for carrying disease to humans – the primary illness in Europe being Tick-Borne Encephalitis (TBE). Ticks live in long grass, shrubs and bushes, and can survive up to 1500m, attaching themselves to humans and animals as they pass. Walkers and campers are especially vulnerable. Victims often do not realise they have been bitten, because the tick injects a toxin which anaesthetises the bite area. Since ticks prefer warm, moist, dark areas of the body, it is advisable to check for bites in those pressure points where clothing presses against the skin, at the back of the knee, armpits and groin. Should you discover a tick, remove it by firmly grasping the insect as close to the skin as possible (tweezers are best), and using a steady movement pull the tick's body outwards without twisting or jerking. The following methods of prevention are suggested:

- before travelling, seek advice from your GP or travel clinic; consider immunisation (2 injections a month apart)
- use a tick-effective insect repellent
- do not wear shorts, but tuck trousers into socks and wear long-sleeved clothing
- inspect your skin (and that of your companions) for ticks, and remove with tweezers.

For further information visit www.masta.org/health-brief.

- Headtorch plus spare batteries and bulbs
- Water bottle (1 litre minimum)
- Sunglasses, high factor suncream and lip salve
- First aid kit, including tweezers
- Map and compass (and GPS if available)
- Whistle
- Watch
- Guidebook
- Penknife
- Camera
- Toilet kit (soap, towel, toothbrush, toothpaste)

- Emergency food
- Anti-tick insect repellent

RECOMMENDED MAPS

A variety of maps cover much of Austria, the best being those published by the ÖAV/DAV under the heading *Alpenvereinskarten*. Accurate and beautifully drawn, they have a robust quality missing on some of the commercial maps available, and are usually published at a scale of 1:25,000. However, the amount of detail included at this scale is perhaps more than most

Graukogel from the Palfnerscharte (Hohe Tauern, Route 83)

routes in this guide require. Sheets at a scale of 1:50,000 are available from Kompass, Freytag & Berndt, and Mayr, with some districts treated to 1:30,000, 1:35,000 and 1:40,000 scale.

Kompass *Wanderkarte* sheets have huts, hotels, and paths (with numbers) clearly marked in red for ease of identification. Be warned that some of the older maps were produced on poor-quality paper which tears easily, especially on the folds, and you may find that a single sheet will not last a full week. More recently-published sheets are slightly more weatherproof. A slim booklet (in German) accompanies these maps, with local information and brief walk suggestions.

Freytag & Berndt produce sheets of a similar quality to those of Kompass, this time with huts being ringed. The accompanying booklets are perhaps less useful than those of Kompass, although the latest ones include GPS information.

Mayr maps are produced in Innsbruck and, once more, are of similar quality to F&B and Kompass sheets. The paper tears easily and wears quickly at the folds, but the associated booklets give rather more detail with their walk suggestions than those of Kompass.

Specific sheets recommended for routes in this guide are outlined at the head of each walk description, but please note that in some instances names on maps do not match those that appear on local signposts. And the altitude measurements shown on some sheets may be at variance with those quoted on maps produced by different publishers.

USING THIS GUIDE

In this guide we begin in the west of Austria and work eastwards, exploring some of the finest valleys and their neighbouring mountains from resort bases, visiting mountain huts, lakes and viewpoints, and sampling a few multi-day hut tours.

Each mountain group is treated to a separate chapter, for which a map is provided as a locator. While individual walks are marked on the basic maps produced especially for this book, you will need a detailed topographical map to follow the route as described. The introduction to each chapter includes a note of specific map requirements, with details of the various villages or valley resorts, their access, facilities, tourist offices, huts and so on, followed by a number of walks based in the district. All the walks are listed in Appendix E at the back of this book, while an explanation of the grading system is found above.

Distances and heights are quoted throughout in kilometres and metres. This information is sourced directly from the recommended map where possible, but because of countless zigzags on some

routes, it has been necessary to resort to estimates in terms of actual distance walked. Likewise times quoted for each walk are approximations only. They refer to **actual walking time and make no allowances for rest stops, picnic breaks or interruptions for photography** – such stops can add considerably (25 to 50 per cent) to the overall time you're away from base, so it is important to bear this in mind when planning your day's activity. Although such times are given as an aid to planning they are, of course, subjective, and each walker will have his or her own pace which may or may not coincide with those quoted. By comparing your times with those given here, you should soon gain a reasonable idea of the difference and be able to compensate accordingly.

Abbreviations are used sparingly, but some have been adopted through necessity. While most should be easily understood, the following list is given for clarification:

From the frontier ridge above the Tübinger Hut, the twin Seehorn summits rise above their glacier (Route 11)

AAC	Austrian Alpine Club (UK branch)	km	kilometres
		m	metres
ATM	Automated Teller Machine ('hole in the wall' cash machine)	mins	minutes
		ÖAV	Österreichischer Alpenverein (Austrian Alpine Club)
AV	Alpenverein (maps)		
DAV	Deutscher Alpenverein (German Alpine Club)	PTT	Post Office (Post, Telephone, Telegraph)
FB	Freytag & Berndt (maps)	TVN	Touristenverein Naturfreunde
hrs	hours		

INFORMATION AT A GLANCE

- **Banking hours** These vary, but banks are usually open 8am–12.30pm and 1.30 or 2pm–3 or 4pm on Monday to Friday. Cash machines (ATMs) are located in most major resorts.

- **Currency** The Euro (€) 100 cents = €1. It is safer to carry large amounts of money in the form of travellers' cheques, or use an internationally accepted credit card such as American Express, Eurocard, Mastercard or Visa which are accepted by most banks, hotels and restaurants. Foreign currency can be changed at official exchange rates at all banks. Bureau de Change kiosks usually charge a handling fee.

- **Formalities** Holders of a valid UK passport or the national identity card of an EU country do not need a visa to enter Austria. Citizens of Australia, the USA, Canada and New Zealand can stay up to three months without a visa, but require a valid passport.

- **Health precautions** At the time of writing Austria has no major health concerns for the visitor, but walkers should be aware of an increasing danger of tick bites which can lead to Tick-Borne Encephalitis (TBE) – see box above. In addition avoid too much exposure to the sun, and only take drinking water from approved sources. UK visitors should carry the European Health Insurance (EHI) card which entitles the holder to free or reduced-cost medical treatment in an emergency. Medical insurance cover is essential, even where reciprocal health arrangements exist.

- **International dialling codes** When calling Austria from the UK, the code is 0043. To dial the UK from Austria, use 0044. When making an international call from a public phone booth, it is preferable to use a phone card (*Telefonkarte*) available from post offices and tobacconists. The majority of phone booths, however, have coin operated telephones.

- **Language** German is the national language of Austria. English is understood in most major resorts, but not everywhere. A basic German–English glossary is given in Appendix D.

41

- **Tourist information** Holiday Service of the Austrian National Tourist Office (☎ 0845 101 1818 – calls charged at local rate; e-mail: holiday@austria.info website: www.austria.info).

- **Weather Forecast** Recorded regional weather forecasts can be heard on ☎ 0900 91 1566 81 On the internet, a forecast for the Tyrol region can be found on www.tirol.at/wetter. Local forecasts can also be found on morning TV channels.

The path to the Stüdl Hut above the Lucknerhaus, with Grossglockner ahead (Hohe TauernRoute 98)

1 RÄTIKON ALPS

Carrying the borders of Liechtenstein and Switzerland southwest of the Montafon valley, this small group of limestone mountains provides an attractive backdrop to a variety of walks. Although several peaks remain the preserve of rock climbers, a few summits such as the 2818m Sulzfluh, and the Rätikon's highest – the Schesaplana (2965m), attract experienced mountain walkers and scramblers and reward with extensive panoramic views.

ACCESS AND INFORMATION	
Location	In the Vorarlberg, Austria's westernmost province. The Rätikon group forms the southwest wall of the Montafon valley and spreads across the borders of both Liechtenstein and Switzerland.
Maps	Kompass Wanderkarte 032 *Alpenpark Montafon* 1:35,000
	Freytag & Berndt WK371 *Bludenz-Klostertal-Brandnertal-Montafon* 1:50,000
Bases	Brand, Schruns, Tschagguns, Gargellen
Information	Vorarlberg Tourismus, Postfach 302, 6901 Bregenz (e-mail: info@vorarlberg.travel; website: www.vorarlberg.travel)
	Bludenz Tourismus (website: www.bludenz.at)
	Brand Tourismus, 6708 Brand (e-mail: tourismus@brandnertal.at; website: www.brandnertal.at)
	Montafon Tourismus, 6780 Schruns (e-mail: info@montafon.at; website: www.montafon.at)
	Schruns-Tschagguns Tourismus, 6780 Schruns (e-mail: schruns-tschagguns.at; website: www.schruns-tschagguns.at)
	Gargellen Tourismus, 6787 Gargellen (e-mail: info@gargellen.at; website: www.gargellen.at)
Access	By mainline train to Bludenz and the narrow-gauge Montafonerbahn to Schruns and Tschagguns. There are bus services from Bludenz to Brand and throughout the Montafon valley from Schruns to the Bielerhöhe.

At the northwestern end of the Rätikon group the Gamperdonatal is the first of the tributary valleys to give access to these mountains. Opening at Nenzing it stretches up

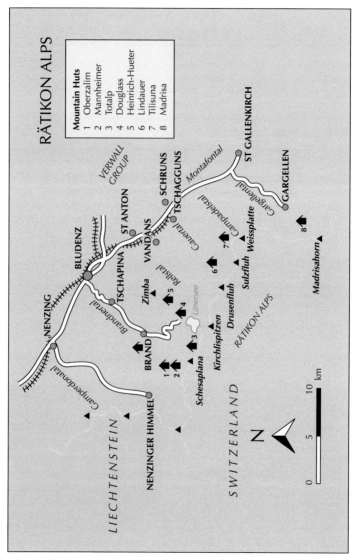

RÄTIKON ALPS

Mountain Huts
1 Oberzalim
2 Mannheimer
3 Totalp
4 Douglass
5 Heinrich-Hueter
6 Lindauer
7 Tilisuna
8 Madrisa

to the Liechtenstein border, its highest settlement being Nenzinger Himmel at 1370m, from where a variety of trails splay onto and across neighbouring ridges.

In the Montafon valley, Bludenz is an important transport hub lying mostly on the north bank of the river Ill at 561m. Although it boasts a cable-car to the Muttersberg with commanding views of the Rätikon and Silvretta Alps, the town is really too low to serve as a useful base. But about 12km away to the southwest, and almost 500m higher in the Brandnertal, Brand (1037m) acts as the main base for walkers and climbers at this end of the district. On the southern outskirts of this popular little resort the Zalimtal branches southwest, while the main valley continues southward to the roadhead where a cable-car carries visitors up to the Douglass Hut overlooking the Lünersee. From here a number of excellent walks and scrambles can be made, including the ascent of the Schesaplana.

Between Bludenz and St Gallenkirch the Montafon valley is largely flanked by wooded slopes, with a string of villages on either side of the river – St Anton im Montafon, Vandans, Tschagguns and Schruns. Cutting into the southern wall of mountains are the Rellstal, Gauertal, Gampadelstal and finally, the Gargellental which effectively forms a division between the Rätikon and Silvretta Alps. Mountain huts grace each of these tributary valleys, and in their upper reaches trails climb to the wonderland of craggy peaks that give the district much of its allure.

Gargellen, at the end of the Rätikon Höhenweg Nord

Visitors staying in any Montafon resort are given a **Guest Card** on arrival. This gives access to a number of services within the district free of charge or at a reduced rate. In addition it could be worth buying a **Montafon season ticket** (the *Sommerkarte*) for unlimited use of cable-cars in the Montafon valley, Bludenz and the Brandnertal; or the **Montafon-Silvretta Card** which allows unlimited use on numerous cable lifts and public transport on 3, 5, 7, 10 or 14 consecutive days, not only in the Montafon district, but also in the neighbouring Paznaun and Samnaun valleys.

Main Bases

Brand (1037m) A small health resort and low-key ski station, the village has more than a dozen hotels and *pensionen* up to 4-star, plus a number of private rooms and apartments, shops, restaurants, two banks with ATMs and a post office. For information contact Brand Tourismus (☎ 05559 5550 tourismus@brandnertal.at www.brandnertal.at). There's a campsite 4km to the north at Bürserberg.

Schruns (690m) Together with neighbouring Tschagguns across the Ill, Schruns is the main tourist centre in the Montafon valley. With a campsite and no shortage of hotel or apartment accommodation, the resort makes an obvious base, not only for the Rätikon group, but also for the Verwall mountains at the head of the Silbertal which stretches behind it. There are plenty of shops and restaurants, tourist information, banks with ATMs and a post office, while use of the Hochjochbahn cable-car gives access to some high trails east of the village. The tourist office is on Silvrettastrasse (☎ 05556 721660 info@schruns-tschagguns.at www.schruns-tschagguns.at).

Tschagguns (687m) Lying on the south bank of the Ill, Tschagguns is slightly smaller than its neighbour Schruns, but is close enough to share many of its facilities, including tourist office. It also has plenty of accommodation, including a campsite, a bank with ATM, restaurants and supermarket.

Gargellen (1423m) Located deep inside the Gargellental on the southern edge of the Rätikon Alps, Gargellen is served by bus from St Gallenkirch in the Montafon valley. It has limited facilities, but a good range of hotels, apartments and private rooms, a supermarket, post office and tourist information (☎ 05557 6303 info@gargellen.at www.gargellen.at).

Other Bases

Other Montafon villages offering accommodation at the foot of the Rätikon range include **St Anton im Montafon** (652m) on the right bank of the Ill, and **Vandans** (648m) which has a wide variety of hotels, apartments and private rooms located a short distance downstream from Tschagguns at the mouth of the Rellstal.

Mountain Huts

Douglass Hut (1976m) The original Douglass Hut was the first built by the DAV in 1872, and named after the British mountaineer John Sholto Douglass. With the creation of the Lünersee reservoir the former hut was flooded; its replacement dates from 1960, and is adjacent to the Lünersee cable-car station on the north shore of the lake at the head of the Brandnertal. Owned by the ÖAV's Bludenz section, this Category II hut is staffed from the end of May to mid-October, has 50 beds in rooms, and 100 dormitory places (☎ 05559 206).

Heinrich-Hueter Hut (1766m) Set below the impressive 2643m Zimba above the Rellstal and reached either in 2½hrs from the Douglass Hut or in 3–3½hrs from Vandans, this Category I hut is fully staffed from mid-June to the beginning of October. It has 20 beds in rooms and 90 dormitory places, and is owned by the Vorarlberg section of the ÖAV (☎ 05556 76570 www.hueterhuette.at)

Lindauer Hut (1744m) A popular hut standing among pinewoods below the Drusenfluh at the head of the Gauertal, it is owned by the Lindau section of the DAV and is manned from the end of February to the end of March, and from June to mid-October. With 40 beds in rooms and 120 dormitory places, it may be reached by a walk of 2½hrs from Latschau near Tschagguns (☎ 0664 5033456). Category I.

Madrisa Hut (1660m) Located southwest of Gargellen, this is an unmanned Category I hut owned by the Karlsruhe section of the DAV. It has just 15 dormitory places and may be reached by a walk of about 45mins from Gargellen. Prospective users should enquire at the tourist office in Gargellen for the key holder.

Mannheimer Hut (2679m) The highest of the Rätikon huts, it makes a popular base for climbs on the north side of the Schesaplana. Situated close to the shrinking Brandner glacier it stands south of the Oberzalim Hut, albeit almost 800m higher than its neighbour. Owned by the DAV's Mannheim section, it has 25 beds in rooms, and 150 dormitory places, and is staffed from July to mid-September (☎ 0664 3524768). A Category I hut, it is reached in about 5hrs from Brand via the Oberzalim Hut.

Oberzalim Hut (1889m) Reached by a walk of about 2½hrs from Brand, this Category I hut is located near the head of the Zalimtal. Owned by the Mannheim section of the DAV, it has a total of 28 places and is staffed from mid-June to the end of September (☎ 0664 1229305).

Tilisuna Hut (2211m) Overlooking a small tarn northeast of the Sulzfluh, and owned by the Vorarlberg section of the ÖAV, the Tilisuna Hut has places for 142 in beds and dormitories. A Category I hut, it is manned from mid-June to mid-October (☎ 0664 1107969) and may be reached in 2½–3hrs from Tschagguns.

Totalp Hut (2385m) Reached by a walk of a little under 1½hrs from the Douglass Hut, this Category I building lies in a stony landscape below and to the east of the Schesaplana. Owned by the Vorarlberg section of the ÖAV, it is manned from the end of May to mid-October, and has 85 dormitory places (☎ 0664 2400260).

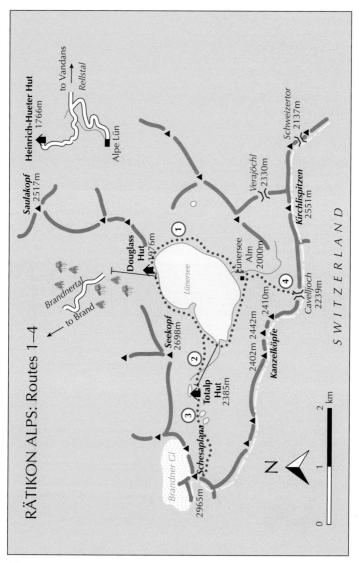

RÄTIKON ALPS: Routes 1–4

Saulakopf 2517m

Heinrich-Hueter Hut 1766m

to Vandans

Rellstal

Alpe Lün

Douglass Hut 1976m

Brandnertal

to Brand

Lünersee

Lünersee Alm 2000m

Verajöchl 2330m

Schweizertor 2137m

Kirchlispitzen 2551m

Seekopf 2698m

Totalp Hut 2385m

Schesaplana

Brandner Gl

2965m

Kanzelköpfe

2402m 2442m 2410m

Cavelljoch 2239m

SWITZERLAND

N

km

0   1   2

ROUTE 1

Douglass Hut (1976m) –
Lünersee Circuit – Douglass Hut

Location	At the head of the Brandnertal
Valley base	Brand
Grade	1
Distance	5.5km
Height gain	c100m
Height loss	c100m
Time	1¾ hrs

Lying in a natural basin below and to the east of the Schesaplana, the Lünersee was enlarged in the late 1950s by the construction of a dam at its northern end, which flooded the original Douglass Hut. Being accessible by cable-car, the undemanding lake circuit described here is understandably popular and likely to be very busy in summer. Although it is perfectly feasible to walk all the way from Brand to the Douglass Hut along the Schattenlagantweg and Böser-Tritt-Steig (3hrs), the normal approach is by car or bus to the Brandnertal roadhead, with the final 400m ascent via cable-car. The Douglass Hut is located a few metres east of the upper cable-car station, and its terrace is usually crowded with visitors when the sun shines.

Lünersee Alm

49

For the clockwise lake circuit simply continue eastwards across the lake along the Lünersee-Uferweg. Ignore the path breaking left to the Heinrich-Hueter Hut and follow the lake's curving outline heading south and southwest towards a building on the **Lünersee Alm** (2000m) where there's another junction. The left branch here climbs to the Cavelljoch on the Austro–Swiss border, and is also taken by the Rätikon Höhenweg Nord. For the lake circuit, however, wander westwards to yet another junction by the goods lift for the Totalp Hut, then veer right to return to the Douglass Hut along the lakeside in a further 30mins.

ROUTE 2

Douglass Hut (1976m) – Totalp Hut (2385m) – Lünersee Alm (2000m) – Douglass Hut

Location	Southwest of the Douglass Hut at the head of the Brandnertal
Valley base	Brand
Grade	3
Distance	7km
Height gain	409m
Height loss	409m
Time	3hrs

This is a longer variation of the Lünersee circuit described above. Heading anti-clockwise it breaks away from the lake shore and climbs to the Totalp Hut, before descending again to the Lünersee Alm to complete the circuit.

From the **Douglass Hut** pass the cable-car station heading west and follow the lakeside track for 15mins. A signed path now breaks away to the right, rising across a hillside dotted with alpenroses. In another 15mins or so it comes to a second junction at 2080m. The Totalp Hut route continues to twist up the hillside which becomes increasingly rocky,

and about 40mins from the junction you come over a lip to find the hut just ahead (1hr 15mins from the Douglass Hut). Refreshments can be taken here.

Kirchlispitzen, viewed from the Totalp Hut

The timber-built **Totalp Hut** (2385m) is staffed from the end of May to mid-October; 85 dormitory places, Category I (☎ 0664 2400260).

To return to the Lünersee descend the stony path used on the ascent, but in 20mins or so branch right at the 2080m junction signed to the Lindauer Hut, Cavelljoch and Schweizertor. This takes you down to the Totalp Hut's goods lift and a crossing path. Turn right, and rising gently round the southern end of the lake over grass hummocks starred with flowers, come to the **Lünersee Alm** and yet another junction at 2000m. Take the left fork, and 45mins later arrive back at the Douglass Hut.

ROUTE 3
Douglass Hut (1976m) – Schesaplana (2965m)

Location	West of the Lünersee at the head of the Brandnertal
Valley base	Brand
Grade	3
Distance	5km (ascent only)
Height gain	989m
Time	3hrs (+ 2hrs descent)

The ascent of the Schesaplana, highest of the Rätikon peaks, will no doubt be on the list of most experienced mountain walkers and scramblers visiting the area. By this route the mountain is not technically difficult to climb under 'normal' summer conditions, but snow patches should be expected, and there's a certain amount of loose rock, grit-covered ledges and some exposed passages to be wary of. Caution should be exercised, and the ascent taken seriously.

Follow Route 2 above as far as the **Totalp Hut** (1hr 15mins) where a sign directs you onto a path west into the stony basin of the Totalp ('dead alp') which, despite its name, displays a rich variety of alpine plants. Across the basin the path, waymarked blue and white, climbs in zigzags and in a further 50mins arrives at a junction with the Gemslücken path which cuts to the left.

The way now climbs more steeply in numerous zigzags to gain an upper basin choked either by scree or snow. From here the route slants up the right-hand side of the basin, then angles across to the left in order to reach the frontier ridge. The large cross on the summit of the **Schesaplana** is now visible for the first time as you turn right to climb the ridge directly to it. The views are extensive and varied. Near at hand both Drusenfluh and Sulzfluh attract in the southeast, the Brandner glacier is seen below to the north, while the Swiss side falls away to a mass of green valleys.

Descend by the same route in 2hrs, taking special care to avoid knocking loose stones onto others below.

From the Schesaplana, the vivid Lünersee captures your attention

ROUTE 4

Douglass Hut (1976m) –
Cavelljoch (2239m) – Douglass Hut

Location	South of the Lünersee
Valley base	Brand
Grade	2
Distance	8km
Height gain	263m
Height loss	263m
Time	3hrs

The Cavelljoch is a broad saddle on the Austro–Swiss border flanked by the abrupt west wall of the Kirchlispitzen. In the early summer the saddle is ablaze with alpine flowers, and views are beautiful both north and south. An easy but extremely pleasant walk leads to it from the Douglass Hut.

Cotton grass betrays a marshy area above the Lünersee Alm

Take the lakeside path in either direction as far as the **Lünersee Alm** on the south side of the lake, to find a signed junction (50–60mins). Follow the trail which rises to the rear of the hut into a hanging valley, and at the next junction 5mins later, branch half-right and mount grass slopes above a marshy area to gain the saddle of the **Cavelljoch** about 40–50mins from the Lünersee Alm. On a calm day this is a very pleasant site for a picnic. To return to the **Douglass Hut** (1½hrs) reverse the outward route, but take a different lakeside path for variety.

Cutting across the southern flank of the mountains the path of the **Rätikon Höhenweg Sud** is the Swiss equivalent of the Rätikon Höhenweg Nord described below. By following this trail westward, the Schesaplana Hut can be reached in 1hr 45mins; to the east the Carschina Hut is 3hrs away.

ROUTE 5
Rätikon Höhenweg Nord

Location	West to east across the north flank of the mountains
Grade	3
Distance	23km
Highest point	Sarotlapass (2389m)
Start	Douglass Hut (1976m)
Finish	Gargellen (1423m)
Time	3 days

Making a traverse of the north flank of the Rätikon mountains, this is a justifiably popular hut-to-hut tour that makes an excellent introduction to this form of mountain activity. Each stage is comparatively short. Paths are mostly good and well marked. The route is not too demanding, yet it has a few strenuous sections and in places a brief sense of isolation. Huts are comfortable and the scenery superb.

Day 1 From the **Douglass Hut** follow the lakeside path in either direction as far as the **Lünersee Alm** where there's a signed junction. Take the upper path climbing into a hanging valley, and keep ahead at the next junction 5mins later. (The right branch goes to the Cavelljoch on the Swiss border – see Route 4.) Aiming for the Verajöchl the path rises alongside a little stream leaking through pastures. Ignore a second path branching right to the Cavelljoch, continue ahead and cross the stream by footbridge, then skirt a marshy basin fluffed with cotton grass.

Passing below an abandoned customs hut, the way climbs left into an upper region littered with rocks and boulders, then becomes more grassy on the final approach to the 2330m **Verajöchl**. From the saddle a splendid view ahead shows the great gash of the Schweizertor cleaving the limestone wall that runs from the Kirchlispitzen to the Drusenfluh. Looking back the Schesaplana is equally impressive.

Descend grass slopes on the east side of the saddle to another one-time customs hut close to the **Schweizertor** at

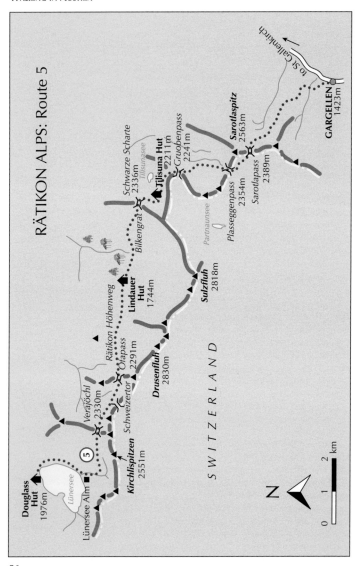

RÄTIKON ALPS: Route 5

Douglass Hut 1976m

Lünersee

Lünersee Alm

Kirchlispitzen 2551m

Verajöchl 2330m

Schweizertor

Drusenfluh 2830m

Öfapass 2291m

Rätikon Höhenweg

Bilkengrat

Lindauer Hut 1744m

Sulzfluh 2818m

S W I T Z E R L A N D

Schwarze Scharte 2336m

Tilisunasee

Tilisuna Hut 2211m

Gruobenpass 2241m

Partnaunsee

Plasseggenpass 2354m

Sarotlaspitz 2563m

Sarotlapass 2389m

Sarotlaspitz

to St Gallenkirch

GARGELLEN 1423m

N

0 1 2 km

Sulzfluh, seen from Sporeralpe near the Lindauer Hut

2137m, then keep ahead to climb through a narrow grass valley below the contorted limestone of the Drusenfluh, and gain the 2291m **Ofapass** about 40mins from the Verajöchl. The Lindauer Hut can now be seen below to the east, and a sign suggests a rather generous 1hr 15mins to get there.

With the hut in sight virtually all the way, the path descends steeply in places, with the Drusenfluh's rock scenery growing more impressive with each step. Shortly after passing a very small *alm* hut, wander past the complex of buildings of Obere Sporalpe to reach the **Lindauer Hut**, about 3½hrs from the Douglass Hut.

The Category I **Lindauer Hut** (1744m) has 40 beds in rooms and 120 dormitory places, is staffed from the end of February to the end of March, and from June to mid-October (☎ 0664 5033456). A notable alpine garden is located next to it.

Day 2 The second stage of the tour is also short (3hrs 15mins), but full of interest and notable for the long, steep ascent of the Bilkengrat. It begins by following a signed path heading east. This becomes a track, and when it curves left you continue ahead on a footpath sloping down among bilberry, dwarf pine and alpenrose, then twisting through light pinewoods with the big walls of the Sulzfluh towering overhead.

Edging below these walls the way forks at the entrance to a hanging valley.

An alternative route here ascends the **Sulzfluh** and crosses to the **Tilisuna Hut** in 3hrs 45mins.

Taking the path to the **Bilkengrat**, wander a short distance into this valley, cross its stream, then climb steeply up the left-hand slope. Passing through a belt of conifers emerge to a stunning view back to the Drei Turme of the Drusenfluh. Continuing the steep climb of the Bilkengrat spur there are consistently fine views to enjoy. You then come to a junction at 1990m where a sign gives 1hr 15mins to the Tilisuna Hut. But the climb is by no means over, for there's almost 350m yet to gain before reaching the 2336m **Schwarze Scharte** overlooking the Tilisunasee which lies below in a green basin. The Tilisuna Hut is unseen from here, although it's only 20mins away. The path now swings round the mountainside, contours for a while, then angles easily down to turn a spur which reveals the hut just below.

The Tilisuna Hut (2211m: Category I) is manned from mid-June to mid-October with 142 places in rooms and dormitories (☎ 0664 1107969). Given time and energy on arrival, it would be worth making the ascent of the Sulzfluh – see Route 7.

Day 3 This final stage of the Rätikon Höhenweg Nord strays briefly onto the Swiss flank of the mountains before descending to Gargellen. A sign outside the hut directs the way to the Gruobenpass (25mins), the first of the day's three passes. It heads across pastures above the Tilisunersee and forks near a much smaller tarn. Ignore the left branch and keep ahead, rising above the tarn and skirting the base of limestone crags. The way then twists among them, and squeezing through narrow clefts, gains the gap of the **Gruobenpass** where there's a small wooden customs hut. There are two signs giving the altitude; the Austrian says 2241m, the Swiss sign gives 2232m.

Do not cross this pass, but descend briefly left towards the pastures of the Gampadelstal, then rise again over grass hummocks, skirting little pools as the path works its way round the head of the valley. After weaving a devious course, the trail then makes a more direct approach to the **Plasseggenpass** (2354m). Just below it you pass another small one-time customs hut.

The Plasseggenpass is not only the border between Austria and Switzerland, but also marks the divide between limestone on the west, and crystalline rock on the east. Once again the path forks. Branch left (southeast) to cut along the Swiss flank of the Sarotlaspitzen on a narrow path that picks a route across the steep broken slope. One section crossing a band of rocks is safeguarded with a length of fixed cable, and moments later you arrive at the **Sarotlapass** (2389m) to gain an exciting view ahead of the Silvretta group – a range of jaunty, rocky peaks, some wearing glaciers and snowfields.

There follows a descent of more than 900m to Gargellen, at first taking a series of long loops down a steep hillside before contouring across the right-hand slope. The descent then resumes among alpenroses, crosses a gully and makes a traverse among lush vegetation, including thickets of alder. On turning a spur you gaze down into the head of the Gargellental, with the 2770m Madrisa directly ahead.

On reaching the solitary *alm* building of Obere Röbialpe at 1913m, the path descends beside it, cuts down the right flank of a spur, then more steeply to Untere Röbialpe and a junction. Both options lead to Gargellen. The right branch cuts along the edge of woodland, then goes through it. Over a stream you then wander through a meadow to another farm and barn, then descend again into forest where a signed path slopes to the right and moments later you gain a direct view onto the village. A footpath takes you over a stream at the outflow from a gorge, and across a final meadow enters **Gargellen** (3hrs 15mins from the Tilisuna Hut).

Gargellen (1423m) has a range of hotels, apartments and private rooms, a supermarket, post office and tourist information (☎ 05557 6303). Buses go from here to St Gallenkirch in the Montafon valley.

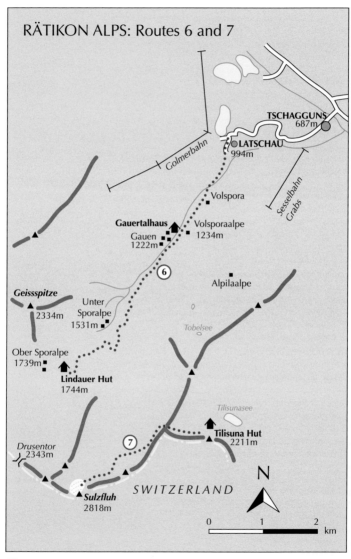

RÄTIKON ALPS: Routes 6 and 7

TSCHAGGUNS
687m

⊙**LATSCHAU**
994m

Golmerbahn

Sesselbahn Grabs

Volspora

Gauertalhaus

Gauen
1222m

Volsporaalpe
1234m

⑥

Alpilaalpe

Geissspitze
2334m

Unter
Sporalpe
1531m

Tobelsee

Ober Sporalpe
1739m

Lindauer Hut
1744m

Tilisunasee

Tilisuna Hut
2211m

⑦

Drusentor
2343m

Sulzfluh
2818m

SWITZERLAND

N

0   1   2
km

ROUTE 6

Tschagguns (Latschau: 994m) –
Lindauer Hut (1744m)

Location	Southwest of Tschagguns, at the head of the Gauertal
Valley base	Tschagguns
Grade	2
Distance	6km (one way)
Height gain	750m
Time	2½hrs (+ 2–2¼hrs return)

The Lindauer Hut makes a popular destination for a day-walk, as well as a good base for climbing a variety of peaks, and an overnight halt for walkers on the Rätikon Höhenweg. The following approach is one of the easiest; a delight of grassy alms, woodland and fine views.

Lying some 300m above Tschagguns, **Latschau** is a collection of chalets overlooking a reservoir. Reached by local bus via a road that twists between meadows and chalets, there's plenty of parking space for visitors with their own cars, while the area is also served by a two-stage gondola lift system from Vandans.

Wander along the narrow tarmac road heading south above the reservoir. Passing a number of chalets take the left branch when it forks. A few paces after this you pass to the left of Hotel Montabella. Once again the road forks, but this time take the right branch. Almost immediately the road becomes a stony track.

The way goes through a wooded gorge, then forks. Both routes lead to the Lindauer Hut, but on this occasion keep to the left branch. After going through mixed woods you emerge to open meadows and the scattered chalets and haybarns of **Volspora**. Ahead can be seen the Sulzfluh and its glacier.

At the far end of the meadows another track breaks left to Alpilaalpe, but ignore this and keep ahead to **Volsporaalpe** (1234m) where, should you be in need of refreshment, a path

The Drei Turme above the Lindauer Hut

descends to the river, then climbs the opposite bank to the **Gauertalhaus**. If refreshment is not required, remain on the track which now rises to another level where long fingers of coniferous trees come down into the valley. When the track forks again, keep ahead, remaining on the east side of the river.

After crossing another alpine meadow with a solitary barn in it, the track twists up through forest (unmarked footpath shortcuts), and above this you rise through more pastures to a T junction of tracks. Bear left. As the track returns to forest more footpath shortcuts can be taken. One of these makes a long, steady uphill slant, and on rejoining the track, the hut can be seen ahead. Walk up the track, bear left when it forks, and shortly after, arrive at the **Lindauer Hut**. Note the alpine garden located on its western side.

The Category I **Lindauer Hut** has 40 beds and 120 dormitory places. Staffed from the end of February to the end of March, and from June to mid-October, it is owned by the Lindau section of the DAV (☎ 0664 5033456 www.alpenverein-lindau.de).

For an alternative return to Latschau, try the left-bank path and track by way of **Gauen**. Although steep in places in the early stages, the way eases lower down and makes a very pleasant walk in its own right.

Note A 3hrs 15mins link with the **Tilisuna Hut** is described from the Lindauer Hut as part of the Rätikon Höhenweg Nord (Route 5), and is recommended.

ROUTE 7
Tilisuna Hut (2211m) – Sulzfluh (2818m)

Location	Southwest of the Tilisuna Hut at the head of the Gampadelstal
Valley base	Tschagguns
Grade	3
Distance	3km (one way)
Height gain	607m
Time	2hrs (+ 1hr descent)

The Sulzfluh is a mountain with two faces. Its south (Swiss) side soars above screes in a formidable wall, but its northeast flank is much less severe with an approach dominated by a vast region of limestone pavement that leads to the final lumpy tower of the summit. The route described here is probably the easiest on the mountain, being little more than a walk, although care should be taken when crossing the limestone pavement – especially in misty conditions, as there are numerous deep fissures – and the snow patches that often linger on the upper slopes.

On leaving the **Tilisuna Hut** take the path signed to the Lindauer Hut, then keep ahead when it forks after 5mins. The trail rises through a shallow grass scoop, then up a spur before angling left to gain height at a steady gradient. About 30mins from the hut you come onto a ridge and the start of the limestone pavement where cairns and paint flashes guide the way.

The 2818m Sulzfluh can be climbed by an undemanding route from the Tilisuna Hut

This is a broad, almost featureless terrain that demands concentration, but views include the Drusenfluh and distant Schesaplana, while the cross on the Sulzfluh's summit is clearly seen ahead. The trail meanders across the pavement, avoiding numerous deep fissures that have been cut into it, then goes up a slope (the path breaking into several strands) to gain an upper section of ridge and a signed junction. (The right branch is used on the ascent from the Lindauer Hut.)

The ridge narrows after this junction, and the path works along limestone ribs to be joined by a trail bringing a route from the Swiss side. It is here that the final ascent begins up rough slopes (sometimes snow ramps), still guided by cairns and paint flashes to mount the summit tower by its easiest side. The summit of the **Sulzfluh** is crowned by a huge wooden cross, and the panoramic view is immense.

OTHER ROUTES IN THE RÄTIKON ALPS

The seven routes described above represent some of the best walking opportunities in the Rätikon Alps, but there are, of course, scores more. A glance at the map is sufficient to reveal numerous walks of varying length and degree of difficulty, and the following outline suggestions may help focus your attention.

• From **Brand** a 2½hr route heading southwest through the Zalimtal leads to the **Oberzalim Hut** at 1889m near the head of the valley beneath the Schesaplana.

• An extension of the Oberzalim Hut walk takes the demanding Leibertsteig route up to the **Mannheimer Hut**, the highest in the Rätikon Alps at 2679m; while another trail heads roughly westward, crosses the **Spusagangscharte** (2237m), descends to **Nenzinger Himmel** (accommodation) in the Gamperdonatal, and returns to Brand via the 2028m **Amatschonjoch**, for a rewarding two-day trek.

• Several walks have already been described from the **Douglass Hut**, but instead of either following the Rätikon Höhenweg Nord, or descending to Brand at the end of your visit, an alternative way out follows the Saulajochsteig north of the Lünersee, crosses the Saulajoch (2065m), descends to the **Heinrich-Hueter Hut**, then wanders down the length of the Rellstal to **Vandans** in the Montafon valley – a walk of about 4hrs.

• A *Wanderbus* operates a daily service in summer from Vandans through the Rellstal to **Alpengasthof Rellstal** at 1490m. This gives access to a number of trails that explore the mountains to south, east and west, among them the Lünerweg leading to the **Douglass Hut** via the Lünerkrinne, and a straightforward route continuing south to the Obere Zaluandialpe, up to the Schweizertor, then east across the Öfapass to the **Lindauer Hut**.

• The *Golmerbahn* from Vandans provides a fast and easy way to reach the sprawling ridge which forms a divide between the Rellstal and Gauertal. From the top **Bergstation Golmerbahn** at 1880m a large number of walks become possible, among them one which goes to the **Lindauer Hut** in just 1½hrs, and another leading to **Alpengasthof Rellstal** in 2hrs on a walk via Platzisalpe.

• A very pleasant 2½–3hr high route takes walkers from the Tschagguns-Grabs chairlift (1393m) up to the scenic **Tobelsee**, and across the 2166m Schwarzhornsattel to gain the **Tilisuna Hut**. A longer alternative walk from Tschagguns to the Tilisuna Hut follows a farm road into the Gampadelstal, but then breaks off on a footpath known as the *Herrawegli* from the Gampadels Alpe. This leads to the hut via the Walseralpe and Tilisunasee.

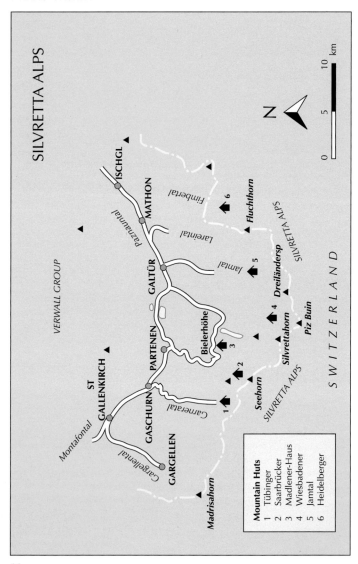

SILVRETTA ALPS

Mountain Huts
1 Tübinger
2 Saarbrücker
3 Madlener-Haus
4 Wiesbadener
5 Jamtal
6 Heidelberger

2 SILVRETTA ALPS

The main ridge of the Silvretta group carries the frontier south and east of the Rätikon Alps, extending beyond the boundaries of Vorarlberg into the Tyrol, and across the border into the Swiss canton of Graubunden. But while the Rätikon is limestone, the Silvretta is crystalline, and a number of its mountains are daubed with snowfields and glaciers, which add a certain majesty to their 3000m summits.

ACCESS AND INFORMATION	
Location	Spreading east from the Vorarlberg province into Tyrol south of the Arlberg Pass, and carrying the Austro–Swiss border south and east of the Rätikon Alps. The Montafon and Paznaun valleys, linked by the Bielerhöhe, form the northern boundary and divide the Silvretta from the Verwall range.
Maps	Alpenvereinskarte 26 *Silvrettagruppe* 1:25,000
	Kompass Wanderkarte 032 *Alpenpark Montafon* 1:35,000
	Kompass Wanderkarte 41 *Silvretta Verwallgruppe* 1:50,000
	Freytag & Berndt WK373 *Silvretta Hochalpenstrasse-Piz Buin* 1:50,000
Bases	St Gallenkirch, Gaschurn, Bielerhöhe, Galtür, Ischgl
Information	Vorarlberg Tourist Board (e-mail: info@vorarlberg.travel; website: www.vorarlberg.travel)
	Tirol Info, 6010 Innsbruck (e-mail: info@tirol.at; website: www.tirol.at)
	Montafon Tourismus, 6780 Schruns (e-mail: info@montafon.at; website: www.montafon.at)
	St Gallenkirch Tourismus, 6791 St Gallenkirch (e-mail: info@ stgallenkirch.at; website: www.stgallenkirch.at)
	Gaschurn Tourismus, 6793 Gaschurn (e-mail: info@gaschurn-partenen.com; website: www.gaschurn-partenen.com)
	Tourismusverband Paznaun, 6563 Galtür (e-mail: info@galtuer.com; website: www.galtuer.com)
	Tourismusverband Paznaun, 6561 Ischgl (e-mail: info@ischgl.com; website: www.ischgl.com)
Access	West of the Bielerhöhe, the Montafon valley has mainline train services to Bludenz, then via the narrow-gauge Montafonerbahn

to Schruns. Bus services run throughout the valley between Schruns and the Bielerhöhe. For the Paznauntal east of the Bielerhöhe, buses connect the mainline railway network at Landeck with villages up to the Bielerhöhe. Visitors with their own transport should note that the Silvretta Hochalpenstrasse, the route over the Bielerhöhe, is a toll road.

Linked across the watershed pass of the Bielerhöhe by the serpentine road of the Silvretta Hochalpenstrasse, both the Montafon and Paznaun valleys are luxuriously green and attractive, and having the Verwall mountains on one side and the Silvretta Alps on the other, they provide numerous walking opportunities. Apart from Ischgl, their village resorts are mostly small and fairly low-key, public transport is good, and waymarked trails abundant within the main valleys. But it is the tributary valleys and the mountains they drain that are the main focus of attention here. Mountain huts are found in virtually all of these southern tributaries, and there are some rewarding routes that link one with another, often over scenic passes.

The high mountain landscapes are some of the most impressive in all Austria. Notable among Silvretta summits are the rock pinnacle of the Gross Litzner (3109m), the glacier-draped Piz Buin (3312m) and neighbouring 3197m Dreiländerspitz.

Piz Buin, seen from the Mittelrücke

The **Montafon-Silvretta Card** offers reductions for guests staying in resorts in either valley. The card allows unlimited use of buses, trains and numerous cable lifts on 3, 5, 7, 10 or 14 consecutive days. Enquire at your nearest tourist office for details and up-to-date prices.

Main Bases

St Gallenkirch (878m) Sprawling along the north bank of the Ill in the Montafon valley near the entrance to the Gargellental, St Gallenkirch has most facilities, including shops, supermarkets, bank with ATM, post office and restaurants. It has a good selection of hotels, *pensionen*, *gasthöfe*, apartments and private rooms. There's also a campsite here and in neighbouring Gortipohl. Contact the tourist office for an accommodation list (☎ 05557 66000 info@stgallenkirch.at)

Gaschurn (979m) This is perhaps the best resort base in the Montafon valley for Silvretta walks. It has a gondola lift on the south side of the valley giving access to some high trails, and the Garneratal reaches into the mountains opposite the village. The local tourist office makes much of the 4000 steps that climb above Partenen to the top station of the Vermuntbahn at 1732m. As for resort facilities, Gaschurn has a choice of shops, supermarkets, restaurants, a bank, post office and tourist information. There are plenty of hotels of all grades, as well as *pensionen*, private rooms and apartments. For information ☎ 05558 82010 (info@gaschurn-partenen-com).

Bielerhöhe (2036m) Crowning the Silvretta Hochalpenstrasse, the Bielerhöhe overlooks the reservoir of the Silvretta Stausee and the 3223m Schneeglocke with its glacial scarf. There's a large car park, café and kiosk at the dam, where bus routes from Schruns and Landeck terminate. Above the road the 2-star Berggasthof Piz Buin has 55 beds (☎ 05558 4231 info@pizbuin.at; www.buin.at). There's also the slightly more expensive Silvretta Haus (☎ 05558 4246) opposite the car park. The only other accommodation is at the Madlener-Haus below the dam (see under Mountain Huts).

Galtür (1584m) A small, compact village at the eastern foot of the Silvretta Hochalpenstrasse, it is somewhat limited in facilities, with a handful of shops, two banks with ATMs, a post office and restaurants. It has a tourist office and a choice of hotels and *pensionen*. For details contact info@galtuer.com or visit www.galtuer.com.

Ischgl (1376m) Both a winter resort and a useful walking base, with the long Fimbertal cutting into the mountains to the south (its headwall is on the Swiss side of the range). A gondola lift rises to Idalpe (2311m) from where it's possible to walk across the border, descend to duty-free Samnaun and return by bus via Landeck. Ischgl has a wide range of facilities and lots of accommodation in various categories. Visit the tourist office in the centre of the village for details, or try www.ischgl.com.

Mountain Huts

Heidelberger Hut (2264m) Built by the Heidelberg section of the DAV in 1889 and enlarged several times since, this Category II hut is located within Swiss territory, but approached by a long walk from Ischgl through the Fimbertal, which is mostly Austrian. Payment for services is in Euros. With 84 dormitory places and 72 beds in rooms, it is fully manned from the end of June to early October (☎ 0664 4253070 www.heidelbergerhuette.com).

Jamtal Hut (2165m) This large Category I valley hut is built near the head of the Jamtal south of Galtür, from which it is reached by a 3–3½hr walk. Property of the DAV's Schwaben section, it was rebuilt in 1999 after being destroyed by avalanche. Fully staffed from mid-February to early May, and the end of June to the end of September, it has 90 beds in rooms, and 100 dormitory places (☎ 05443 8408 info@jamtalhuette.at; www.jamtalhuette.at).

Madlener-Haus (1986m) Built in 1884, but enlarged and improved in 1906 and 1975, this Category II hut is located just below the Bielerhöhe dam amongst a complex of buildings. Owned by the Wiesbaden section of the DAV, it has 60 beds in rooms and 20 dormitory places, and is staffed from February to Easter, and from June to mid-October (☎ 05558 4234 www.madlenerhaus.at).

Saarbrücker Hut (2538m) Property of the DAV Saarbrücken section, this large, traditional Category I hut stands amid rocky country below the Klein Litzner in the upper Kromertal. With 80 dormitory places and 20 beds in rooms, it may be reached by a 3hr walk from the Bielerhöhe, or in 2½hrs along a track from the Vermunt reservoir. Fully staffed at Easter and Whitsun, and from July to the end of September (☎ 05558 4235 www.alpenverein-saarbruecken.de).

The Saarbrücker Hut

The Kromerbach, below the Saarbrücker Hut

Tübinger Hut (2191m) Built on a shelf near the head of the Garneratal with 79 dormitory places and 40 beds in rooms. A Category I hut, owned by the Tübingen section of the DAV, it is staffed from July to the end of September and reached by a walk of about 4–4½hrs from Gaschurn (☎ 0664 2530450 www.dav-tuebingen.de)

Wiesbadener Hut (2443m) One of the most popular of Silvretta huts on account of its location and pleasant 2–2½hr approach walk from the Bielerhöhe, it is owned by the Wiesbaden section of the DAV. With Piz Buin and the Dreiländerspitz nearby, this Category I hut makes a good base for climbs and glacier tours. It has 160 dormitory places and 40 beds in rooms, and is fully staffed from the end of February to early May, and from the end of June to early October (☎ 05558 4233 www.wiesbadener-huette.com).

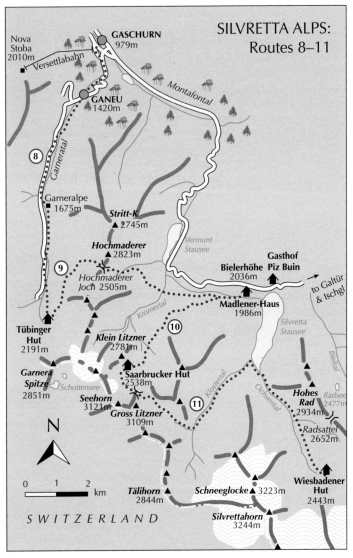

SILVRETTA ALPS:
Routes 8–11

Nova Stoba 2010m

GASCHURN 979m

Versettlabahn

GANEU 1420m

Montafontal

⑧

Garneratal

Garneralpe 1675m

Stritt-K ▲ 2745m

Hochmaderer ▲ 2823m

Vermunt Stausee

⑨

Hochmaderer Joch 2505m

Bielerhöhe 2036m

Gasthof Piz Buin

to Galtür & Ischgl

Kromertal

Madlener-Haus 1986m

Silvretta Stausee

Tübinger Hut 2191m

⑩

Bieltal

Klein Litzner ▲ 2781m

Garnera Spitze 2851m

Schottensee

Saarbrucker Hut 2538m

Klostertal

Ochsental

Hohes Rad 2934m

Radsee
2477m

Seehorn 3121m

⑪

Gross Litzner 3109m

Radsattel 2652m

N

0   1   2 km

Tälihorn 2844m

Schneeglocke ▲ 3223m

Wiesbadener Hut 2443m

Silvrettahorn 3244m

S W I T Z E R L A N D

ROUTE 8

Gaschurn (979m) – Tübinger Hut (2191m)

Location	In the Garneratal south of Gaschurn
Valley base	Gaschurn
Grade	2–3
Distance	9km
Height gain	1212m
Time	4–4½hrs

The Tübinger Hut sits high up on the east side of the wild Garneratal in the rocky cirque that carries the Austro–Swiss border. Built in 1908 it has been enlarged and improved at least twice since then, but it retains a cosy atmosphere with its wood-burning stove glowing in the *stube* when storm clouds broil outside. The valley is narrow, steep-walled and rugged; at its head rise mountains of 2700–2800m, but a wooded gorge squeezes its northern end from which the Garnera Bach spills out to the Montafontal.

There are at least two routes to the hut from Gaschurn. This is the shortest and easiest, but a good alternative begins by taking the Versettla gondola lift to Nova Stoba on the western ridge at 2010m, from where a waymarked path heads south to cross several modest summits before coming to the 2515m Vergaldajoch, after which the way cuts across the valley's upper reaches with a final climb to the hut (5–6hrs).

A signpost by the tourist office in **Gaschurn**'s main street directs the way down a side road towards the river. Do not cross at the first opportunity, but turn left along a side road, then cross at the next bridge, arriving on the main road opposite the **Versettla Bahn**. Take a service road left of the cableway entrance, and when this ends by a restaurant, go ahead on a stony track, cross a stream and turn right on another service road.

Following the Garnera Bach upstream, the tarmac ends by some houses, but an unmade road continues, twisting uphill through the wooded gorge (Garneraschlucht) at the Garneratal's entrance. At the first hairpin a footpath breaks away to climb alongside the river's waterfalls, and about 1hr from Gaschurn it brings you to the large and attractive group of timber buildings of **Ganeu** (1420m) set among pastures. The track also reaches this hamlet, then continues upvalley, crossing the stream several times.

Although it's perfectly feasible to follow the unmade road/track all the way to the Tübinger Hut's goods lift about 6km beyond Ganeu, a better option is to take the path which remains on the east bank of the stream as far as a bridge where you rejoin the track. The valley is surprisingly level for while, then it rises on the approach to the **Garneralpe** (1675m). Once again it's possible to take a path on the east bank, rejoining the track where it crosses the stream a little over 1km further on.

At about 1890m a signed path breaks away to make a rising traverse of the eastern hillside. The Tübinger Hut is now 40mins away. Rising among lush vegetation the path climbs steeply in places up what is an old glacial sill, and the final few paces to the hut are over rocks.

The **Tübinger Hut** (2191m: Category I) has 40 beds in rooms and 79 dormitory places, and is fully staffed from July to the end of September (☎ 0664 2530450).

ROUTE 9
Tübinger Hut (2191m) – Hochmaderer Joch (2505m) – Bielerhöhe (2036m)

Location	Northeast and east of the Tübinger Hut
Valley base	Gaschurn or Bielerhöhe
Grade	3
Distance	9km
Height gain	430m
Height loss	585m
Time	4–4¼hrs

A natural departure from the Tübinger Hut takes a route over the Garneratal's east-walling ridge, down to the Kromertal and up to the Bielerhöhe, from where buses run through both the Montafon and Paznaun valleys. This is a very fine mountain walk, with some exposure on the way to the Hochmaderer Joch, and a very steep initial descent from it.

A sign outside the hut indicates the way to the Bielerhöhe, at first picked out with waymarks across a bouldery wilderness, but then a path becomes clearer as it slants across the hillside heading northeast. As you gain height, retrospective views reveal that the hut is perched on a glacial sill.

The path to the *joch* is mostly good, but there are several fairly exposed sections where caution is advised. About 40mins after leaving the hut the way turns a spur into the hanging valley of the Gatschettatäli headed by the 2823m Hochmaderer. About 6mins later reach a path junction at 2300m. Ignore the left branch (a high route to Ganeu and Gaschurn) and keep ahead with cairns and red paint flashes guiding the way ever higher through the rocky little valley.

Descending from the Hochmaderer Joch, the Vermunt Stausee can be seen in the valley below

Shortly before gaining the pass, an alternative path strikes off left to make the ascent of the **Hochmaderer** – a recommended diversion. Allow 50–60mins for the ascent, plus 40mins descent back to this junction.

From the junction the path makes a traverse to the right (south) and 2mins later comes onto the **Hochmaderer Joch** (2505m), about 1hr 40mins from the hut. A sudden eastward view shows the Silvretta Stausee at the Bielerhöhe with the road snaking to it; but best of all is the sight of snow-gleaming peaks of the Silvretta Alps.

The initial descent is very steep and demands care. But the gradient eases as you come down to a rocky hollow, cross a stream then work round the right-hand hillside and turn a spur to gain a view onto the milky blue waters of the Vermunt reservoir. A few minutes after this the view is to the south, where rocky peaks block the Kromertal.

Descend into the bed of the Kromertal, crossing several minor streams on the way to a track where you turn right along it for just 2mins. A signed junction at 1920m directs you left, and moments later you cross the Kromer Bach on a plank footbridge and continue across pastures. Here the way becomes less distinct, although there's a path of sorts which weaves among bilberry, juniper and alpenrose, crosses several more minor streams and comes to the **Madlener-Haus**

(60 beds, 20 dormitory places; ☎ 05558 4234). Unless you need accommodation here follow a service road beyond the hut, then take a slanting footpath up to the car park at the **Bielerhöhe**.

At the **Bielerhöhe** you will find bus stops (for Montafon and Paznaun village services), a kiosk, toilets, public telephone and café. There is also a tourist boat on the Silvretta Stausee. For accommodation note the 2-star **Berggasthof Piz Buin** (55 beds; ☎ 05558 4231) just above the road, and the large Silvretta Haus hotel opposite the car park.

ROUTE 10
Bielerhöhe (2036m) – Saarbrucker Hut (2538m)

Location	Southwest of the Bielerhöhe
Valley base	Bielerhöhe or Galtür
Grade	2
Distance	6km
Height gain	502m
Time	3hrs

Built upon a rocky spur projecting from the Klein Litzner at the head of the Kromertal, the Saarbrucker Hut is used by climbers tackling an assortment of neighbouring peaks, as well as by hut-to-hut trekkers, for there are several passes nearby that link with other refuges on both sides of the frontier. It's a traditional hut, easily accessible and often very busy. There are two routes to it through the Kromertal, the shorter of which follows a track all the way from the southern end of the Vermunt reservoir. The route described here, though longer and slightly more demanding, is the more scenic option.

From the western side of the Bielerhöhe car park take a waymarked path which descends below the road to the **Madlener-Haus**. Pass along its left-hand side and, a few paces later, follow the red-and-white waymarked path (no 302) cutting left ahead along the edge of a gully. It then

The Grosser Seehorn overlooks the Saarbrücker Hut

descends into the gully and crosses a stream before working along the lower hillside to a signed fork at 1950m.

Branch left and angle across the hillside, rising to turn a spur and reach a sloping shelf above the entrance to the **Kromertal**. Crossing minor streams the path rises again, making a few twists, then over a rocky shoulder and a rock tip beyond. A succession of shoulders are crossed or turned before coming to two small tarns. Soon after, the way descends a little to cross the Kromer Bach by footbridge. A few paces later come onto the track which serves the hut. A sign here indicates 50mins to reach it.

Either follow the track as it winds up into a stony basin below glacial remnants, or take the more direct, but steeper, waymarked path leading directly to the **Saarbrucker Hut**.

The **Saarbrucker Hut** is a large Category I hut with 20 beds in rooms, and 80 dormitory places. It is manned at Easter and Whitsun, and from July to the end of September (☎ 05558 4235).

ROUTE 11

Wiesbadener Hut (2443m) – Litzner Sattel
(2737m) – Saarbrucker Hut (2538m)

Location	Northwest of the Wiesbadener Hut
Valley base	Bielerhöhe
Grade	3
Distance	10km
Height gain	696m
Height loss	641m
Time	4½hrs

Classified as an 'Alpine route' suitable for experienced mountain walkers only, this is a popular cross-country trek for climbers moving from one hut to the next. The Litzner Sattel lies in a ridge running northeast of the elegant rock pinnacle of the Gross Litzner, and on its northern side lie the remnants of a small glacier – mostly snow now, but it could be icy in its upper reaches.

From the Wiesbadener Hut (see Route 12) walk down the track/dirt road to the southern end of the **Silvretta Stausee** reservoir. Cross the bridge over the torrent which drains the Ochsental, and at the next junction branch left into the Klostertal (about 1hr to here).

A good path keeps to the left of the Klostertaler Bach, and about 45mins after entering the valley, you come to a sign stating that the unmanned Klostertaler Hut is just 20mins ahead. Fork right here on a narrow trail which soon crosses two branches of the stream on what was found to be a some-what dubious footbridge during research.

The trail now weaves alongside the stream, then climbs a steep grass slope in the little side valley known as the Verhupftäli. Where there are brief rock slabs to mount, fixed ropes provide aid, and once you've climbed above these the way continues up to a plateau at about 2500m. This leads to the upper basin which is topped by the ridge connecting the Gross Litzner to the Sattelkopf and Verhupfspitz.

A line of small cairns and waymarks direct the path up a steep ramp of rocks to a prominent cairn. Bear left (west) along the ridge, descend to a saddle and pass along the left-hand side of a small lake, then curve north to reach the **Litzner Sattel** (about 3½hrs from the Wiesbadener Hut).

Descend the northern side of the pass to a steep snow slope (caution). Angle a little leftwards down this slope, and at the foot of the snow you'll find blue and white waymarks taking the trail down to a second snow slope. Below this more waymarks lead into a basin below the Saarbrucker Hut. Join its service road/track and follow it up to the hut, whose details are found under Route 10.

ROUTE 12

Bielerhöhe (2036m) – Wiesbadener Hut (2443m)
– Radsattel (2652m) – Bielerhöhe

Location	Southeast of the Bielerhöhe
Valley base	Bielerhöhe or Galtür
Grade	2–3
Distance	13km
Height gain	616m
Height loss	616m
Time	5–6hrs

A circular tour with close views of Piz Buin and the Dreiländerspitz, visiting a popular mountain hut and crossing an easy pass, this makes an excellent day's walk.

From the **Bielerhöhe** car park cross the dam wall and wander along a good path on the western side of the **Silvretta Stausee**. When the path forks near the end of the lake take the left branch (the right branch is for the Klostertal). Shortly after cross the Klostertaler Bach and continue round the southern end of the lake, and having crossed a second stream join the east bank trail and bear right into the Ochsental. Mountain

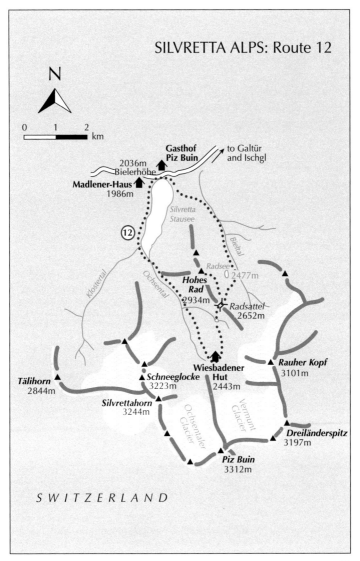

The Silvretta reservoir at the Bielerhöhe

views increase in grandeur, and glaciers and snowfields of the Dreiländerspitz, Piz Buin, Signalhorn and Silvrettahorn form a gleaming white backrop. Several minor streams are crossed as the path rises to the **Wiesbadener Hut** (2443m) about 2–2½hrs from the Bielerhöhe.

The **Wiesbadener Hut** (Category I) has 160 dormitory places and 40 beds, and is fully staffed from the end of February to early May, and from the end of June to early October (☎ 05558 4233).

A few paces beyond the hut bear left on the Edmund Lorenz Weg, a trail climbing northward with a few zigzags up to a high, stone-littered meadow – a good vantage point from which to study Piz Buin and its neighbours. Cairns and way-marks guide the continuing way into a rolling pastureland where a few minor pools are found in early summer. From here the path climbs a final slope to the 2652m **Radsattel** by a series of zigzags. This saddle, or pass, on the south-east ridge of the Hohes Rad marks the boundary between Vorarlberg and Tyrol.

The ascent of the **Hohes Rad** (2934m) is recommended if you have the time and energy. Take the left-hand path at the Radsattel. Heading north it cuts along the east side of the ridge to a point about 200m above the little Radsee, where a sign painted on a rock directs the ascent route up to the left. The way is a little exposed, and some easy scrambling is involved, but the summit is reached about 30–45mins from the Radsattel. The panoramic view makes the effort worthwhile.

At the Radsattel take the right fork at the path junction to descend northeastwards. Snow patches often lie well into summer on this side of the ridge, so caution is advised. The initial descent is steep and over rocks, then in tight zigzags down to the floor of the Bieltal shortly after passing the **Radsee** tarn at 2477m.

The Bieltal is a gentle, narrow valley with a rich variety of alpine flowers in early summer, and the path follows its stream most of the way through it. Towards the northern end of the valley the way curves left among hillsides thick with alpenroses, and finally brings you back to the Bielerhöhe above the Silvretta Stausee.

Piz Buin and its glacier, from the Radsattel

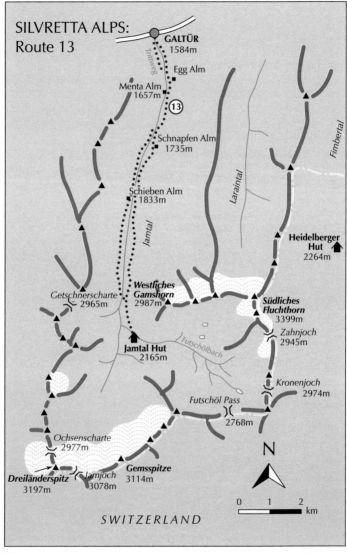

SILVRETTA ALPS:
Route 13

GALTÜR
1584m

Trittweg

Egg Alm

Menta Alm
1657m

(13)

Schnapfen Alm
1735m

Schieben Alm
1833m

Jamtal

Laraintal

Fimbertal

Heidelberger
Hut
2264m

Getschnerscharte
2965m

*Westliches
Gamshorn*
2987m

Südliches
Fluchthorn
3399m

Futschölbach

Zahnjoch
2945m

Jamtal Hut
2165m

Kronenjoch
2974m

Futschöl Pass

2768m

N

Ochsenscharte
2977m

0   1   2
km

Dreiländerspitz
3197m

Jamjoch
3078m

Gemsspitze
3114m

SWITZERLAND

ROUTE 13

Galtür (1584m) – Jamtal Hut (2165m)

Location	South of Galtür, at the head of the Jamtal
Valley base	Galtür
Grade	1–2
Distance	10km (one way)
Height gain	581m
Time	3hrs (+ 2½hrs return)

The head of the Jamtal is bounded by a group of 3000m summits and a neat curtain of glaciers. Streams drain from them to gather in a little plain below the Jamtal Hut which stands amid a rocky landscape at the mouth of the wild tributary valley of the Futschölbach. The hut is a large one with good facilities, and this walk to it travels almost the full length of the valley without any complications, so you can swing along the track and enjoy the scenery without frequent reference to either guidebook or map. The route only warrants a grade slightly higher than 1 because of its length.

A sign in the village square near the tourist office in **Galtür** indicates the way to the hut. Heading south, a narrow road rises between buildings, then forks. Take the right branch, and soon after a sign gives two options: one (the main route) continues straight ahead, the other branches right and is signed Trittweg – see box.

Trittweg option: Turn right and walk down a tarmac drive towards a house named Büntalihof. Pass alongside the house and beyond a few other buildings to a footbridge over the Jambach. Across the stream turn left on a track. At first rising under forest, it then goes between meadows, recrosses the Jambach and joins the standard route a little north of Egg Alm.

Above Galtür the main route continues on the road on the east side of the valley, and shortly after being rejoined by the Trittweg option, an alternative track (for those in need of refreshment) crosses the Jambach to **Menta Alm**. For the Jamtal Hut remain on the road and you will soon come to a parking area, which marks the limit for private vehicles. Beyond this point the road is unsurfaced.

The dirt road crosses the Jambach to its west bank at 1697m. A footpath alternative route is marked on the map as beginning at the bridge, but during research this was closed. Should it be reopened, it may be worth taking this option, which remains on the east bank all the way to the hut, and has sections of farm track as well as narrow footpath to follow. It is however, slightly more demanding than the main route described. Meanwhile, in 30–40mins from the bridge over the Jambach the dirt road/track passes just below **Schieben Alm** (1833m, refreshments) where it then forks. Take the upper branch, in effect continuing directly ahead.

As you progress deeper into the valley, so more mountains are revealed – the Gamshorn for example, showing itself as a craggy peak with a block of moraine concealing a glacial remnant. Then the mountains that carry the Swiss border appear, with daubs of snow and small glaciers.

Galtür, where the route to the Jamtal Hut begins

In a little over 2½hrs the track crosses the Jambach for the last time at 2005m, before angling up and across the hillside below the Gamshorn. Topping a rise you pass a stone-built hut on the right and an alm building on the left, with the large **Jamtal Hut** seen ahead. Sloping down a little, cross the boisterous Futschölbach and walk up the final slope to the hut which stands among rocks and alpenroses at 2165m.

> The **Jamtal Hut** belongs to the Schwaben section of the DAV, and following avalanche damage, was rebuilt in 1999. A large Category I hut, it is fully manned from mid-February to early May, and from the end of June to the end of September, with 90 beds and 100 dormitory places (☎ 05443 8408). Unusually, the hut also contains an indoor climbing wall. It has been wardened by members of the Lorenz family since the hut was first built in 1882.

ROUTES FROM THE JAMTAL HUT

Numerous summits, of varying degrees of difficulty, are accessible from the Jamtal Hut, among them the 3197m glacier-hung Dreiländerspitz (so-named because it links the borders of Vorarlberg, Tyrol and Switzerland), the Gemsspitze (3114m), Südliches Fluchthorn (3399m), and the 2987m Westliches Gamshorn.

Perhaps of greater relevance to users of this guide, though, is the number of pass crossings that exist in the neighbourhood.

- On the west side of the valley lies the 2965m **Getschnerscharte** whose crossing leads to the **Bielerhöhe** in 4½–5hrs.

- The 2977m **Ochsenscharte**, north of the Dreiländerspitz, enables experienced trekkers to reach the **Wiesbadener Hut** in 5–6hrs.

- In the valley's headwall east of the Dreiländerspitz, the **Jamjoch** is a 3078m glacier pass on the frontier ridge, on the south side of which lies the **Tuoi Hut** (6hrs).

- Another pass on the frontier ridge, but this one approached through the Futschöl valley, is the 2768m **Futschöl Pass**

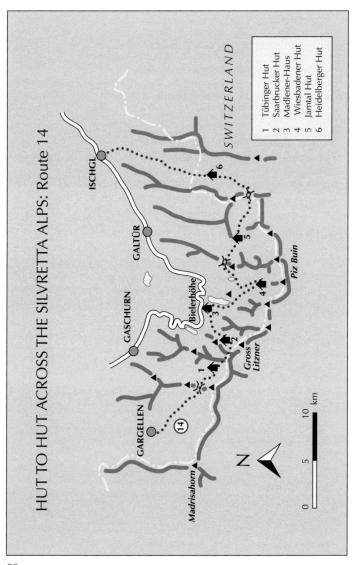

HUT TO HUT ACROSS THE SILVRETTA ALPS: Route 14

1 Tübinger Hut
2 Saarbrucker Hut
3 Madlener-Haus
4 Wiesbadener Hut
5 Jamtal Hut
6 Heidelberger Hut

SWITZERLAND

ISCHGL

GALTÜR

GASCHURN

Bielerhöhe

Piz Buin

Gross Litzner

GARGELLEN

14

Madrisahorn

N

0   5   10 km

whose crossing leads into the Swiss Val Urschai which drains into the Lower Engadine (5½hrs to Ardez).

• At the head of the Futschöl valley, two cols give access to the **Heidelberger Hut** in the Val Fenga/Fimbertal. The **Zahnjoch** (2945m, 2½hrs) is unmarked for some of the way, and the 2974m **Kronenjoch** (3hrs from the Jamtal Hut) is the current recommended crossing, taking 5hrs in all to the Heidelberger Hut.

ROUTE 14
Hut to Hut across the Silvretta Alps

Location	Eastward from Gargellen
Grade	3
Distance	59km
Highest point	Kronenjoch (2974m)
Start	Gargellen (1423m)
Finish	Ischgl (1367m)
Time	5 days

Making an eastward traverse of the Silvretta Alps, this outline hut tour is often added as an extension to the Rätikon Höhenweg Nord (Route 5) by strong mountain walkers. It's a very fine route, challenging in places, less demanding in others, but almost always scenically inspiring.

Day 1 The tour could begin in either Gargellen or Gaschurn, for the first stage leads to the Tübinger Hut in the upper reaches of the Garneratal. If it is to be added to the Rätikon Höhenweg, the most obvious choice is to head upvalley a short distance from **Gargellen**, then branch left into the Vergaldatal in order to cross the **Vergaldajoch** at 2515m. A second ridge is crossed beyond the *joch* from which the Tübinger Hut can be seen across the head of the Garneratal, and some 300m lower than your vantage point. The way then contours round the lower slopes of the valley's headwall and

The alternative and more direct route from Gaschurn is described as Route 8 above.

on to the **Tübinger Hut**, which is gained about 4–4½hrs from Gargellen. ◂

Day 2 A longer stage than yesterday's, taking about 7hrs by the main route. This crosses the 2728m Plattenjoch above and southeast of the Tübinger Hut, by way of a crevasse-free glacier, then along the Austro–Swiss border to the Schweizerlücke and another small glacier bordered by the 2750m Mittelrücke above the **Saarbrucker Hut**. This hut is reached in 3–4hrs. From there an easy valley walk leads to the **Bielerhöhe** overlooking the Silvretta Stausee, but it should be noted that a more direct route from the Tübinger Hut to the Bielerhöhe crosses the Hochmaderer Joch, and is described in detail as Route 9. Once at the Bielerhöhe, follow directions given in Route 12 as far as the **Wiesbadener Hut** with its view of Piz Buin and attendant peaks and glaciers.

Day 3 In order to reach the Jamtal Hut in the next valley to the east of that in which the Wiesbadener Hut is located, a rather devious route is chosen. A more direct crossing than that which is suggested here connects the two huts, but is only recommended for experienced trekkers. The 2965m Getschnerscharte chosen here gives an interesting 4–4½hr day, that begins along a trail heading north to cross the

Piz Buin dwarfs the Wiesbadener Hut

Radsattel, described in Route 12. Having crossed this easy saddle a path is taken down into and across the Bielstal to join another trail (adopted by the Zentralalpenweg) coming from the Bielerhöhe, which climbs steadily southeastward over snow remnants of the former Madlener Ferner to reach the Getschnerscharte. The descent into the Jamtal is steep but not difficult, and after crossing the Jambach, a short climb brings you to the **Jamtal Hut**.

Day 4 Above the Jamtal Hut, at the head of the little Fütschol valley, a choice of two cols give access to the Fembertal which drains down to the Paznauntal at Ischgl. The lower of these, the Zahnjoch, is the more direct route to the Heidelberger Hut, but it is the 2974m **Kronenjoch** which is preferred by the Zentralalpenweg, and is recommended here. This col lies south of the Zahnjoch between the Krone and the Bischofspitze and is reached about 3hrs after leaving the Jamtal Hut. The col is on the Austro–Swiss border, although the Fembertal into which the descent is made, is north of the watershed and shared between the two countries. A remnant glacier (snowfield) is crossed on the Swiss side of the col before a well marked path is joined north of Fuorcla Val Tasna. This path soon descends steeply northwestward, then eases past a small tarn on a more northerly course to the left of the stream, finally joining the Zahnjoch trail shortly before reaching the large white building of the **Heidelberger Hut**, set among lovely meadows at 2264m.

Day 5 A long valley walk of about 14km concludes this tour. The hut's access road leads all the way to Ischgl, but there are sections of footpath that enable you to avoid it in places. An easy, pleasant walk of about 3hrs, at the end of which **Ischgl** will no doubt seem like a teeming metropolis after days spent among the mountains.

3 ÖTZTAL ALPS

Despite advanced recession caused by climate change, the Ötztal Alps contain more glaciers than any other group in Austria, and from certain vantage points the landscape is reminiscent of the larger Western Alps. These glaciers are mostly gathered along or just north of the Austro–Italian frontier where many of the range's 3000m peaks are located, although the highest of its summits, and the second highest in Austria (the 3772m Wildspitze), stands some way forward of the border at the head of the Pitztal.

The Wildspitze, from the Ölgrubenjoch (Route 15)

It's an extensive region of high mountains, and more than 170 of its 600-odd summits exceed 3000m in height. Its boundaries are easily defined. Although the Inn's valley north of the Swiss border marks its western limit, so far as this guide is concerned, we will concentrate on the region's other three main north-flowing valleys, the Kaunertal, Pitztal and the Ötztal and its tributaries. This latter valley, some 65km long, also forms a boundary of the Stubai Alps, so anything rising on the east side of that valley belongs to the next chapter.

ACCESS AND INFORMATION

Location	Between the Silvretta and Stubai Alps in Tyrol. The western boundary is marked by the River Inn south of Landeck, the eastern by the Ötztal. The group extends south of the frontier ridge, but is limited on the north by the Inn's valley spreading east of Landeck.
Maps	Alpenvereinskarten 30/1 *Gurgl*, 30/2 *Weisskugel*, 30/3 *Kaunergrat*, 30/4 *Nauderer Berge*, 30/5 *Geigenkamm*, 30/6 *Wildspitze* 1:25,000
	Kompass Wanderkarte 43 *Ötztaler Alpen* 1:50,000
	Freytag & Berndt WK251 *Ötztal, Pitztal, Kaunertal, Wildspitze* 1:50,000
Bases	Feichten (Kaunertal), Plangeross and Mandarfen (Pitztal), Längenfeld, Sölden and Obergurgl (Ötztal)
Information	Tirol Info, 6010 Innsbruck (e-mail: info@tirol.at; website: www.tirol.at)
	Tourismusverband Tiroler Oberland und Kaunertal, 6531 Ried im Oberinntal (e-mail: info@tiroleroberland.at; website: www.tiroleroberland.at)
	Tourismusverband Pitztal, 6473 Wenns/Pitztal (e-mail: info@pitztal.com; website: www.pitztal.com)
	Tourismusverband Längenfeld, 6444 Längenfeld (e-mail: info@laengenfeld.com; website: www.laengenfeld.com)
	Ötztal Tourismus, 6450 Sölden (e-mail: info@oetztal.com; website: www.solden.com)
	Ötztal Tourismus, 6456 Obergurgl (e-mail: info@obergurgl.com; website: www.obergurgl.com)
Access	The Kaunertal is reached from Landeck via Prutz, with buses to Feichten and (less frequently) as far as the Gepatsch Haus. For the Pitztal, road access is from Imst, with buses to the roadhead at Mittelberg. The Ötztal itself is gained from Ötztal Bahnhof (mainline railway) in the Inn valley. At its southern end the 2474m Timmeljoch road pass takes traffic over the mountains to St Leonhard in Italy. A bus service from Imst goes as far as Obergurgl.

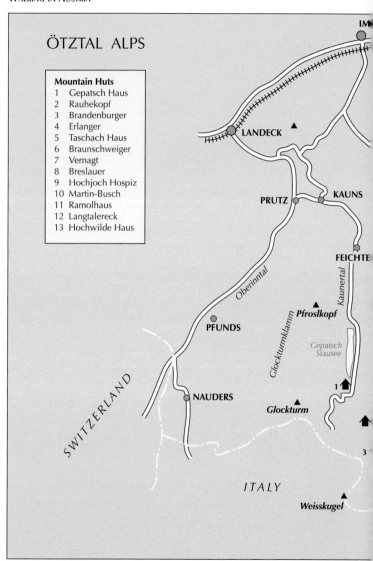

ÖTZTAL ALPS

Mountain Huts
1 Gepatsch Haus
2 Rauhekopf
3 Brandenburger
4 Erlanger
5 Taschach Haus
6 Braunschweiger
7 Vernagt
8 Breslauer
9 Hochjoch Hospiz
10 Martin-Busch
11 Ramolhaus
12 Langtalereck
13 Hochwilde Haus

IM

LANDECK

PRUTZ   KAUNS

FEICHTE

Oberinntal

Kaunertal

Pfroslkopf

PFUNDS

Glockturmklamm

Gepatsch Stausee

1

NAUDERS   *Glockturm*

3

SWITZERLAND

ITALY

Weisskugel

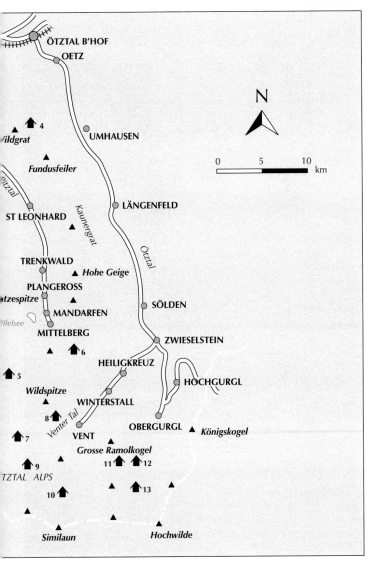

The Taschachferner seen from the Fuldaer Höhenweg (Route 15)

Dividing the Ötztal valleys, long ridge systems push forward from the frontier crest. The Glockturmkamm is the most westerly of these; a comparatively little visited stretch of high country between the Inntal and Kaunertal, whose highest summit is the 3353m Glockturm.

East of the Kaunertal, the Kaunergrat is dominated by the Watzespitze (3533m), a serious mountain and one of the real gems of the Ötztal Alps, as far as climbers are concerned. At its southern end the Kaunergrat is connected to the Weisskamm, a major source of glaciers above which the Wildspitze is undisputed monarch.

And then there's the Geigenkamm rising between Pitztal and Ötztal. This too is attached to the Weiskamm at its northeastern end. While the Geigenkamm is mostly ice-free and running roughly south to north, the Weiskamm's southwest to northeast alignment flanks one of the Ötztal's major tributaries, the Ventertal, and is the most heavily glaciated section of the range.

Then there's the Ramolkamm, a secondary ridge of high mountains dividing the Ventertal from the Gurglertal, this last-named valley being the location of the well-known Obergurgl, the highest Tyrolean parish, which is a first-rate walking and climbing centre in summer, and a major ski resort in winter.

So much for an outline of the mountain blocks and their valleys, what of their attraction to walkers? Suffice to say that the Ötztal Alps provide a bewilderingly wide range of opportunities for walkers of all ages, abilities and ambitions, with multi-day hut tours, scrambles to summits, and *klettersteig* adventures at the upper end of the scale.

Main Bases

Feichten (1286m) The highest village in the Kaunertal, Feichten is located 11km from Prutz, and a short distance from the toll booths of the Gletscherstrasse which extends a further 26km up to a ski complex at the Weisseeferner, passing close to the Gepatsch Haus on the way. Feichten has a tourist office, post office, a bank with ATM, a supermarket and a number of hotels and *gasthöfe* up to four-star standard. The nearest campsite is located a short way downvalley at Platz, by Sporthotel Weissseespitze (Camping Kaunertal, open May to October).

Plangeross (1617m) One of many small villages in the long and narrow Pitztal, Plangeross is reckoned one of the best valley bases with basic facilities such as small grocery, post office, restaurant, several hotels and *pensionen*.

Mandarfen (1682m) Lying a short distance to the south of Plangeross, Mandarfen is the highest resort in the Pitztal, with tourist information, restaurants, a bank with ATM, but limited shopping. It has plenty of hotel and *pension* accommodation, there's also an artificial climbing wall, and a gondola lift to the Riffelsee.

Längenfeld (1170m) Situated midway along the Ötztal between Oetz and Sölden, Längenfeld is a pleasant village standing astride the main road at the entrance to the Sulztal which cuts into the Stubai Alps, and was the birthplace of Franz Senn, the so-called 'glacier priest' (see box in Stubai Alps section). The village has a tourist office, a few shops, restaurants, post office, a bank with ATM, a number of hotels, *pensionen*

Gurgler Alm on the trail to the Langtalereck Hut

and holiday apartments, and a campsite with first class facilities, Camping Ötztal (www.camping-oetztal.com). There are two *klettersteige* (*via ferrata*) in the vicinity; *Klettersteig Reinhard Schiestl* (grade C/D), and the *Lehner Wasserfall Klettersteig* (grade B/D).

Sölden (1377m) The main village in the Ötztal, with no shortage of tourist facilities and plenty of hotel and *pension* accommodation, as well as holiday apartments and a campsite, Camping Sölden. There's a good selection of shops and restaurants, banks with ATMs, a post office and tourist office. Being primarily a ski resort, the slopes above Sölden are laced with cableways.

Obergurgl (1927m) Though noted as a winter resort, Obergurgl has plenty to offer walkers and climbers, and unlike some ski resorts, it retains a lively atmosphere in summer. Accommodation should not be a problem, for there are more than 40 hotels and *pensionen*, as well as apartments for rent. There's a supermarket, tourist office and banks with ATMs, and the resort is served by bus from Imst and Sölden. In the heart of the village near the church stands a statue of Martinus Scheiber (1856–1939), a local guide and entrepeneur who built the first hotel here (he was also responsible for building the Ramolhaus, the first mountain hut in the valley) and effectively put Obergurgl on the map.

Other Bases

Numerous other villages could effectively be used as a holiday base in the Ötztal Alps. At the entrance to the **Kaunertal**, for example **Prutz** has six hotels, *gasthöfe* or *pensionen*, and a large campsite; it also has banks with ATM, a post office and shops. But it's a long way from the action, so your own transport would be a benefit.

In the lower **Pitztal** the village of **St Leonhard**, which extends its influence over several neighbouring communities, has plentiful accommodation and facilities that may be lacking further upvalley.

The **Ötztal** has perhaps the largest choice of valley bases, in addition to Längenfeld, Sölden and Obergurgl mentioned above. The lower valley especially, with **Oetz** (820m) being one of the best with hotels and *pensionen* of all standards, and all facilities within the town. **Umhausen** is much smaller than Oetz, with limited accommodation and considerably fewer facilities. But it does have a campsite and bathing lake and, situated below the entrance to the Horlachtal (admittedly part of the Stubai Alps), its range of available walks is extended somewhat.

Mountain Huts

Braunschweiger Hut (2758m) Standing on rocks overlooking the Mittelbergferner 2½hrs from Mittelberg at the head of the Pitztal, this Category I hut belongs to the Braunschweig section of the DAV. With 35 beds and 61 dormitory places, it's fully staffed from mid-June to the end of October (☎ 0664 5353722 www.braunschweiger-huette.at).

Breslauer Hut (2844m) Originally built in 1882 by the Breslau section of the DAV, this Category I hut stands on the southern slopes of the Wildspitze 3hrs from Vent. Staffed from mid-June to the end of September, it has 64 beds and 107 dormitory places (☎ 05254 8156 breslauer.huette@aon.at).

Erlanger Hut (2541m) Reached by a walk of about 4½hrs from Umhausen, this small Category I hut, owned by the Erlangen section of the DAV, stands by the little Wettersee tarn on the northeast slopes of the Wildgrat. It has just 8 beds and 40 dormitory places, and is manned from the end of June to the end of September (☎ 0664 3920268).

Gepatsch Haus (1925m) Built in 1873 the Gepatsch Haus is one of the oldest huts in Austria. Until the Gepatsch reservoir was created, and the Gletscherstrasse built to the head of the Kaunertal, it enjoyed a remote location, but it's now possible to take a bus almost to its door. A Category II building owned by the Frankfurt-am-Main section of the DAV, it has 35 beds and 43 dormitory places, and is fully staffed from mid-June to the end of September (☎ 0664 4319634).

Hauersee Hut (2331m) This tiny, unmanned self-catering hut, with places for just 14, replaces an earlier building destroyed by avalanche. It stands beside the beautiful little lake after which it is named, below the Luibiskogel, about 3½hrs from Längenfeld. The hut is open from June to the end of September.

Hochjoch Hospiz (2412m) This very popular Category I hut stands far up the Rofental, about 2½hrs from Vent. Owned by the Berlin section of the DAV it has 20 beds and 50 dormitory places, and is fully staffed from mid-March to the beginning of May, and from the end of June to the end of September (☎ 0676 6305998 www.dav-berlin.de).

Hochwilde Haus (2866m) Cecil Davies reckoned the situation of this hut to be second to none. Jeff Williams (in his guide to the Öztaler Alps) claimed it has 'one of the most beautiful outlooks anywhere in the Alps'. It would be hard to disagree with either comment. Built beside a small tarn by the Karlsruhe section of the DAV on the west flank of the Schwärzenkamm overlooking the fast-shrinking Gurgler Ferner, the hut has 30 beds and 60 dormitory places, and is manned from the end of June to mid-September (☎ 0664 4245824 www.alpenverein-karlsruhe.de). The approach from Obergurgl takes about 4½hrs via the Langtalereck Hut.

Kaunergrat Hut (2811m) A strenuous 3½hr approach from Plangeross in the Pitztal leads to this Category I hut which stands on the northeast flank of the Watzespitze. Owned by the Mainz section of the DAV, it has 55 dormitory places and is staffed from the end of June to mid-September (☎ 05413 86242 www.kaunergrathuette.de).

Langtalereck Hut (2430m) Formerly known as the Karlsruher Hut, this Category I hut once enjoyed a direct view of the Gurgler Ferner's icefall cascading into the Gurglertal, but the fast receding glacier can no longer be seen from it. The hut is nevertheless a very pleasant one, reached in about 2½hrs from Obergurgl. With 22 beds and 45 dormitory places, it is fully staffed from early March to early May, and from the end of June to the end of September (☎ 0664 5268655 www.alpenverein-karlsruhe.de).

Ludwigsburger Hut (1935m) Previously known as the Lehnerjoch Hut, and still shown as such on some maps, it stands below the treeline 2hrs above Zaunhof in the lower Pitztal. A Category I hut belonging to the Ludwigsburg section of the DAV, with 8 beds and 48 dormitory places, it is fully staffed from the end of June to the end of September (☎ 0664 4632543 www.alpenverein-ludwigsburg.de).

Martin-Busch Hut (2501m) Extremely popular with day visitors from Vent, from which it's gained by an easy 2½hr walk through the Niedertal, this Category I hut was formerly known as the Samoar Hut. Owned by the Berlin section of the DAV, it has 49 beds and 72 dormitory places, and is fully staffed from March to mid-May, and from the end of June to the end of September (☎ 05254 8130 www.dav-berlin.de).

Ramolhaus (3005m) Built between 1881 and 1883 and owned by the Hamburg section of the DAV, the Ramolhaus is perched on a rocky promontory on the west side of the Gurglertal opposite the Langtalereck Hut. Reached from Obergurgl by a walk of about 4hrs, it has 28 beds and 38 dormitory places, and is manned from July to mid-September (☎ 05256 6223 www.alpenverein-hamburg.de).

Rheinland-Pfalz Bivouac Hut (3247m) A bright orange bivouac shelter perched close to the summit of the Wassertalkogel on the Geigenkamm high above Mandarfen. Useful in emergencies for climbers and those tackling the Mainzer Höhenweg, it has 9 places, is fully equipped and always open. Amazing panoramic views; reached in 4½–5hrs from the Rüsselsheimer Hut.

Riffelsee Hut (2293m) Popular with visitors to Mandarfen near the head of the Pitztal, this hut can be reached by gondola lift, or by a 2½hr walk. Standing above the south-eastern end of the small lake after which it's named, it's owned by the Frankfurt-am-Main section of the DAV, has 21 beds and 38 dormitory places. Category II, and fully staffed from mid-June to the end of September and from mid-December to Easter for group bookings (☎ 0664 3950062 www.alpenverein-frankfurtmain.de).

Rüsselsheimer Hut (2323m) Previously known as the Chemnitzer Hut, this Category I hut can sleep 47 in its dormitories, and is manned from mid-June to the end of September (☎ 0664 2808107 www.dav-ruesselsheim.de). Gained in about

The Langtalereck Hut is owned by the Karlsruhe section of the DAV

2hrs from Plangeross on the east flank of the Pitztal, the view across the valley to the Watzespitze is very fine.

Similaun Hut (3019m) Standing on the Niederjoch on the international border at the very head of the Niedertal, this privately owned hut has 60 dormitory places and is manned from March to the end of September (☎ 0473 669711). A long walk of 5hrs leads to it from Vent, or 2hrs from the Martin-Busch Hut.

Taschach Haus (2434m) Often used as a base for climbing courses, due to its ideal location close to the Taschachferner and Wildspitze, this large Category I hut is invariably very busy. Owned by the Frankfurt-am-Main section of the DAV, it has 40 beds and 85 dormitory places, and is fully staffed from mid-June to the beginning of October (☎ 0664 8368769 www.alpenverein-frankfurtmain.de). It can be reached by a walk of 2½hrs from Mittelberg, or 3hrs from the Riffelsee Hut along an extremely scenic path.

Vernagt Hut (2755m) Built among the moraines of the Vernagtferner about 3½hrs from Vent, this Category I hut has room for 50 in beds, and 81 dormitory places. It belongs to the Würzburg section of the DAV and is fully staffed from March to mid-May, and July to the end of September (☎ 0664 1412119 www.dav-wuerzburg.de).

Verpeil Hut (2025m) Pleasantly situated among meadows in the Verpeiltal east of Feichten, by which it is reached in 1½–2hrs, this Category I hut is another owned by the Frankfurt-am-Main section of the DAV. It has 45 dormitory places and is manned from the end of June to mid-September (☎ 0664 2501408 www.alpenverein-frankfurtmain.de).

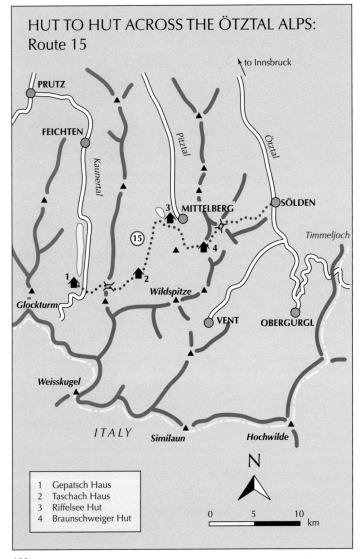

HUT TO HUT ACROSS THE ÖTZTAL ALPS: Route 15

↑ to Innsbruck

PRUTZ

FEICHTEN

Kaunertal

Pitztal

Ötztal

SÖLDEN

Timmeljoch

3 **MITTELBERG**

(15)

4

Wildspitze

1

2

Glockturm

VENT

OBERGURGL

Weisskugel

ITALY   *Similaun*   *Hochwilde*

N

1	Gepatsch Haus
2	Taschach Haus
3	Riffelsee Hut
4	Braunschweiger Hut

0   5   10
km

ROUTE 15

Hut to Hut across the Ötztal Alps

Location	From the Kaunertal to the Ötztal
Grade	3
Distance	33km
Highest point	Ölgrubenjoch (3095m)
Start	Gepatsch Haus (1925m)
Finish	Sölden (1377m)
Time	3 days
Accommodation	Gepatsch Haus, Taschach Haus, Braunschweiger Hut

Crossing the Ötztal Alps from west to east, this magnificent short trek is both strenuous and rewarding. There are two high passes to cross, exciting views of the highest Ötztal mountain (the Wildspitze), glacier scenery of the very best, and three diverse mountain huts in which to stay overnight. The best time to tackle the traverse is from July to September. Snow will no doubt be encountered on some sections, ice is a possibility too, but in a normal summer neither crampons nor ice-axe are likely to be needed.

To reach the Gepatsch Haus to start this route, take the *postbus* from Landeck to Feichten via Prutz. At least two buses a day continue through the Kaunertal to the Gepatsch Haus which is set very close to the toll road at the southern end of the Gepatsch reservoir.

The Category II **Gepatsch Haus** (1925m) is a fine old inn-like building set among pine trees, with glimpsed views to the Gepatschferner glacier upvalley. It has 35 beds and 43 dormitory places, and is fully staffed from mid-June to the end of September (☎ 0664 4319634).

Day 1 The first stage of the tour begins with a climb of 1170m to gain the Ölgrubenjoch, a pass located between the Hinterer Ölgruben-Spitze and the Ölgruben Kopf on the east side of the Kaunertal. The path to it is found about 200m south of the Gepatsch Haus where a sign beside the road indicates 3½–4hrs to the *joch*.

Climbing steeply at times, the trail twists up the hillside among shrubs, flowers and boulders, then swings right to a bluff with an ornate crucifix before making zigzags up to a junction after about 1½hrs. Ignore the right branch and continue ahead, rising alongside an old moraine to gain a rocky basin, with traces of glacier plastered on the face of the Hinterer Ölgruben-Spitze above a small lake. Waymarks and a few small cairns direct the onward route, with a final slope of rock and scree leading to the broad and stony **Ölgrubenjoch** (3095m) about 3½hrs from the start.

The view that greets you on arrival is magnificent, with the Wildspitze rising above a sea of ice and snow directing your attention a little south of east. Below lies the Taschachtal, with the Taschach Haus clearly seen to the north-east.

From the lowest part of the *joch* a marked route veers left along the top edge of a cliff, then descends glacial slabs

Exercise caution as you make this descent.

and grit-covered ledges to a snowfield. ◀ Then go down the snow to a rain gauge above and to the left of a small lake. A path now continues down moraines extravagant with alpine flowers, to a braiding of streams draining the Sexegertenferner. These streams will be lively with snowmelt during the afternoon, but whilst you will no doubt ford one or two of these, the trail will eventually bring you to a footbridge that enables you to cross the main stream just below the hut. Walk up the slope to gain the **Taschach Haus** about 5½–6hrs after leaving the Gepatsch Haus. Close views of the Taschachferner's icefall make this a memorable place in which to spend the night.

The **Taschach Haus** (2434m) is invariably busy with climbers, for it is used as a base for a number of ascents, as well as climbing courses. Owned by the Frankfurt-am-Main section of the DAV, this Category I hut has 40 beds and 85 dormitory places, and is fully staffed from mid-June to the beginning of October (☎ 0664 8368769).

Day 2 There are two ways to descend to Mittelberg at the head of the Pitztal before climbing to the Braunschweiger Hut: a direct route which follows the stream all the way, and an alternative which takes the highly scenic Fuldaer Höhenweg to the

Riffelsee before descending steeply to Mittelberg. The recommended second option is described here.

Begin the day by reversing yesterday's trail of approach, then take the lower of two paths to cross the Taschachbach, after which the way climbs north-eastward as the Fuldaer Höhenweg. ▶ A truly great walk on a well-made path, a few sections are secured with fixed chains or cables, but places where protection is needed are few. The trail edges round rocky bluffs, meanders over meadows loud with marmots and starred with flowers, and crosses numerous streams before arriving at the **Riffelsee** (2232m) about 3hrs from the Taschach Haus. The **Riffelsee Hut** (refreshments) overlooks the lake from its south-eastern end.

The Taschachferner, seen from the Fuldaer Höhenweg

This magnificent walk takes you high above the valley with eye-watering views across to the cascading Taschachferner and its rim of glistening peaks.

The **Riffelsee Hut** (2293m) is a Category II refuge owned by the Frankfurt-am-Main section of the DAV. With 21 beds and 38 dormitory places, it's fully staffed from mid-June to the end of September, and from mid-December to Easter for group bookings (☎ 0664 3950062).

On the Pitztaler Jöchl above the Braunschweiger Hut

Unless you need refreshments here take a path breaking sharply to the right at a signed trail junction before reaching the lake, and descend steeply to a track leading to **Mittelberg** (3½hrs), which consists only of the **Berghof Steinbock** hotel (accommodation and refreshments ☎ 05413 86238) and a small parking area at the start of the route to the Braunschweiger Hut.

Cross the bridge just beyond the hotel, and turn right along a track signed to the Gletscherstube (in 30mins) and Braunschweiger Hut (in 2½hrs). This track is invariably very busy with day visitors, most of whom venture no farther than the **Gletscherstube** (1891m, refreshments). The track ends at the hut's goods lift, where a stony path continues heading south towards a waterfall pouring down a rock barrier. On reaching this barrier the path works its way up via ledges, weaving to and fro and almost into the spray from the waterfall.

The way eases, with glacier views growing in extent as you make progress. Then the gradient increases, you come to another rocky section, then a long uphill ramp of a path bordered by alpine plants. There are rocky staircases, and more switchbacks, and a final bit of effort required with the hut teasing above before you arrive at last at the **Braunschweiger Hut**, about 6–6½hrs after leaving the Taschach Haus.

From its rocky perch overlooking the receding Mittelbergferner north-west of the Wildspitze, the **Braunschweiger Hut** (2758m) is used by climbers as a base for tackling a number of 3000m peaks that rise above the glaciers. Crevasse rescue techniques are often practised nearby. This large Category I hut has 35 beds and 61 dormitory places, and is fully staffed from mid-June to the end of October (☎ 0664 5353722).

Day 3 The final stage of the Ötztal Alps crossing involves a short climb to the Pitztaler Jöchl, followed by descent into a landscape sadly scarred by the ski industry, before you turn away from this on paths and tracks down to Sölden.

The route to the Pitztaler Jöchl starts behind the hut with an undemanding ascent (ibex may be seen here) that brings you onto a rocky ridge giving a view of the Riffelsee backed by mountains of the Kaunergrat. The way scrambles along the ridge to the east, using natural ledges on the right of the crest where necessary, to gain the 2995m **Pitztaler Jöchl**, a narrow dip in a shattered ridge, about 1hr from the hut.

Descend with care to a small glacier/snowfield and wander down its left-hand edge to a car park at the head of the Ötztaler Gletscherstrasse which serves the Rettenbach ski area. Beyond the car park a path drops down a slope to join then cross a lower section of road, after which you follow the route of E5 taking you down to the milky-blue Rettenbach stream. Remain on the right bank until the track brings you onto the road again just below Rettenbach Alm (2145m, refreshments).

Walk down the road until, just before reaching a toll building, a path on the left leads down to the Stabele chair-lift and a broad *piste* curving into forest. Wandering through the forest come to a footpath sign directing a way more steeply down the wooded slope, twice crossing the road and eventually coming into **Sölden** about 3½–4hrs from the Braunschweiger Hut.

Sölden (1377m) has all the usual tourist facilities, plenty of accommodation of all standards, and a tourist office in the town centre. Frequent buses travel down valley to link with mainline rail services at Ötztal Bahnhof.

WALKS IN THE KAUNERTAL

Much less busy than either the Pitztal or Ötztal, the Kaunertal nevertheless has plenty to offer the visiting walker.

- East of Feichten, for example, the **Verpeiltal** is worth exploring. The 2hr route to the charming **Verpeil Hut** may be steep for much of the way, but the hut's setting in meadows at 2025m rewards your arrival, and if you spend a night there, you have the temptation to continue to viewpoints such as the 2532m **Mooskopf** (1½hrs) and the **Madatsch Kopf** (2783m) in 2hrs.

- More demanding than the above, is the 2½hr ascent (steep but not difficult) of the **Schweikert**, a modest rock peak of 2881m on the ridge west of the Hochrinnegg and northwest of the Verpeil Hut.

- For experienced mountain walkers a crossing of the Kaunergrat ridge to the **Kaunergrat Hut** and **Plangeross** in the Pitztal is possible via the 3010m **Madatsch Joch** below the Watzespitze. However, there's a small glacier on the Kaunertal side, and if icy, crampons may be needed; 3hrs from the Verpeil Hut to the Kaunergrat Hut, or 5½–6hrs to Plangeross.

WALKS IN THE PITZTAL

Stretching north for some 38km from Mittelberg at the roadhead to where it spills into the Inn's valley at Imst, the Pitztal has plenty of walks to consider. The following is just a small sample.

- On the west side of the Pitztal a little south of Trenkwald, the Lorbachtal is a small hanging valley below the Vorpeilspitze. In it lies the little **Mittelberglesee** at 2450m. A path takes you there from Trenkwald to give a pleasant round trip of 4½–5hrs.

- From Plangeross the 2hr walk up to the **Rüsselsheimer Hut** at 2323m is steep, but the switchback path has been so well-made that the effort needed for the 700m or so of height gain is less than one might fear. And the hut's outlook, especially across the valley to the Watzespitze is splendid.

- The **Mainzer Höhenweg** is generally reckoned to be one of the finest long walks in the Ötztal Alps – allow 9–10hrs. Beginning at the **Rüsselsheimer Hut** it climbs southeast to the 2959m **Weissmaurach Joch**, then works a way southward along the ridge (fixed cables in places) skirting some summits, crossing others. The 3247m **Wassertalkogel** is the highest, with the bright orange Rheinland-Pfalz Bivouac Hut nearby, and a fabulous panoramic view to make you want to linger.

An easy descent south takes the route over the **Gschrappkogel** (3191m) and continues south before veering southeast and eventually coming down to the Ötztaler Gletscherstrasse, with a long and tiring walk down to **Sölden** to finish, as described in the final stages of Walk 15.

- From the top of the Riffelsee gondola (the valley station is at Mandarfen) the **Cottbuser Höhenweg** is a narrow path which, heading north, crosses the steep flanks of the Brandkogel and Steinkogel before swinging west above the Plangerosstall and eventually joining the standard approach to the **Kaunergrat Hut**. Allow at least 4hrs from the Riffelsee, but note there are some sections of fixed cable, and easy scrambling is required in places.

- Also from the **Riffelsee** (reached in 2½hrs from Mandarfen, or by gondola if you prefer) the **Fuldaer Höhenweg** is a highly recommended trail leading in 3½hrs to the **Taschach Haus**. It is described in reverse as part of Route 15 above.

WALKS IN THE ÖTZTAL

The longest, best known and most developed of the three valleys, as mentioned above, the Ötztal acts as the boundary between Ötztal and Stubai Alps; Ötztal Alps to the west, Stubai Alps to the east. For walks on feeder valleys on the east side of the Ötztal, please see the Stubai Alps chapter; here we concentrate on the western tributaries and their flanking hillsides.

The valley is 55km long. It's broad and fertile in its lower reaches; more narrow with a series of gorges interrupted by open meadows about halfway up, and rising from one level to the next, becomes more dramatic and challenging as you approach the valley's head where above Sölden it breaks into three stems – the Ventertal (with Zwieselstein at its entrance), Gurglertal (with Obergurgl its only village), and the Timmelstal which leads to the Timmelsjoch and Italy. Sölden and Obergurgl see the greatest concentration of visitors attracted to the district for its walking potential, and the two resorts are linked by a reliable bus service.

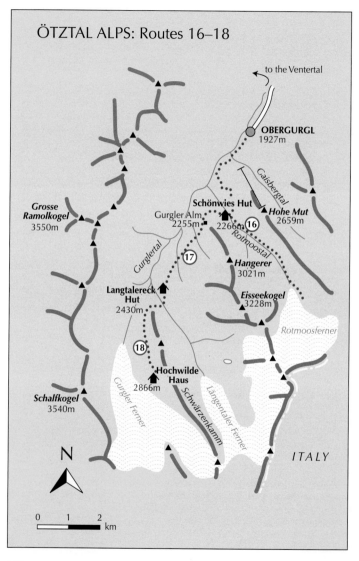

ÖTZTAL ALPS: Routes 16–18

to the Ventertal

OBERGURGL
1927m

Gaisbergtal

Schönwies Hut
Gurgler Alm
2255m   2266m (16) *Hohe Mut*
                        2659m
*Grosse
Ramolkogel*
3550m   Rotmoostal

                (17)   *Hangerer*
                        3021m
**Langtalereck
Hut**   *Eisseekogel*
2430m   3228m

                                    Rotmoosferner
            (18)

        **Hochwilde
         Haus**
Schalfkogel 2866m
3540m

Gurgler Ferner   Schwärzenkamm   Längentaler Ferner

N   *ITALY*

0   1   2
|___|___| km

ROUTE 16

Obergurgl (1927m) –
Schönwies Hut (2266m) – Rotmoostal (c2500m)

Location	In the Gurglertal south of Obergurgl
Valley base	Obergurgl
Grade	2–3
Distance	7km (one way)
Height gain	573m
Time	3hrs (+2½hrs return)

Of the two main ways to reach the Schönwies Hut, this is by far the nicer. The walk is utterly delightful, with wonderful trees, shrubs and flowers, good views and a fine waterfall. On arrival at the Schönwies Hut (no accommodation, refreshments only) you gaze into the Rotmoostal, a valley of considerable charm and of particular appeal to anyone with an interest in mountain flowers. There is no specific destination for this walk, for the Rotmoostal is the sort of valley where one could wander for hours and harvest pleasures with every moment.

From the church in **Obergurgl** walk to the nearby junction of streets where the statue of Martinus Schieber points upvalley. Take the left fork (Ramolweg), and just beyond Hotel Jenewein branch left again on the Gaisbergweg, a narrow road rising up the slope, then fork right where a sign announces 1½hrs to the Schönwies Hut.

After passing several apartment houses, the metalled road becomes a dirt road flanked by meadows and leading to the Steinmannbahn (refreshments), where it ends. A path now continues, curving right among trees, then left above a gorge. Having turned a corner the path forks. Take the upper option, and when this divides a few paces later, take the right branch (the lower path) – a narrow trail cutting across a steep slope among pine and alpenrose. At first contouring, the way then rises, and with a few twists comes to a junction on a bluff clothed with alpenrose, juniper and pine.

Turn right to climb a slope smothered in bilberry and alpenrose, and shortly come to another junction where once again you turn right. On the way up the slope the path veers to the right in order to gain a view of the Rotmoos waterfall crashing through a ravine, then twists above the ravine to join a dirt road (the alternative route from Obergurgl). Turn right and you will shortly arrive at the **Schönwies Hut** (2266m, 1½hrs, refreshments) approached across a timber bridge.

Privately owned, the **Schönwies Hut** stands above the left bank of the river which forms the Rotmoos waterfall, with a direct view into the Rotmoostal which stretches away to the southeast, headed by the Heuflerkogel. The hut has no accommodation, but caters for day visitors, and is open throughout the summer from mid-June to early October. The man-made lake nearby is used for snow-making in winter.

Stretching beyond the Schönwies Hut, the Rotmoostal rewards an exploration

From the bridge a footpath entices into the **Rotmoostal** on the east side of the Rotmoosache, and very soon divides, with one stem forking left to climb the 2659m Hohe Mut (in 1½hrs). Ignore this and keep ahead through pastures lavish

with wild flowers in the early summer, and with increasingly fine views of the valley's headwall mountains, from which the Rotmoosferner spreads an icy apron. The path is almost level for some way, and for the first 30mins or so from the Schönwies Hut, it strikes through meadows or pastureland. But then the valley grows wilder, becomes more stony, yet the variety of alpine flowers is even richer than before, and the views more dramatic.

The way eventually rises along the lateral moraine of the **Rotmoosferner**, but it's not essential to go that far, for there's much to enjoy at all levels in this valley, so when you've absorbed enough of its beauty, simply return by the same path.

MOUNTAIN FLOWERS OF THE GURGLERTAL

The Gurglertal and its tributaries are noted for the rich alpine flora that regularly attracts botanical tours to use Obergurgl as a base. Among the many outstanding flowers to be found here, one of the loveliest is the deep blue-violet *Primula glutinosa* which grows in tight clusters amid the turf and survives both dry and damp areas. It is sometimes discovered almost swamped by mattresses of the tiny pink-flowered creeping azalea, *Loiseleuria procumbens*. One of the first flowers to emerge as the snows melt, *Soldanella pusilla* (the dwarf snowbell) brings a contrast to the sometimes drab early-spring meadows with its pendulous violet, narrow bell-shaped flowers. Similar, but even smaller than *pusilla*, the so-called least snowbell (*Soldanella minima*) is also seen high in the valley from May to June. Later, from July onwards, the slender short-leaved gentian, *Gentiana brachyphylla*, can be found, as can the brilliant blue, but tiny flowers of *Gentiana nivalis*, the snow gentian, and dense pink rosettes of *Androsace obtusifolia* spreading among dry turf or around the rocks. If you want to know more about the wonderful flora of the mountains, there are several beautifully illustrated pocket guides available.

ROUTE 17

Obergurgl (1927m) – Schönwies Hut (2266m) –
Langtalereck Hut (2430m)

Location	In the Gurglertal SW of Obergurgl
Valley base	Obergurgl
Grade	2–3
Distance	7.5km (one way)
Height gain	503m
Time	2½hrs (+ 2hrs return)

A natural extension of Route 16, this walk leads to a traditional mountain hut situated on a spur high in the Gurglertal. It was formerly known as the Karlsruher Hut, in Cecil Davies's guide which preceded the present volume (*Mountain Walking in Austria*), and he described it as 'overlooking the great ice-fall of the Gurgl Glacier'. But he was there in the 1960s, and since then glacial recession has led to the glacier's complete disappearance from the hut's view. It was on that glacier (in the days when it extended much farther down the valley) that Auguste Piccard and his companion crash-landed their balloon in May 1931 after making the first flight into the stratosphere.

Follow directions given in Route 16 to reach the **Schönwies Hut** (1½hrs), then take the continuing dirt road/track beyond as it rises to a broad grassy saddle with splendid views back through the Rotmoostal. In just 2mins from the hut, note the path breaking to the left, signed to the Hangerer (in 2½hrs), and 2mins beyond this another path to the right, leading to the viewpoint of the Schönwiesskopf (a 15min diversion).

The **3021m Hangerer** can be clearly seen from Obergurgl as an obvious pointed mountain – as you draw closer the summit cross can also be seen. The ascent is steep but not difficult, with a path virtually all the way to the top. Summit views are said to be excellent.

Across the saddle the track descends, then curves along the east flank of the Gurglertal and past the tiny building of the **Gurgler Alm** (2255m). From here you should be able to see a building on a shoulder some way ahead, with the track rising to it. This is not the Langtalereck Hut, but an old customs hut, now locked and unused. The track contours beyond the Gurgler Alm, then twists up the slope ahead, passes to the left of the customs hut, then drops down to the **Langtalereck Hut** about 1hr after leaving the Schönwies Hut. Instead of a large glacier in view, the outlook is now dominated by slabs of red rock that flank both sides of the Gurglertal. The narrow Langental, with the Hochwilde at its head, cuts back into the mountains behind the hut.

Gurgler Alm goats

Built by the Karlsruhe section of the DAV in 1929/30, the **Langtalereck Hut** (2430m) has 22 beds and 45 dormitory places, and is fully staffed from March to the beginning of May, and from the end of June to the end of September (☎ 0664 5268655).

ROUTE 18

Langtalereck Hut (2430m) –
Hochwilde Haus (2866m)

Location	South of the Langtalereck Hut
Valley base	Obergurgl
Grade	3
Distance	3km
Height gain	429m
Height loss	83m
Time	2hrs

Like the Langtalereck Hut, the Hochwilde Haus is owned by the Karlsruhe section of the DAV, and has an outstanding location overlooking the Gurgler Ferner from the well-named Steinerner Tisch (*Stone Table*) below the Schwärzenkamm ridge. A small pool lies beside it. The hut is unquestionably a magnificent place in which to spend the night, whether or not you have plans to climb any of the peaks above it.

From the **Langtalereck Hut** take the path directly ahead and branch right when it forks shortly after. It now descends frustratingly into the narrow ravine-like Langental to cross the glacial stream flowing through it. Across this the path now climbs the steep and in places exposed northern end of the Schwärzenkamm ridge – a fixed cable safeguards the most exposed section.

After turning the Schwärzenkamm spur the gradient slackens as the outlook grows in drama, and you rise along the lateral moraine wall to reach the group of four buildings that includes the **Hochwilde Haus**. Allow 3–3½hrs for the return to Obergurgl.

Built in 1938–39 the **Hochwilde Haus** (2866m) enjoys a wonderful vista of mountain and glacier from its platform of stone. It has 30 beds and 60 dormitory places, and is manned from the end of June to mid-September (☎ 0664 4245824).

OTHER ROUTES FROM OBERGURGL

- The grassy knoll of **Hohe Mut** (east of the Schönwies Hut) is a much-favoured vantage point easily reached in 2½hrs from the village, or by gondola all the way to the summit. The Hohe Mut Haus restaurant exploits a view said to include 21 peaks of 3000m. Many visitors use the gondola to gain the top, then walk back down by a direct path. But there's also a route which goes southeast down the broad ridge where another breaks left to descend into the **Gaisbergtal** for a longer return to Obergurgl. But the trail which continues along the ridge soon slips down the south side into the **Rotmoostal**, where you gain close views of the Rotmoosferner before cutting back to the Schönwies Hut and thence to Obergurgl.

- Upvalley from Obergurgl on the west side of the Gurgler Ache is **Beilstein** (2117m), reached by a reasonably short walk on a path branching from the Ramolhaus trail. Studies of the site show that it was frequented more than 9500 years ago, and its pastures cultivated as long ago as 4300BC.

- A 4hr walk along the west side of the Gurglertal leads to the **Ramolhaus** at 3005m. Despite the 1000m of height gain and some steep sections, the walk is not too demanding, and the view from the hut of the Hochwilde above the Gurgler Ferner is ample reward for getting there.

- For strong walkers, crossing the 3186m **Ramoljoch** above the **Ramolhaus** gives an opportunity to make a recommended over-the-mountains walk to either **Vent** (in 3hrs) or the **Martin-Busch Hut** in 5–6hrs. On the Gurglertal side of the pass there's a short metal ladder to ascend, and on the Ventertal side, remnants of a small glacier to descend.

WALKS IN THE VENTERTAL

Cutting into the mountains south-west of Zwieselstein, the Ventertal is a sparsely-populated valley whose only real village, and that a very small one, is **Vent** at 1896m. The village has a modest amount of hotel accommodation and limited shopping facilities, but makes a good walking centre (www.vent.at). The valley forks just beyond Vent, with the Niedertal extending to the south, and the Rofental to the west. A steep road climbs briefly into the latter valley to reach the hamlet of Rofenhöfe (2014m), with footpaths that continue from it.

- One of the nicest walks from Vent is the 2½hr approach to the 2412m **Hochjoch Hospiz**. The path initially goes along the south bank of the Rofen Ache, then crosses to the north bank at Rofenhöfe. The most notable section is where it goes through a gorge (fixed cable safeguards) north-east of the valley of the Vernagtbach. Several other routes pan out from the hut, including a popular link with the Schöne Aussicht Hut on the Italian side of the border.

- The route to the **Schöne Aussicht Hut** (Gasthof Schöne Aussicht or Albergo Bella Vista: 2842m) leads along the west side of the Hochjochferner and crosses the Hochjoch on the Austro–Italian border about 20m above the hut. It's an uncomplicated 2½hr walk from the Hochjoch Hospiz, with a height gain of less than 600m. Sadly its former beauty has been marred by ski lifts on the nearby glacier.

- Closer to Vent, but high above Rofenhöfe and set below the Wildspitze, a path climbs steep pastures to gain the **Breslauer Hut** (2840m) in 3hrs, but this could be reduced to about 2hrs by use of a chairlift to Stablein Alm.

- Above and to the east of the Breslauer Hut, an easy ascent of the 3019m **Wildes Mannle** can be made by footpath from either the Stablein Alm (3hrs) or the Breslauer Hut itself. Views are said to be very fine.

- Near the head of the Niedertal at 2501m, the **Martin-Busch Hut** is the destination for many visitors to Vent, for it's an easy walk of just 2½hrs along a track, with the attractive 3606m Similaun rising above its glaciers to the south. The privately owned **Similaun Hut** on the Italian border at the Niederjoch may be reached in 1½hrs by a straightforward route. It was near this latter hut that 'Ötzi the Ice Man' was found in 1991 (see box opposite).

- Above and to the northwest of the Martin-Busch Hut rises the 3457m **Kreuzspitze**, an easy but steep summit and a noted viewpoint, reached by a 2½hr ascent. Could be problematic or even dangerous in snowy conditions, but not unduly difficult otherwise. The little Samoarsee (also known as the Brizzisee: 2920m) lies between the hut and the summit and may be reached by a recommended diversion. It makes a superb foreground to photographs of the Similaun.

Lichen patterned rocks brighten many trails

ÖTZI THE ICE MAN

In September 1991 two German walkers discovered a body protruding from the Similaun glacier. Although it was found on the Italian side of the border, the corpse was removed from the ice and taken to Innsbruck University for examination. At first thought to be a walker who'd perished after being overtaken by a storm, speculation then focused on a Viennese music professor who had disappeared in 1939. However, carbon dating later revealed the body to be around 5500 years old! The tools and clothing found with him confirmed that Ötzi belonged to the late Stone Age, his diet consisting of ibex meat and cereals. He would have weighed around 45kgs, and died at the age of about 45. With worldwide interest aroused, Ötzi became the subject of an ownership dispute between the Austrian and Italian authorities, but since it was proven that the body was found 90m inside the Italian border, he was eventually taken to the Museo Archeologico in Bolzano where he has become the prize attraction. Not to be outdone, at Umhausen in the lower Ötztal, there's now an 'Ötzi Dorf' – a replica village based on Ötzi's period in history.

The lovely Sulztal on the way to the Amberger Hut

4 STUBAI ALPS

Spreading northeast of the Ötztal Alps, and easily reached from Innsbruck, the Stubai range is a complex block of mountains slashed by numerous valleys. Understandably popular, it has a well-earned reputation for its wealth of rewarding walks and climbs of all grades of difficulty. The highest summits are snow- or ice-covered, and a number of glaciers and glacial lakes add much to the quality of the landscapes. Headed by some of the most impressive peaks, the Stubaital (from which the range takes its name) attracts the majority of visitors, while several of its outlying valleys, though undeniably attractive, are comparatively little known.

ACCESS AND INFORMATION

Location	East of the Ötztal and west of the Wipptal headed by the Brenner Pass.
	The northern boundary is the Inn's valley, while the southern limit, so far as we are concerned, is the Austro–Italian border.
Maps	Alpenvereinskarten 31/1 *Hochstubai*, 31/2 *Sellrain* at 1:25,000; 31/3
	Brennerberge, 31/5 *Innsbruck und Umgebung* 1:50,000
	Kompass Wanderkarte 83 *Stubaier Alpen* 1:50,000
	Freytag & Berndt 24 *Stubaier Alpen* 1:100,000, WK241 *Stubai-Sellrain* 1:50,000
Bases	Längenfeld and Sölden (Ötztal), Kühtai (Nedertal), Gries im Sellrain (Sellraintal), Neustift (Stubaital)
Information	Stubai Tirol (e-mail: info@stubai.at; website: www.stubai.at) Tourismusverband Längenfeld, 6444 Längenfeld (e-mail: info@laengenfeld.com; website: www.laengenfeld.com)
	Ötztal Tourismus, 6450 Sölden (e-mail: info@oetztal.com; website: www.solden.com)
	Tourismusbüro Kühtai, 6183 Kühtai (e-mail: info@kuehtai.co.at; website: www.pollenfrei.at)
	Tourismusbüro Gries im Sellrain, 6182 Gries im Sellrain (e-mail: gries@innsbruck.info; website: www.tiscover.at/gries-sellrain)
	Tourismusbüro Neustift (website: www.neustift-stubaital.net)

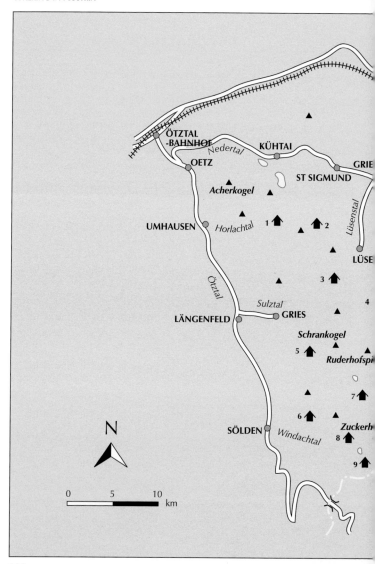

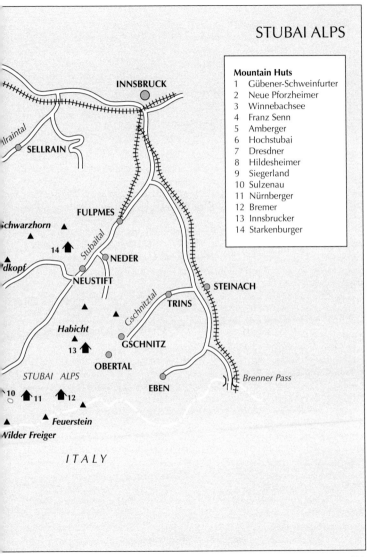

STUBAI ALPS

Mountain Huts
1 Gübener-Schweinfurter
2 Neue Pforzheimer
3 Winnebachsee
4 Franz Senn
5 Amberger
6 Hochstubai
7 Dresdner
8 Hildesheimer
9 Siegerland
10 Sulzenau
11 Nürnberger
12 Bremer
13 Innsbrucker
14 Starkenburger

Access	Western valleys draining into the Ötztal (Windachtal, Sulztal and Horlachtal) are accessed from Sölden, Längenfeld and Umhausen. Linked by the Kühtai Sattel, the Nedertal and Sellraintal are served by buses running between Oetz (in the Ötztal) and Innsbruck. The Stubaital is reached from the Brenner Pass road by way of Schönberg, with train and bus services from Innsbruck. The Gschnitztal also breaks away from the Brenner Pass road at Steinach am Brenner, and is served by *postbus*.

Of the four westernmost Stubai valleys draining into the Ötztal, the most southerly is the uninhabited Windachtal above Sölden, with the Zuckerhütl at its head. A paved road goes part-way into it, with a track extending further. Some of the highest Stubai mountains line the Austro–Italian border that forms its headwall, a number of small tarns lie on the mid-height slopes of the flanking mountains, and several huts are accessible from the valley.

Next comes the Sulztal with a road climbing to it from Längenfeld. This is a charming valley with Gries at the roadhead its only village. From here paths lead to the Amberger and Winnebachsee Huts, from both of which more trails extend across the mountains to other refuges. The Stubai Alps, of course, is the ultimate district for multi-day hut-to-hut tours.

In the peaceful Horlachtal, reached from Umhausen (between Längenfeld and Oetz), lies the Guben-Schweinfurter Hut at the end of a track, from which paths tease across neighbouring cols to multiply its walking opportunities, while the Horlachbach stream crashes out of the valley in spectacular fashion at the Stuibenfall.

The most northerly of the Stubai valleys spilling into the Ötztal is the Nedertal, an unremarkable wooded valley at its lower end, where the road from Oetz climbs into it, but rising to a promise of more open country as you approach Kühtai on the saddle leading to the Sellraintal. Two reservoirs have been created at Kühtai, and development for skiing has not been kind to the landscape. But there are plenty of paths that allow escape to less-tamed regions on the south side of the immediate neighbourhood.

Considerably longer than the Nedertal, the Sellraintal has several small villages and a choice of feeder valleys. These feeders all cut into the main Stubai block and are well worth exploring. The Lüsenstal is the longest. With Gries im Sellrain at its entrance, a road invades the valley as far as Praxmar, a hamlet built on the western hillside, while a secondary road continues along the valley bed to Alpengasthof Lüsens and a trailhead full of promise.

By comparison, the Stubaital on the eastern side of the range is heavily populated. With Schönberg at its entrance, the road into the valley either runs through or bypasses a whole string of villages before coming to Neustift, after which the Stubaital divides into the Oberbergtal (the northerly stem) and Unterbergtal. At the head of the former lie one or two *alms* and a crescent of mountains, with the Franz Senn Hut making a near-perfect base from which to explore them. The road into the Unterbergtal passes two impressive waterfalls, goes through several tiny hamlets, and ends in a massive car park at the Mutterbergalm where cableways serve the main Stubai ski grounds above the Dresdner Hut on the south side of the valley. The Dresdner is just one of many huts in the region, a number of which are linked to form a classic hut to hut tour known locally as the Stubaier Höhenweg.

The final valley in this survey of the Stubai Alps is the Gschnitztal which runs south of, and parallel to, the Stubaital. Entered from Steinach am Brenner, a little north of the Brenner Pass, the valley begins modestly enough among broad pastures, but narrows towards its head where a group of 3000m peaks closes it in. There are two proper villages, Trins and Gschnitz with prospects of accommodation and limited shopping, and several hamlets spread through the valley as far as Gasthof Feuerstein at the roadhead. At least five huts can be reached by good paths, and other undemanding trails within the valley appeal to walkers of modest ambition.

Main Bases

Sölden (1377m) A major summer and winter resort, and the most important walking centre in the Ötztal, it has plenty of accommodation of all standards, including holiday apartments and a campsite. A good selection of shops and restaurants, banks with ATMs, a post office and tourist office.

Längenfeld (1170m) Located below the Sulztal, midway between Oetz and Sölden in the Ötztal, this is a pleasant village with a number of hotels, *pensionen* and holiday apartments, a campsite with excellent facilities, a few shops and restaurants, a post office, a bank with ATM, and a tourist office in the main street. Buses run from here to Gries-im-Sulztal throughout the summer. Längenfeld was the birthplace of Franz Senn, the so-called 'glacier priest' who was influential in opening both the Stubai and Ötztal Alps to mountain tourism, and worked tirelessly to establish alpine huts in the region (see box p127).

Kühtai (2017m) Primarily a ski resort, and lacking in atmosphere in summer, Kühtai nonetheless has several hotels and holiday apartments, and the Dortmunder Hut (details below) located beside the road on the edge of the resort. There's a small grocery, an ATM and a tourist office. The nearest bank is in Gries im Sellrain (10km), and the village is served by bus from both Oetz and Innsbruck.

Gries im Sellrain (1187m) A small and compact village with some attractive painted houses at the entrance to the Lüsenstal, it has plenty of accommodation, a few shops, a post office, a bank with ATM, and tourist information.

Neustift (993m) The village may be smaller than its neighbour Fulpmes, but Neustift is without question the most important resort of the Stubai Alps. It has more than a dozen hotels, plus holiday apartments and a campsite. There's a reasonable selection of shops, a supermarket, post office, banks with ATMs, a *Bergführer Büro* (mountain guides' office with guided trips organised for walkers and climbers) and a tourist office. The Stubaital may be reached by bus from Innsbruck, or by train as far as the railway terminus at Fulpmes, then bus from there to Neustift and on to Mutterbergalm at the head of the valley. A minibus service also links Neustift with Oberiss at the head of the Oberbergtal.

Mountain Huts

Adolf Pichler Hut (1960m) Owned by the Academic Alpine Club of Innsbruck, this hut is located on the western slopes of the Kalkkögel massif at the head of the Senderstal, about 3hrs from Grinzens. It has 25 beds and 50 dormitory places, and is manned from mid-June to the beginning of October (☎ 05238 53194).

Amberger Hut (2136m) Overlooking meadows of the upper Sulztal with the Schrankogel to the east, this Category I hut belongs to the Amberg section of the DAV. It has 10 beds and 59 dormitory places, and is fully staffed from February to the end of April, and from mid-June to the beginning of October (☎ 05253 5605 www.dav-amberg.de). It may be reached by a walk of about 2hrs from Gries im Sulztal.

Bielefelder Hut (2112m) Easily reached in 30mins from the Oetz-Acherkogel gondola lift, the Category II Neue Bielefelder Hut replaces a former building which was destroyed by avalanche. It stands below the Wetterkreuzkogel with a very fine view of the Ötztal Alps. Owned by the Bielefeld section of the DAV, it is fully staffed from mid-June to the end of September and from mid-December to Easter, and has 36 beds and 22 dormitory places (☎ 05252 6926 www.alpenverein-bielefeld.de).

Bremer Hut (2411m) Situated by a small tarn at the head of the Gschnitztal, and used by walkers on the Stubaier Höhenweg, this is an atmospheric Category I hut owned by the Bremen section of the DAV. Reached by a walk of 3hrs from the Gschnitztal roadhead, it has 23 beds and 46 dormitory places, and is manned from the end of June to the end of September (☎ 0664 4605831 www.dav-bremen.de).

The Amberger Hut near the head of the Sulztal

Dortmunder Hut (1949m) A large, inn-like building standing beside the road on the western outskirts of Kühtai, this Category II hut was built by the Dortmund section of the DAV in 1931–1932. It has 32 beds and 40 dormitory places, and is fully staffed from June to the end of October, and December to the beginning of May (☎ 05239 5202).

Dresdner Hut (2308m) The first hut to be built in the Stubai Alps (in 1875), it was rebuilt in 1887 and has since been enlarged and extensively modernised. A Category II hut, sadly its immediate environs have been savaged by the ski industry. Nevertheless, the hut itself is comfortable and welcoming, and used by trekkers on the Stubaier Höhenweg. A 2hr walk from Mutterbergalm at the Stubaital roadhead leads to it, or 2½–3hrs from the Sulzenau Hut on the *höhenweg*. It has 150 beds and 20 dormitory places, and is manned from June to the end of October (☎ 05226 8112 www.alpenverein-dresden.de).

Franz Senn Hut (2147m) A large and very popular Category I hut used by walkers and climbers, it is reached by an easy walk of 1–1½hrs from Oberiss at the Oberbergtal roadhead. Property of the Innsbruck section of the ÖAV, it is fully staffed from mid-February to early May, and from mid-June to the beginning of October (☎ 05226 2218 www.frankhauser.at). It has 84 beds and 176 places and is named in memory of the mountaineering pastor (see box).

Gubener Schweinfurter Hut (2028m) A very pleasant Category I hut set among pastures at the end of a track from Niederthai in the Horlachtal (a 2hr walk), it has 20 beds and 30 dormitory places, and is manned from mid-June to mid-September (☎ 05255 50029 www.dav-sw.de).

Hildesheimer Hut (2900m) Overlooking the Pfaffenferner west of the Zuckerhütl above the Windachtal, the Category I Hildesheimer Hut is reached in 4½–5hrs from Sölden in the Ötztal. Owned by the Hildesheim section of the DAV it has 24 beds and 56 dormitory places, and is fully staffed from the end of June to the end of September (☎ 05254 2300 www.dav-hildesheim.de).

Hochstubai Hut (3174m) The highest in the Austrian Stubai, this Category I hut has a magnificent perch on the insignificant Wildkarspitze high above the Windachtal. A steep but well-made path climbs to it in 5–6hrs from Sölden. Owned by the Dresden section of the DAV it has 4 beds and 60 dormitory places, and is manned from July to mid-September (☎ 0664 2665290 www.alpenverein-dresden.de).

Innsbrucker Hut (2369m) A large Category I hut built close to the Pinnisjoch with a tremendous view of the Tribulaun peaks across the Gschnitztal, it is usually approached from Neder through the Pinnistal in 4–4½hrs. Property of the Innsbruck section of the ÖAV, it has 30 beds and 100 dormitory places, and is fully staffed from mid-June to the beginning of October (☎ 05276 295 www.innsbrucker-huette.at).

Neue Pforzheimer Hut (2310m) Formerly known as the Adolf Witzenmann Haus, this Category I hut stands near the head of the Gleirsch valley 2½hrs from St Sigmund im Sellrain. Manned from mid-February to the beginning of May, and mid-June to the end of September, it has 28 beds and 20 dormitory places (☎ 05236 521 www.alpenverein-pforzheim.de), and belongs to the Pforzheim section of the DAV.

Neue Regensburger Hut (2287m) Standing in the Falbeson valley below the Ruderhofspitze, this cosy Category I hut is the property of the Regensburg section of the DAV, and is on the route of the Stubaier Höhenweg. With 27 beds and 56 dormitory places, it is staffed from mid-June to the end of September (☎ 0664 4065688 www.alpenverein-regensburg.de).

Nürnberger Hut (2278m) Another hut used by walkers tackling the Stubaier Höhenweg, this one stands at the head of the Langental below the Hohe Wand. Reached in 3–3½hrs from the Bremer Hut, or 2½hrs from a car park/bus stop south of Ranalt, this Category I hut belongs to the DAV's Nürnberg section. With 50 beds and 92 dormitory places, it's fully staffed from the end of June to the end of September (☎ 05226 2492 www.dav-nuernberg.de).

Potsdamer Hut (2009m) Built by the Potsdam-Dinkelsbühl section of the DAV in 1931/32, this attractive Category I hut is located in the Fotschertal 3½hrs from Sellrain. With 20 beds and 38 dormitory places, it is manned from the end of January until Easter, and from mid-June to the beginning of October (☎ 05238 52060).

Siegerland Hut (2710m) Reached through the Windachtal in 5hrs from Sölden, the Siegerland Hut stands below the Schwarzwandspitze. A Category I hut, and the property of the Siegerland section of the DAV, it has 32 beds and 29 dormitory places, and is staffed from July to the end of September (☎ 05254 2142 www.dav-siegerland.de).

Starkenburger Hut (2237m) Standing high above Neustift on the slopes of the Hoher Burgstall, this Category I hut has 27 beds and 30 dormitory places. Owned by the Starkenburg-Darmstadt section of the DAV, it is manned from June to the beginning of October (☎ 0664 5035420 www.alpenverein-darmstadt.de).

Sulzenau Hut (2191m) A pleasant 2hr walk from Graba Alm in the Unterbergtal leads to this Category I hut set on a meadow below the Wilder Freiger. Property of the DAV's Sulzenau section, it has 90 beds and 40 dormitory places, and is staffed from June to the end of September (☎ 05226 2432 www.davsektionsulzenau.de).

Tribulaun Hut (2064m) Property of the Touristenverein Naturfreunde (TVN) this hut stands at the foot of the Gschnitzer Tribulaun south of Gschnitz, from which it is reached in about 2½hrs. With 2 beds and 48 dormitory places, it's manned from mid-June to mid-October (☎ 0664 4050951 www.naturfreunde.at).

Westfalenhaus (2276m) Situated on the west bank of the Längental spur of the Lüsenstal, 2½hrs from the Lüsens trailhead, this Category I hut belongs to the Münster/Westfalen section of the DAV. Fully staffed from early February to the beginning of May, and from the end of June to the end of September, it has 15 beds and 50 dormitory places (☎ 05236 267 www.dav-muenster.de).

Winnebachsee Hut (2361m) Built on the southern shore of the little Winnebachsee 2½hrs above Gries in the Sulztal, this small Category I hut has 8 beds and 40 dormitory places. Staffed from March to the beginning of May, and from the end of June to mid-October, it is owned by the Hof/Bayern section of the DAV (☎ 05253 5197 www.alpenverein-hof.de).

FRANZ SENN, THE GLACIER PRIEST

Born the son of a Längenfeld farmer in 1831, Franz Senn was educated by Jesuits in Innsbruck and entered the priesthood in Brixen, South Tyrol (now Italy) in 1856. After serving in both Serfaus and Landeck, he was then sent to the remote parish of Vent in the Ötztal Alps in 1860. There he became a keen mountaineer, and concerned by the poverty and hardship of his parishioners and those of neighbouring mountain communities, he saw a way of improving the local economy through tourism. Campaigning for new roads, creating paths, developing huts and encouraging local men to use their skills to guide visitors to the summits, he became known as the *Gletscherpfarrer* (Glacier Priest). A founder member of the Tyrolean branch of the Austrian Alpine Club (ÖAV), and also of the German Alpine Club (DAV), he made a number of first ascents among his local mountains, including the Fluchtkogel, Weissseespitze and Vorderer Brochkogel. Tireless in his efforts to improve the training of guides, he also campaigned for better maps and guidebooks, and the provision of more alpine huts, whilst continuing to look after the spiritual needs of his parishioners. Franz Senn died of TB in the Stubaital in 1884 and is buried in the churchyard at Neustift. A year later the ÖAV built a hut at the head of the Oberbergtal, and named it in his honour.

WALKS IN THE WINDACHTAL

Most routes in this valley, which lies to the east of Sölden, lead to huts. The majority of them are quite long and with the reputation of being something of a slog.

- On the north side of the valley, and at its entrance, the **Kleble Alm** can be reached by a combination of paved road and footpath. Accommodation and refreshments are available here, and at 1983m the *alm* makes a splendid vantage point from which to view some of the high peaks of the Ötztal Alps.

- About 2hrs from Sölden, the walk to **Gasthaus Fiegl** (Fiegl Hut, 1956m) is said to be one of the nicest in the Windachtal. On paved road for a short distance, then by track in woodland the rest of the way, the *gasthaus* stands among pastures on the north bank of the Windache stream. Open from June to the end of September, it has 20 beds and 10 dormitory places (☎ 05254 2571).

- North of the Gasthaus Fiegl, and 700m higher, the **Seekarsee** (2658m) can be reached by a steep zigzag path, about 1½–2hrs from the *gasthaus*.

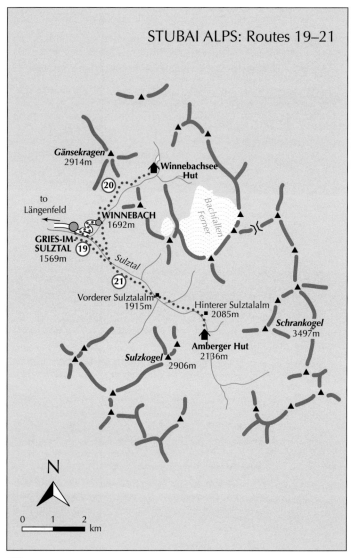

STUBAI ALPS: Routes 19–21

Gänsekragen
2914m

Winnebachsee
Hut

to
Längenfeld

⟨20⟩

Bachfallen Ferner

WINNEBACH
1692m

GRIES-IM-
SULZTAL
1569m

⟨19⟩

Sulztal

⟨21⟩

Vorderer Sulztalalm
1915m

Hinterer Sulztalalm
2085m

Schrankogel
3497m

Amberger Hut
2136m

Sulzkogel
2906m

N

0   1   2
km

WALKS IN THE SULZTAL

This is a delightful valley of meadow and forest which grows in drama the deeper you penetrate. Buses run daily from Längenfeld to Gries-im-Sulztal, its only village, which has a car park at its eastern end. This serves as the trailhead for the main walking interest leading to the Winnebachsee and Amberger Huts, described below, but a much shorter circular walk is also given which remains close to Gries.

ROUTE 19
Circular Walk from Gries-im-Sulztal

Location	East of Gries
Valley base	Längenfeld or Gries
Grade	1
Distance	6km
Height gain	130m
Height loss	130m
Time	1½hrs

Using a combination of footpaths and tracks, a short and pleasant circular walk can be made which gives an introduction to the valley.

From the bus stop by the tourist office, walk through the village heading upvalley, then take a side road on the left which slopes uphill between hay meadows, makes a couple of loops and brings you to the buildings of **Winnebach** (1692m, accommodation and refreshments). On coming to the first building on the right, leave the road and take a signed path climbing above it. This swings to the right and crosses a bridge over the Winnebach torrent. A track then takes you among trees, and shortly afterwards contours along the hillside to provide lovely views down to Gries and the lower valley.

Before long the way eases downhill and brings you onto a dirt road. Turn left along the road, and about 6mins on it crosses the Fischbach river. Immediately across the bridge fork right and descend a slope on a track among trees. You then follow the river all the way back to Gries, sometimes among trees, sometimes along the edge of hay meadows. Ignore two bridges, and continue on the track until you reach a third bridge near the Tiroler Hütte. Cross this into the centre of Gries.

ROUTE 20

Gries-im-Sulztal (1569m) –
Winnebachsee Hut (2361m)

Location	Northeast of Gries
Valley base	Längenfeld or Gries
Grade	3
Distance	5km (one way)
Height gain	792m
Time	2½hrs (+1½–2hrs return)

The approach to the Winnebachsee Hut is persistently steep, but as almost every step is uphill, height is quickly gained. The hut is popular with day visitors, so don't expect to have the path to yourself.

At the eastern end of **Gries** walk up the side road which rises between hay meadows, then makes a couple of turns to reach the buildings of **Winnebach** (1692m, accommodation and refreshments) after about 20mins. The road ends by a large barn, with a footpath rising behind it, soon giving views onto the rooftops of Gries. It's a broad and well-made path that twists up the wooded slopes of the narrow Winnebachtal.

The way is clear throughout, and there are no junctions to watch out for. Above the forest the path cuts through dwarf

The Winnebachsee Hut and its little tarn

pine, then angles across scree, turns a bend and enters an upper level of the Winnebach Alm. Across the flat meadows the spectacular Bachfalle waterfall streaks the opposite wall. For a short spell the path eases across the left-hand slope, then the gradient steepens, with a few twists to gain the hut.

The **Winnebachsee Hut** (2361m) occupies a position at the southern end of the little lake after which it is named. Above the lake rocky peaks curve in a horseshoe, several of which exceed 3000m. Built in 1901, it's a small, traditional hut with very fine views from the terrace. There are 8 beds and 40 dormitory places, and it's fully staffed from March to the beginning of May, and from the end of June to mid-October (☎ 05253 5197).

ROUTES FROM THE WINNEBACHSEE HUT

- Making a **circuit of the Winnebachsee** is a natural temptation, but beware that whilst it is possible, a path only goes along the west bank, and crossing the powerful stream that feeds the lake at its northern end involves the use of semi-submerged rocks. Caution is advised. Allow 30–40mins.

- The ascent of the 2914m **Gänsekragen** west of the hut by a very steep path will take about 1½–2hrs. The summit is marked by a cross, and the views are impressive – especially to the glacier-clad Ötztal Alps.

- Northeast of the hut, the **Winnebachjoch** (2782m) provides a way over the mountains to the **Westfalenhaus** in the Längental stem of the Lüsenstal (3½hrs). In the words of Cecil Davies, the way is long and laborious to the *joch*, but without difficulty on descent to the Westfalenhaus.

ROUTE 21
Gries-im-Sulztal (1569m) – Sulztalalm (1915m) – Amberger Hut (2136m)

Location	Southeast of Gries
Valley base	Längenfeld or Gries
Grade	2
Distance	6km (one way)
Height gain	567m
Time	2hrs (+ 1½hrs return)

The Amberger Hut overlooks such an idyllic scene that this walk would be worthwhile even if the rest of the valley held little of interest. But the Sulztal is delightful throughout its length, which compensates for the fact that this hut approach follows a dirt road all the way.

Walk through **Gries** heading upvalley, passing the car park at the eastern end of the village. The paved road soon become a dirt road, at first on the north side of the river, then

crossing to the south side and twisting uphill through woodland. For some way views are restricted, but now and again
a gap in the trees reveals the unmistakable pointed 3497m
Schrankogel directly ahead. About 12mins after crossing the
river, the road forks – the right branch goes to Nisslalm and
the Schönrinnen See – but we continue ahead in the direction of the Sulztalalm.

▶ About 1hr 15mins from Gries, the path comes to
Vorderer Sulztalalm (1915m, refreshments) where a sign
gives 45mins to the Amberger Hut. The way rises at a steady
angle, then curves through a narrowing gap to emerge to the
secluded meadows of **Hinterer Sulztalalm** (2085m).

The dirt road eases through the meadows, crosses the
river for the last time, then angles above a minor gorge before
turning rocks for a final short rise to the **Amberger Hut**.

*Meadows of the upper
Sulztal, seen from the
Amberger Hut*

When you emerge
from woodland the
valley opens out to
reveal its true nature,
with broad pastures
littered with rocks,
and a great rim of
peaks ahead.

The **Amberger Hut** (2136m) overlooks a vast meadowland sliced by the Fischbach
which flows directly from the Sulztalferner, the valley's most important glacier
hanging from the Windacher Daunkogel. The Category I hut has 10 beds and 59
dormitory places, and is fully staffed from early February to the end of April, and
from mid-June to the beginning of October (☎ 05253 5605).

WALKS IN THE HORLACHTAL

The valley is hidden from the Ötztal into which it drains at Umhausen, but as you take the winding access road through forest above the village, so the impressive Stuibenfall may be seen thundering over a sudden drop. Accessible from the road, the granite Tauferberg is a popular local *klettergarten* with routes of 10–30m. The paved road ends at the tiny village of Niederthai (1535m) which has a handful of hotels, *gasthöfe*, holiday apartments, and a small tourist office (Information Umhausen-Niederthai, ☎ 05255 5400, e-mail niederthai@oetztal-mitte.com; www.oetztal-mitte.com). Beyond the village the valley reaches northeastward into a lovely mountain landscape, not as dramatic perhaps as some other Stubai districts, but it's undeniably seductive to the walker.

- From Niederthai a dirt road twists into a side valley cutting into the Horlachtal's south wall. A trail extends beyond the road up to the **Grastalsee** at 2533m, and from there it's possible to make the ascent of the 2759m **Hemerkogel** which looks down on Niederthai, but also enjoys a fine series of views across the Ötztal.

- Niederthai is the start of another dirt road which pushes on through the Horlachtal on the true left bank of the Horlachbach as far as the **Gubener Schweinfurter Hut** (2028m), making an easy but not uninteresting walk of about 2hrs. It's one that many visitors make in the summer, for it has much to commend it.

- The Gubener Schweinfurter Hut sits at a junction of trails. One of these (the Gubener Weg) goes northeast then north to cross the 2719m **Finstertaler Scharte**, then descends alongside a dammed lake to end at **Kühtai** above the Sellraintal.

- Southeast of the Gubener Schweinfurter Hut a good trail continues along the Zwiselbachtal a short distance, then rises across its right flank before climbing to the 2751m **Gleirschjöchl** on the way to the **Neue Pforzheimer Hut** (3–4hrs), with another 2hrs needed to walk down the Gleirsch valley to **St Sigmund** in the Sellraintal.

WALKS IN THE NEDERTAL

Above and to the east of Oetz the Nedertal and Sellraintal, linked by the resort village of Kühtai, effectively define the northern limits of the Stubai Alps. Drained by the Nederbach, the Nedertal is narrow and heavily forested, but on the approach to Kühtai it opens out, the woodland cover is less constricting and three tributary valleys cut into the south flanking mountains: Wörgetal, Mittertal, and Längental. The last of these has a reservoir at its entrance beside which the road from Oetz makes its final approach to Kühtai at 2017m. Since Kühtai is primarily a ski resort, it has a number of cableways on slopes to north and south, and a distinctly out-of-season atmosphere in summer. Above and to the south lies a second reservoir, the Speicher Finstertal, and alongside it a trail entices into less-managed country. There are, in fact, several opportunities to explore the high country south of the Nedertal, among them a series of waymarked paths promoted locally as the Knappenweg – usually starting at the Bergstation Hochoetz (2020m) reached by the Acherkogelbahn cable-car from Oetz. There are, of course, plenty of other paths, tracks and cairned routes worth following.

- In the Wörgetal a path entices towards the head of the valley then, less defined, it swings west to climb the **Wetterkreuzkogel** (2501m).

- The Mittertal is a little longer than its neighbour to the west, but is still fairly short. Two thirds of the way through this valley, the Theodor-Streich-Weg suggests an interesting ascent of the **Wörgegratspitze** above the Mittertaler Scharte – a grade 3 route for walkers with a good head for heights.

- Better still, the Längental is worth exploring, and at its head a devious cairned route with ladder assistance leads to the **Hochreichkopf** at 3010m. Once again, this is a route for walkers with a good head for heights.

- From Kühtai the Drei-Seen-Bahn carries visitors southeastward to the upper chairlift station at 2420m. From there a 20min walk leads to a two-section *klettersteig* on the 2807m **Pockkogel**.

- A 20min walk also leads from the upper station of the Drei-Seen-Bahn to the Finstertal reservoir south of Kühtai. From there it's possible to take a path which climbs above the southwest shore to the summit of the **Sulzkogel** (3016m), while another crosses the **Finstertaler Scharte** at 2719m, and descends on the south side to the **Gubener Schweinfurter Hut** in the Horlachtal in 4–5hrs (see above).

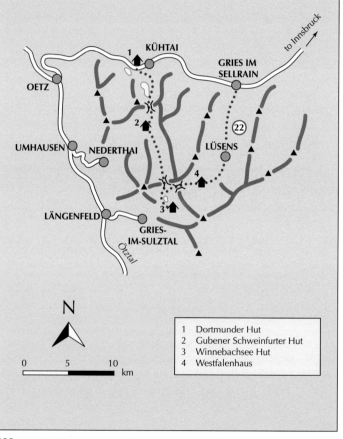

HUT TO HUT IN THE NORTHWEST STUBAI ALPS:
Route 22

to Innsbruck

KÜHTAI

1

GRIES IM
SELLRAIN

OETZ

2

22

UMHAUSEN

NEDERTHAI

LÜSENS

4

LÄNGENFELD

3

GRIES-
IM-SULZTAL

Ötztal

N

| 0 | 5 | 10 | km |

1 Dortmunder Hut
2 Gubener Schweinfurter Hut
3 Winnebachsee Hut
4 Westfalenhaus

ROUTE 22

Hut to Hut in the northwest Stubai Alps

Location	A counter-clockwise tour starting from Kühtai
Grade	3
Distance	36km
Highest point	Zwiselbachjoch (2868m)
Start	Kühtai (2017m)
Finish	Gries im Sellrain (1187m)
Time	4 days

Although the majority of hut-to-hut interest in the Stubai Alps focuses on the Stubaier Höhenweg (see Route 28 below), the following tour was described by the late Cecil Davies as 'one of the best round walks in the Stubai Alps, full of interest, variety and beauty, yet without serious difficulties' (*Mountain Walking in Austria*).

Day 1 The tour begins on the south side of the road opposite the Dortmunder Hut at the western end of Kühtai, and soon comes to the Finstertalbach which it follows upstream to the Finstertal reservoir. The way continues along the eastern side of the lake, and at its southern end climbs to the Finstertaler Scharte at 2719m (the Kompass map gives the height of this pass as 2777m). On the south side of the *scharte* the descent is on scree, then grass through the Weites Kar, following the Gubener Weg all the way to the **Gubener Schweinfurter Hut** (2028m) in 4–5hrs.

   Day 2 Another 4–5hr stage, the route continues along the cairned Gubener Weg which extends through the gently curving Zwiselbachtal, and climbs the headwall to the right (west) of the last remnants of a glacier plastered just below the summit ridge. Arriving at the 2868m Zwiselbachjoch, you're suddenly confronted by the snowy Breiter Grieskogel (3287m) which looms a short distance away to the south-west. Waymarks guide the descent down steep scree, heading roughly south then southeast, before aiming round the west shore of a tiny lake to reach the **Winnebachsee Hut** at 2361m.

Day 3 A shorter stage than the previous two, the Westfalenhaus can be reached in 3½hrs, given reasonable conditions. It begins by retracing the last part of yesterday's route, to a point beyond the lake where the trail forks. The path to the Winnebachjoch takes the right branch, heading north then northeast to make a laborious climb through a wild, boulder-strewn hanging valley below the Winnebacher Weisskogel. The 2782m *joch* lies below and southeast of this peak, and is reached in a little under 3hrs. Once across, a short, easy and uncomplicated descent leads to the **Westfalenhaus** (2276m).

Day 4 In his guide, Cecil Davies was rather dismissive of the final stage of this tour, apart from the initial section which takes an easy, pleasant path down the Längental to Alpengasthof **Lüsens** at the Lüsener Alm, from where an infrequent minibus service carries passengers through the Lüsenstal to Gries im Sellrain. He says the 2–2½hr walk down the road would be tedious. He may be correct, but this can be avoided by remaining above Lüsens and following a footpath to the hamlet of Praxmar, then walking north along the road for about 2km where a *panoramaweg* then offers an alternative almost all the way to **Gries im Sellrain**. Should you need to return to Kühtai, catch the *postbus* in Gries.

WALKS IN THE SELLRAINTAL

East of Kühtai the Sellraintal is fed by five tributary valleys draining the block of mountains on its south side. Reading from west to east, these tributaries are the Kraspestal, with Haggen at its entrance; the Gleirschtal cutting back from St Sigmund; then the longest of the five, the Lüsenstal which spills out at Gries; followed by the Fotschertal, south of Sellrain; and finally the Senderstal above Grinzens. Making a traverse of the region, a variante of the Zentralpenweg links all but the first of these, and other than the Kraspestal each tributary has a hut to visit, or to use as a base for further explorations.

- The most obvious walk in the **Kraspestal** leads to the little **Kraspessee** lying at 2549m in the head of the valley below converging ridges. An alternative, cairned route breaks to the west about halfway through the valley, rises through the Steintal to cross the ridge below the Pockkogel, and descends to **Kühtai**.

- St Sigmund has plenty of parking space for walkers heading into the **Gleirschtal**. Among its tempting routes, one leaves the valley floor near Gleirschalm and climbs the west slope to make the ascent of the 2420m **Mutenkogel**, but the main interest here lies in the 2½hr approach to the **Neue Pforzheimer Hut** which stands at 2310m a short distance inside the upper, westerly stem of the valley. A 4hr extension of this walk crosses the **Gleischjöchl** (2751m) south-west of the hut, and continues on the far side of the ridge to the **Gubener Schweinfurter Hut** in the Horlachtal (see above).

- A more demanding, and less well-defined route heads east from the Neue Pforzheimer Hut, crosses the 2735m **Satteljoch** and descends to **Praxmar** in the Lüsenstal.

- A minibus service feeds the steeply walled, V-shaped Lüsenstal from Gries im Sellrain. North of Praxmar the road divides. The main route rises along the west slope to Praxmar at 1689m, while the other stem continues in the valley to the Lüsener Alm (1634m), where there's an Alpengasthof with rooms and dormitory accommodation. From here a 2hr walk leads to the **Westfalenhaus**, while an extension of that route continues south through the upper valley towards the Längentalferner.

- The roadhead by **Alpengasthof Lüsens** is also the start of a route to the **Lüsener glacier**, but arguably the finest route here is the 5hr crossing of the 2812m **Horntaler Joch** which leads to the **Franz Senn Hut** at the head of the Oberbergtal.

- About 9km south of Sellrain, and 1100m higher than the village, the **Potsdamer Hut** stands at 2009m towards the head of the Fotschertal, and may be reached by a walk of 3½hrs. Strong walkers could make the ascent, and a crossing, of the 2832m **Roter Kogel** with a steep descent into the **Lüsenstal** in 5hrs from the hut. On the east side of the valley above the Potsdamer Hut, it's feasible to climb the **Schwarzhorn** (2812m) in 3hrs to gain a splendid overview of the district.

- And finally, in this selection of routes in and around the Sellraintal, mention must be made of the 3hr walk from Grinzens to the **Adolf Pichler Hut** (1960m) deep inside the Senderstal. This hut nestles below the lovely limestone Kalkkogel peaks which form a section of the Stubaital's west flank, and a linking route with that valley goes from the Adolf Pichler Hut over the **Seejöchl** hard against the Schlicker Seespitze, then cuts across screes on the way to the **Starkenburger Hut** in a little over 2hrs.

*Kalkkogel peaks –
an outburst of
limestone in the
crystalline Stubai Alps*

WALKS IN THE STUBAITAL

Longest of all the valleys in the range to which it lends its name, the Stubaital is entered from the busy Wipptal. At Neder, a short distance before reaching Neustift, a major tributary valley, the Pinnistal, slices into the southern wall of mountains, and again, just beyond Neustift at Milders, the Stubaital breaks into two stems. The Oberbergtal is a pastoral valley rimmed at its head by a lovely group of 3000m peaks daubed with snow and hanging with small glaciers. The ever-popular Franz Senn Hut is located 1½hrs above Oberiss at the roadhead (minibus from Neustift), and makes a fine base from which to explore further. The Unterbergtal, the southern stem of the Stubaital, is heavily wooded, but above the forests another group of attractive snow- and ice-bound summits rise well above the 3000m mark, including Zuckerhütl, Wilder Pfaff and Wilder Freiger. Just below the snowline a whole string of huts has been built, with trails leading to them from the valley, and across intervening ridge spurs to create a truly classic hut to hut tour. Sadly, mass ski development above the Mutterbergalm roadhead has devalued the immediate area around the Dresdner Hut, but the rest of the district remains largely free from commercial exploitation, and walkers can wander from tarn to tarn or hut to hut in what must surely count among Austria's finest mountain landscapes.

ROUTE 23

Neder (964m) – Pinnisalm (1560m) –
Innsbrucker Hut (2369m)

Location	South of Neder
Grade	2
Distance	10km
Height gain	1405m
Time	4–4½hrs

Standing close to the Pinnisjoch on a ridge dividing the Stubaital from the Gschnitztal, the Innsbrucker Hut is large, comfortable, and busy with both walkers and climbers. This approach is usually adopted as the first stage of the Stubaier Höhenweg (Route 28 below), but is worth tackling in its own right, for the Pinnistal through which the route journeys is a joy to wander in. It has neat pastures, soaring rock walls, and a handful of *alm* restaurants to relax by. The walk is easy and gently inclined as far as Karalm, but then steepens considerably for the 600m climb to the pass, from where the Tribulaun peaks suddenly burst into view across the deep Gschnitztal.

Note In his guide, Cecil Davies cautioned against walking through the Pinnistal, suggesting you'd be covered with dust raised by 'jeeps filled with gaping tourists'. My own experience has been very different, for my wife and I had the valley to ourselves (it was in July too), and the walk was a delight.

From **Neder** follow the road southeast a short distance to Schmieden at the Pinnistal entrance, beyond which the road is unpaved. Remain on this dirt road all the way through the valley, alongside the Pinnisbach and with neat fenced meadows, forested slopes, and impressive rock walls soaring above them. The left-hand wall (east flank of the valley) has the 2840m Kirchdachspitze as its highest summit, while at the head of the valley, to the right (west) of the Pinnisjoch, the 3277m Habicht is the main focus of attention.

After passing one or two *alms*, in 2hrs come to the **Pinnisalm** (1560m, refreshments). This can also be reached

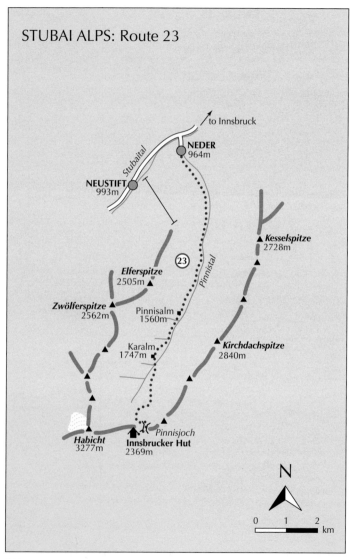

STUBAI ALPS: Route 23

Stubaital

NEUSTIFT 993m

NEDER 964m

to Innsbruck

㉓

Pinnistal

▲ **Kesselspitze** 2728m

Elferspitze ▲ 2505m

Zwölferspitze ▲ 2562m

Pinnisalm 1560m ■

Karalm 1747m ■

▲ *Kirchdachspitze* 2840m

Habicht 3277m

Pinnisjoch **Innsbrucker Hut** 2369m

N

0   1   2
km

by footpath leading from the Elfer cableway which begins in Neustift. Another path breaks away from the road heading to the right near the alm, climbing the west flank of the valley to cross the ridge between the Elferspitze and Zwölferspitze. The route to the Innsbrucker Hut, however, continues along the dirt road to **Karalm** (1747m, refreshments), after which a footpath strikes south across rough pastureland, then up steeply with zigzags to gain the **Pinnisjoch**. The **Innsbrucker Hut** lies just beyond the pass.

The Innsbrucker Hut enjoys a direct view of the Tribulaun peaks

Built by the Innsbruck section of the ÖAV, the Category I **Innsbrucker Hut** enjoys a glorious view south to the Tribulaun peaks, while the Habicht rises above the hut to the west. The normal ascent of this handsome peak by its east flank is only graded F (some fixed ropes) and takes about 2½–3hrs; there's some scrambling involved, but the descent is notoriously dangerous for anyone straying from the correct route. The hut is also used as a base by activists tackling the *klettersteig* on the nearby Ilmspitze, and (as mentioned above) by hut-to-hut trekkers on the Stubaier Höhenweg. The next stage of the *höhenweg* is a demanding one which leads to the Bremer Hut perched above the head of the Gschnitztal. There is also the option of a steep descent by path to the Gschnitztal from the Innsbrucker Hut, which has 30 beds and 100 dormitory places, and is staffed from mid-June to the beginning of October (☎ 05276 295 www.innsbrucker-huette.at).

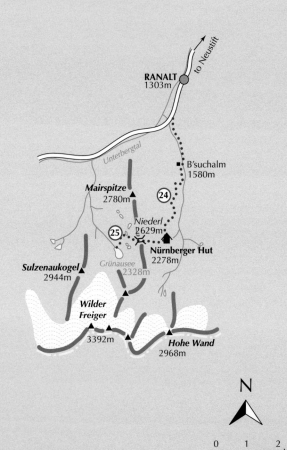

STUBAI ALPS: Routes 24–25

RANALT
1303m

to Neustift

Unterbergtal

B'suchalm
1580m

Mairspitze
2780m ▲

(24)

Niederl
2629m

(25)

Nürnberger Hut
2278m

Sulzenaukogel
2944m ▲

Grünausee
2328m

*Wilder
Freiger*

3392m ▲

Hohe Wand
2968m

N

0   1   2 km

ROUTE 24

Ranalt (1303m) – Nürnberger Hut (2278m)

Location	South of Ranalt, about 12km southwest of Neustift
Grade	2–3
Distance	5km
Height gain	975m
Time	2½hrs

Standing high up in the Langental tributary on the south side of the Stubaital's Unterbergtal stem, the four-storey Nürnberger Hut is another comfortable place in which to stay for a night or two in somewhat wild surroundings. The Wilder Freiger crowns the border ridge to the southwest, and a short stroll above the hut gives a broad view of the headwall peaks and their glaciers.

The start of the walk described here is a bus stop (ask for the Nürnberger halt) about 1km south of **Ranalt** on the road to the Mutterbergalm. There's a small unmade parking area on the east side of the road, and a marked path climbs from it, steeply at first through forest, then after about 15mins the path brings you onto a track rising gently along the east side of the Langental stream. When the track forks, branch right

A 2½hr approach from Ranalt leads to the Nürnberger Hut

147

to cross the stream and reach the **B'suchalm** (1580m, refreshments) about 40–45mins from the bus stop.

Above the *alm* the way zigzags up and across the steep west flank of the valley, climbing some 400m or so before easing to a short contouring section, then rising again through a wild landscape of rocks on the east slope of the Mairspitze. Another steep pull, and at last you reach the **Nürnberger Hut** about 2½hrs from the start.

Standing among rocks and boulders below the long south ridge of the Mairspitze, the Category I, DAV-owned **Nürnberger Hut** has 50 beds and 92 dormitory places, and is fully staffed from the beginning of June until the beginning of October (☎ 05226 2492 www.dav-nuernberg.de). Built in 1886, the hut has been enlarged and improved several times since, but the panelling in the *gaststube* is a throwback to earlier times. A short (20–30min) stroll upvalley brings you to an area of ice-smoothed glacial slabs – textbook geography writ large upon the landscape.

ROUTE 25
Nürnberger Hut (2278m) –
Niederl (2629m) – Grünausee (2328m)

Location	West of the Nürnberger Hut
Grade	3
Distance	2.5km
Height gain	351m
Height loss	301m
Time	1¾–2hrs

First a warning: the crossing of the Mairspitze ridge by the Niederl is marked *Nur für Geübte* – 'only for the experienced' – on account of the descent on the west side which uses a series of narrow shelves on the steep and broken face of the mountain. Fixed cables safeguard the way, but there's considerable exposure, so this route is definitely not for vertigo sufferers. Safely down, the way picks a route across a natural rock garden past a small tarn, then down to the emerald Grünausee in which the Wilder Freiger is mirrored – a truly magnificent scene.

Wayside tarn near the Grünausee

A sign at the hut directs the way to the Sulzenau Hut (the next stop on the Stubaier Höhenweg). Aiming northwest the route is shared with that of the Zentralalpenweg, but when the path forks after about 10mins, take the left branch (the right-hand path offers an alternative crossing further north along the ridge), soon zigzagging up the steep rocks. Sometimes scrambling, sometimes aided by fixed cables, the way climbs in about 1hr to the **Niederl**, a 2629m pass noted for its large wooden cross, a seat and a small shrine (some authorities quote this pass as 2680m).

Note The alternative path on the east flank not only offers a slightly easier crossing of the ridge, but is used for the ascent of the 2780m **Mairspitze**. Once the crossing col is gained, the ridge is then followed northward all the way to the summit – 2hrs from the Nürnberger Hut.

Descend on the west side with great care, for the rock face is steep, and the way is led along and down a series of exposed narrow shelves and ledges protected by fixed cables.

Once down, the trail winds among screes, rocks and boulders, between which in early summer alpine flowers

149

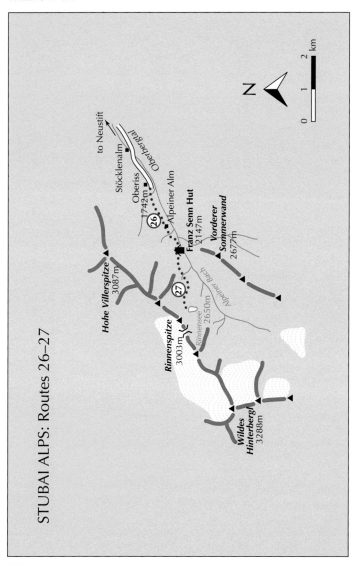

STUBAI ALPS: Routes 26–27

create a surprise of a wild garden. Come to a small pool with lovely reflected views, and beyond that join another path (the higher crossing mentioned earlier) where you turn left and wander over grass slopes to the **Grünausee** (2328m) in full view of the Wilder Freiger and its steep glacier.

Note To return to the Nürnberger Hut by the same route will take about 2hrs. But a better option would be to follow the continuing path northwest and west of the Grünausee, and reach the Sulzenau Hut in another hour, then descend to the Unterbergtal by a good path which brings you onto the valley road about 300m west of the Grabaalm where there's a bus stop.

ROUTE 26
Oberiss (1742m) – Franz Senn Hut (2147m)

Location	At the head of the Oberbergtal
Grade	1
Distance	3km
Height gain	405m
Time	1½hrs

A short and easy walk to the best-known hut in the Stubai Alps, from which a number of fine excursions (walks and climbs) are possible.

The narrow paved road through the Oberbergtal breaks away from the main Stubaital at Milders, near Neustift. A minibus ferries passengers as far as Oberissalm, while a trail (and sometimes track) mirrors the road route for much of the way – a walk of about 3hrs from Milders to Oberissalm. Among other accommodation facilities in the valley, there's the Alpengasthof Bärenbad, and rooms at Stöcklenalm about 1km from Oberiss. Car parking is possible at Oberiss, and it is here that the approach walk to the hut begins.

Go through the gate on the west side of the **Oberiss** car park and continue along the road (no private vehicles). When this ends take the direct path ahead (ignore the left branch) through meadows to the **Alpeiner Alm** (1hr, refreshments). With the hut in view the path continues to rise easily, and about 30mins from the *alm* reaches the **Franz Senn Hut**.

Named after the 'glacier priest' who lies buried in the churchyard at Neustift, the popular Category I **Franz Senn Hut** dates from 1885 when it had just 20 *matratzenlager* places (8 of these were in the hayloft). With a number of extensions and modernisations since then, it can now accommodate a total of 160 in its rooms and dormitories. Fully staffed from mid-February until early May, and from mid-June to the beginning of October, advance booking is advised (☎ 05226 2218 www.frankhauser.at).

ROUTE 27

Franz Senn Hut (2147m) – Rinnensee (2650m)

Location	West of the Franz Senn Hut
Grade	2–3
Distance	3km
Height gain	503m
Time	1½hrs

The view south across the Rinnensee to the snow-capped Seespitzen is a classic feature of Stubai postcards, and this short and easy walk is understandably one of the most popular excursions from the Franz Senn Hut.

Out of the hut head north along a signed path which has a number of destinations marked. After about 10mins the way forks by a stream (about 2200m) where you take the left branch to climb steeply for a while. Rising southwestward, the path then curves northwest in the cirque walled by the Kreuzkamp, Rinnenspitze and Berglasspitze. At about 2600m a cairned route forks right to make the ascent of the Rinnenspitze, while we slant left to reach the northern end of the **Rinnensee**. (Return to the hut by the same path in a little under 1hr.)

OTHER ROUTES FROM THE FRANZ SENN HUT

An almost unlimited variety of walks and easy ascents can be made from a base at the Franz Senn Hut. The following is just a small selection. For more ideas, consult the appropriate map.

*   The 3003m **Rinnenspitze** above the Rinnensee makes a very fine vantage point from which to study the district surrounding the Franz Senn Hut. The normal route via the east flank is not difficult (grade F) and is gained by following the Rinnensee route (see above), to the point where the path forks at about 2600m. The right branch is the one to take for the Rinnenspitze, rising over grass and scree (2hrs).

*   The **Vorderer Sommerwand** (2677m) is one of a group of four summits spreading southsouthwest of the hut in a wall ending at the Kräulscharte. Whilst some scrambling

Named after the 'glacier priest', the Franz Senn Hut makes a popular base for walks and climbs

and climbing of grade III is called for on other peaks, the ascent of the Vorderer Sommerwand is little more than a walk (1½–2hrs) rewarded by a tremendous display of alpine flowers in early summer, and good views.

- An easy walk is worth taking towards the **Alpeiner Ferner** at the head of the valley stretching behind the hut. It follows the Alpeiner Bach stream all the way towards its source in the glacier.

- A full day's walk (6½–7hrs) follows the Franz-Senn-Weg northeastward along the north flank of the Oberbergtal to the **Starkenburger Hut**. This splendid route forms part of the Stubaier Höhenweg (Route 28), and is highly recommended.

The path to the Starkenburger Hut cuts along the left flank of the Oberbergtal

- Another fine hut to hut walk also follows the Franz-Senn-Weg as far as the **Sendersjöchl**. It then crosses the pass and slopes gently down the east side of the upper Senderstal to reach the **Adam Pichler Hut** in 4–5hrs.

ROUTE 28
The Stubaier Höhenweg

Location	A clockwise tour of the Stubaital, starting from Neder
Grade	3
Distance	120km
Highest point	Grawagrubennieder (2881m)
Start	Neder (964m)
Finish	Neustift (993m)
Time	7–9 days

Generally considered to be the finest hut-to-hut route in the Eastern Alps, this well-marked tour rewards with memorable views on every stage. Several of these stages are short (no more than 3hrs long), but the quality of the scenery is such that unless you are really pushed for time, or the weather is poor, a whole day should be given to enjoy the landscape, flora and wildlife seen along the way. As for the huts used for overnight accommodation, each one has its own special atmosphere which adds to the overall *höhenweg* experience.

Whilst there are no really demanding ascents to face, numerous ridges and ridge spurs need to be crossed, a number of which have narrow ledges or exposed sections safeguarded by fixed cables. In places the trail is little more than a row of waymarks painted on rocks, and in poor visibility route-finding could be a challenge. On the descent from the highest pass (the Grawagrubennieder), extreme caution should be exercised where there's much loose rock.

After leaving Neder the route avoids all roads and villages until completion in Neustift. A wonderful tour, recommended to all experienced hillwalkers, it is treated to full description in the excellent *Trekking in the Stubai Alps* by Allan Hartley (Cicerone Press).

Day 1 Conveniently reached by public transport from Innsbruck, **Neder** sits at the entrance to the Pinnistal through which the first stage leads to the Pinnisjoch, with the large and comfortable **Innsbrucker Hut** (2369m, 4–4½hrs) standing just beyond it. This stage is fully described above as Route 23.

THE STUBAIER HÖHENWEG: Route 28

Wildkopf

Ruderhofspitz

Unterbergtal

Habicht

NEUSTIFT

NEDER

FULMES

to Innsbruck

Kalkkogel

(28)

7

6

5

4

3

2

1

8

Wilder Freiger

Zuckerhütl

Feuerstein

ITALY

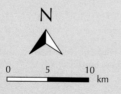

N

0   5   10
km

1	Innsbrucker Hut
2	Bremer Hut
3	Nürnberger Hut
4	Sulzenau Hut
5	Dresdner Hut
6	Neue Regensberger Hut
7	Franz Senn Hut
8	Starkenburger Hut

Walkers en route to the Bremer Hut, on the Stubaier Höhenweg

Day 2 This is undoubtedly one of the most demanding stages on the *höhenweg*. It's a 6hr day with numerous ridge spurs to cross (plenty of fixed cables) on the way to the atmospheric **Bremer Hut** (2411m), overlooking a small tarn at the head of the Gschnitztal. For much of the way views will be enjoyed of peaks that form the south wall of the valley, as well as those that close it off in the west.

Day 3 A much shorter stage beginning with the crossing of the 2754m Simmingjöchl on the south ridge of the Innere Wetterspitze which looms above the Bremer Hut. The route to the *jöchl* involves some modest scrambling, although it's nowhere difficult, while the descent to the **Nürnberger Hut** is a joy of stony basins, tiny meadows, winding streams, more brief scrambling pitches, and a region of glacial slabs at the head of the Langental. The hut is reached in just 3hrs.

Day 4 This is another 3hr stage that could easily take all day to complete, such is the quality of the scenery on the way to the **Sulzenau Hut** (2191m) below the Wilder Pfaff. Once again there are some tricky moves to be made on the descent from the Niederl, where the route uses a series of narrow, exposed ledges protected by fixed cables (see Route 25). The second half of the walk from the Grünausee is partly along an old moraine, now grassed over and flower-starred. All in all, an utterly delightful day's walking.

Day 5 Continuing the westward trend taken by the *höhenweg* on Day 3, this stage has a choice of either crossing the 2672m Peiljoch, overlooking the Sulzenauferner, or of making the ascent of the Grosser Trögler (2902m) to gain

The glacier-hung Wilder Freiger above the Sulzenau Hut

a far-reaching panorama – especially fine is the view of the Zuckerhütl. Neither route is unduly difficult, although the Trögler option has some scrambling sections and exposure on part of the descent. Once across either the *jöchl* or the Trögler's summit, an easy trail leads to the **Dresdner Hut** (2308m) – a 3hr stage. Sadly the hut's immediate surroundings have been vandalised by the ski industry, although the building itself is cosy and welcoming.

Day 6 The longest stage of all (in terms of hours), taking 6–7hrs to reach the **Neue Regensberger Hut** on the lip of a hanging valley, by way of the tour's highest pass. From the Dresdner Hut the day begins by heading west, but it soon turns northward, cutting across the Unterbergtal's upper reaches, then trending northeast below the Ruderhofspitze to locate the 2881m Grawagrubennieder, a notch in a long rocky ridge, and with a steep drop on the northern side. It is the descent of this northern side that calls for extra care in order to avoid dislodging loose rocks and stones onto anyone who might be below. In the past a short glacier crossing was involved at the foot of this descent, but this glacier has now withdrawn, and you pick a way over old moraine debris and a boulder field before easing through the Hochmoostal to the hut.

Day 7 Little more than a morning's walk (4hrs) separates the Neue Regensberger and Franz Senn Huts, but it's another interesting stage whose highlight is the crossing of the 2714m Schrimmennieder north of the Regensberger. It's a fairly steep climb to the col, reached about 1½hrs after setting out, and the descent on the north side of the ridge cuts down through the narrow Platzengrube before following a good trail to reach the large and invariably busy **Franz Senn Hut**.

Day 8 This penultimate stage is the longest in actual distance of any previous section of the Stubaier Höhenweg, but there are no cols to cross and for the most part the way follows an easy undulating course along the left-hand wall of the Oberbergtal. Given reasonable conditions, this is a most enjoyable 6hr walk and, unusual for this tour, about 2hrs along the trail refreshments are available at the Seduckalm. Towards the end of this stage you come to the Seejöchl overlooking the Senderstal, but then turn sharply to the southeast to cut across screes at the foot of the impressive Kalkkogel peaks – Dolomite lookalikes – on the final approach to the **Starkenburger Hut**. High above Neustift, and standing at 2237m, the hut has a marvellous view of much of the route taken over the previous week.

Towards the end of the Stubaier Höhenweg, the route crosses screes below the Kalkkogel peaks

Day 9 A short, but knee-achingly steep descent of more than 1200m takes this last stage down through forest to **Neustift** where you can collapse in a restaurant chair and reflect on the delights of the route with a well-earned drink. Or two.

WALKS IN THE GSCHNITZTAL

The final valley in this overview of the Stubai Alps, the Gschnitztal is approached from Steinach am Brenner (railway from Innsbruck) in the Wipptal, north of the Brenner Pass. The valley flows parallel to the Unterbergtal, the southernmost extension of the Stubaital, and at its northeastern end is broad, green and pastoral, but tapering to a convergence of ridges above the Bremer Hut in the southwest. There's a *postbus* service from Steinach all the way through the valley to Gasthof Feuerstein (1281m) at the roadhead, and accommodation can be found in Trins and Gschnitz. There are no campsites in the valley, and little in the way of tourist infrastructure, but at its upper end the south wall which carries the Austro–Italian border is buttressed by the impressive Tribulaun peaks, the Weisswand, Schneespitze and the two Feuerstein summits.

- A series of connecting footpaths and tracks travels along the east side of the Gschnitzbach from **Trins** to **Gschnitz**, continues a little further upvalley before spilling onto the road, then resuming once more beyond the **Gasthof Feuerstein** roadhead; a peaceful, undemanding walk to suit all tastes.

- A direct route to the **Innsbrucker Hut** climbs the steep north slope of the valley just outside Gschnitz in 3hrs. Another 3hr approach to the same hut begins close to Gasthof Feuerstein and climbs more or less under the hut's goods lift most of the way.

- Also from Gasthof Feuerstein a good path heads south through the little Sandesbach valley, then climbs up its east flank to the TVN-owned **Tribulaun Hut** at 2064m, reached in about 2½hrs.

- And finally, the **Bremer Hut**, visited on the Stubaier Höhenweg, is reached by an uncomplicated walk of 3hrs from Gasthof Feuerstein.

5 ZILLERTAL ALPS

With Mayrhofen its main resort base, the Zillertal is one of the best-known valleys in Austria, noted as much for its walking potential as for its skiing. Its glacier-clad peaks provide numerous expeditions for the mountaineer, while the hillsides and lower meadows suggest a botanical paradise. Reliable bus services and cableways give access to most areas, and waymarked trails are plentiful. The whole district is extremely popular, which justifies its ever-expanding tourist infrastructure.

ACCESS AND INFORMATION

Location	East of the Stubai Alps, from which the Zillertal chain is separated by the Wipptal which carries the Brenner Pass road. The mountains spread across the Italian border, and are bounded to the north by the Tuxer and Kitzbüheler Alps. The Zillertal proper runs in an almost straight line south of the Inn Valley to Mayrhofen, where it then branches into several major tributaries.
Maps	Alpenvereinskarte 35/1 *Westliches Blatt*, 35/2 *Mittleres Blatt*, and 35/3
	Östliches Blatt 1:25,000
	Kompass Wanderkarte 037 *Mayrhofen Tuxertal-Zillergrund* 1:25,000
	Mayr 33 *Zillertaler Alpen* 1:35,000
	Freytag & Berndt WK152 *Mayrhofen – Zillertaler Alpen* 1:50,000
Bases	Zell am Ziller, Mayrhofen, Finkenberg
Information	Tirol Info, 6010 Innsbruck (e-mail: info@tirol.at; website: www.tirol.at)
	Zillertal Tourism (e-mail: holiday@zillertal.at; website: www.zillertal.at)
	Zell am Ziller Tourismus (e-mail: service@zillertalarena.com; website: www.zillertalarena.com)
	Mayrhofen Tourismusverbund (e-mail: info@mayrhofen.at; website: www.mayrhofen.at)
	Tux-Finkenberg Tourismus (e-mail: info@tux.at; website: www.tux.at)

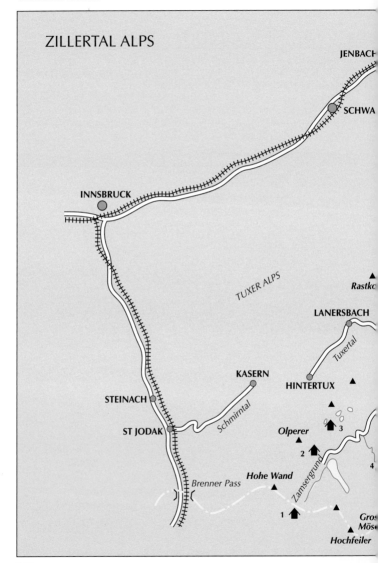

ZILLERTAL ALPS

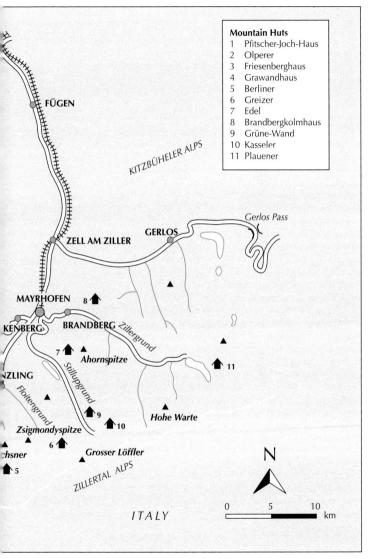

Mountain Huts
1. Pfitscher-Joch-Haus
2. Olperer
3. Friesenberghaus
4. Grawandhaus
5. Berliner
6. Greizer
7. Edel
8. Brandbergkolmhaus
9. Grüne-Wand
10. Kasseler
11. Plauener

FÜGEN

KITZBÜHELER ALPS

ZELL AM ZILLER   GERLOS

Gerlos Pass

MAYRHOFEN   8

KENBERG   BRANDBERG   Zillergrund

7   Ahornspitze

NZLING   Stillupgrund   11

Floitengrund   9

Zsigmondyspitze   10   Hohe Warte

chsner   6

5   Grosser Löffler

ZILLERTAL ALPS

N

ITALY

0   5   10
km

Access	From Jenbach, 38km northeast of Innsbruck, the Zillertal strikes south to Mayrhofen. The valley is served by the Zillertalbahn, a narrow-gauge steam railway running between Jenbach (on the Innsbruck-Salzburg main-line) and Mayrhofen, with bus or minibus services extending to most of the tributary valleys.

The northern part of the Zillertal consists of a great expanse of meadowland walled on the west by the Tuxer Alps, with the Kitzbüheler Alps spreading to the east. But south of Zell am Ziller at the foot of the Gerlos Pass road (linking the Zillertal with Krimml in Oberpinzgau), the valley narrows, and grows increasingly alpine above Mayrhofen where tributary glens, known as *Gründe*, cut deeply into the mountains. Beginning to the east of Mayrhofen and listing clockwise, these tributaries are the Zillergrund, with a minor road via Bärenbad leading to a reservoir at over 1800m; the Stillupgrund, also partially drowned with a reservoir; the long Zemmgrund with three more feeder glens; and the beautiful Zamsergrund extending beyond that with a toll road leading to the Schlegeis reservoir, beyond which the valley reaches up to the Pfitscher Joch on the Italian border. And finally there's the Tuxertal which pushes west and southwest from Mayrhofen. This last-named is the most heavily developed, thanks to year-round skiing on the glacier at its head.

It is in these tributaries that the vast majority of walks are located. For each valley rewards with stimulating scenery, and has at least one mountain hut and, more often than not, an additional restaurant, inn or farmhouse offering refreshments.

Apart from the 3476m Olperer which forms a cornerstone of the Tuxertal, and the steep-sided Schrammacher (3410m) neighbouring it to the south, most of the highest mountains rim the Austro–Italian border. These include the Hochfeiler (3509m), Grosser Möseler (3480m), the 3420m Turnerkamp, 3369m Schwarzenstein and Grosser Löffler at 3379m. All of these are draped with fast-shrinking glaciers which, though not technically difficult to climb, put their summits beyond the range of routes in this book. But as a backdrop to numerous walks, their individual structure and grace of line help make the Zillertal Alps a district of considerable dramatic charm.

Walkers planning to spend a week or more in the Zillertal should consider investing in a **Z-Ticket** (available from June to October) to obtain free use of cablecars, gondolas and chairlifts in the district, as well as trains and buses (not in the Stilluptal), together with unlimited use of the valley's open-air swimming pools. Valid for 6, 9 or 12 consecutive days, the **Z-Ticket** can be purchased from Zillertal tourist offices and railway stations – a passport-sized photograph will be needed. The accompanying booklet includes timetables.

Walkers in the upper Zamsergrund (Route 35)

Main Bases

Zell am Ziller (575m) Formerly a gold-mining village, Zell is the chief resort of the lower valley, with a large ski area to the east served by the Kreuzjochbahn gondola, and an enticing 380m *klettersteig* above the Gerlos Pass road. There are plenty of restaurants, shops, a post office and bank, several hotels, private rooms and a campsite about 400m southeast of the centre, on the way to the Gerlos Pass. The tourist office is located on Dorfplatz in the village centre.

Mayrhofen (633m) One of the major Tyrolean resorts, Mayrhofen is largely dependent on package tourism, but its popularity is entirely justified by its situation, infrastructure, public transport and wealth of attractions. Given half-decent weather, no walker based here for a couple of weeks or so in summer need run short of ideas. The town has numerous hotels of all grades, *gästehäuser* and private rooms, and a campsite at Laubichl. There's no shortage of shops, restaurants, banks and bars, and the well-stocked tourist office is housed in the impressive Europahaus congress centre.

Finkenberg (850m) About 3km west of Mayrhofen at the entrance to the Tuxertal, Finkenberg is a modest-sized village in contrast to Mayrhofen's somewhat crowded atmosphere. Although there's limited accommodation and few other facilities, it makes a pleasant alternative base for a walking holiday. Details may be had from the Tux-Finkenberg tourist office.

Mountain Huts

Berliner Hut (2042m) Standing at the head of the Zemmgrund in view of the Hornkees glacier about 3hrs walk from the Breitlahner bus stop, the Berliner Hut is the largest in the Zillertal Alps. Owned by the Berlin section of the DAV, it was originally built in 1879, has 76 beds in rooms, and 92 dormitory places, and is noted for the chandeliers in its panelled dining room. A Category I hut, it's fully staffed from mid-June to the end of September (☎ 05286 5223 www.dav-berlin.de).

Dominikus Hut (1805m) The original Dominikus Hut was drowned in 1971 when the valley it stood in was dammed to create the Schlegeis reservoir. The replacement is a privately owned hotel-like hut with 13 beds and 18 dormitory places, standing just above the road at the head of the Zamser Tal, reached by bus from Mayrhofen. It is staffed from May to the end of October (☎ 05286 5216).

Edel Hut (2238m) This Category I hut (its full name is the Karl von Edel Hut) is invariably visited by walkers climbing the popular Ahornspitze above Mayrhofen. Easily reached in 1–1½hrs via the Ahornbahn cableway, it has 35 beds and 60 dormitory places, is manned from mid-June to the end of September, and belongs to the DAV's Würzburg section (☎ 0664 9154851 www.dav-wuerzburg.de).

Friesenberghaus (2477m) Standing some 700m above the Zamsergrund, on the route of the Berliner Höhenweg, this Category I hut is owned by the Berlin section of the DAV and is fully manned from mid-June to the beginning of October. It has 11 beds and 30 dormitory places and can be reached in about 2hrs from the bus stop at the Schlegeis reservoir (☎ 0676 7497550 www.dav-berlin.de).

Furtschaglhaus (2293m) Built in 1889 below the Grosser Möseler at the head of the Schlegeisgrund, the Furtschaglhaus has 77 beds and 30 dormitory places. A Category I hut owned by the DAV's Berlin section, it is staffed from mid-June to the end of September (☎ 0676 9579818 www.dav-berlin.de).

Gams Hut (1921m) Located southwest of Finkenberg, the small Category I Gams Hut has just 40 dormitory places, is owned by the Otterfing section of the DAV and is staffed from June to the end of September (☎ 0676 3437741 www.dav-otterfing.de).

Geraer Hut (2326m) Standing on the southwest slope of the Olperer, and usually approached from St Jodok am Bremer in 4hrs, this Category I hut belongs to the DAV's Landshut section. With 16 beds and 80 dormitory places, it's manned from the end of June to mid-September (☎ 0676 9610303 www.geraerhuette.com).

Grawandhaus (1640m) This privately owned hut is located roughly midway along the Zemmgrund valley, about 1½hrs walk from the Breitlahner bus stop. With 20 beds and 15 dormitory places, it's manned from May until the beginning of October (☎ 05286 5213).

Greizer Hut (2227m) A 4hr walk from Ginzling leads to this Category I hut set at the head of the Floitengrund below the Floitenkees glacier. Manned from mid-June to mid-September, and owned by the Greiz section of the DAV, there are 18 beds and 52 places in its dormitories (☎ 0664 1405003 www.alpenverein-greiz.de).

Grüne-Wand Hut (1438m) Reached by either a 4hr walk or by minibus from Mayrhofen, this privately owned hut stands near the roadhead in the Stillupgrund valley. With 14 beds and 15 dormitory places, it's staffed from mid-May to the end of September (☎ 0664 4332107).

Kasseler Hut (2178m) At the head of the Stillupgrund, this Category I hut is reached by a 2hr walk from the Grüne-Wand Hut (minibus from Mayrhofen) on a steep zigzag path. Belonging to the DAV's Kassel section, it has 24 beds and 72 dormitory places, and is manned from mid-June to the end of September (☎ 0664 1141496 www.alpenverein-kassel.de).

Olperer Hut (2388m) Perched about 600m above the Schlegeis reservoir (bus service from Mayrhofen), and gained by a walk of 1½hrs from the bus stop, the Category I Olperer Hut is owned by the Neumarkt section of the DAV. With 42 dormitory places, it's manned from June to the beginning of October (☎ 0664 4176566 www.dav-neumarkt.de).

Pfitscher-Joch-Haus (2275m) Although standing on the Italian side of the pass after which it is named, it's easily reached by a lovely walk of about 2hrs from the bus stop at the Schlegeis reservoir. Privately owned, it is staffed from late June until mid-October, and has 30 beds (☎ 0472 630119).

Plauener Hut (2364m) A very pleasant 1½hr walk from the bus stop at the Zillergrund reservoir dam leads to this Category I hut overlooking the Reichenspitze amphitheatre. Belonging to the Plauen-Vogtland section of the DAV, it's manned from mid-June to the end of September with 6 beds and 74 dormitory places (☎ 0650 2250369 www.plauener-huette.de).

Spannaglhaus (2531m) Owned by the ÖTK, the hut stands at the head of the Tuxertal among the gondolas serving the Tuxer glacier ski area, about 3½hrs from Hintertux, or 10mins from the upper gondola lift station. Open throughout the year, except June, there are 20 beds and 27 dormitory places (☎ 05287 707).

Tuxer-Joch-Haus (2313m) Also owned by the ÖTK, this hut is located southwest of Hintertux, about 2½hrs from the roadhead, but with a chairlift nearby. Open most of the year (not May or November), it has 13 beds and 28 dormitory places (☎ 05287 87216 www.oetk.at).

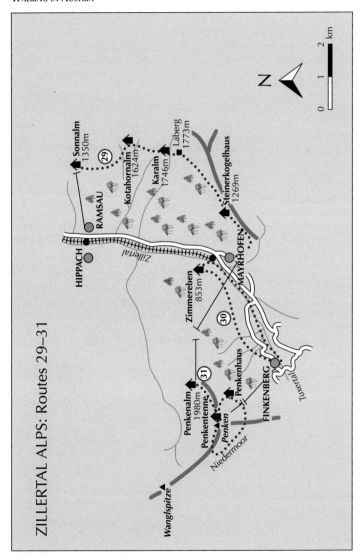

ZILLERTAL ALPS: Routes 29–31

ROUTE 29

Ramsau (Sonnalm: 1350m) –
Laberg (1773m) – Mayrhofen (633m)

Location	North of Mayrhofen, then south along the east flank of the Zillertal
Grade	2
Distance	9km
Height gain	423m
Height loss	1140m
Time	3–4hrs

Ramsau and Hippach face one another across the Ziller about 4km north of Mayrhofen. In the winter, skiing takes place on the slopes above Ramsau on the valley's east flank, and in summer the Ramsberglift carries visitors up to the restaurant of Sonnalm, from where a series of tracks and footpaths can be linked to make a pleasant high walk among pastures, groups of *alm* buildings and steep forest on the way to Mayrhofen. Refreshments can be had at Sonnalm, Kotahornalm and Karalm.

Walkers based in Mayrhofen can take the train or bus to Hippach-Ramsau, or follow an easy footpath alongside the river. From Ramsau take the chairlift (Ramsberglift) to **Sonnalm**, then descend a few paces onto a dirt road and head south (direction Kotahorn). Rising easily the way takes you past a few farms between steep meadows. At a hairpin leave the dirt road and walk ahead on a footpath which zig-zags uphill among trees, then angles south again. When it forks take the upper path which brings you to a grass track in a clearing. Red waymarks take you above this on a continuing path. This leads to another crossing track just beyond the rustic 400-year-old building of **Kotahornalm** (1624m, refreshments).

Walk alongside the *alm* building on a narrow path which soon climbs once more and turns a spur to a view of the Karalm ahead. The path leads directly to it. **Karalm**

(1746m, refreshments) occupies a steeply sloping pasture and is reached about 30mins from Kotahornalm.

The way continues round the hillside and rises a little further to reach more *alm* buildings at **Laberg** (1773m). It is here that you take a grass path heading to the right and wander downhill to pass a whole string of attractive *alm* buildings before entering forest. Signs are for Brandberg and Mayrhofen, and after twice crossing a track, you come in view of the **Steinerkogelhaus** (1269m). Immediately to its left a path winds down to more forest, and at a sharp bend you gain a very fine birdseye view onto Mayrhofen and up the Tuxertal.

Descend through steep forest on countless zigzags, pass a tiny chapel and religious carvings that represent the stations of the cross, and eventually come onto a minor road near Mayrhofen's cemetery.

ROUTE 30

Mayrhofen (633m) –
Finkenberg (850m) – Mayrhofen

Location	Southwest of Mayrhofen
Grade	1–2
Distance	9km
Height gain	370m
Height loss	370m
Time	3–3½hrs

Most of this walk takes place in forest shade, but although views are necessarily restricted, interest is retained throughout. Just outside Finkenberg the deep gorge of the Tuxer Klamm is visited before returning to Mayrhofen alongside meadows, typical Tyrolean chalets, and the river Ziller.

From Mayrhofen's railway station walk downvalley along the main road for a few paces, then cross the railway line by Landhaus Carla. Beyond the Landhaus take a footpath

Zillertal hay meadow

between fields, come to the river and follow it downstream. Cross on a road bridge, and a few metres after passing Gasthof Zillertal, turn left on a marked footpath climbing into woodland. Zigzag up the steep wooded slope to gain a birds-eye view onto Mayrhofen. Beyond this rise alongside a steep little meadow to a crossing path (30mins). A few paces to the right stands **Gasthaus Zimmereben** (refreshments) at 853m.

Turn left along the Mariensteig. This sweeps downhill, passes a shrine and crosses an open area with wild raspberries growing beside the path. A few moments after returning to the forest take the upper branch when the trail forks. You now regain much of the height recently lost, and at the next junction take the right branch once more. Signed to Penken this cuts sharply to the right and climbs to another open area with direct views onto Mayrhofen. Regaining the forest the way forks for a third time. Now take the lower option signed to Finkenberg Dorf. This is the Leonhard-Stock-Weg, named after a former Olympic ski champion from Finkenberg.

Taking an undulating course the path eventually crosses a small stream. At the next junction keep ahead. Losing more height you soon pass a series of cascades and 2mins later cross below a slender waterfall pouring over crags. At a T junction of paths turn right, shortly leave the forest and wander across a meadow to a farm and come onto a service road in the upper part of **Finkenberg** (1½hrs).

Go down to the parish church, and turn right just below it. Bear left beside the post office, go through a parking area and continue ahead beyond the Troppmair hotel where a lane takes you to a bridge spanning the Tuxer Klamm. This is a dramatic ravine, deep and narrow – almost like a rocky crevasse with the Tuxerbach swirling far below.

On the far side of the bridge lies the neat village cemetery. Turn right by the entrance and keep to a woodland path on the left-hand lip of the gorge. Rising easily among trees, the way emerges to a road by another bridge over the gorge. Cross directly ahead to a path which takes you onto the Teufelsbrücke – a covered wooden bridge high above the Tuxer Klamm.

Go over the bridge to the north side of the gorge, cross the road and take a cycle path along the gorge's vegetated lip. This cuts round the right-hand side of the Almbahn gondola lift station, and continues down to the Troppmair hotel again. Return towards the post office, but turn right by the first building (sign to Mayrhofen), then left a few paces later.

Opposite Hotel Eberl turn right on a narrow service road running down past a few houses, and 2mins later branch left on a descending footpath. Take the right branch when it forks, and twist downhill through mixed woodland, then across a meadow and over a bridge. After a few paces on a road, turn right onto another footpath beside Haus Egger. This leads through more woodland on the way to Gstan where you turn right and follow Hochsteg signs before descending to the Zemmbach. Do not cross the river here but take the left bank footpath and follow the river downstream until you reach Gasthof Zillertal once more on the northern edge of **Mayrhofen**.

ROUTE 31

Mayrhofen (Penkenalm: 1980m) –
Niedermoor – Penkenalm

Location	West of Mayrhofen
Grade	1–2
Distance	7km
Height gain	280m
Height loss	280m
Time	2½hrs

Above and to the west of Mayrhofen the slopes of the Penken have been scarred with pistes and laced with cableways and ski tows. In summer it's an eyesore. But this is just one side of the story, for there are also meadows full of flowers, a host of trails and tracks, and splendid views. This walk is just one of a number of possible circuits, best taken in the early summer when the alpine plants are in full bloom. A combination of gondola and chairlift gives quick and easy access.

Take the Penkenbahn gondola from the southern end of Hauptstrasse, then the Penkenlift chairlift to its upper station at **Penkenalm** (1980m). An obvious track rises a little left ahead to pass a group of rocky towers and hillocks, soon gaining fine views left across the Zillertal to the Ahornspitze and into the Stillupgrund. Remain on the track to reach a junction among ski lifts and the large **Penkentenne** restaurant (refreshments).

Curve right on the track which descends briefly, then goes along the ridge crest towards Wanglspitze and Rastkogel. Shortly come to a footpath on the left (No 57) signed to Naudisalm. This is the one to take. At first angling to the right as you descend the Baumgartenalm slope, it then takes a series of zigzags down to a junction and a bench seat with views of Lanersbach in the Tuxertal.

Turn left along the narrow Moorlehrpfad (direction Finkenberg) – a path with occasional nature trail signs that takes you across boggy slopes and through wonderful flower meadows of Niedermoor. There are duckboards in places.

Penkenalm above Mayrhofen makes a very fine vantage point

Eventually come onto a farm track, and a few paces later take a footpath which contours a little below the track. Again this returns you to the track to run along the hillside between meadows with views across the Zillertal.

The track forks with a sign indicating the way to the Penkenhaus restaurant (5mins below to the right). Ignore this option and keep ahead, soon reaching a signed footpath on the left. This now climbs the vegetated slope in long sweeps, and emerges at the **Penkentenne** restaurant and the familiar ridge crest track. Turn right and retrace the outgoing walk along the track to **Penkenalm** and the chairlift for the descent to Mayrhofen.

ROUTE 32

Zillergrund Reservoir (1860m) –
Plauener Hut (2364m)

Location	Southeast of Mayrhofen
Grade	2–3
Distance	4km (one way)
Height gain	504m
Time	1½hrs

Not only is the ascent to the Plauener Hut a very fine walk, but the approach through the long and narrow Zillergrund makes a magnificent start to the day. The soaring walls of the valley are cut in a few places by enticing tributaries, while the brief sections of meadow beside the road are dotted with old *alm* buildings. Private vehicles are allowed as far as Gasthof Bärenbad at 1450m, beyond which a toll is charged. A bus service from Mayrhofen goes all the way to the Zillergründl dam where the walk begins.

Note Zillergrund Linie buses operate a summer service 4–6 times per day between Mayrhofen railway station and the Zillergründl Staumauer (dam).

From the bus terminus on the dam go through a dimly-lit tunnel on the north side of the reservoir, and on emerging continue along a track that takes you past cascading streams. When it slopes downhill note a footpath breaking left, signed to the Plauener Hut. At first gaining a little height, this path then undulates along the hillside among dwarf pine, bilberry and alpenrose, curves left and rises again, then gently angles into the charming little valley of the **Keesbach**, from where the hut may be seen high above on the eastern slope, under craggy summits that rim the Reichenspitze amphitheatre.

The way slopes down to cross a footbridge over the Keesbach, then rises on its far side over an increasingly rocky terrain. From here to the hut is straightforward, on a winding, zigzag trail that tackles the gradient in generous fashion.

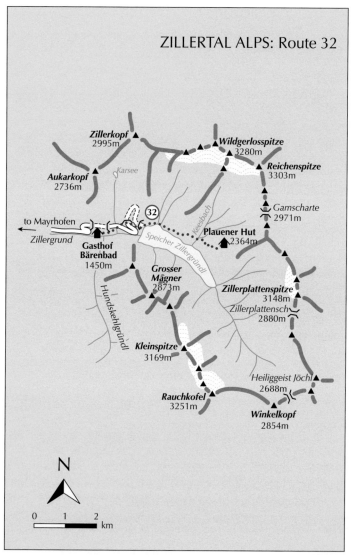

ZILLERTAL ALPS: Route 32

Zillerkopf
2995m

Wildgerlosspitze
3280m

Reichenspitze
3303m

Aukarkopf
2736m

Karsee

Gamscharte
2971m

to Mayrhofen

Zillergrund

32

Keesbach

Plauener Hut
2364m

Speicher Zillergründl

**Gasthof
Bärenbad**
1450m

*Grosser
Mägner*
2873m

Zillerplattenspitze
3148m

Zillerplattensch
2880m

Hundskehlgründl

Kleinspitze
3169m

Heiliggeist Jöchl
2688m

Rauchkofel
3251m

Winkelkopf
2854m

N

0   1   2 km

At the first junction keep on the upper path; in one place it is secured with fixed cable where it crosses a steep section running with a stream, but almost all the way the path is adorned with alpine flowers.

The Zillergrund reservoir lies far below the Plauener Hut

At the next junction take the left branch and, passing beneath the hut's goods lift cable, you gain a ridge spur offering a grand view of the Rauchkofel and the frontier ridge blocking the head of the Zillergründl, and of the Reichenspitze crest above the hut. Turn left and climb the last few metres to the **Plauener Hut** (1½hrs).

The Category I **Plauener Hut** is fully staffed from mid-June to the end of September, and has 6 beds and 74 dormitory places (☎ 0650 2250369). Among the routes from here, one crosses the 2688m Heiliggeistjöchl at the head of the Zillergründl and descends to Kasern in the Italian Ahrntal (4hrs), and another climbs to the Gamscharte (2971m) above the hut, then descends 600m to the Richter Hut in the Hohe Tauern's Rainbachtal (3hrs).

To return to Mayrhofen, descend to the **Zillergründl** dam and take the bus, or continue all the way to **Gasthof Bärenbad**. The path for this is found a short distance west of the bus stop at the dam, just beyond the road tunnel. It descends in zig-zags to the road where you turn right (uphill) for a few paces to find the continuing descent path. This drops in long loops to the road once more near alm buildings. Bear right along the road, and on a bend a descending trail cuts left among trees and leads directly to the *gasthof*.

ROUTE 33

Madseit (1402m) – Höllenstein Hut (1740m) – Lanersbach (1281m)

Location	In the Tuxertal, southwest of Mayrhofen
Grade	2
Distance	10km
Height gain	508m
Height loss	629m
Time	3hrs

The head of the Tuxertal has been sacrificed to the ski industry, with a variety of lift systems lacing the slopes right up to the glaciers. The valley's lower region, above Lanersbach and Finkenberg, is also given over to skiing, leaving only its middle reaches unaffected by cableways and bulldozed pistes. The following route makes the most of this green central valley, with an undulating walk among woodland and meadow, visiting on the way Grieralm and the Höllenstein Hut – a mountain inn which houses a small farming museum.

Take the bus to Madseit in the Tuxertal, then walk along a track which crosses the river heading south then southwest towards **Hintertux**. Keep alert for a footpath which breaks from the track and climbs forested slopes to the small timber building of **Tulferalm**, then takes a steepening route above the hut, crosses a brief line of scree and follows a level-ling section before entering a lovely enclosed meadowland below the Grierer Kar and a craggy ridge. Across the meadow the way continues among alpenroses, then comes onto a dirt

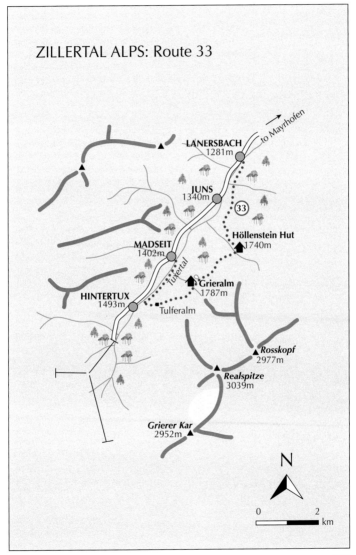

road. Walk ahead for a short distance, then cut left following waymarks down the slope and across a grassy basin drained by the Griererbach, and up to **Grieralm** (1787m, refreshments), about 1–1¼hrs from the start.

A sign for Höllenstein directs you up the continuing dirt road to pass a pond on the right, then twists uphill to a large farm building on a bend. Take the waymarked track climbing to the left to gain a fine grassy bluff with good views at about 1910m. A path then leads easily down the slope ahead overlooking the Tuxertal 600m or so below, and along a line of trees before descending a wooded slope heading roughly northeast to enter the pastures of Loschbodenalm. Here a track takes you past a farm and on to the large **Höllenstein Hut** (1740m, 2hrs; accommodation and refreshments).

Not a mountain hut in the conventional sense, the **Höllenstein Hut** is a modern mountain inn, built with 300-year-old timbers that give the interior an impression of great age. It houses a museum mostly of farming implements.

Hintertux at the head of the Tuxertal

Continue down the track into woodland, then take a descending path on the left. This eventually returns you to

the track/dirt road lower down. Having rejoined it you then walk ahead to a hairpin where the track forks. Ignore the branch signed to Lanersbach, go round the bend, and a few paces after this, turn right on a footpath. This fine woodland path (signed Klausboden) eventually brings you onto a narrow road where you turn right.

The road becomes a track just beyond some houses. Now take a path on the right, rising gently along the edge of a forested slope. Another pleasant path, this comes onto another track which cuts back to the left to cross the Tuxbach into **Lanersbach**.

ROUTE 34
Breitlahner (1257m) – Berliner Hut (2042m)

Location	Southwest of Mayrhofen
Grade	2
Distance	8km (one way)
Height gain	785m
Time	3hrs (+ 2–2½hrs return)

The Zemmgrund is enclosed at its head by a great arc of glaciers spilling from the frontier crest topped by Grosser Möseler, Turnerkamp, the Hornspitze, Schwarzenstein and Grosser Mörchner. That crest continues round to the Zsigmondyspitze which thrusts out a spur to the 3107m Ochsner. Below the Ochsner and with a full-on view of three linking glacier-draped cirques, nestles the Berliner Hut. It's a fabulous site for a hut, and it makes a first-class destination for a walk.

The Zemmgrund valley itself is full of variety, and views are constantly being rearranged as you progress through it. There are forests, gorges, alpine meadows, rock faces, waterfalls and clear-flowing streams – and flowers. In early summer the Zemmgrund is a botanical paradise, its upper reaches no less than one immense natural rock garden.

Take the Schlegeis Stausee bus from Mayrhofen's railway station, and alight at the Breitlahner stop at the mouth of the

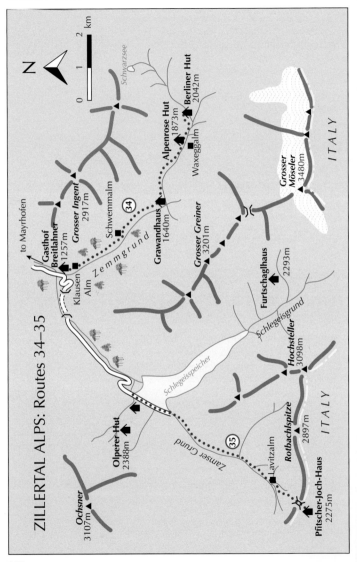

ZILLERTAL ALPS: Routes 34–35

upper stem of the Zemmgrund valley, 18km from Mayrhofen.
If you have your own car there's limited parking space
available.

Gasthof Breitlahner is open from May to October, and at Christmas and Easter,
with 45 beds and 35 dormitory places (☎ 05286 5212).

Walk through the car park and pass the impressive **Gasthof
Breitlahner** (accommodation and refreshments) where
a well-made dirt road/farm track cuts through woodland
alongside a small gorge. As you wander through, note
how a number of trees and shrubs have grown on top of
rocks and boulders to create a romantically wild scene.
Emerging from the woods you pass the farm buildings of
Klausen Alm.

The track curves between meadows, with the valley's
left-hand wall showing a series of steep cliffs and slabs. Then
it rises, angling towards a wall of rock down which spectacular waterfalls stream in bounding cascades, and shortly
before reaching these you come to the privately owned
Grawandhaus (1640m, 1hr 15mins) where refreshments are
available.

The **Grawandhaus**, or Grawand Hut as it's also known, is manned from May
to the beginning of October, with 20 beds and 15 dormitory places (☎ 05286
5213).

A footpath shortcut avoiding several hairpin bends goes up
beside the house, climbs among trees, then emerges across
a little meadow bright with alpenroses to rejoin the track
east of the hut. Having now gained a higher valley level,
the gradient eases for a while before rising again on the
left-hand side, tight against the rocks where the track has
been carved across slabs above another gorge. This leads
to yet another level with glaciers, snowfields and moraine
walls seen ahead. The valley is broader too, and the river
partly dammed with an alternative route across it that leads
to the Jausenstation Waxeggalm (refreshments) below the

The Alpenrose Hut near the head of the Zemmgrund

Waxeggkees glacier. Ignore this option and remain on the left side of the river, and shortly after you will come to the privately owned **Alpenrose Hut** (1873m, 2hrs; accommodation and refreshments ☎ 05286 5222).

The track ends just beyond the Alpenrose, where a signed continuing path cuts to the left then zigzags uphill. This stone-slab path gives increasingly fine and varied views, and turning a corner it passes a memorial to members of the German and Austrian Alpine Clubs who perished in two world wars. The path continues to rise and before long the **Berliner Hut** can be seen just ahead.

At 2042m the large Category I **Berliner Hut** enjoys stimulating views. With its dining room hung with chandeliers, and exquisite hallway and staircase, this is far removed from most people's idea of a 'hut'! There are 76 beds and 92 dormitory places, and it's open and fully staffed from mid-June to the end of September (☎ 05286 5223). The hut is used by climbers, walkers and hut-to-hut trekkers and forms an essential overnight halt for those tackling the 3–4 day Berliner Höhenweg (Route 36) and the 8–9 day Zillertaler Höhenweg (Route 37). Among local walks worth considering is the 1½hr route to the Schwarzsee tarn at 2472m below the Plattenkopf, and the 4hr ascent of the Schönbichler Horn.

ROUTE 35

Schlegeis Reservoir (1805m) –
Pfitscher-Joch-Haus (2275m)

Location	At the head of the Zamser Tal southwest of Mayrhofen
Grade	2
Distance	7km (one way)
Height gain	470m
Time	1¾–2hrs (+ 1½hrs return)

The Pfitscher Joch is a 2246m saddle on the Austro–Italian border at the head of the Zamsergrund, a charming valley of pasture, waterfalls and streams flanked by the Schramacher on the west and Hochsteller on the east. On the Italian side of the border a privately owned hut commands a fine view down the Pfitschertal, and makes a prime goal for a walk.

Either ride the local bus from Mayrhofen, or drive the length of the toll road to the Schlegeisspeicher (reservoir) where parking is available. The bus stop is by the Schlegeis Bergrestaurant, and the view along the reservoir to a glacial ribbon spreading from Hochfeiler to Grosser Möseler is truly impressive. But stretching to the southwest the Zamsergrund is even more enticing.

Make your way from the bus stop to the **Zamsergrund**'s entrance where you cross a bridge and bear right on a broad path to pass a small café/souvenir kiosk. Keeping left of the Zamserbach you soon gain a view of a waterfall crashing out of a cirque high on the opposite side of the valley. Easing through pastures adorned with alpenrose and dwarf pine, the path rises in a series of steps from one level to the next. A second waterfall is passed halfway upvalley before you climb again to see a small hut on a rise ahead. This is **Lavitzalm** (refreshments) and an alternative path offers a short diversion to it.

The Schlegeis reservoir, starting point for several walks

On the upvalley side of Lavitzalm cross one of the early tributaries of the Zamserbach on stepping stones, and continue across what appears to be the bed of a one-time glacial lake. Ahead the ridge dips between 3000m peaks, while the path rises once more over rocks to gain the saddle of the **Pfitscher Joch** (2246m) where a stone marker indicates the international border. Ignore the building on the right (an old customs house) and continue ahead on a road between small tarns, to reach the **Pfitscher-Joch-Haus** shortly after.

Also known as Rifugio Passo di Vizze, the **Pfitscher-Joch-Haus** (2275m) is manned from late June until mid-October. With 30 beds it is in a good position to be useful as a base for climbs on Hochsteiler (3½hrs) and Schrammacher (4–5hrs), and for a 2½hr descent to Stein in the Pfitschertal (☎ 0472 630119).

HUT TO HUT IN THE ZILLERTAL ALPS

Any number of multi-day hut-to-hut tours could be created in this magnificent range of mountains. The following outline routes will give an idea of the possibilities.

ROUTE 36
The Berliner Höhenweg

Location	Counter-clockwise, from Finkenberg to Breitlahner
Grade	3
Distance	42km
Highest point	Schönbichler Scharte (3081m)
Start	Finkenberg (850m)
Finish	Breitlahner (1257m)
Time	3–4 days

This splendid route links five huts positioned along the flanks of the Zemmgrund and Zamsergrund valleys above Mayrhofen. Given settled conditions the route should be feasible between mid-June and the end of September, when the huts are wardened. Please note that at the start of the season an ice axe and crampons may be required.

Day 1 The route begins in **Finkenberg**, the small village 3km upvalley of Mayrhofen at the entrance to the Tuxertal. From the village at just 850m, the way climbs southwestward more than 1200m up the Gamsberg to reach the **Gams Hut** at 1928m in 3½hrs.

    Day 2 A much longer and more demanding stage, this follows the trail at mid-height across the west flank of the valley, linking several *alms* on a 14km walk which gains and loses a lot of height. After a tough day of 10hrs plus rests, the stage ends at the **Friesenberghaus**, built at 2477m near a small tarn on the slopes of the **Hoher Riffler**.

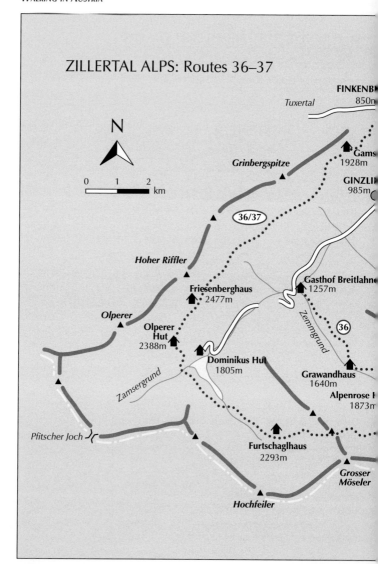

ZILLERTAL ALPS: Routes 36–37

N

0   1   2 km

Tuxertal

FINKENB
850m

Grinbergspitze

Gams
1928m

GINZLI
985m

36/37

Hoher Riffler

Gasthof Breitlahne
1257m

Friesenberghaus
• 2477m

Olperer

Olperer Hut
2388m

Dominikus Hut
1805m

Zemmgrund

36

Grawandhaus
1640m

Zamsergrund

Alpenrose H
1873m

Pfitscher Joch

Furtschaglhaus
2293m

Grosser Möseler

Hochfeiler

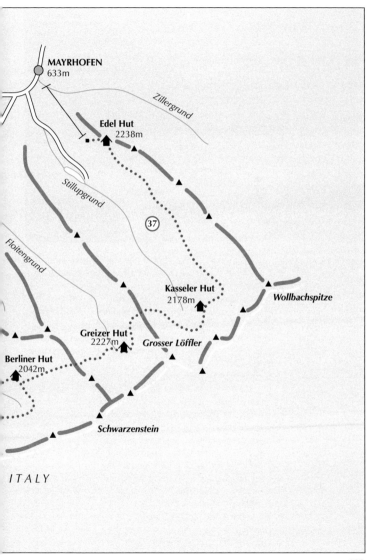

Stream crossing in the upper Zemmgrund

Day 3 With the scenery becoming ever more dramatic, this stage angles down to the **Olperer Hut** (1½hrs) overlooking the Schlegeis reservoir, then drops to the bed of the **Zamsergrund** and goes along the southwest side of the reservoir to its upper end. From there the trail climbs a short distance to the **Furtschaglhaus** at 2293m (5½hrs in all). Above the hut the shrinking glacial scarf of the Schlegeiskees hangs across the valley headwall between the Hochfeiler and Grosser Möseler.

Day 4 Good settled weather is needed for this stage, as the *höhenweg* crosses the highest part of the route at the 3081m Schönbichler Scharte (fixed ropes and considerable exposure). From the start of the day the trail makes directly for the *scharte* with a climb of 788m. Both sides of the col are steep, and snow often lies well into the summer. Extra caution is needed. After the initial difficulties across the col have been dealt with, the route cuts down into the head of the **Zemmgrund** (several streams to cross) to reach the magnificent **Berliner Hut** (2042m) after 6–7hrs of exhilerating trekking.

Day 5 The Berliner Höhenweg ends with an easy valley walk on a track most of the way to the **Gasthof Breitlahner** (2½hrs) and the bus stop for Mayrhofen.

ROUTE 37
The Zillertal Höhenweg

Location	A clockwise tour of the Zillertal, starting from Mayrhofen
Grade	3
Distance	75km
Highest point	Schönbichler Scharte (3081m)
Start/Finish	Mayrhofen (633m)
Time	8–9 days

This is a well-established hut-to-hut tour, also known as the Zillertaler Rundtour. At least half the route is used by the Berliner Höhenweg described above – but in the opposite direction. As may be imagined, the tour is quite demanding, but the scenery is spectacular, and the huts comfortable and welcoming. A full route description is contained in Allan Hartley's highly recommended guide devoted to the route, *Trekking in the Zillertal Alps* (Cicerone Press), in which the author calls the tour the 'Zillertal Rucksack Route'.

Day 1 The first stage climbs southeastward from Mayrhofen to the **Edel Hut** (2238m), some 600m above the town on the slopes of the Ahornspitze. All but the purist will ease this ascent by riding the Ahornbahn cable-car to Filzen Alm at 1955m and walking from there to the hut (1–1½hrs), thus saving at least 2½hrs of uphill climbing. If you've just arrived in Mayrhofen with the intention of tackling the route as soon as possible, the Ahornbahn makes good sense.

Day 2 A long day's effort, with much height gain and loss and plenty of fixed cables where the terrain could be difficult, takes the *höhenweg* high above the Stillupgrund to the **Kasseler Hut** (2178m) under the valley's curving headwall. This is a stage of 8–10hrs, depending on conditions underfoot and fitness of the party. With a whole series of ridge spurs to cross, plus some serious rock- and boulder-hopping, it can be a tiring stage, but the landscape maintains interest throughout.

Day 3 A much easier stage than that of Day 2, the route traces the Zentralalpenweg below the Stillupgrund headwall. Heading roughly westward it crosses the rocky 2701m Lapenscharte on the ridge forming the east wall of the Floitengrund, before descending to the **Greizer Hut** (2227m) in 6hrs.

Day 4 The day begins with a descent of almost 400m to a footbridge spanning the torrent draining the Floitenkees glacier. Frustratingly, that gives a 1000m climb up the west flank of the valley to reach the 2872m Mörchenscharte, negotiating a 5m length of ladder and fixed ropes on the way. The pass slices the ridge linking the Grosser Mörchner with the Zsigmondyspitze, and once over it the way descends past the Schwarzsee (beautiful views from the tarn's north shore looking south to the glacier-hung Hornspitze), and easily down to the **Berliner Hut** (2042m) at the head of the Zemmgrund – about 7–8hrs.

The final approach to the col is steep, rocky, and aided by fixed cable, and the initial descent on the western side is often plastered with snow or ice.

Day 5 Reversing Day 4 of the Berliner Höhenweg, several streams are crossed below the Zemmgrund headwall as the route works its way up and over glacial debris towards the highest point on the tour, the 3081m Schönbichler Scharte. ◄ On the continuing descent to the **Furtschaglhaus** (2293m, 7½–8hrs), views are exciting to the Grosser Möseler and Hochfeiler, with the glacial apron of the Schlegeiskees draped between them.

Day 6 A mostly easy walk, but with a sting in the tail; it begins with a descent to the southern end of the Schlegeis reservoir, followed by a gentle stroll along a track above the west bank. This leads to a road at the far end of the reservoir, from where a 580m climb leads to the **Olperer Hut**, which looks back across the valley of approach from its 2388m perch. After a 5hr walk, this is a splendid hut in which to relax and take stock of the route so far.

Day 7 A pleasant 3hr walk high above the valley takes the *höhenweg* northeastward to its highest hut, the 2477m **Friesenberghaus**, below the Friesenberg tarn on the slopes of the Hoher Riffler.

Day 8 This penultimate day of the Zillertaler Höhenweg is long and, in places, a rough stage of 8hrs or so, during which the scenery changes dramatically. Once again reversing the Berliner Höhenweg, there are several *alms* to visit, spurs to cross, much more vegetation than on any previous

stage, and the distinct possibility of sighting chamois and marmots. At the end of the day you arrive at the **Gams Hut** (1921m), more than 580m lower than the Friesenberghaus.

Day 9 The final stage is virtually downhill all the way, on the Herman-Hecht-Weg to Finkenberg, 3km from **Mayrhofen**.

The historic and ever-popular Berliner Hut

6 KITZBÜHELER ALPS

Spreading east of the lower Zillertal, the Kitzbüheler Alps cover an extensive region of mostly grass-covered mountains indented with numerous relatively short valleys. Named after the well-known ski resort, the district is a firm favourite with first-time visitors to the Alps, and the walking potential, though not as demanding as in the majority of other areas covered in this guidebook, is richly rewarding, with hundreds of kilometres of good paths along broad ridges and easily-accessible summits. There are some very fine villages to use for a holiday base: among the best of these are Saalbach and Hinterglemm, Söll, Scheffau and Ellmau, Westendorf and Brixen in the Brixental west of Kitzbühel and, to a lesser extent, Zell am See and Kitzbühel itself.

ACCESS AND INFORMATION

Location	A large rectangular block lying east of the Zillertal. Its southern limit is drawn by the road running from Zell am Ziller to Zell am See, its northern extent marked by the Inn Valley as far as Wörgl, then by the road to St Johann in Tirol, and Saalfelden downstream from Zell am See.
Maps	Alpenvereins Karte 34/1 *Kitzbüheler Alpen Westliches Blatt* and *Östliches Blatt* 1:50,000
	Kompass Wanderkarte 9 *Kaisergebirge* and 29 *Kitzbüheler Alpen* 1:50,000
	Mayr 51 *Wilder Kaiser*, 55 *Kitzbühel*, 56 *Brixental* and 72 *Saalbach Hinterglemm* 1:25,000
	Freytag & Berndt WK301 *Kufstein, Kaisergebirge, Kitzbühel* 1:50,000
Bases	Westendorf, Brixen, Kitzbühel, Söll, Scheffau, Ellmau, Saalbach, Hinterglemm, Zell am See
Information	Kitzbüheler Alpen-Brixental (e-mail: info@kitzbuehel-alpen.at; website: www.kitzbuehel-alpen.com, www.kitzalps.com/en)
	Westendorf Tourismus (website: www.westendorf.com)
	Brixen im Thale Tourismus (website: www.brixenimthale.at)
	Kitzbühel Tourismus (e-mail: info@kitzbuehel.com; website: www.kitzbuehel.com)
	Infobüro Söll (e-mail: soell@wilderkaiser.info; website: www.wilderkaiser.info)

Infobüro Ellmau (e-mail: ellmau@wilderkaiser.info; website: www.wilderkaiser.info)

Saalbach Tourismus (e-mail: contact@saalbach.com; website: www.saalbach.com)

Zell am See Tourismus (e-mail: welcome@zellamsee-kaprun. com; website: www.zellamsee-kaprun.com)

Access   Mainline trains serve Kitzbühel, Wörgl, St Johann, Saalfelden and Zell am See. Bus services feed most resorts neighbouring mainline train stations. Good roads serve all sides of the district, with the Gerlos Pass (toll road) and 1274m Pass Thurn carrying traffic to and from the Zillertal and Kitzbühel respectively.

Around Kitzbühel the gently domed ridges and sparsely wooded slopes have made this one of Austria's most popular ski areas, but elsewhere there are large swathes of hill and valley that remain piste-free. Traditional dairy farms dot the pastures through which walkers' trails and farm tracks entice the visitor. From some of the highest of these the snowy Venediger and Glockner groups can be clearly seen to the south and southeast, while views in the opposite direction often reveal various compact groups of the Northern Limestone Alps.

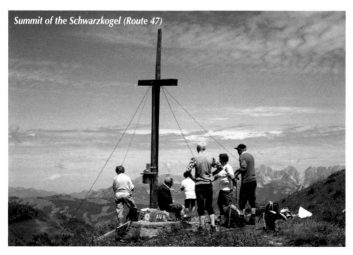

Summit of the Schwarzkogel (Route 47)

KITZBÜHELER ALPS

N

0   5   10
km

KAISERGEBIRGE

SCHEFFAU

ELLMAU

SÖLL

WÖRGL

HOPFGARTEN   BRIXEN

KIRCHBER

WESTENDORF

2   4

3   ASCH

KITZBÜHELER ALPS

Grosser Rettenstein

1

Salzachgeier

Gerlos Pass

Oberpinzgau

Kreuzjoch

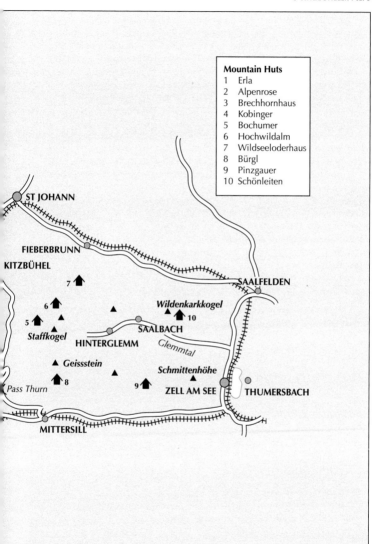

Mountain Huts

1 Erla
2 Alpenrose
3 Brechhornhaus
4 Kobinger
5 Bochumer
6 Hochwildalm
7 Wildseeloderhaus
8 Bürgl
9 Pinzgauer
10 Schönleiten

ST JOHANN

FIEBERBRUNN

KITZBÜHEL

SAALFELDEN

7

6

5

Staffkogel

Wildenkarkkogel

10

HINTERGLEMM

SAALBACH

Glemmtal

Geissstein

Schmittenhöhe

8

9

ZELL AM SEE

THUMERSBACH

Pass Thurn

MITTERSILL

The highest of the Kitzbüheler Alps is the 2558m Kreuzjoch in the southwest corner, but the most striking of its summits has to be the 2362m Grosser Rettenstein above Aschau in the Spertental. But it's not so much individual mountains that encourage the visitor to return time and again, but the wealth of walking opportunities that exist for all the family.

The northern limit of the region is scored by a broad green valley running between Wörgl and St Johann. Nestling in that valley lie the small resort villages of Söll, Scheffau, Ellmau and Going. With the rolling hills of the Kitzbüheler Alps spreading to the south, and the stark limestone wall of the Kaisergebirge to the north, this makes an idyllic base for a walking holiday, as does the Brixental which slices through the hills between Wörgl and Kitzbühel a little south of the valley in which Söll and Ellmau reside; the two valleys separated by big hills criss-crossed with trails accessed by cable lifts.

Close to Zell am See the Glemmtal cuts into the eastern edge of the region, and makes an excellent introduction to alpine walking. There are no great rock peaks here, no glaciers nor permanent snowfields, but many undemanding routes from which the quintessential Alps can be seen as a distant backdrop. One of these routes gives a wonderful ridge-walk and acts as a link with Zell am See. From it the Venediger and Glockner groups dazzle their snowpeaks across the valley of the Salzach.

Main Bases

Westendorf (783m) An attractive, typical farming village, Westendorf stands among open meadows at the western end of the Brixental about 15km from Kitzbühel, close to

Nestling between the Wilder Kaiser and Kitzbüheler Alps,
Ellmau makes a near-perfect base for a walking holiday

the Windautal. Although small, it has most services required for a week's holiday, with a choice of hotels and holiday apartments and a tourist office. The railway station lies on the north bank of the Brixentaler Ache near Bichling, and there's also a bus service to Kitzbühel and Wörgl. Chairlifts and gondolas carry visitors onto the Hohe Salve to the north and Nachsöllberg to the southeast where a network of footpaths and tracks offers plenty of walking possibilities.

Brixen (794m) With Lauterbach adjacent, Brixen (or Brixen im Thale to give its full title) is a little larger than Westendorf, and lies about 4km from it on the railway to Kitzbühel. It has an attractive twin-towered parish church, a few hotels and *pensionen*, shops, restaurants and a tourist office. Behind the village lift systems are useful for quick access to the broad, flat-topped ridge that stretches out from Hochbrixen and provides easy walking.

Kitzbühel (766m) One of Austria's largest and best-known ski resorts, the town lies in the heart of the Kitzbüheler Alps at the foot of the Kitzbüheler Horn on the road from St Johann to the Thurn Pass. With no shortage of accommodation, plenty of restaurants, bars and shops, a bank, post office, hospital and railway station, the town is less glitzy and more egalitarian in summer than in winter. There's a campsite at the Schwarzsee about 2km north of the town centre. The tourist office stocks hiking maps and in summer organizes free walks for local guests.

Söll (698m) This fairly small, modern resort nestles at the foot of the Wilder Kaiser mountains south of Kufstein, but has gondola access to the nearby Hochsöll and Hohe Salve on the Kitzbüheler Alps. The Hintersteiner See lies in a wooded basin to the northeast (see under Kaisergebirge section), and buses link the village with Scheffau, Ellmau and Going on the way to St Johann. Facilities are somewhat limited, but there's plenty of accommodation to meet most needs, and the tourist office in the heart of the village can provide details.

Ellmau (810m) A very pleasant village lying below the Hartkaiser with views across the valley to the limestone peaks of the Wilder Kaiser, like Söll it is equally suited for walks on both the gentle Kitzbüheler Alps and the more challenging mountains to the north. It has several hotels and *pensionen*, holiday apartments and a few private rooms. There are shops, restaurants and a useful tourist office, and the village is on a bus route between St Johann (9km) and Kufstein (19km). From Ellmau a funicular carries passengers up to the Hartkaiser for a wealth of gentle walks with big views.

Saalbach (1002m) Located in the Glemmtal northwest of Zell am See, by which it is linked by bus, Saalbach and its neighbour Hinterglemm are among the most popular walking centres in the Kitzbüheler Alps. Located midvalley, Saalbach has plenty of accommodation of all standards. Its main street has shops, bars, restaurants, a bank with ATM and a tourist office. The Schattberg to the south and Kohlmaiskopf to the north are accessible by cablecar or gondola, and well-marked trails abound.

Hinterglemm (1035m) Just 4km upvalley from Saalbach, Hinterglemm is primarily known as a winter resort suitable for beginners and intermediates, but in the context of this guide, it makes a good base for a walking holiday. Quieter than its neighbour,

Zell am See, the ultimate 'lakes and mountains' resort

the village has hotels, *pensionen*, holiday apartments and private rooms, and a modest number of shops, restaurants and bars.

Zell am See (750m) The ultimate 'Lakes and Mountains' resort, Zell is crowded on the west shore of the Zeller See below the 1965m Schmittenhöhe. On the opposite bank, a romantic ferry ride away, Thumersbach lies at the foot of the grassy Hundstein range. To the south rises the snowy spike of the Kitzsteinhorn, while to the north the valley appears to be blocked by the limestone wall of the Steinernes Meer which carries the border with Bavaria. Among the many accommodation possibilities, there's a youth hostel at the southern end of the lake, and campsites on the north shore. The town has all facilities, including banks and a large tourist office. Mainline trains call at the station, and buses serve neighbouring valleys and villages.

Other Bases

Numerous other villages and small resorts would make decent walking centres for holidays based on the Kitzbüheler Alps. Among these, **Scheffau** and **Going** in the so-called Berg-Welt region near Söll and Ellmau, or **Hopfgarten** and **Kirchberg** in the Brixental to the west of Kitzbühel. **St Johann in Tirol** at a crossroads north of Kitzbühel is another, as is **Saalfelden** downvalley from Zell am See.

Mountain Huts

Alpenrose Hut (1534m) This Category II hut stands on the slopes of the Nachsöllberg southeast of Westendorf, from which it is reached by a 2½hr walk, or a 20min descent from the Talkaser gondola station. Owned by the Schorndorf section of the DAV it has

20 beds and 40 dormitory places, and is staffed throughout the year except November, and mid-April to mid-May (☎ 05334 6488).

Bochumer Hut (1430m) Standing high in the Kelchalmgraben valley, and reached in 1½hrs from Hechenmoos (south of Kitzbühel), this Category I hut belongs to the DAV's Bochum section (www.dav-bochum.de). With 22 beds and 48 dormitory places it is fully staffed all year except November and part of April (☎ 0664 4150575). In addition to local walks and modest ascents, a cross-country route could be made via any one of several walkers' cols to Hinterglemm in the Glemmtal.

Brechhornhaus (1660m) A privately owned *berggasthaus*/hut located below the 1957m Gampenkogel south of Brixen, it has 30 beds and 20 dormitory places, and is fully staffed throughout the year except November to mid-December (☎ 0664 3807011).

Bürgl Hut (1699m) Basically a dairy farm with hut-style accommodation, below the Geissstein on the Pinzgauer Spaziergang east of Pass Thurn. Privately owned, it is manned from June to the end of September, and has 15 beds and 20 dormitory places (☎ 0676 9439141).

Hochwildalm Hut (1557m) Another privately owned hut, this stands near the head of the Aurach Graben valley (also known as the Wildalmgraben) east of Aurach near Kitzbühel. Manned from June to the end of October it has just 10 dormitory places (☎ 0664 3819179).

Kobinger Hut (1504m) The privately owned Kobinger Hut is located above Rettenbach and may be reached in 1½hrs from the Brechhornhaus. With 20 beds and 14 dormitory places, it's staffed from May to the end of October (☎ 0664 3218553).

Pinzgauer Hut (1700m) Standing below the Hahnkopf near the Schmittenhöhe, this hut is owned by the Naturfreunde of Zell am See, and could be useful for walkers tackling the Pinzgauer Spaziergang. It has 46 places and is staffed from June to mid-October, and from Christmas to mid-April (☎ 06549 7861).

Schönleiten Hut (1804m) Built on the ridge crest of the Glemmtal, and reached by cableway from Vorderglemm, this privately owned *berghotel*/hut has 40 beds and 40 dormitory places, and is fully staffed from mid-June to mid-October, and from December to mid-April (☎ 06541 7649). It stands on the route of the Saalachtaler Höhenweg west of the Grosser Asitz.

Wildseeloderhaus (1854m) Owned by the Fieberbrunn section of the ÖAV, this Category I hut stands on the bank of the little Wildsee tarn high above Fieberbrunn southeast of St Johann. Reached by a 1hr walk from the upper gondola lift from Fieberbrunn, or a 3½hr approach from the Hochwildalm Hut, it has 38 dormitory places and is manned from June to the end of September (☎ 0664 325483 www.alpenverein-fieberbrunn.at).

The Kitzbüheler Alps are clearly seen from the deep U-shaped col of Elmauer Tor

WALKS FROM SÖLL AND ELLMAU

With bus routes travelling the Wörgl-St Johann road, with a feeder route from Kufstein, the valley of the Weissache has reasonable access by public transport (Wörgl, Kufstein and St Johann are all on rail routes). It's a beautiful, broad valley flanked in the north by the abrupt limestone wall of the Wilder Kaiser, and in the south by the modest heights of the Kitzbüheler Alps. Below the hills Söll, Scheffau, Ellmau and Going are all attractive little resorts standing back from the main road. Söll has a gondola lift rising to Hochsöll, Scheffau a cable-car up to the Brandstadl, and Ellmau a funicular railway climbing to the Hartkaiser, all of which give good walking with views across the valley to the Wilder Kaiser – a range which has no mechanical uplift.

Note For walks on the north side of the Weissache, please refer to the Kaisergebirge section.

ROUTE 38

Söll (698m) – Scheffau (744m)

Location	Northeast of Söll
Grade	1
Distance	7km
Height gain	Negligible
Time	2hrs

An easy valley walk which links two attractive villages, visits a small lake, and clearly shows the marked difference between mountains that wall either side of the valley; the abrupt limestone peaks of the Wilder Kaiser on the north, the green wooded hills of the Kitzbüheler Alps to the south.

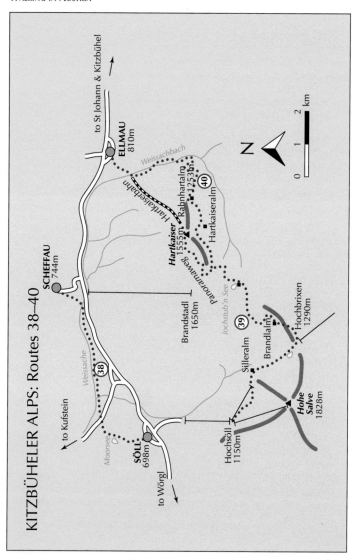

KITZBÜHELER ALPS: Routes 38–40

to St Johann & Kitzbühel

ELMAU
810m

Weissachbach

SCHEFFAU
744m

Rabnhartalm
1253m

40

Hartkaiser
1555m

Hartkaiseralm

Hartkaiserbahn

Panoramaweg

Brandstadl
1650m

Jochstub'n See

Hochbrixen
1290m

39

Brandlalm

Silleralm

to Kufstein

Weissache

38

Hohe
Salve
1828m

Hochsöll
1150m

Moorsee

SÖLL
698m

to Wörgl

Begin in the pedestrian heart of **Söll** and, with the church behind you and Hotel Postwirt to your left, walk down a narrow street where a sign directs the way to the Moorsee. Branch right when the road forks and 20mins from the church you will come to the little lake of **Moorsee** in a shallow basin of grass and trees.

As the road descends to the lake take a footpath on the right, signed to Scheffau. This goes along the east shore and, at the far end, veers right to the edge of woods where there's a junction. Bear left, and ignoring an alternative path heading into the woods, continue ahead on the forest edge before sloping downhill into the trees. About 10mins from the Moorsee cross open meadows to the Kufstein road.

Cross with care and walk ahead on a track which passes farm buildings, then takes you through flat valley meadows. Just after passing a small barn, cross a footbridge over a stream and continue on a narrow tarmac lane.

With the main road off to the right, the Wilder Kaiser mountains flanking the valley on the left, and the block of the Loferer Steinberge ahead to the east, a very pleasant and uncomplicated walk takes you to **Gasthof Blaiken** (refreshments), smothered with flowers and standing by a stream, about 1½hrs from Söll. Immediately beyond the *gasthof* turn left, and when the road forks by a farm, take the right branch through more open meadows, to reach **Scheffau** by the church. There's a bus stop here for the ride back to Söll.

ROUTE 39

Ellmau (Hartkaiser: 1519m) – Hochsöll (1150m)

Location	Southwest of Ellmau
Grade	1–2
Distance	11km
Height gain	161m
Height loss	530m
Time	4hrs

By use of the Hartkaiser funicular to access the broad range of hills which separates the valley of the Weissache from the Brixental, a variety of fairly gentle walks can be made. Following the path known as the *Berg-Welt Panoramaweg*, this outing is one of the longest, and it leads to a gondola lift on the north flank of the Hohe Salve, enabling a quick descent to Söll. The actual walk is mostly undemanding, and there are several places en route where refreshments can be had. If your base is Ellmau, before you set out don't forget to check the bus timetable for the return journey from Söll.

Leaving the top station of the **Hartkaiserbahn** walk ahead along a path signed to Hochbrixen. When this forks 2mins later you have a choice of either crossing the Hartkaiser summit, or skirting it on a broad path. Whichever you choose, when you come to another junction, branch right to follow the *panoramaweg* which, true to its name, enjoys a splendid panoramic view across the valley to the Wilder Kaiser mountains.

About 30mins from the start the *panoramaweg* footpath brings you to a track where you turn right, and 3mins later branch left at another junction. This track now leads across the broad grass ridge with the Kitzbüheler Alps to the south and east, and snowpeaks of the Hohe Tauern forming a distant horizon. Another junction is met 5mins after coming onto this track. Continuing along the track takes you past several *alms*, while the recommended footpath cutting right visits the **Jochstub'n See** with its little restaurant. This is reached in another 20mins.

Skirt the end of the lake on a path which then eases along a crest of pasture, zigzags up a short rise to a high point of 1680m from where the Hohe Salve can be seen to the west, then twists downhill to the track of the Berg-Welt Panoramaweg. Passing to the left of the Zinsbergalm building, about 5mins later turn right on a footpath descending along the line of a ski tow, but when an alternative breaks off to the right, follow this to the **Brandlalm Jausenstation** (refreshments). Take the track leading from the Jausenstation, then bear right at a crossing track and soon come to the complex of buildings of **Hochbrixen** (1290m) about 2½hrs from the Hartkaiser.

Maintain direction ahead, then branch right at a fork. Once again the track forks, but this time you continue ahead, and about 30mins from Hochbrixen you pass the **Silleralm** building, after which the track briefly rises. Söll can now be seen in the valley below. The track divides at a hairpin bend, and you take the right-hand option which shortly descends

Walkers on the Hartkaiser

through pastures below the Antlasseealm building, and continues downhill to pass through a belt of forest, eventually reaching **Hochsöll**. Here you'll find restaurants, chairlifts to Hohe Salve, and the gondola lift which descends to Söll.

ROUTE 40
Ellmau (Hartkaiser: 1519m) – Panoramaweg –
Rahnhartalm (1253m) – Ellmau (810m)

Location	Southwest of Ellmau
Grade	1
Distance	12km
Height loss	745m
Time	3hrs

For visitors to the Hartkaiser by funicular, this route suggests an easy but interesting way back down to Ellmau. First it samples the delights of the *panoramaweg*, with its great views across the valley to the Kaisergebirge mountains, then descends via a series of farm tracks, visiting remote *alms* on the way, before wandering through the Weissachbach valley. There's plenty of fine scenery to enjoy, and in the early summer a wealth of alpine flowers in the meadows. Later in the year, there'll be bilberries or wild raspberries to pick.

Leave the top station of the Hartkaiserbahn and take the marked path to the summit of the **Hartkaiser** (1555m) in a little under 10mins, then descend by a more narrow trail through forest and out to a grass slope leading to a broad track and a path junction. Here you join the *panoramaweg*, a lovely footpath crossing slopes carpeted with bilberries, and with a magnificent view to the right where the Wilder Kaiser mountains make a formidable wall on the far side of the valley.

On coming to a broad track at the end of the *panoramaweg* footpath, turn left to gain a view of the Kitzbüheler Horn in the distance. When the track forks, with the left branch returning to the Hartkaiserbahn, continue ahead sloping downhill, and 5mins later bear right at another junction. Wander down towards the **Hartkaiseralm**, where a path swings left and descends to a pleasant farm track cutting through steeply sloping pastures and belts of woodland, with *alms* seen scattered across distant hillsides where the Kitzbüheler Alps stretch among countless ridges and undemanding summits.

Arriving at a double hairpin bend, ignore another track which breaks away to the right, and remain with the Ellmau route. Soon reach a multi-junction of tracks near the **Rahnhartalm** (1253m) and keep ahead towards *alm* buildings. Passing along the left-hand side of the first building, descend to the second, beyond which a footpath slopes down to a farm road where you bear left.

This road will eventually lead to the valley station of the Hartkaiser funicular, but serving only a few outlying farms, it's not at all busy. Where alternatives arise, the Ellmau route is signed, and on entering the **Weissachbach** valley you first walk along the left bank, then cross to the right, only to revert back to the left bank once more. On reaching the Hartkaiserbahn, bear right across the Weissache for the last time and walk along the road into Ellmau.

The Hartkaiser Panoramaweg

WALKS FROM WESTENDORF
AND BRIXEN

The Brixental is a valley of gentle proportions, and set among its meadows traditional farming communities appear still to maintain a way of life unaffected by tourism, despite the close proximity of Kitzbühel to the east. It's a lush green valley of woodland and pasture, and its string of villages are modest in size and ambition. On the northern side above Westendorf and Brixen a range of hills, rising to little more than 1800m, form an effective divide between the Brixental and the valley of the Weissache in which Ellmau, Söll and Scheffau are settled. A cable lift from Brixen gives access to a veritable wealth of footpaths criss-crossing those hills, while on the south side of the valley a cableway from Westendorf carries walkers onto the upper slopes of the wooded Nachsöllberg where numerous walks are accessed.

ROUTE 41
Westendorf (783m) – Brixen (794m) – Westendorf

Location	Northeast of Westendorf
Grade	1
Distance	11km
Height gain	92m
Height loss	92m
Time	3hrs

Gentle walking on paths and trackways through meadows and woodland of the Brixental, makes this circuit a good introduction to the soft country of the Kitzbüheler Alps. It's a walk for all weathers and all the family. Refreshments may be had in Winkl, Brixen and Bichling.

Facing the tourist office in **Westendorf**, walk along the narrow road which cuts along its right-hand side, rising between

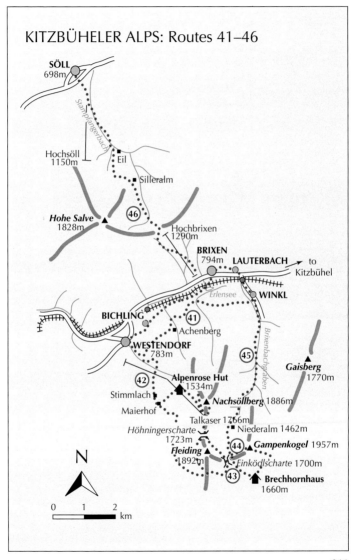

KITZBÜHELER ALPS: Routes 41–46

SÖLL
698m

Stampfangerbach

Hochsöll
1150m

Eil

Silleralm

Hohe Salve
1828m

(46)

Hochbrixen
1290m

BRIXEN
794m

LAUTERBACH — to Kitzbühel

Erlensee

WINKL

BICHLING

(41)

Achenberg

WESTENDORF
783m

(45)

Brixenbachgraben

Gaisberg
1770m

(42)

Alpenrose Hut
1534m

Stimmlach

Nachsöllberg 1886m

Maierhof

Talkaser 1766m

Höhningerscharte
1723m

Niederalm 1462m

(44) **Gampenkogel** 1957m

Fleiding
1892m

Einködlscharte 1700m

(43) **Brechhornhaus**
1660m

N

0 1 2
km

211

Westendorf

houses towards the wooded slopes of Nachsöllberg. Once clear of the village open meadows spread to either side, and in 10mins or so you leave the road and take a footpath on the left along the forest edge. When it forks, take the lower option (direction Bichling) which soon becomes a woodland path. This forks again when you emerge from the trees. On this occasion ignore the Bichling branch and keep ahead across a small meadow and onto a rising stony track. Continue through a series of meadows to reach a group of farm buildings at **Achenberg** (40mins).

A few paces beyond these, bear left on a narrow farm drive. Shortly after, turn sharply to the right on a paved drive (direction Kandleralm and Brixen). Passing a few houses you will come to a large farm on the left. Now go alongside the farm on a path which takes you across a small meadow, then swings to the right to enter a patch of forest.

This becomes a delightful forest walk, joins a track and slopes downhill to the forest edge where there's a picnic site, about 20mins from Achenberg. Immediately beyond this turn right along a track, and when it forks after crossing a bridge, take the upper branch rising steadily in the forest. About 10mins later ignore a path descending to Brixen. Shortly after, when the track makes a sharp right-hand hairpin, go ahead on a minor track.

At another junction, ignore the path slanting up to Kandleralm, and branch left a few paces later to head down the slope, across an open ski piste, and continue to the hamlet of **Winkl** (1½hrs refreshments). A narrow road now takes you down to Brixen's railway station.

Cross both the railway line and the main road, and continue along a minor road opposite. This takes you over a stream where you then turn left and immediately right. Passing houses, rise steeply above a farm on the Schneckgasse which develops as a delightful path above first Lauterbach, then Brixen proper. On coming to an opening with a view down to Brixen's impressive church, descend the grass slope, go through a gate and onto a metalled drive which eventually brings you into **Brixen** (2hrs, refreshments) a short distance from the church.

Directly opposite your entry into the village, cross the main road and walk down a narrow road signed to the Fischerstadl. The way crosses the railway line, and shortly afterwards you will reach the anglers' lake of **Erlensee** (refreshments). Over a stream turn right onto a good path, and when this reaches a junction of tracks near the railway line, keep ahead for the walk via **Bichling** which leads back to **Westendorf**.

ROUTE 42

Westendorf (783m) – Nachsöllberg (1886m) –
Einködlscharte (1700m) – Westendorf

Location	Southeast of Westendorf
Grade	3
Distance	17km
Height gain	1103m
Height loss	1103m
Time	6½–7hrs

Nachsöllberg, Westendorf's 'home mountain', is usually ascended by the Alpenrosenbahn gondola lift. The following route is for keen walkers who may wish to climb it on foot. There's nothing difficult about it, but with a tour of the upper mountainside, it makes for a fairly long and strenuous day out. There are plenty of opportunities for refreshment, and a good choice of lunch spots with fine views, while the descent is on a trail that visits several waterfalls. The walk could always be cut short if needed, by descending via the gondola lift.

Take the narrow road which passes to the right of the tourist office (as on Route 41). At the top of the slope bear right for a short distance, still on the road, then take a path on the left signed to Zieplhof and Nachsöllberg. Climbing through forest, about 30mins from the tourist office come to the Jausenstation Zieplhof (970m, refreshments).

Walk up the road until it ends by a house, and go ahead on the continuing track until a footpath breaks to the right. This is the Wanderweg Nachsöllberg which takes you into forest again. Blue waymarks are your guide when the path forks, and following these you continue a steady ascent. Leaving forest, the way crosses open grass slopes, passes beneath the gondola lift, and brings you to the farm of Ellmerer. Pass along the right-hand side of the house, then up a fence-enclosed footpath to another stretch of forest. There are alternative crossing tracks, but blue waymarks sign the correct route.

Out of the forest once more you cross another meadow and come to **Gasthof Stimmlach** (1½hrs, refreshments). Wander up the road as far as **Gasthof Maierhof** (refreshments), then take a signed path climbing to the right, heading for the Alpenrose Hut. Winding through forest and steep open slopes, about 2¼–2½hrs from Westendorf you arrive at the **Alpenrose Hut** (1534m, refreshments) which enjoys views across the valley to the Höhe Salve.

> The Category II **Alpenrose Hut** belongs to the Schorndorf section of the DAV. With 20 beds and 40 dormitory places it is manned all year except in November and from mid-April to mid-May (☎ 05334 6488).

A few paces beyond the hut take a red-and-white waymarked path climbing to the right. This soon becomes a track or piste which you follow winding up the hillside, eventually reaching the **Talkaser** restaurant (refreshments) and the top station of the Alpenrosenbahn gondola lift at 1760m.

The 1886m Guggenkogel summit covered with summer snow

Bear left and take the *panoramaweg*, a narrow path at first skirting trees to edge the eastern slopes of the **Nachsöllberg** peak whose summit is known as the Guggenkögele, with views steeply down into the Brixenbachgraben valley. Soon leave the trees and twist up to the large summit cross of the Guggenkögele at 1886m (3–3¼hrs).

Continue heading north over the summit down to a tiny chapel nestling on the ridge near the top station of the Choralmlift. Turn sharp left onto a track which leads back to the gondola station and **Talkaser** restaurant. Passing the restaurant on your right head south along the broad track towards Fleidingalm, descending gently to the saddle of the **Höhningerscharte** (1723m) and a junction of tracks. Take the left-hand path to make a contour overlooking the head of the Brixenbachgraben valley, and about 20mins later come to a path junction at the **Einködlscharte** (1700m).

Keep ahead for a few paces, then branch right for Fleidingalm. The trail slopes down to a crossing track above the Windauberg Hochalm. Turn right and follow the track as it curves round the southern flank of the **Fleiding**. Just before coming to the Fleidingalm restaurant (refreshments) by a ski tow, turn left down another track and follow this until, at a left-hand hairpin, a minor track breaks directly ahead signed *Wasserfallweg* and Westendorf.

When this track forks take the lower branch, but you later leave this on the contining *Wasserfallweg* footpath which cuts to the right, crosses the hillside, goes through a strip of forest and emerges to a lovely view of Höhe Salve ahead, and Westendorf in the valley below. Descending to forest once more join another path, cross a stream and come to the very tiny wooden chapel at Hampferalm.

The way now climbs above the three *alm* buildings, enters forest yet again, and crosses a series of waterfalls, the last of which is glimpsed through the trees before you actually reach it. Emerging from forest the trail descends to a narrow road where you turn right and walk uphill. After crossing a bridge come to a junction of roads just below **Gasthof Maierhof** (refreshments) and turn left, now on the familiar route used earlier for the ascent. Follow this down to **Gasthof Stimmlach** (refreshments) and turn right to retrace the route back to Westendorf.

ROUTE 43

Westendorf (Talkaser: 1766m) –
Brechhornhaus (1660m) – Talkaser

Location	Southeast of Westendorf
Grade	1
Distance	7km
Height gain	148m
Height loss	148m
Time	2–2½hrs

This high-level walk demands very little climbing – all the main height gain is achieved by taking the Alpenrosenbahn gondola as far as the Talkaser top station on the Nachsöllberg above Westendorf. For much of the walk, views are far-reaching and inspiring, and as the route makes a circuit of the Fleiding peak, those views are continually rearranged. There are three refreshment opportunities, all in scenic locations.

Note A longer and more demanding variation of this walk is described as Route 44.

Begin by riding the Alpenrosen gondola to the **Talkaser** top station, then turn right along a broad track which soon slopes down to the **Höhningerscharte** saddle at the foot of Fleiding. This saddle, or col, is gained in about 10mins. Remain on the track as it curves right and eases gently round the mountainside with views virtually all the way, and about 25–30mins from the start reach the Jausenstation Fleidingalm (refreshments).

Keep on the track until it forks, then take the upper branch, from which the Brechhornhaus is about 30mins walk away. Rising gently in a long curve, the track forks again just before the Windauberg Hochalm buildings. Stay with the upper track, and about 20mins from Fleidingalm, note a path cutting back to the left with a stream running alongside it. This will be taken later. But for now keep on the track and in another 10mins you will come to the tall, shingle-walled **Brechhornhaus** (1660m refreshments).

Berggasthaus Brechhornhaus has 30 beds and 20 dormitory places, and is open throughout the year, except between November and mid-December (☎ 0664 3807011).

Return along the track to the footpath junction noted above, and turn right along it. The way is signed to the Gondelbahn Bergstation, Alpenrosehütte and Westendorf. Rising easily along the hillside it brings you to the **Einködlscharte** (1700m), a neat pass from which you can see down into the Brixenbachgraben valley to the north.

Continue on the path as it now makes a contour along the northeast face of the Fleiding mountain, and at the next col, the **Höhningerscharte**, bear right on the track which climbs back to **Restaurant Talkaser** (refreshments) and the top station of the Alpenrosen gondola.

Signpost on the way to the Brechhornhaus

ROUTE 44

Westendorf (Talkaser: 1766m) –
Gampenkogel (1957m) – Talkaser

Location	Southeast of Westendorf
Grade	3
Distance	8km
Height gain	423m
Height loss	423m
Time	3–3½hrs

This is a longer and more strenuous variation of Route 43, but given good conditions it will reward with outstanding views from the summit of the Gampenkogel. The path to this summit is very steep, as is the descent to the Einkögelscharte, and extra caution will be needed should snow be lying on it. Once again there's plenty of opportunity for refreshment along the way.

Ride the Alpenrosen gondola from Westendorf to the top station, follow Route 43 as far as the **Brechhornhaus** (1hr, refreshments), then continue on the track as it winds above and beyond it to reach a grass-covered saddle and three small buildings on the Streischlagalm (1685m), about 10mins later. ▶

The path strays left of the *alm* buildings and before long enters woodland. Just before emerging from the trees, take a path breaking left which immediately attacks the steep slope of the Gampenkogel. The slope is heavily vegetated with alpenrose, juniper and bilberry, and the path picked out with red-and-white waymarks on rocks jutting through.

The 1957m summit of the **Gampenkogel** is marked by a large wooden cross, and a splendid panoramic view unfolds from it – a vast collection of mountains and valleys of the Kitzbüheler Alps, with the Kaisergebirge seen to the north.

Descend the steep west flank of the mountain. Initially the way is on grass, but then a more dense vegetation covers the slope, and 20–30mins from the summit you arrive at the **Einködlscharte** (1700m) saddle and a path junction. A clear

From here you gain fine views into the Spertental, its east flank being part of the Hahnenmoos ridge complex pushing south from Kitzbühel.

path, signed Gondelbahn, cuts across the face of the Fleiding mountain and leads to the track on the **Höhningerscharte** used at the start of the walk. Follow this up the slope to the Alpenrosenbahn lift station.

ROUTE 45

Westendorf (Talkaser: 1766m) –
Einködlscharte (1700m) –
Brixenbachgraben Valley – Brixen (794m)

Location	Southeast of Westendorf
Grade	2–3
Distance	8km
Height loss	972m
Time	2½–3hrs

Another walk using the Alpenrosenbahn gondola lift onto Nachsöllberg, practically every step of the way is downhill, for the route descends into a peaceful valley that flows north into the Brixental. Although the actual walking time and distance covered is modest, it feels like a much longer and more enterprising outing. Since the Brixenbachgraben valley is undeveloped, with only an *alm* farm or two, it would be worth taking a picnic lunch and plenty of liquid refreshment with you.

Out of the gondola top station (Talkaser) take the broad track to the **Höhningerscharte** saddle and veer left on the contouring path which skirts the north and northeast flank of the Fleiding mountain to bring you to the 1700m **Einködlscharte** about 20mins from Talkaser. At the trail junction turn sharp left, cross a fence and take a narrow path along the right-hand side of a stream to enter the Brixenbachgraben valley, with the wall of the Wilder Kaiser mountains apparently blocking the northern horizon.

The path briefly improves and takes a zigzag course down towards the upper valley basin. It then fades, but a line

Talkaser Niederalm

of red-and-white waymarks directs the way, taking you to the left-hand side of the stream and down to the *alm* buildings of **Talkaser Niederalm** (1462m). From here you have a choice of routes. The easier of the two takes the farm track which angles off to the right and winds its way down the east side of the valley. But the recommended way remains on the west flank. Here the continuing waymarked path steadily loses height, slips into a gully, crosses a stream and then descends near a small wooden chalet to join a track which you follow northwards in the bed of the valley.

This is a charming valley in which there's a sense of isolation – despite the fact that it's popular with walkers. (Several other trails show possibilities for more days of exploration – see below.) ▶ There should be no route-finding difficulties as the track remains on the left of the Brixenbach until it discharges from the valley just short of **Winkl**. It now crosses to the right bank and becomes a metalled road, along which you pass at least two refreshment opportunities about 5mins before reaching **Brixen Bahnhof,** where you can take the train to Westendorf, if needed. However, should you prefer to walk, follow directions given for Route 41 – in which case allow another hour.

With forest, open pastures, leafy glades and a cheerful stream rumbling through, the walk is a delight.

OTHER ROUTES IN THE BRIXENBACHGRABEN VALLEY

A range of possibilities exists in the Brixenbachgraben, including easy walks from Brixen to **Brixenbachalm** (1hr) or to the **Wiegenalm** (2hrs).

• A more energetic route leads to the summit of the 1770m **Gaisberg** (3hrs from Brixen).

• Another crosses a saddle above the Wiegenalm and cuts round the Gaisberg flank to the **Kobinger Hut**, or from there down to **Rettenbach** in the Spertental.

• Yet another makes the ascent of the 2031m **Brechhorn** south of the Brechhornhaus. Study the map for further ideas.

ROUTE 46
Brixen (794m) –
Hochbrixen (1290m) – Söll (698m)

Location	Northwest of Brixen
Grade	3
Distance	9km
Height gain	496m
Height loss	592m
Time	3½hrs

The north side of the Brixental above Westendorf and Brixen is dominated by the 1828m Hohe Salve whose upper slopes have been transformed on behalf of the winter ski trade. Lifts abound, as they do on the Hochbrixen Sonnberg region directly above Brixen. This is an extensive area of high land, a broad ridge which divides the Brixental from the lovely valley which lies below the Wilder Kaiser mountains. On this ridge numerous tracks and pathways exploit long views, and some of these trails are described from a base at Ellmau (see above). The following route, however, makes a crossing of this ridge at one of its narrowest points. It could, of course, be shortened by riding the gondola from Brixen to Hochbrixen, but that would defeat the object.

Make your way to the valley station of the Hochbrixen gondola lift, which is located at the western side of **Brixen**. Walk up through the car park and continue along a drive between houses, then ahead on a track. Bear left on another road (signed to Hohe Salve) and follow this uphill.

Snaking its way up the hillside the road leads to the lovely farms of Mölling. Just above these, where the road makes a right-hand hairpin, break away left on a footpath waymarked red and white. Rising up the left-hand side of a steep meadow to a barn, it then cuts left into woodland, and

The impressive parish church of Brixen im Thale

enters a narrow wooded cleft of a valley with a stream cascading through it. Cross the stream and climb to a junction of paths on the woodland edge, and take the upper branch, remaining just inside the trees.

The way climbs steeply in places, with occasional views across the valley. Eventually recross the stream and resume the ascent, and about 1hr from Brixen come to a crossing path and bear right. Moments later emerge from the trees, cross open pasture and reach a track near the top station of the gondola at **Hochbrixen** (1290m), a broad open saddle with Hohe Salve rising to the west.

Bear left on the track, and at the next junction take the Bergwelt Panoramaweg on the right. Keep ahead at the next junction, and about 30mins from Hochbrixen pass the small farm of **Silleralm** (1211m).

The track rises, makes a couple of hairpin bends and then forks. Continue ahead, still on the *panoramaweg* signed to Hochsöll. After rising a little further, the track then starts its long winding descent. Coming out of tree cover to an open pasture with a small *alm* building on the left, and cableways strung overhead, pass beneath the cables then take a narrow path on the right, marked to Söll.

Waymarked red, the path crosses the pastureland and enters forest, where it then makes a steep descent before emerging to more grass slopes. At the foot of these come onto a track by the farm of **Eil**, and remain on this all the way down to Söll. About 2km further on, pass an attractive little chapel (Stampfangerkapelle) perched on a rock above the track. The track forks. Bear left, cross the **Stampfangerbach** stream and shortly after come to a restaurant and the Hochsöll lift station. More restaurants are passed on the final walk into **Söll**.

For a return to the Brixental, either use the local bus service, or a combination of bus and train (for timetable information visit the tourist office in Söll).

WALKS FROM KITZBÜHEL

Primarily known as a ski resort, Kitzbühel is also popular in summer with package tourists, yet somehow it still retains an air of gentility. The colourful painted houses give the town its character, and in summer the streets throng with visitors drawn there for a whole range of activities – tennis, golf, mountain biking, paragliding and walking. Several cable lifts give access either to summits, the upper slopes of mountains, or the green ridges that allow easy walking with far-reaching views.

ROUTE 47

Kitzbühel (Hahnenkamm: 1668m) –
Schwarzkogel (2030m)

Location	Southwest of Kitzbühel
Grade	2
Distance	8km (one way)
Height gain	385m
Time	3½hrs (+2½hrs return)

Reached by gondola lift, the Hahnenkamm is Kitzbühel's star attraction, so far as competitive skiers are concerned, for this is the start of a celebrated World Cup downhill course on which top racers reach 90km an hour on their 2min descent. For walkers speed is not a priority, and the following walk is one to take at ease. It mostly follows broad and easy paths and tracks heading south along a grassy crest scarred (it must be admitted) in places by ski tows and pistes, but rewarding with extensive panoramic views. The destination is the summit of the Schwarzkogel, gained by an uncomplicated but reasonably strenuous ascent of its steep north ridge. Marked by a wooden cross, the summit serves as both a physical and a visual high point.

The top station of the Hahnenkamm gondola gives a view across the town to the 1996m Kitzbüheler Horn, and northwest to the Wilder Kaiser mountains. A museum has been set up in the nearby restaurant, which tells the story of alpine sport in the region, with a virtual ski simulator enabling you to descend at breakneck speed to Kitzbühel without leaving the building!

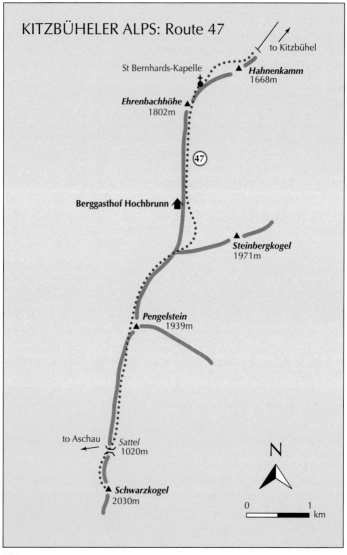

KITZBÜHELER ALPS: Route 47

to Kitzbühel

St Bernhards-Kapelle

Hahnenkamm
1668m

Ehrenbachhöhe
1802m

47

Berggasthof Hochbrunn

Steinbergkogel
1971m

Pengelstein
1939m

to Aschau

Sattel
1020m

N

Schwarzkogel
2030m

0   1
km

Out of the top station follow signs for the *panoramaweg* foot-path which takes you among trees, then along a belvedere skirting the right-hand side of a grassy crest. The way passes the Berghaus Tirol restaurant, comes to St Bernhardskapelle and continues up to the **Ehrenbachhöhe**, the top station of the Fleckalm gondola at 1802m (1hr).

Heading south you now descend along the line of a ski tow, then joining a broad track rise to **Berggasthof Hochbrunn** (refreshments) and continue up the slope to a junction of tracks west of the Steinbergkogel. Keep ahead past a small pond at Jufenalm where a splendid panorama opens to reveal the snowy range of the Hohe Tauern in the distance. It's a view to absorb, and it lures you on to the **Pengelstein** (1939m), reached in about 2hrs from Hahnenkamm.

The small pond at Jufenalm

Descend past assorted buildings and ski lifts on a foot-path along a grassy ridge with lovely views, but on reaching a saddle at 1904m, you then begin the ascent of the easy but steep north ridge of the **Schwarzkogel** (2030m, 3½hrs). ◄ The view encompasses a sea of green ridges and summits of the Kitzbüheler Alps, the rugged Grosser Rettenstein to the southwest, the bare slab walls of the Loferer and Leoganger Steinberge to the northeast, and the snow and ice peaks of the Hohe Tauern to the south and southeast.

The uncluttered summit makes a worthy goal, for the 360° panorama is outstanding.

Return to Hahnenkamm by the same route or, alterna-tively, descend the north ridge for 100m to a path junction, then take the left branch which winds down via Kleinmoos-Niederalm to **Aschau** in the Spertental (2½–3hrs from the Schwarzkogel). From there catch a bus back to Kitzbühel.

ROUTE 48

Hechenmoos (936m) – Bochumer Hut (1432m)

Location	Southeast of Kitzbühel
Grade	2
Distance	5km (one way)
Height gain	496m
Time	1½hrs (+1hr return)

Formerly known as the Kelchalm Berghaus, the Bochumer Hut stands on the right flank of the Kelchalmgraben valley with several walkers' mountains accessible from it. A very pleasant hut owned by the Bochum section of the DAV, it's staffed throughout the year, except in November and part of April, and makes a good destination for a walk, or a base for further exploration. The small village of Hechenmoos, where the approach walk begins, stands beside the road to Pass Thurn, and is served by bus from Kitzbühel.

From the **Hechenmoos** bus stop cross the road and enter the Kelchalmgraben valley by Gasthof Hechenmoos, soon passing several other *gasthofs* and hotels. When the road forks after about 3mins take the right branch, and in 20mins

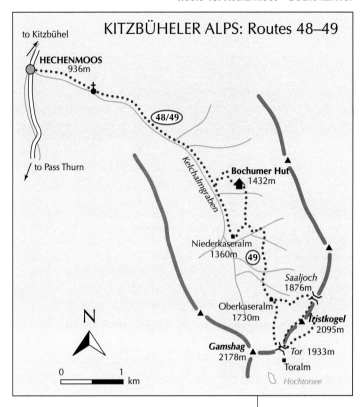

KITZBÜHELER ALPS: Routes 48–49

you will reach the tiny Grüntal chapel where a track breaks left to Oberaurach. Ignoring this track continue up the farm road which remains on the north side of the Wieseneggbach torrent. ▸

About 40mins from Hechenmoos the dirt road makes a sharp left-hand bend. Leave it here and take the track ahead which serves as a shortcut. The track narrows to a footpath rising through woodland beside the river, and eventually reunites with the road.

The road brings you to the ruins of a mine, about 1hr from Hechenmoos, and 5mins later you leave the road for

The valley is narrow, wooded and very pleasant, and in season wild strawberries and raspberries may be gathered.

The Bochumer Hut

a signed track heading left. This snakes uphill and leads
directly to the **Bochumer Hut.**

ROUTE 49

*Hechenmoos (936m) –
Tristkogel (2095m) – Saaljoch (1876m) –
Bochumer Hut (1432m) – Hechenmoos*

Location	Southeast of Kitzbühel
Grade	3
Distance	15km
Height gain	1159m
Height loss	1159m
Time	6–6½hrs

The Tristkogel is one of several accessible peaks above the Bochumer Hut. Standing
on the borders of Tyrol and Salzburg province it overlooks the Glemmtal (home of
Saalbach and Hinterglemm) to the east. This walk makes a full day's outing, and
although refreshments are available at the Bochumer Hut, this is not visited until
the return, so it is advisable to carry food and plenty of liquid with you.

Follow directions given in Route 48 as far as the point, about 5mins beyond the mine ruins, where the track to the Bochumer Hut breaks to the left. Ignore this and continue upvalley along the dirt road. Soon after, emerge from woodland to a view of Tristkogel and Gamshag rising either side of an obvious col at the head of the valley. Tristkogel is the peak on the left of the col.

When you reach the farm of **Niederkaseralm** (1360m, 1½hrs), take a footpath which rises behind it then curves left to gain a view downvalley to the distant Wilder Kaiser mountains. Briefly rejoin the dirt road, and almost immediately cut to the right on the continuing path. This returns you to the road once more, and when it forks you go ahead through a gateway. The route continues to the dairy farm of **Oberkaseralm** (1730m, 2½hrs) from where the path to the col rises steadily among alpenroses and marmot burrows.

The 2178m Gamshag may be climbed in 30mins from the Hochtorsee

About 30mins from Oberkaseralm come onto the col of **Tor** at 1933m, and overlook undulating pastures with the buildings of the **Toralm** a little below.

Note A 15min diversion south of the col leads to the little reedy tarn of the **Hochtorsee**, which makes a good site for a picnic. Another option is to make the ascent of the 2178m **Gamshag** by a clear path rising above the lake in 30mins.

Turn left at the col on a path which climbs the south ridge of the Tristkogel. This path soon forks – the right-hand option avoids the summit climb, makes a traverse of the mountain's south-east flank, and comes onto the ridge northeast of the Tristkogel near the Saaljoch (30–40mins from Tor). The continuing route to the summit is not difficult, but there are fixed cables in places which could be useful in descent. At about 2050m you come onto the mountain's shoulder, and shortly after this reach the summit cross in little more than 20mins from the col. At 2095m the **Tristkogel** makes a fine vantage point, and the summit rocks are adorned with alpine flowers.

The lovely Hochtorsee, one of the gems of the Glemmtal

The short but steep descent by the northeast ridge is trickier than the ascent from Tor, and is marked *Nur für Geübte* ('only for the experienced'), so if you feel unsure

about tackling it, return to Tor and take the traverse path across the southeast flank, and rejoin the other route shortly before reaching the saddle of the 1876m **Saaljoch**.

At the Saaljoch turn left on a thin waymarked path heading west across grassland rich with alpenrose, bilberry, gentian and cotton grass, and with views ahead to the Wilder Kaiser. Descending easily you come once more to the Oberkaseralm dairy farm and rejoin the route used on the ascent. However, when the footpath brings you onto the dirt road a little above Niederkaseralm, bear right, then almost immediately take a footpath on the left signed to the Bochumer Hut. Cutting across a steep hillside, then through a patch of forest, you emerge to the **Bochumer Hut** (1432m, 5–5½hrs; accommodation and refreshments).

The walk to Hechenmoos for the bus back to Kitzbühel is straightforward and takes about 1hr. Simply descend the track below the hut, which leads to the main dirt road in the Kelchalmgraben valley. You then follow this all the way downhill to Hechenmoos.

OTHER ROUTES FROM KITZBÜHEL

On the northwest outskirts of Kitzbühel the attractive lake of **Schwarzsee** makes a popular destination for a walk. Visited in the early morning or at dusk, the lake reflects the magical light conditions, and with the Wilder Kaiser mountains as a backdrop, it has an ethereal quality. Allow 1hr for a circuit.

- A walk to the **Seidlalm** (1203m) on the slopes of the Hahnenkamm is steep and fairly strenuous, but views are breathtaking, and if linked with a return via a dreamy visit to the **Schwarzsee**, a very fine 3½hr walk can be turned into a full day's outing.

- The **Kitzbüheler Horn** (1996m) dominates the town and surrounding area, and the summit view is very extensive. Reached by a steep walk or by cableway from Kitzbühel.

- A long and demanding full day's hike takes strong walkers from **Hechenmoos** (southeast of Kitzbühel) through the Kelchalmgraben valley (see Routes 48–49) and over the 1933m pass of Tor, followed by descent to **Hinterglemm** in the Glemmtal. Accommodation would need to be found in Hinterglemm or Saalbach – see details above.

WALKS FROM SAALBACH
AND HINTERGLEMM

With more than 400km of marked paths, giving the opportunity for walks of all grades, from gentle strolls to more challenging ascents, the Glemmtal has plenty to offer. Guided walks are often arranged by the local tourist offices for guests staying in their resorts, but with abundant signs and reasonably accurate maps, it should be possible to work out routes for yourself. As skiing has become a major attraction in the Glemmtal, more than 60 lifts and cable-cars now lace the slopes. It is worth noting, however, that not all cableways operate in summer – and unsightly pistes are not in most places a major hindrance.

ROUTE 50
Saalbach (1002m) –
Hinterglemm (1035m) – Lindlingalm (1310m)

Location	West of Saalbach
Grade	1
Distance	11km (one way)
Height gain	308m
Time	3hrs

This undemanding riverside walk is an excellent way of getting to understand the valley's layout, and gives an opportunity to visit Hinterglemm on the way to Lindlingalm, an *alm* restaurant nestling within the arc of mountains that encloses the Saalgraben, from where a variety of more strenuous walks begin.

Begin in **Saalbach** on the south bank of the Saalach, which is reached by one of three bridges. The first of these is located near the Saalbach tourist office, the second is directly opposite the Schattberg cableway station, and the third is found near Gasthof Auwirt at the western end of the village.

Across the river turn right and walk upstream along a well-made footpath. Approaching Hinterglemm, about 30mins from Saalbach, the path veers away from the river, edges a large meadow, then curves right to meet the valley road at the Wieshofbrücke. Cross the bridge towards the Theresa Gartenhotel, then immediately turn left where a gravel path continues between the river and meadows and soon goes beneath the road as it enters a tunnel.

Cross the river on the Mühlfeldbrücke, then turn right and walk into **Hinterglemm** (1035m, 45mins). At the western end of the village the road emerges from its tunnel. Continue upvalley, and about 8mins from the centre of Hinterglemm, recross to the right-hand side of the Saalach by a bridge in front of the Forellenhof, and follow the river upstream once more.

A little under an hour from Hinterglemm come onto the road near the valley station of the Zwölferkogel Nordbahn, cross to the south bank of the Saalach and resume upstream on a broad gravel path which soon narrows. Rising in easy stages, the path takes you high above the river among trees, then slopes down again with views ahead to the Tristkogel, the central peak in the horseshoe ridge which closes the head of the valley and forms the border between the provinces of Salzburg and Tyrol.

The Glemmtal near Mitterlengau

235

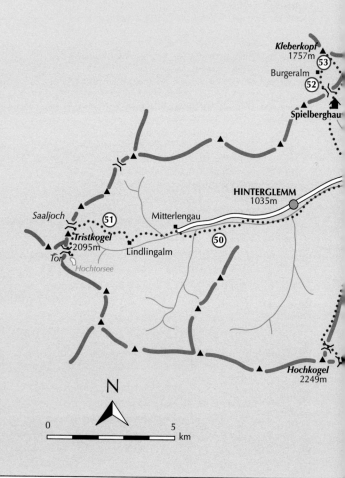

KITZBÜHELER ALPS: Routes 50–56

Kleberkopf
1757m
(53)

Burgeralm
(52)

Spielberghau

HINTERGLEMM
1035m

Saaljoch
(51)

Mitterlengau

Tristkogel
2095m
Tor
Hochtorsee

Lindlingalm

(50)

Hochkogel
2249m

N

0   5
|____|____| km

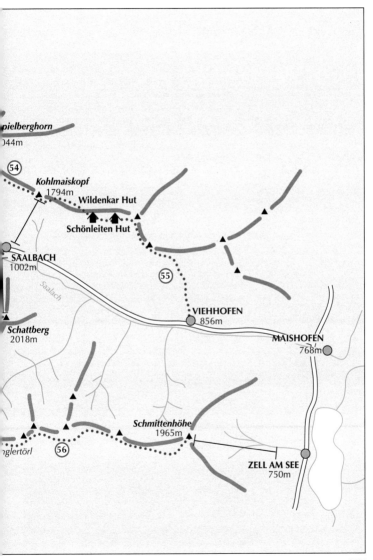

As you draw near to **Mitterlengau** (Lengau on the map) a tributary stream, the Vogelalpbach, appears from the south to join the Saalach. Here the path briefly veers left before crossing the tributary, cutting through meadows, then crossing the Saalach for the final time at the valley's bus terminus by Hotel Lengauerhof (1120m, 2hrs 15mins).

Keep ahead, and in another 10mins you come to the end of the public access road at the Stefflalmbrücke. Now follow a track branching right. Heading between streams, through pasture and forest, it winds high above the river and, about 35mins from Mitterlengau, arrives at the **Lindlingalm** (1310m, refreshments).

To return to Saalbach, either walk back to Hotel Lengauerhof and catch a bus, or take the tourist 'Noddy Train' (the Talschlusszug) from Lindlingalm to the Lengauerhof bus stop.

WALKS AND ASCENTS FROM LINDLINGALM

* North of Lindlingalm a route (farm track, then waymarked path) leads to the **Henlabjoch**, a saddle at 1960m on the valley rim between the Sonnspitze and Staffkogel. From the joch bear left and make the ascent of the 2115m **Staffkogel** – about 3hrs from Lindlingalm.

* An alternative ascent to be made from the Henlabjoch, is that of the **Sonnspitze** (2062m), an excellent viewpoint reached in 2½hrs from Lindlingalm.

Overlooking the Hochtorsee at the head of the Glemmtal

ROUTE 51

Mitterlengau (1120m) –
Tristkogel (2095m) – Hochtorsee (2000m)

Location	West of Hinterglemm
Grade	2–3
Distance	8km (one way)
Height gain	880m (+95m for Tristkogel ascent)
Time	3–3½hrs (+2–2½hrs return)

The reedy little Hochtorsee lies in a grass-and-rock basin at the foot of the 2178m Gamshag at the head of the valley. In July the west slope of the basin is bright with alpenroses, and the idyllic scene makes a natural site for a picnic. The walk to it is reasonably strenuous but not at all difficult, while the optional ascent of the Tristkogel, whilst recommended for its splendid summit panorama, is only for those with a good head for heights.

The walk begins at the bus stop near Hotel Lengauerhof, **Mitterlengau**, where you walk west along the continuing road for about 10mins. This is as far as private vehicles are allowed. A track then branches right ahead, and takes you on a pretty walk between streams, across pastureland and through forest. Winding above the Saalach, past squat hay-barns in the meadows, about 35mins from the bus stop the track brings you to the *alm* restaurant of **Lindlingalm** (1310m, refreshments).

Bear right and follow a farm track twisting up the hill-side. About 10mins from Lindlingalm the track forks, with the right branch going to Forstofalm and the Henlabjoch. Ignore this option and continue on the main track heading west, and about 15mins later come to Ossmannalm (1464m, refreshments) and another junction.

Take route no 2 ahead, a minor track rising gently as far as a stream at 1565m. Here the track becomes a footpath which soon descends to cross the Saalachbach on rocks, after which you climb a steep bank to gain a crossing path. Bear

At the head of the Glemmtal, near the Hochtorsee

right along a narrow, stony trail which climbs north among bilberry, heather and alpenrose below the Saalkogel, and about 1hr 45mins from the start, you come to yet another junction at 1800m and turn left. The way now rises out of a grassy shelf, climbs through a small rocky 'pass' and continues a short distance to the 1876m **Saaljoch** on the ridge. (If you take a few paces across the saddle, a fine view can be had to the Wilder Kaiser mountains in the distance, and down to Kitzbühel.)

Follow the grass ridge to the left (south) towards the rocky Tristkogel and skirt round its left (east) flank, adorned with alpine flowers, to a junction about 10mins from the Saaljoch. It is here that the normal ascent route to the Tristkogel breaks to the right.

TRISTKOGEL ASCENT

Take the path climbing to the right. Though steep, it is not unduly difficult, and fixed cables have been fitted that could be useful in descent. The way climbs to a shoulder at about 2050m, then continues up for about 40m or so to gain the summit cross, about 20mins from the path junction. Summit views from the **Tristkogel** (2095m) make the effort worthwhile. Descend by the same route to the path junction.

From the junction continue ahead and shortly reach the saddle of **Tor** at 1933m where there's yet another path junction. Take the upper of two paths ahead to cut across the hillside above the buildings of Toralm. The way curves to cross a low grass ridge, beyond which you come to the charming little **Hochtorsee** (2000m) about 3hrs from Mitterlengau, or 3½hrs if you've climbed the Tristkogel. To return by the same route, allow about 2hrs.

OPTIONS FROM THE HOCHTORSEE

* Immediately above the lake to the northwest, the 2178m **Gamshag** may be climbed in 30mins by a direct path.

* An alternative descent to Mitterlengau takes a way-marked path south to the **Hochtor** (2005m), then along a broad, rolling grass ridge to the **Schusterscharte** at 2010m. From here red waymarks take the route below the Schusterkogel (fixed ropes in places) and down to the Saalach where you wander gently through meadows to Mitterlengau (about 2½hrs from the Hochtorsee).

ROUTE 52
Saalbach (1002m) –
Spielberghaus (1319m) – Burgeralm (1256m)

Location	Northwest of Saalbach
Grade	1–2
Distance	5km (one way)
Height gain	317m
Height loss	63m
Time	1½hrs

A short and easy walk with a modest amount of height gain, which crosses a minor saddle and leads to a charming *alm* restaurant with views to the Northern Limestone Alps. This outing is perfect for those occasions when you prefer an undemanding but rewarding day out; not quite a 'rest day', but one in which you can afford to take your time and relax.

It begins by following a woodland path up the west flank of the narrow Spielberggraben 'behind' Saalbach. At its head the Spielberghaus stands at a junction with many options for longer walks. The Burgeralm lies among pastureland on the far side of the Spielberg saddle.

Spielberghaus above Saalbach

From **Saalbach** make your way to the valley station of the Bernkogel lift and wander along the service road which goes to the left of the building. When it forks by some houses branch right, then snake up the hillside with views down to the village. About 10mins from the start, when the road makes a left-hand bend, go through a gate onto a track, the Grubenweg, which cuts through a meadow and curves by a barn. Here you take a footpath to pass beneath the Bernkogel lift and enter forest. The path forks. Take the upper option (the Pascherweg) with its red-and-yellow waymarks, and at the next junction keep ahead on an easy contour across the steep hillside.

About 1hr after leaving Saalbach the path brings you onto a track at 1230m. Keep ahead along this and 15mins later come to the **Spielberghaus** (1319m, accommodation and refreshments), with its small chapel and open views to the north. A goodly choice of walks can be made from here, with paths to left and right, and a track continuing ahead across the narrow saddle. Walk ahead to the Innere Spielbergalm (1320m), and the **Gasthof Burgeralm** (1256m, refreshments), the latter reached in a little over 10mins from the Spielberghaus.

Allow about 50mins to return to Saalbach by the track which descends all the way through the Spielberggraben valley.

Note The continuing track beyond the Gasthof Burgeralm eventually leads to Fieberbrunn in the valley of the Schwarzachbach, one of the divisions between the Kitzbüheler Alps and the Northern Limestone Alps, which has a scenic road running through it from St Johann in Tirol to Saalfelden.

ROUTE 53
Saalbach (1002m) –
Spielberghaus (1319m) – Kleberkopf (1757m)

Location	North of Saalbach
Grade	2–3
Distance	7km (one way)
Height gain	755m
Time	3hrs

The modest Kleberkopf stands to the west of the loftier Spielberghorn, which is climbed on the following route. Despite its modest height, summit views are truly inspiring and justify time spent reaching it.

Grassy saddle between the Kleberkopf and Spielberghorn

Follow directions given for Route 52 as far as the **Spielberghaus** (1319m, 1hr 15mins; refreshments) and turn right between the *gasthof* and the chapel, onto a footpath climbing steeply to a track. Turn right and follow the track to the buildings of Wirtsalm and a junction, about 10mins from the Spielberghaus.

Take the left-hand track where a sign suggests 1½hrs to the Kleberkopf. Ignoring path options, after about 15mins come to a narrow footpath on the right of the track at 1475m and break away along it. This path climbs steep grass slopes, goes through woodland and comes to another junction with a stile. Cross the stile and continue uphill to yet another junction at the Spielbergtörl (1671m, 2hrs 10mins).

Bear left, and in 1min the path divides, with one branching right for the ascent of the Spielberghorn (see below). Keep ahead for the Kleberkopf, crossing the grass flank of the Spielberghorn and soon gaining views to the Kitzbüheler Horn and the enticing block of the Wilder Kaiser beyond it.

Curving among dwarf pine and juniper, views are now of the Loferer Steinberge range as you approach a saddle at 1645m where you gain an even bigger view. A concrete cowshed stands on the saddle, from which the path rises up the mountain's flowery southeast flank to gain the summit of the **Kleberkopf** (1757m) about 20mins from the cowshed. Predictably the summit is marked with a cross, and the wonderful panorama now includes the Leoganger Steinberge range, as well as rumpled green heights of the Kitzbüheler Alps and snowy Tauern peaks in the south.

To return to Saalbach by the same route, allow 2hrs. Alternatively, return to Wirtsalm, then take the Saalbacher Höhen-Rundweg southeast to the Panorama Alm, from where a footpath descends steep grass slopes to Ronach, a little east of Saalbach – a very fine descent, for which you should allow 2hrs from Wirtsalm.

ROUTE 54
*Saalbach (Kohlmaiskopf: 1794m) –
Barnkogel (1709m) – Spielberghorn (2044m) –
Saalbach (1002m)*

Location	North of Saalbach
Grade	2–3
Distance	12km
Height gain	373m
Height loss	1127m
Time	5½hrs

Above Saalbach the Spielberghorn is a prominent summit at a junction of grass ridges overlooking a series of valleys that splay out like open fingers. From it a vast panoramic view captures numerous individual ranges, making it one of the finest vantage points of the entire Glemmtal. The walk described here offers the easiest approach to the mountain, for it begins with a gondola lift to the Kohlmaiskopf, followed by an easy, undulating path among trees and bilberry slopes, but with enticing views here and there. The final climb to the summit is steep, but not difficult, and the long descent to the valley can be rather tiring. Note that after leaving the Kohlmaiskopf there are no refreshment facilities until you're well on the way back to Saalbach, so carry plenty of liquid and food for the day.

From the upper station of the Kohlmais gondola, descend by a zigzag path for about 4mins to a small saddle east of the summit where a signboard indicates numerous destinations. Turn immediately left onto a narrow path (a section of the Saalachtaler Höhenweg) which edges along the steep north flank of the **Kohlmaiskopf**. The Spielberghorn can be seen for much of the way across the head of the lush green valley of Schwarzleograben.

About 40mins from the start the path brings you onto the forested ridge crest where a handful of tiny pools will be seen lying just below among the trees. A few minutes later come to a path junction at 1635m, where the left branch descends to the Spielberghaus and Saalbach. Remain along the wooded ridge, but soon rise to a more open area where the gradient steepens for a while. Come to a brief open saddle, crossed by three electricity pylons, and continue uphill to the 1709m Barnkogel (1hr 15mins) and an emergency shelter enjoying a very fine outlook.

A fine view of the Leoganger Steinberge can be had from the Kohlmaiskopf

Beyond the hut the way descends among trees to another path junction. To the right a path descends into the head of the Schwarzleograben and continues from there to Leogang. We, however, keep ahead and very shortly come to

the depression of the Spielbergtörl (1671m, 1hr 25mins) and, a minute later, yet another junction.

For the Spielberghorn take the steeply climbing path heading north up a grass slope. The gradient is maintained virtually all the way to the summit, and the path is clearly waymarked. In early summer the slopes are starred with alpine flowers, and as you make progress, so the views grow in extent and variety. The 2044m summit of the **Spielberghorn** is marked with a large wooden cross, and is reached about 1hr 15mins from the Spielbergtörl. As indicated above, the 360° panorama is simply magnificent, and among the many individual groups of mountains on show, the Leoganger Steinberge is the nearest to the northeast, with the Steinernes Meer to the right of that, and the Loferer Steinberge to the left and farther away, while the blue wall of the Wilder Kaiser is off to the west, and to the south a snowy sea of peaks of the Hohe Tauern contrast with the green hills of the nearer Kitzbüheler Alps.

Descend with care by the route of ascent ▶ as far as the Spielbergtörl, where you continue to descend quite steeply to two further junctions and on as far as a track. Bear left along the track to a junction by the alm buildings of Wirtsalm. Turn right, and about 2mins later take a narrow path on the left which descends to the **Spielberghaus** (1319m, refreshments).

Special care should be taken when descending rocky sections.

The Spielberghaus stands on a small saddle at the head of a track. Turn left onto this track and follow it downhill through the narrow wooded valley of Spielberggraben, which spills out in Saalbach, about 1hr 45mins from the Spielbergtörl.

ROUTE 55

Saalbach (Kohlmaiskopf: 1794m) –
Geierkogel (1853m) – Viehhofen (856m)

Location	Northeast and east of Saalbach
Grade	2–3
Distance	14km
Height gain	195m
Height loss	1230m
Time	4½–5hrs

The Saalachtaler Höhenweg traces the Glemmtal's north walling ridge crest from the Spielbergtörl to the ridge's far northeastern end overlooking Leogang and Saalfelden. The previous walk adopted a section of this *höhenweg* above Saalbach, while the following route takes it eastward above the Vorderglemmtal before descending to Viehhofen, from where a return to Saalbach can be made by bus. The route is a long one, and the descent to Viehhofen can seem endless, but refreshments are available at the large Wildenkar Hut on the summit of the Wildenkarkogel, and at the Schönleiten Hut, while a gondola lift (Schönleitenbahn) provides an early 'escape' from the walk – should one be necessary – from the Wildenkarkogel.

As its name implies, the Saalachtaler Höhenweg is a high path which keeps to the crest of the ridge as much as possible. With nothing to impede the views, this is a very scenic trail with the limestone massifs of the Leoganger Steinberge and Steinernes Meer seen in one direction, the snow-crested Hohe Tauern in the other.

Take the gondola to the **Kohlmaiskopf**, descend to the saddle which lies just below and wander ahead (eastward) above a chairlift; then cut along the north side of the ridge overlooking the valley of the Schwarzleograben to the Leoganger Steinberge beyond. Bear left at a path junction (in 10mins) and make your way round the north flank of the 1817m Mardeckkopf, then return to the ridge near an emergency shelter, the Grüne-Böden-Hut, where views become more extensive.

Beyond the Pründlkopf (with its ski tow), the ridge crest narrows with the trail edging along it – a delightful section with big open views all around. A short, sharp ascent is then made to the Wildenkarkogel (1910m, 1hr) where the semi-circular, shingle-walled **Wildenkar Hut** provides refreshment.

The Saalachtaler Höhenweg

Beyond the Schönleitenbahn keep ahead along a track for a few paces before you take a grass path slightly left ahead, passing avalanche fences as you descend to a saddle with the **Schönleiten Hut** (refreshments) at 1804m, reached about 15mins from the Wildenkarkogel. At a junction of tracks go up the slope ahead to a small white chapel, and then continue up the slope on a waymarked path above the track.

Rejoin the ridge a little south of the Grosser Asitz (1914m) and follow the path southeastward below the summit to a four-way junction at 1855m (1hr 40mins). Continue ahead and 20mins later gain the summit of the Schabergkogel (1888m), a splendid viewpoint. ▶ Reach the Geierkogel (1805m) in 2hrs 20mins, after which the trail leaves the ridge, skirts to the right, then descends for 10mins to the emergency shelter of the Geierkogel Hut. Continue down the slope among trees, bilberries and alpenroses, and when the way becomes boggy, use the boardwalks provided.

The broad green ridge spreads to the east, and the trail along it to the Geierkogel represents one of the best sections of the walk.

About 30mins from the Geierkogel Hut the trail forks. Now, leaving the Saalachtaler Höhenweg, take the lower branch, soon emerging from woodland where you descend to a track near the **Lochalm** (1670m). Turn right and follow this track all the way down to Viehhofen, much of the way being through forest. Where alternative tracks appear, the main route is obvious, and when **Viehhofen** (856m, accommodation and refreshments) is reached, turn right along the main road to find the bus stop for Saalbach nearby.

ROUTE 56

Saalbach (Schattberg: 2018m) – Klinglertörl (2059m) – Zell am See (Schmittenhöhe: 1965m)

Location	South and southeast of Saalbach
Grade	3
Distance	18km
Height gain	475m
Height loss	525m
Time	5–6hrs

The ridge walk of the Pinzgauer Spaziergang is reckoned to be one of the classic routes of the region. In truth the *Spaziergang* has two stems: the one described here, which links the Glemmtal with Zell am See, and the other – a longer route – which goes from Zell to the Burgl Hut above Mittersill.

The following walk begins at the top station of the Schattberg gondola, and heads roughly southward to skirt the Stemmerkogel and Saalbachkogel before reaching a major east–west ridge system at the Klinglertörl above the Pinzgau district valley of the Salzach. The route now turns eastward with splendid views across that valley where the needle-sharp Kitzsteinhorn dominates with its steep glacier and snowfield. The walk ends on the Schmittenhöhe for a cable-car ride down to Zell am See, from where a bus returns you to Saalbach.

Since there's very little shelter on this walk, and no easy 'escape routes' should the weather turn bad, wait for a settled forecast before committing yourself to it. And take a packed lunch and plenty of liquids with you.

Note When buying a ticket for the Schattberg lift, explain that you will be using the Schmittenhöhe cable-car at the end of the walk. A ticket can be bought that is valid for both lifts.

Bearing in mind the length of this route, it is advisable to take an early gondola to the **Schattberg**'s east summit (Ostgipfel) at 2018m. You then descend by a track to a saddle between the two peaks – the other being the Westgipfel. On reaching the saddle leave the track, which curves sharply to the left, and go ahead along a path which crosses the east flank of the Mittelgipfel.

Curving to the right, cross another track (20mins) and continue to a rocky minor ridge where you bear left for a few paces, then rise up a grass ridge to the Marxtenscharte (2015m), gained about 30mins from the start of the walk. Bear left, and 2mins later when the *Familienweg* breaks away to the right, keep ahead to contour along the west side of a ridge among bilberry and (later) alpenrose, and pass below the Stemmerkogel to gain the 1963m Samersattel about 1hr from the Schattberg.

There's another path junction at the Samersattel, but ignoring the right-branching trail, the *Spazierweg* eases southward with the Saalbachkogel ahead. The path rises along the ridge for about 5mins, then veers to the right below this peak, with the Hohe Tauern range now coming into view as you approach the Seetörl (1964m, 1hr 15mins), a narrow

*Walkers on the
Pinzgauer Spaziergang*

saddle with a couple of small ponds (the Hackelberger Seen)
and yet another choice of paths.

Cross to the left of the ridge on the continuing trail that
curves round the northeast flank of the 2249m Hochkogel
and brings you to the **Klinglertörl**, about 1½hrs walking time
from the Schattberg. From this saddle you have an uninter-
rupted view across the broad Salzach valley to the massed
peaks of the Hohe Tauern – a lovely vista of snow- and
ice-capped mountains, a large number of which are drawn
within a national park. Keep ahead, and sloping downhill,
in another 7mins you come to a path junction by a small
timber-built emergency shelter at about 2000m.

Bear left to make a long traverse of the southern slope of
the Niedernsiller Hochsonnberg; about 30mins after crossing the Klinglertörl the path turns a spur, and in another
30mins comes to a second emergency shelter below the
Klammscharte (1993m, 2½hrs). From here the path now
heads southeastward before turning another spur, this one
descending from the Gernkogel. The path forks here, with
one descending steeply to Niedernsill which can be seen
about 1200m below.

The path for the Schmittenhöhe and Zell am See curves
left, heading northeast to regain the ridge at the 1918m
Rohrertörl from where you look north to the Leoganger
Steinberge. Continue along the ridge for a short distance to
a signpost, then veer right along a track. About 30mins later
the Pinzgauer Spaziergang leaves the track for a footpath
at 1885m.

Note Should you need refreshment, remain on the track for a further 4mins to the Hochsonnbergalm.

The Kesselscharte (1844m) is the next point on the ridge, gained in about 4hrs 10mins. ▶ This is a charming little saddle with a few tiny pools and glorious views to north and south, and beyond it the way heads northeast among more trees and shrubs, passes beneath the Hahnkopflift ski tow, then goes down a slope used as a ski run in winter. At the foot of the slope there's a ski hut and a junction of tracks.

Climb the opposite slope, at first steeply before the track assumes a more user-friendly gradient to loop up the hillside, finally reaching the summit of the **Schmittenhöhe** (1965m) with its famed view, and with Zell am See and its lake lying 1200m below.

Ride the cable-car down to Zell, and either take a bus into town, or walk the straightforward road route to the bus station located behind the post office, and there catch a bus for Saalbach.

Rising gently the path winds among trees and shrubs, with Kaprun and the Kapruner Tal seen to the southeast across the Salzach valley.

OTHER ROUTES FROM SAALBACH AND HINTERGLEMM

- A recommended full day's walk (5hrs one way) goes all the way through the Vogelalpgraben valley south of **Mitterlengau** upstream from Hinterglemm, crosses the 1959m **Murnauer Scharte** below the Geissstein, and descends to a working dairy farm which doubles as the **Bürgl Hut**. This could be turned into a two-day trek by returning along the Pinzgauer Spaziergang from the hut to the Schattberg above Saalbach.

- Another suggestion is for a fairly demanding day's trek from Mitterlengau which goes through the Vogelalpgraben valley to the Murnauer Scharte. This route then turns along the ridge east of the *Scharte* to make the easy ascent of the 2092m **Mittagskogel**, continues to the **Zehetner Stange** (2114m), then heads north along a *Höhenweg*, returning to the Vogelelpgraben near the Saalhof-Grundalm.

- From Hinterglemm a marked route goes up the northern hillside to the Pfeffer Alm, continues up to the Rosswald Hut, then heads northeast along a ridge to the summit of the **Reiterkogel** (1818m). Views are very fine, but it has to be said that there are rather too many cableways to make this a 'must-do' outing – unless you've done just about everything else!

WALKS FROM ZELL AM SEE

Romantically situated on the west shore of the Zeller See and backed by the Schmittenhöhe, Zell am See is one of the most popular of holiday destinations, not only in the Kitzbüheler Alps, but in all of Austria. Compact and picturesque, the town almost spills into the lake on a spit of land below wooded hills. Across the lake to the east rise the gentle green heights of the Hundstein. The majestic, snowy spire of the Kitzsteinhorn raises its signature to the south, while the impressive wall of the Steinernes Meer in the north can appear seductive to walkers with plenty of time at their disposal. In winter and summer alike the resort throngs with visitors. It has all facilities, is served by mainline train from Innsbruck and Salzburg, and has access to several neighbouring valleys. But it has to be admitted that the walking potential in the immediate surroundings is somewhat limited in scope.

Hohe Tauern peaks seen across the Zeller See

ROUTE 57

Zell am See (750m) –
Thumersbach (756m) – Zell am See

Location	Around the Zeller See
Grade	1
Distance	11km
Height gain	Negligible
Time	2½–3hrs

Here's a walk that makes no demands, yet has its own undeniable attractions, including lovely views and no shortage of refreshment opportunities. It's one that could be walked at any time, especially when higher routes should be avoided because of bad conditions. But tackled early on a calm summer's morning – or in the evening – this lake circuit has a tranquil, dreamlike quality, for the crystal waters of the Zeller See mirror the surrounding mountains undisturbed by day-time activity. The shoreline is not accessible everywhere, although you're never far from it. On the eastern side, Thumersbach is a small village with neat public gardens and a ferry link with Zell, while at the southern end of the lake the route passes through a marshy area (the Zeller Moos) protected as a nature reserve. Being a circular route it could be tackled in either direction, but on this occasion it is described as a clockwise walk, beginning and ending near Zell's Grand Hotel which virtually projects its imposing edifice into the lake.

Approaching the Grand Hotel from the heart of **Zell am See**, turn left on a broad tarmac path beside the railway line; before you've gone far the lake is edged by a neat greensward. Heading north, the distant wall of the Steinernes Meer above Saalfelden, which carries the Bavarian border, represents the unfailingly attractive chain of the Northern Limestone Alps, on which the evening light can be extremely colourful.

Little more than 30mins will be required to reach the northern end of the lake where the path curves eastward. At first among trees and shrubs, the way then goes through a marshy area of reeds and alder before reaching the Zell am See Yacht Club with its small marina. Skirt the boundary

KITZBÜHELER ALPS: Routes 57–59

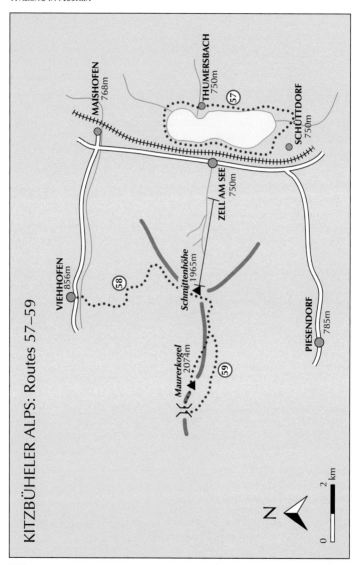

MAISHOFEN
768m

THUMERSBACH
750m

57

SCHÜTTDORF
750m

ZELL AM SEE
750m

VIEHHOFEN
856m

58

Schmittenhöhe
1965m

PIESENDORF
785m

Maurerkogel
2074m

59

N

0   2 km

of a campsite, remaining along the lake shore, but shortly after passing the campsite restaurant the way veers left to the Zell–Thumersbach road opposite Gasthof Wieshof. Turn right along the road and follow it into **Thumersbach** (55mins).

In the heart of the village you come to a crossroads with a stream draining the horseshoe of hills behind it. A short stroll to the right leads to shady public gardens, café/restaurants, and the lakeside jetty from where it's possible to catch a ferry back to Zell.

Continue along the road through Thumersbach, on the south side of which you pass several hotels and restaurants. A short distance beyond Restaurant Konigshof (1½hrs) turn right by a football pitch. At the end of a parking area join a footpath (the Thomas-Bernhard-Weg) which takes you through the Zeller Moos nature reserve, bordered by tall reeds at the southern end of the Zeller See.

On the western side of the nature reserve you reach the first houses of **Schüttdorf** and continue ahead, passing more refreshment facilities and a residential area. At a minor crossroads by the railway line, turn right, and 5mins later come to the southwestern corner of the lake. Now follow the lakeside path ahead to the Grand Hotel in Zell am See.

The Zeller See

ROUTE 58

Zell am See (Schmittenhöhe: 1965m) –
Viehhofen (856m)

Location	Northwest of Zell am See
Grade	2–3
Distance	7km
Height loss	1109m
Time	2½hrs

No visit to Zell am See would be complete without a cable-car ride to the Schmittenhöhe, for the panorama which unfolds from the summit ridge is said to include no less than thirty 3000m peaks, and the wealth of footpaths and tracks accessible from it offer a great variety of walks. The following route is downhill almost all the way, and although much of it is in forest, there's plenty of interest, not least of which is the possibility of sighting deer, chamois, red squirrels and numerous birds. At the end of the walk, Viehhofen, in the Vorderglemmtal, has bus connections with Zell or, if you were so inclined and had the time and energy, you could continue the walk all the way back along the valley via Maishofen.

Leaving the cable-car station and restaurant on the **Schmittenhöhe**, turn right in front of the Elisabethkapelle to the start of the Höhenweg Sonnkogel, a gentle walk which follows the so-called *Höhenpromenade* to the Sonnkogel lift at 1856m. This well-made path goes down the slope on the east side of the ridge and soon passes just below the Hochzeller restaurant (10mins, refreshments). About 5mins beyond this, at 1904m, take the upper path at a junction. This brings you onto a broad path rising to the ridge-crest and a collection of ski tows a little below the crown of the Salersbachköpfl.

Bear left beside a small hut used by the ski tow attendant where a narrow and somewhat vague trail slopes off to the north among trees – as you progress the path becomes more evident. Cross a bluff 1min beyond the hut, then descend

The Schmittenhöhe, high above Zell am See

a narrow vegetated crest along a ridge spur. This is the Schmittenweg which makes a steady descent of assorted ribs and spurs, sometimes crowded with trees, and after passing a seat about 40mins from the Schmittenhöhe, the gradient increases within mature forest, and 6mins later you come onto a forestry road at 1526m.

Wander down the road for about 2mins to a left-hand hairpin where the continuing path descends through more forest with a view into the Glemmtal. After losing height quite steeply, the trail then makes a long leftward contour before descending again to a water trough. From there the way angles down to the right and rejoins the forestry road where you turn right. Just 1min later another path drops to the left to shortcut a hairpin, where you then continue along the road/track until it forks at 1318m.

Turn right, and wander along the left-hand side of an open flat area to the start of the next footpath section indicated by a signpost. Once again the continuing descent is among trees, losing 200m before coming to another forestry track junction. The path forks just before reaching this track, at 1100m. One path goes ahead to Viehhofen via Kreuzerlehen, but the recommended route crosses the right-hand track and continues down through lush vegetation (including lots of wild raspberries), then in a dense section of forest which squeezes the trail on a steep descent to a crossing path.

Bear right and soon slope down to cross a minor stream easing through a gully by another path junction. Keep ahead, soon rising to a lovely bilberry-carpeted area before descending yet again. Over a second small gully the way rises briefly and, at the next junction, continues ahead, now sloping downhill with Viehhofen seen to the left. Moments later come to yet another junction. Bear left and go down to a broad crossing path. Turn right, then left to cross the Saalach river on a bridge, and enter **Viehhofen** (856m). On the opposite side of the road there's a foodstore, public telephone and a bus stop for Saalbach and Hinterglemm. But you'll find the bus stop for Zell am See about 100m to the right.

ROUTE 59

*Zell am See (Schmittenhöhe: 1965m) –
Maurerkogel (2074m) – Rohrertörl (1918m) –
Schmittenhöhe*

Location	West of Zell am See
Grade	2–3
Distance	10km
Height gain	479m
Height loss	479m
Time	4–4½hrs

The Maurerkogel is a modest summit on the ridge of the Piesendorfer Hochsonnberg west of the Schmittenhöhe. From it a formidable view is gained of the various groups of the Northern Limestone Alps spreading between the Kaisergebirge and the Dachstein massif, and south across the Salzach valley to the Hohe Tauern. Walkers tackling the Pinzgauer Spaziergang (Route 56 above) pass below it, but this particular route follows the ridge-crest onto and over the summit as far as the saddle of the Rohrertörl, then returns to the Schmittenhöhe along the *Spaziergang*.

Out of the **Schmittenhöhe** cable-car station go up to the Elisabethskapelle, and turn left on a broad track which slopes down to the south with a direct view of the Kitzsteinhorn and a crowd of snowpeaks which includes the Grossglockner, Austria's highest peak. About 7mins down the track turn right at a junction to follow the continuing track (a ski piste in winter) which swings to the northwest, exchanging views of the Hohe Tauern for those of the limestone range carrying the border with Bavaria. The track twists down to a saddle at 1780m (25–30mins) and a multi-junction of paths and tracks.

Take a path up the slope directly ahead. Near the head of this slope waymarks direct the path to the left, to pass beneath a ski tow. This becomes a delightful trail, rising gently among trees, clumps of bilberry and juniper, with a lovely panorama to the left, but soon regaining views to the Northern Limestone Alps. Almost 1hr from the Schmittenhöhe you come to the Kesselscharte (1844m), an attractive dip in the ridge with several small pools lying in hollows.

It is here that you leave the route of the Pinzgauer Spaziergang and take the path which forks slightly right (red waymarks), tracing the crest of the ridge northwestward. ▶

The summit of the 2074m **Maurerkogel** is gained in about 1hr 45mins, and if conditions are favourable, it makes

This ridge separates the Glemmtal in the north, and the Pinzgau valley of the Salzach in the south, and rewards with lovely views virtually every step of the way.

Hohe Tauern mountains from near the Schmittenhöhe

a perfect place to stop for a picnic. Then, continuing with the walk, keep to the ridge-crest and slope down to the **Rohrertörl** (1918m, 2hrs 15mins) where there's a signpost. Turn sharply to the left onto a track used by the *Spaziergang* and follow directions back to the Schmittenhöhe given above as Route 56.

OTHER WALKS FROM THE SCHMITTENHÖHE

- The **Pinzgauer Spaziergang** has been mentioned several times, and one stem of this classic route has been described from the Schattberg above Saalbach to the Schmittenhöhe. But there is another stem heading west from the Schmittenhöhe to the **Bürgl Hut**, a dairy farm with basic accommodation nestling at 1695m below the Geisstein. From the hut a farm road snakes down through the Mühltalgraben to Stuhlfelden near Mittersill in the Salzach valley (11–12hrs in all).

- The Schattberg stem of the **Pinzgauer Spaziergang** is every bit as enjoyable when walking *from* the Schmittenhöhe to the **Schattberg** as the route *to* the Schmittenhöhe described as Route 56.

- An interesting descent can be made to **Piesendorf** in the Salzach valley by taking a series of paths and trackways via the **Pinzgauer Hut** and **Kottingeinöden Alm**.

- Numerous shorter and less demanding walks can be had from the Schmittenhöhe. One of the best follows the trail of the **Pfaffenkendelsteig** on a 3hr descent to Zell via the Mittelstation *gasthof*.

- Another 3hr descent to Zell, this time northeast and east of the Schmittenhöhe, takes the **Sonnkogel Hohenpromenade**, and from the Sonnkogel restaurant continues along a track into the **Schmittental** by way of the Sonnalm.

7 KAISERGEBIRGE

The north flank of the Wilder Kaiser, seen from Feldberg

This compact group of mountains forms just one section of the extensive range known as the Northern Limestone Alps which either carries, or runs close to, the Austro–German border. It's an abrupt, dramatic group effectively contained between the Inn Valley at Kufstein in the west, and the minor road which links Kössen and St Johann in Tirol in the east. The mountains are ranged along two parallel ridges: the Wilder Kaiser, whose south face overlooks the resort villages of Söll, Scheffau, Ellmau and Going, and the lower Zahmer Kaiser whose northern flank is reflected in the Walchsee. Between the two lie the valleys of the Kaisertal and Kaiserbachtal, with a rib breached by the Stripsenjoch dividing them, in effect creating a topographical letter H laid on its side.

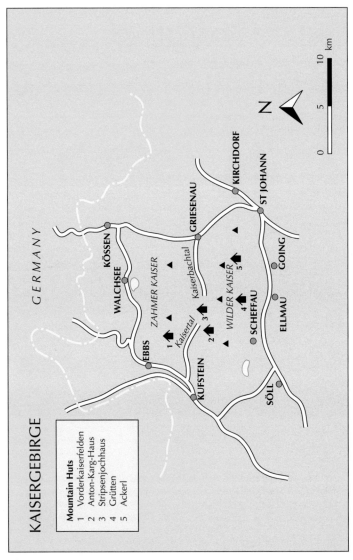

KAISERGEBIRGE

Mountain Huts
1 Vorderkaiserfelden
2 Anton-Karg-Haus
3 Stripsenjochhaus
4 Grütten
5 Ackerl

GERMANY

KÖSSEN

WALCHSEE

ZAHMER KAISER

Kaiserbachtal

GRIESENAU

KIRCHDORF

ST JOHANN

Kaisertal

EBBS

KUFSTEIN

WILDER KAISER

SCHEFFAU

ELLMAU

GOING

SÖLL

N

km
10
5
0

ACCESS AND INFORMATION

Location	North of the Kitzbüheler Alps, and contained by the Inn Valley in the west and the valley of the Grossache in the east.
Maps	Alpenvereinskarte 8 *Kaisergebirge* 1:25,000
	Kompass Wanderkarte 9 *Kaisergebirge* 1:50,000
	Mayr 51 *Wilder Kaiser* and 60 *Kaiserwinkl* 1:35,000
	Freytag & Berndt WK301 *Kufstein, Kaisergebirge, Kitzbühel* 1:50,000
Bases	Kufstein, Söll, Scheffau, Ellmau, Going, St Johann in Tirol
Information	Holiday Region Kufstein (e-mail: info@kufstein.com; website: www.kufstein.com)
	Infobüro Söll (e-mail: soell@wilderkaiser.info; website: www.wilderkaiser.info)
	Infobüro Scheffau (e-mail: scheffau@wilderkaiser.info; website: www.wilderkaiser.info)
	Infobüro Ellmau (e-mail: ellmau@wilderkaiser.info; website: www.wilderkaiser.info)
	Infobüro Going (e-mail: going@wilderkaiser.info; website: www.wilderkaiser.info)
	Infobüro St Johann in Tirol (e-mail: info@ferienregion.at; website: www.ferienregion.at)
Access	By mainline train to Kufstein or St Johann, then bus connections with neighbouring resorts. Kufstein is on the A12 autobahn route, while good roads serve other towns and villages in the area.

Features such as the Fleischbank, Predigstuhl and Totenkirchl have long given the Kaisergebirge a reputation among rock climbers. It was here that Hans Dülfer opened the cult of difficult climbing shortly before the First World War by making the ascent of the smooth slabs of the Fleischbank's East Face; a route that is still highly respected almost a century later. During the inter-war years, and every decade since, other top German and Austrian climbers have used the steep walls as a training ground, and in so doing pushed the standards of difficulty to new levels. Hermann Buhl (who climbed Nanga Parbat solo in 1953) was one. Describing the Steinerne Rinne which forms a narrow gorge between the Totenkirchl and Predigstuhl, he wrote of 'walls that towered to the sky, sensationally steep and smooth; a landscape fashioned by primaeval forces.' As for activity on those walls,

Buhl said that 'from every route, wall, *arête*, gully, crack and chimney you could hear the exchange of climbers' talk, the voices, shouts and yodelling accomplishments of those at work on the rocks. From opposite, the climbers looked like tiny flies on sky-raking walls.' (*Nanga Parbat Pilgrimage*)

But it would be wrong to imagine that the Kaisergebirge is only for climbers, for the massif is also criss-crossed with walkers' trails; paths that skirt the steep cliffs, that meander through forest and across utterly charming alpine meadows. Other trails invite the wanderer onto vegetated crests or undemanding summits with far-flung views; yet more intrude into the near-vertical arena of rock and scree; some routes are safeguarded with fixed ropes or cables; full-blown *klettersteigs* teeter above a dark-shadowed abyss, beckon up a perpendicular crag, then top-out on some airy pinnacle bombarded by choughs.

Several huts and *alm* restaurants exploit idyllic locations, add much to the walker's day and provide opportunities for multi-day tours around, along or across the range from one side to the other, and no mountain walker with imagination and a head for heights should run short of ideas to fill an active holiday among the Kaisergebirge.

Main Bases

Kufstein (499m) Crowded above the Inn close to the Bavarian border, and easily reached by the Innsbruck–Munich autobahn or by mainline train, Kufstein is an historic town dominated by a 13th century sandstone fortress. Immediately to the east rise the wooded outer slopes of the Kaisergebirge mountains, accessed by the Wilder Kaiser chairlift which ascends to the Weinbergerhaus at 1272m. The town has a choice of hotels and *pensionen*, and campsites within easy reach; it has a range of restaurants, bars and cafés, plenty of shopping facilities, banks, and local bus services. The tourist office, on the opposite bank of the river to the railway station, can provide full accommodation details, or go to www.kufstein.com

Söll (698m) A small, fairly modern resort village with an impressive Baroque church, Söll is conveniently situated between the Wilder Kaiser mountains and the Kitzbüheler Alps and is well placed for walks at the western end of the range, and in particular for visiting the lovely Hintersteiner See. The village has a variety of hotels, *gasthöfe* and apartments, but is somewhat limited in other facilities, although it does have banks, a few shops, restaurants and a helpful tourist information office.

Scheffau (744m), or Scheffau am Wilden Kaiser to give its full title, is little more than a one-street village nestling at the foot of the mountains. Although severely limited in facilities (other than a bank and tourist information), it has several large and modestly-sized hotels, *pensionen* and apartments.

Ellmau (810m) Facing north towards the Wilder Kaiser, Ellmau has its back to the Kitzbüheler Alps. A neat and popular resort with good walking opportunities on its doorstep, the village has a modest number of shops and restaurants, but it has a bank, tourist office and a wide variety of accommodation, ranging from a 5-star hotel to holiday apartments, bed and breakfast, and just about everything in between.

Going (722m) Located a few kilometres east of Ellmau, Going also faces across the valley to the Wilder Kaiser mountains. Rather more low-key than its neighbour, it nonetheless has a similar range of facilities, a small selection of hotels but a number of *pensionen*, bed and breakfast opportunities and holiday apartments.

St Johann in Tirol (659m) A bustling resort with a lively atmosphere and good views of the Wilder Kaiser, it lies at a junction of valleys at the foot of the Kitzbüheler Horn. Popular in winter and in summer, St Johann has no shortage of facilities or accommodation, with a good selection of hotels, *gasthöfe*, *pensionen* and apartments, and a well-run campsite, the Michelnhof (www.camping-michelnhof.at), located just to the south. The town has an attractive church, a useful tourist office, and a station on the Innsbruck–Salzburg railway line.

Other Bases

Northeast of St Johann, **Kirchdorf** sits on the left bank of the Grossache, and gives access to the eastern end of the Kaisergebirge. It too has plenty of accommodation (e-mail: kirchdorf@fereinregion.at). Between the Zahmer Kaiser and the Bavarian border, the small lakeside resort of **Walchsee** provides opportunities to explore the northern side of the massif, with a four-man chairlift nearby which rises to 1012m below the Pyramidenspitze.

Mountain Huts

Ackerl Hut (1460m) This small, unmanned hut lies on the south flank of the Wilder Kaiser at the foot of the Ackerlspitze. Owned by the Kitzbühel section of the ÖAV, this Category I hut has 15 places and limited facilities, and may be reached by a walk of about 1½hrs from Going.

Anton-Karg-Haus (829m) Dating from 1899, this Category I hut is a large, rambling timber building set deep in the heart of the Kaisertal at what is known as Hinterbärenbad. It's an atmospheric place with 30 beds and 70 dormitory places, and is fully manned from May to the end of October (☎ 05372 62578).

Fritz-Pflaum Hut (1868m) This unmanned climbers' hut is located high above the Kaiserbachtal (2–2½hrs from Griesner Alm) at the foot of the Kleinkaiser. Owned by the Bayerland section of the DAV, there are 23 dormitory places, but a guardian is present only for group bookings (www.alpenverein-bayerland.de).

Gaudeamus Hut (1263m) Very popular with day visitors, the Gaudeamus Hut is easily reached from both Ellmau and Going via a public road that ends at the Wochenbrunner Alm, just 30mins away. Built in 1927 by the DAV's Main-Spessart section, it has 15 beds and 50 dormitory places, and is fully staffed from the middle of May to mid-October (☎ 05358 2262).

Grutten Hut (1620m) Standing on a spur projecting from the foot of Ellmauer Halt, the highest of Kaisergebirge mountains, the Grutten Hut is a large building which dates from 1899. From it there are splendid views south across the Kitzbüheler Alps, and east to the ragged tops of the Wilder Kaiser. A walk of 1–1½hrs from the roadhead

The privately owned Riedl Hut

at Wochenbrunner Alm is all that's needed to reach this Category I hut, which is fully staffed from June to mid-October, and has 50 beds and 102 dormitory places (☎ 05358 2242).

Hans-Berger-Haus (936m) Also known as the Kaisertalhaus, this hut belongs to the Touristenverein die Naturfreunde (TVN) and stands near the head of the Kaisertal, about 15mins beyond Hinterbärenbad and the Anton-Karg-Haus. Manned from May to the beginning of November, it has 29 beds and 45 dormitory places (☎ 05372 62575).

Riedl Hut (1268m) This small, privately-owned hut/*gasthof* stands among the wooded lower slopes of Treffauer southwest of the Grutten Hut, about 1½hrs from Scheffau, or just 35mins from the Wochenbrunner Alm roadhead. With 12 beds, it is manned from mid-May to the end of October.

Stripsenjochhaus (1577m) Built in 1902 by the Kufstein section of the ÖAV, this large and very popular Category I hut is patronised as much by climbers as it is by walkers, as it's used as a base for climbs on the Fleischbank, Totenkirchl, Ellmauer Halt and numerous other challenging crags. As its name suggests, it stands on the Stripsenjoch which forms a bridge between the Zahmer and Wilder Kaiser mountains at the head of both Kaisertal and Kaiserbachtal, most conveniently reached by a walk of 1½hrs from Griesner Alm. With 50 beds and 130 dormitory places, it's the largest of all Kaisergebirge huts, and is fully staffed from mid-May to the end of October (☎ 05372 62579).

Vorderkaiserfelden Hut (1388m) Standing in a little meadow on the edge of woodland overlooking the Inn Valley at the western end of the Zahmer Kaiser massif, the Vorderkaiserfelden Hut is manned throughout the year. Owned by the Munich-based Oberland section of the DAV, and reached by a walk of 2½hrs from Kufstein, it has 33 beds and 60 dormitory places (☎ 05372 63482).

ROUTE 60

Kufstein (Eichelwang: 500m) – Hinterbärenbad
(829m) – Hans-Berger-Haus (936m)

Location	Northeast of Kufstein
Grade	2
Distance	9km (one way)
Height gain	531m
Height loss	95m
Time	3hrs (+ 2hrs return)

This walk explores the deep and romantic Kaisertal which carves a trench between the Zahmer ('tame') Kaiser and dramatically abrupt slabs of the Wilder Kaiser. Although heavily wooded, the valley is scenically impressive, for when lit by the sun, the great north face of the Wilder Kaiser is breathtakingly beautiful. Two mountain huts are visited, and in the early stages of the walk a couple of *gasthöfe* provide additional opportunities for refreshment.

Eichelwang, where the route begins, is a suburb of Kufstein northeast of the town centre, and is reached by local bus (ask for the Kaisertal stop). Should you have your own transport, there's a pay-and-display car park at the entrance to the Kaisertal gorge.

From **Eichelwang** a seemingly endless flight of steps, in woodland all the way, carries the start of the walk up the north side of the Kaiserbach ravine. A sign near the foot of the steps announces several destinations, including the Anton-Karg-Haus and the Stripsenjoch, and after climbing about 100m the gradient eases along a contouring track. Should you see vehicles parked on this track, and wonder how they managed to get there, the answer is – they were winched up!

Before long the broad path/track makes a steady rise and leaves woodland for open sloping meadows. About 30mins from the start you come to Gasthof Vietenhof (709m, refreshments) from which there are fine views upvalley. When the track forks about 10mins later, take the right branch (the upper path goes to Ritzenalm and the Vorderkaiserfelden

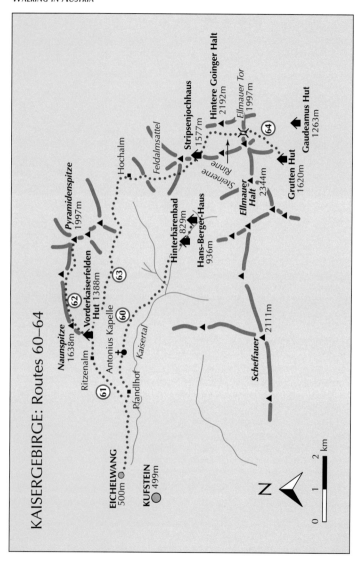

KAISERGEBIRGE: Routes 60–64

Hinterbärenbad

Hut), but when it forks again in another 3mins, this time you take the upper route. Immediately after passing a shrine, an alternative path slopes down ahead to Gasthof Enzian. Ignoring this keep on the main track to pass the **Pfandlhof Alpengasthof** (refreshments) and cross a sloping meadow with a clear view of the Stripsenjoch at the head of the valley.

Once again the track forks about 1hr from the start of the walk. Both options go to Hinterbärenbad, but the recommended route here is the upper, left-hand trail which goes through mixed woodland, then emerges shortly before reaching the pretty **Antonius Kapelle** (840m) – the perfect foreground for a photograph.

Just 1min beyond the chapel there's a large farm and another junction where you leave the main track and go straight ahead, across meadowland and into more mixed woodland. This is a delightful path, and when it forks you take the lower branch signed to the Hans-Berger-Haus. Making a long and steady descent, eventually rejoin the original track shortly after it leaves a tunnel.

Now in the valley bed, pass a memorial to Anton Karg (1835–1919) with its tiny alpine garden and two bench seats. Keep on the track which continues upvalley, and about 30mins from the Antonius Kapelle you cross a bridge, wander past an attractive chapel built upon a rock, and come to **Hinterbärenbad**, otherwise known as the Anton-Karg-Haus (829m, accommodation and refreshments), backed by the smooth walls of the Wilder Kaiser giants.

Continue up the track, passing on the right a rock plastered with memorials to climbers who perished in the mountains, just after which you take a narrow footpath going ahead into the woods. This charming woodland trail crosses a stream on a footbridge, rises up a steep flight of steps, recrosses the stream before tackling more steps, then arrives at the **Hans-Berger-Haus** (936m, accommodation and refreshments) with yet more soaring crags in view. Either this, or the Anton-Karg-Haus, will make a good place to have lunch before returning to **Kufstein**.

ALTERNATIVE RETURN ROUTES

- The most direct route back follows the track all the way and will take about 2hrs – although a sign suggests a rather generous 2¾hrs.

- The track which continues past the Hans-Berger-Haus soon runs out, but a footpath then climbs to the **Stripsenjoch** in another 1¾hrs.

- An alternative trail breaks away below the Stripsenjoch and offers a challenging route across the 2058m **Kopftörl** to the **Grutten Hut** in 4½hrs.

- Yet another 4½hr option heads south from the Hans-Berger-Haus to climb through the Scharlingerboden in order to cross the **Rote Rinnscharte** (2089m) on the south side of Ellmauer Halt, followed by descent to the **Grutten Hut**.

Note These last two routes are reserved for strong walkers with a good head for heights

ROUTE 61

Kufstein (Eichelwang: 500m) –
Vorderkaiserfelden Hut (1388m)

Location	Northeast of Kufstein
Grade	2
Distance	5km (one way)
Height gain	888m
Time	2½hrs (+ 1½hrs return)

A fairly steep walk, but in its upper reaches it's scenically uplifting with great views across the Kaisertal to the Wilder Kaiser mountains. The Vorderkaiserfelden Hut is often busy with day visitors and walkers intent on making the ascent of the Pyramidenspitze (see Route 62).

For the first 30mins as far as Gasthof Vietenhof (709m, refreshments) the route is identical to that of Route 60. When the track forks 10mins later, branch left and rise through mixed woodland. Eventually pass through a gate and leave

Tiny chapel at Ritzenalm

the woods behind, now crossing an open hillside from where the blue wall of the Wilder Kaiser looks especially fine. Rounding a bend you come to the **Ritzenalm** restaurant at 1160m (1½hrs, refreshments).

Continuing along the track, pass a tiny chapel and wander up the slope ahead towards more woodland. The track forks and you swing left up the final slope to reach the **Vorderkaiserfelden Hut** at 1388m.

The **Vorderkaiserfelden Hut** is over 100 years old. Built in 1900, it was enlarged a year later, and again in 1913, and was extensively renovated in the 1970s. Staffed all year round, it has a very fine outlook, with views across the Kaisertal in one direction, and the Inn Valley with the Rofangebirge on the far side in the other. Cecil Davies summed up the romance of the place when he described the 'Evening light on the Wilder Kaiser and mornings when the mist-filled Inn valley resembles a mighty glacier [being] memorable experiences.' (*Mountain Walking in Austria*)

ROUTE 62
Vorderkaiserfelden Hut (1388m) – Pyramidenspitze (1997m)

Location	East of the Vorderkaiserfelden Hut
Grade	3
Distance	4km
Height gain	609m
Time	2½hrs (+ 2hrs return)

As one of the highest summits in the Zahmer Kaiser range, it is not surprising that the Pyramidenspitze makes a popular ascent, and it will be a rare day in summer if you have the route to yourself. Though strenuous in places, there's nothing technically difficult in the ascent, but there are one or two minor sections with a certain amount of exposure.

The map shows two routes from the **Vorderkaiserfelden Hut**; that which is described here climbs the extreme western end of the Zahmer Kaiser ridge on path no 95. As you gain height the way skirts along the south side of the 1638m **Naunspitze**, ▶ then kinks right to gain the 1745m summit of the Petersköpfl.

A 10min diversion left rewards with dramatic views.

The route now eases along a plateau among dwarf pine below the crags of Einserkogel and Zwölferkogel, descends a short and narrow gully, the so-called *Vogelbadkimmen*, after which you then cross the Elferkogel (1916m) to gain the summit of the **Pyramidenspitze** about 2½hrs after leaving the hut. **Note:** *Via ferrata (klettersteig)* enthusiasts may be interested

The summit panorama is extensive, stretching along the Northern Limestone Alps from the Zugspitze to the Hochkönig. It also includes the glacial Stubai Alps and looks down on the Walchsee and across the Kaisertal to major peaks of the Wilder Kaiser. A short distance to the south rises the highest of Zahmer Kaiser summits, the 2001m Vordere Kesselschneid.

to know that a 400m protected route makes the ascent of the Pyramidenspitze from the east, and is usually approached from Winkelalm (see *Klettersteig – Scrambles in the Northern Limestone Alps* by Paul Werner (Cicerone Press)).

ROUTE 63

Kufstein (Eichelwang: 500m) –
Vorderkaiserfelden Hut (1388m) –
Stripsenjochhaus (1577m)

Location	Northeast and east of Kufstein
Grade	3
Distance	12km
Height gain	1077m
Height loss	186m
Time	5½–6hrs

The map highlights this route as a *Höhenweg*, and that sums it up precisely. It is indeed a 'high path' which makes a west-to-east traverse of the north slope of the Kaisertal, edging the crags of the Zahmer Kaiser. It's a classic walk across an ever-varied landscape. It is however quite strenuous, and since the trail is on the sunny side of the valley the heat on a bright summer's day can be quite debilitating. Take plenty of liquids with you.

Note Since the Stripsenjochhaus is very busy in the summer, you are strongly advised to telephone ahead to book bed-space, should it be your intention to spend the night there.

Follow directions given for Route 61 as far as the trail junction immediately below the **Vorderkaiserfelden Hut** (2½hrs, accommodation and refreshments). The left branch climbs to the hut, but we go ahead on a woodland path which forks 2mins later. Take the right branch, a narrow undulating trail which cuts across the steep forested slope for almost an hour before it brings you to a scree slope, where another path breaks away left to climb the Pyramidenspitze.

Stripsenjoch, backed by Ellmauer Halt

After crossing the scree you come to another trail junction within the forest. Ignore the right-hand option (which descends to the Anton-Karg-Haus) and continue ahead, soon emerging from the trees. ▸

The path climbs to about 1480m, then contours among dwarf pine before entering forest once more. Cross a second narrow scree, then rise across a third scree before edging through more dwarf pine, and finally descend to **Hochalm** (1403m) on a broad saddle of pastureland. The first *alm* hut you reach often has drinks for sale.

Veer right after passing the first hut, and rise across the pasture to an eroded path leading up to and through more dwarf pine to gain a pleasant grass saddle at 1522m. Contour among trees round the right-hand side of a pastureland basin, then descend to the **Feldalmsattel** at 1433m, where a sign indicates 45mins to the Stripsenjochhaus.

Climb the southern slope to a grass- and tree-clad ridge, where you then veer left along the steep wooded flank, soon gaining a terrific view of the cliffs of Ellmauer Halt and the Totenkirchl. Then the **Stripsenjochhaus** is seen ahead, backed by impressive rock slabs. The hut is reached shortly after.

Note Set in a sort-of 'lay-by' on the left of the path, you'll find an important water source.

Though invariably busy in summer, the **Stripsenjochhaus** is a splendid place to spend a night. Given good conditions, the alpenglow which flushes the soaring backdrop mountain walls with hues of pink, scarlet and gold, will be among your richest memories. Seated on the terrace, drink in hand, the efforts of the day now past, the mountains seem to gather round – not threatening or oppressive, but welcoming and hospitable. The Stripsenjoch has an atmosphere all its own.

See **Route 64** below for a challenging, exciting and rewarding route from here to the Grutten Hut, and also **Routes 70** and **71** which describe other walks to and around the Stripsenjochhaus from the Kaiserbachtal.

ROUTE 64

Stripsenjochhaus (1577m) – Steinerne Rinne –
Ellmauer Tor (1997m) – Grutten Hut (1620m)

Location	East and south of the Stripsenjoch
Grade	3
Distance	5km
Height gain	582
Height loss	520m
Time	3½–4hrs

This exhilarating route, which crosses the Wilder Kaiser ridge at the deep U-shaped cleft of Ellmauer Tor, is notable for the long sections of *klettersteig* (*via ferrata*) used to ascend the 'stone groove' of the Steinerne Rinne, and the airy nature of the Jubilaumssteig which leads to the Grutten Hut. The first is perhaps less demanding than the second, but takes you among some of the most impressive rock scenery in the Kaisergebirge, while the Jubilaumssteig negotiates a way between bizarre pinnacles with giddy exposure at every turn. As a result, this route cannot be recommended to anyone who might suffer from vertigo.

Note Stonefall is a danger on this route; safety helmets are advised. Note too, that standard *via ferrata* protection (harness, slings and karabiners) should also be used.

The Jubilaumssteig leading to the Grutten Hut

Begin by descending the east side of the Stripsenjoch on a broad switchback path which goes down into the Kaiserbachtal. Having lost about 100m of height, 8mins from the hut take a path which cuts to the right, signed to Eggersteig and Ellmauer Tor. The path now makes a long slanting rise against the cliffs of the Fleischbank and soon brings you to the first of numerous sections of fixed cable.

> The **Eggersteig** was one of the first such protected routes in the Alps, having been developed in 1903. Beginning at the foot of the Schneeloch crags, it tackles the slabs of the Fleischbank before entering the Steinerne Rinne, which it climbs for about 250m using a series of fixed cables, wires and artificial steps.

Before long the exposure is sensational, especially as you turn a corner and the Griesner Alm suddenly appears several hundred metres below. The way now makes a lengthy descent, working round into the base of the Steinerne Rinne – the immense gash, sliced between soaring rock walls of Fleischbank and Predigstuhl, at whose head will be found the Ellmauer Tor.

Weaving back and forth from one fixed cable section to the next, or scrambling up stone- and grit-covered ledges (beware of knocking stones onto others below), the route makes its tortuous way up the Rinne. In many places it's possible to watch climbers in action on the nearby slabs; the rattle of karabiners and calling voices echo from wall to wall, while the Eggersteig simply goes up and up, gaining height with practically every step.

When the fixed cables end, a line of red waymarks indicates the stony path in the upper reaches of the Steinerne Rinne. Surprisingly, the pass of **Ellmauer Tor** (1997m, 2hrs) is not seen until shortly before you reach it. It makes a fine vantage point, for you gaze south through the Tor to the modest green hills of the Kitzbüheler Alps, beyond which rise the snow mountains of the Venediger group. The Grossglockner stands 'behind' the Kitzbüheler Horn to the southeast, while high peaks of the Zillertal Alps ruffle the southwest horizon.

Note Whilst at the Ellmauer Tor, you might be tempted to make the uncomplicated ascent of the 2192m **Hintere**

Goinger Halt which rises northeast of the pass, and whose path can be clearly seen to the left. It will take about 5mins to reach the path by scrambling over rocks and scree, and another 30–35mins up the path to the summit, which is marked by a cross.

The continuing route from Ellmauer Tor to the Grutten Hut initially negotiates some minor slabs before cutting down screes to a false col dominated by a large cross. Below this a vast sweep of scree has to be tackled. This scree consists of tiny, unconsolidated pieces of rock which makes the descent quite tricky. As you lose height so you have a choice of two major descent paths. The one to take for the Jubilaumssteig and the Grutten Hut slants to the right, while the other cuts down through the centre of the scree and leads to the Gaudeamus Hut.

Once off the scree a series of fixed cables leads into an open rock tip that acts as a furnace in full summer sunlight, but on emerging from this you come to a path junction. Once again the left branch descends to the Gaudeamus Hut, while we take the continuing path which is also used by the Wilder-Kaiser-Steig (see Route 68).

Rising up a brief slope you turn a spur and come onto the luxury of grass with a glorious view across the Kitzbüheler Alps. The path turns another corner, around which you come to the start of the Jubilaumssteig; an adventurous *klettersteig* that will demand your concentration for the next 35–40mins. Aided by fixed cables, wires, metal stanchions and ladders, the protected path makes its way round a curious landscape of rocky pinnacles, turrets and towers, with impressive exposure to add a frisson of excitement. At one point you pass through a hole in the rocks, a little later you use three metal stanchions and a horizontal ladder; then, after passing through a narrow gap, the way descends two near-vertical connecting iron ladders, before continuing with fixed cables and a third ladder. After this you begin to climb once more, and emerge from the last of the Jubilaumssteig onto a lovely path on a grass spur, and there, just ahead, stands the **Grutten Hut**.

Built in 1899–1900 the **Grutten Hut** is extremely popular with day visitors, for it's easily accessible from both Ellmau and Going. The hut is one of several buildings occupying a spur projecting from the foot of Ellmauer Halt, and enjoys spectacular views in all directions. As well as being patronised by day visitors and walkers tackling the Wilder-Kaiser-Steig, for whom it serves as an obvious overnight base, it's often used by climbers making the ascent of **Ellmauer Halt** (2344m), one of whose routes is a recommended *klettersteig* of about 550m which begins immediately behind the hut.

ROUTE 65

Söll (698m) – Hintersteiner See (883m) – Söll

Location	Northeast of Söll
Grade	2
Distance	18km
Height gain	299m
Height loss	299m
Time	6½–7hrs

Partially surrounded by trees, the Hintersteiner See is a charming lake nestling below the western reaches of the Wilder Kaiser mountains. At the lake's eastern end there's a bathing beach, but its western end rises to pastureland and an *alm* farm or two. The walk described here makes a circuit of the lake, visits isolated *alms* and descends hundreds of steps of the Steinerne Stiege (although the name means 'stone staircase' the steps are actually timber-braced) into the valley of the Weissachgraben.

From the pedestrian heart of **Söll**, walk down a narrow street between Gasthof Feldwebel and Hotel Postwirt where a sign indicates the way to the Moorsee. When it forks, branch right and soon leave the village behind. About 20mins from the church, you approach the **Moorsee**, a small lake set in a shallow basin of grass and trees. Leave the road and branch right

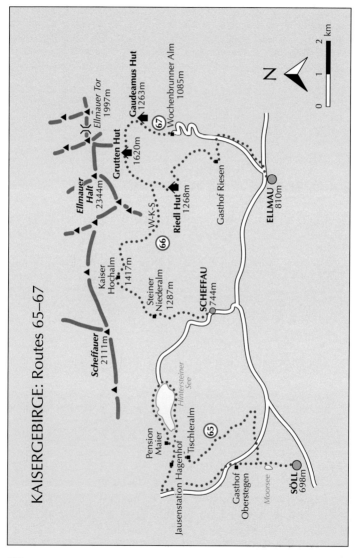

KAISERGEBIRGE: Routes 65–67

Ellmauer Tor
1997m

Gaudeamus Hut
1263m

Wochenbrunner Alm
1085m

67

Grutten Hut
1620m

Ellmauer
Halt
2344m

W-K-S

Riedl Hut
1268m

Gasthof Riesen

Gasthof Riesen

ELLMAU
810m

66

Kaiser
Hochalm
1417m

Steiner
Niederalm
1287m

SCHEFFAU
744m

Scheffauer
2111m

Hintersteiner See

Pension
Maier

Tischleralm

65

Jausenstation Hagenhof

Gasthof
Oberstegen

Moorsee

SÖLL
698m

N

0   1   2 km

on a path signed to Scheffau and Pension Berghof. This goes along the lake's east shore, and at the far end veers right to a junction on the edge of woodland.

Bear left, and ignoring another path heading into the woods, go ahead along the forest edge. Sloping downhill, the path now cuts through the trees, and about 10mins from the Moorsee you cross a meadow to the Kufstein road. Take care crossing this road and continue ahead along a track to a narrow tarmac road where you cut sharply back to the left. After crossing a stream come to Pension Berghof.

Bear right on a service road rising up the hillside in long sweeps. Having turned a sharp right-hand bend by some houses, bear right on a track which goes up the edge of a sloping meadow, through woodland and onto a road where you turn right. After a few paces go left at a junction, and on coming to a junction of roads by a farm, take the upper option, but leave it soon after at a sharp right-hand bend. Now go ahead on a track, first among trees, then along the forest edge. At a fork take a path slanting uphill (marked Tischleralm and Hintersteiner See) following blue waymarks.

Climbing steadily through forest the trail suddenly turns sharp right just before reaching a prominent rock slab. Zigzagging uphill, come to a crossing trail and turn left, and

The path to the Hintersteiner See

a few moments later this path takes you across the top of the rock slab. The way continues among mixed forest with small rock outcrops here and there. Reaching a high point of about 997m you gain a partial view into the deep valley of the Weissachgraben, and shortly after emerge to an open meadow with the solitary farm of **Tischleralm** (the map names this as Schiesswiesalm) with the Wilder Kaiser mountains as a backdrop.

Beyond the *alm* building follow a farm track through pastures, then downhill to a junction. Bear right on a broad forest path which leads to the southwestern end of the **Hintersteiner See** (2hrs 45mins). A footpath skirts the southern shore, while a road traces the northern shoreline.

It will take a little over an hour (plus rests) to make a recommended anti-clockwise circuit of the lake. At its eastern end there are restaurants and a grassy strand for bathing from; at the northwestern end there are two more restaurants. Immediately before reaching **Pension Maier** above the lake's western end, turn left (south) on a narrow roadway. On coming to the next junction turn right on a track signed to the Steinerne Stiege, and 5mins later reach **Jausenstation Hagenhof** (refreshments), set among meadows.

Curve left and wander downvalley through pastures, and 10mins later come to the head of the Steinerne Stiege – a remarkable stairway consisting of hundreds of steps from which you gaze directly down into the Weissachgraben valley draining north into the Inn at Kufstein. ◄

The steps will require added caution by anyone with vertigo problems.

At the foot of the steps the path continues ahead into forest. When it forks take the lower option, and at the next junction bear left. On coming to a track, bear left again, and about 3mins later you come to road level. In another 3mins take a minor road on the left which rises gently to a farm. Go round the buildings, then bear right down the narrow farm road as far as a sharp right-hand bend, where you then take a footpath across a meadow on the left. Once across the meadow the path becomes clearer, easing along a shelf among trees, before descending to river level. Continue alongside the river (the Weissache), then cross by a bridge to the Kufstein road opposite **Gasthof Oberstegen**.

Cross the main road with care and take the minor road left of the *gasthof*, which leads back to **Söll** via the Moorsee.

ROUTE 66

Scheffau (744m) – Wilder-Kaiser-Steig –
Riedl Hut (1268m) – Ellmau (810m)

Location	North and northeast of Scheffau
Grade	3
Distance	14km
Height gain	726m
Height loss	668m
Time	5hrs

The Wilder-Kaiser-Steig is a long waymarked trail which runs along the south flank of the Wilder Kaiser from Kirchdorf (or St Johann in Tirol) to Kufstein, a journey of around 35km (see Route 68). This central section of the route makes a rewarding day's exercise, giving a near-circular walk with a variety of scenery: soaring rock slabs, the chaos of scree chutes, trim forest, and rough pastureland. There's also a strong possibility of sighting chamois along the way.

From **Scheffau** village square walk up the road in the direction of the Hintersteiner See; when it makes a sharp left-hand bend, go ahead on a footpath leading to a narrow service road at Leitenhof. Maintain direction, but when the road curves towards a farm, take a footpath signed to Kaiser Hochalm, Schiessling and Hintersteiner See.

This charming forest path rises through the Gaisgraben valley, and about 30mins from Scheffau brings you onto another narrow road at 911m. Turn left, and 1min later break away on a track going ahead, rising to a house. Bear right on a track which you follow all the way to the **Steiner Niederalm** (1087m, 1hr).

Passing the *alm* house follow a narrow trail waymarked with red flashes, climbing the steep hillside for another 15–20mins to a path junction. Turn right along the Wilder-Kaiser-Steig – although there's no indication here that this is the WKS path, other than yellow-and-black waymarks.

Above Scheffau a link path leads to the Wilder-Kaiser-Steig

After rising over somewhat rough ground, the path enters beechwoods, from which you eventually emerge to be confronted by a scene of wild, ragged mountains ahead and above, but a pleasant green and pastoral valley below. Approaching the *alm* buildings of **Kaiser Hochalm** the path contours, then crosses a slope ablaze with alpenroses in early summer, before rising to the *alm*. This is gained about 1¾–2hrs after leaving Scheffau. Pass the three buildings at 1417m and continue up the slope ahead.

After gaining a high point of 1470m, the way descends a short, steep pitch on hewn-out steps with a fixed cable serving as a handrail. Thereafter the trail heads towards screes and comes to a path junction at 1409m, where the left-hand option makes the ascent of the 2304m Treffauer. Continue down among trees to another junction and, ignoring the right branch, keep ahead.

Cross the southern flank of the Tuxeck where a scree slope is being invaded by a mass of dwarf pine. The path eases through, fringed with heather and horizontal layers of juniper, with glorious views across the valley to the right to the rolling hills of the Kitzbüheler Alps.

Shortly after passing another footpath branching left to climb the Tuxeck, the trail forks in woodland. The left branch goes directly to the Grutten Hut, but we take the right branch and descend through forest to a major track. Bear right and wind downhill to the **Riedl Hut** (1268m, 3½hrs; accommodation and refreshments).

Note The altitude of the Riedl Hut is variously quoted on maps as 1268m, 1230m and even 1224m; the height quoted here is taken from the official hut book.

Immediately beyond the hut take a footpath cutting left. This soon brings you onto a plateau above the Biedringeralm where you bear left along a track. Follow this down to **Gasthof Riesen** (951m), beyond which a road continues to **Ellmau** via Wimm.

Note Should you need to return to Scheffau, there is a linking bus service from Ellmau, although some services do not go into the village itself, but drop passengers off at the Wilder Kaiser Gasthof on the main road below Scheffau Dorf.

ROUTE 67

Ellmau (Wochenbrunner Alm: 1085m) –
Gaudeamus Hut (1263m) – Grutten Hut (1620m)
– Riedl Hut (1268m) – Ellmau (810m)

Location	Northeast and north of Ellmau
Grade	3
Distance	10km
Height gain	535m
Height loss	810m
Time	4–4½hrs

A short hut-to-hut tour on the south side of the Wilder Kaiser, this walk is mostly easy and undemanding, with ever-changing views. However the Klammlweg which links the Gaudeamus and Grutten Huts tackles a steep and narrow cleft among rocks, and here the route is briefly strenuous, though aided by iron rungs for hand- or footholds. This section alone warrants a grade 3 listing.

To walk from Ellmau would take about 1½hrs; a very pleasant walk, part of which is alongside the valley stream. ◄

Take a taxi through the Badhausgraben valley which lies on the northern side of the valley between Ellmau and Going. The road ends at a parking area at the **Wochenbrunner Alm**, where there's a restaurant and deer park at the foot of the Wilder Kaiser mountains. ◄

From the roadhead an obvious stony path continues ahead among trees, with enticing views of the Wilder Kaiser peaks and the deep U-shaped cleft of Ellmauer Tor. In 30–40mins you arrive at the **Gaudeamus Hut** (1263m, accommodation and refreshments), a very popular hut backed by woodland at the foot of steep crags.

At the hut a sign directs the way to the Grutten Hut and Ellmauer Tor; a continuing stony trail that winds up grass slopes speckled with dwarf pine and alpenroses, and in 15mins brings you to a junction among trees. Take the narrow left branch which stumbles among rocks and boulders, and as you gain height, so the big limestone peaks tower

Rugged ramparts of the Wilder Kaiser soar above the Grutten Hut

overhead. Zigzagging steeply upwards, it is not immediately clear where the path is leading, but you suddenly enter a narrow cleft and climb a stairway littered with small stones – take care not to dislodge any onto other walkers below.

Near the top of the Klamml the route is aided by iron rungs, above which you come onto a narrow rib and bear left. The path now climbs a little higher to gain a grassy bluff, from which you look directly onto the Grutten Hut. The bluff is carpeted with alpenroses, providing a magnificent splash of colour in early summer, and from it there's a very fine view across the Kitzbüheler Alps to the snowy mountains of the Hohe Tauern.

The **Grutten Hut** (1620m, 1½hrs; accommodation and refreshments) makes a perfect lunch stop, with views from the terrace to linger over. On its west side a broad trail (the Wilder-Kaiser-Steig) makes a gentle slant below grey crags and scree fans, and about 40mins from the Grutten Hut you will notice a path breaking left to the Wochenbrunner Alm. Ignore this and remain on the track for another 5mins to reach the **Riedl Hut** (1268m, 2hrs 15mins, accommodation and refreshments).

Immediately past the hut turn left on a trail signed to Gasthof Riesen and Ellmau. Initially up a few steps into forest, this trail provides a remarkable transformation, for instead of the soaring rock walls of the Wilder Kaiser, you now enjoy open glades and rolling, green wooded hills turning blue with distance. In the glades there's cotton grass and orchids, dwarf pine and bilberries, while a glance over your shoulder reminds you of that other, vertical world of limestone.

A few minutes later come onto a beautiful green terrace (with bench seats to exploit the views) overlooking the solitary building of Biedringeralm. Ellmau can be clearly seen across the valley, backed by the Kitzbüheler Alps. Bear left along a track which curves down the hillside, and when you come to a small hut standing just off the track on the left, look for a sign indicating path no 10 which breaks left to Going. At first rather narrow, this path leads into forest and soon improves. When you come to a track, you bear right for a few paces, then left on a continuing path. Soon another junction appears. Ignore the right branch to Gasthof Riesen and continue in the direction of Going and Ellmau. This eventually leads to the Wochenbrunner road where you walk uphill for a short distance until you see a footbridge on the right.

Cross the Hausbach stream and follow the Wanderweg Ellmau–Going down its left bank, and finally through meadows and on a track to an underpass beneath the main valley road. Through this enter **Ellmau**.

ROUTE 68

The Wilder-Kaiser-Steig

Location	A west-bound traverse of the Wilder Kaiser's south flank
Grade	3
Distance	35km
Highest point	Ackerl Hut ruins (1720m)
Start	Kirchdorf (641m) or St Johann in Tirol (659m)
Finish	Kufstein (499m)
Time	2 days

Making a traverse of the south flank of the Wilder Kaiser, the Wilder-Kaiser-Steig was created in 1990 by linking a number of existing trails into a very fine *höhenweg* suitable for moderate-to-strong walkers. Waymarked with yellow and black paint flashes, the route is guided here and there with WKS signs. Well-maintained, and with a few fixed chain safeguards, the most challenging section lies between the Gaudeamus and Grutten Huts where the route tackles the *klettersteig* of the Jubilaumssteig (see Route 64). This is a full-blown 'protected route' (*via ferrata*), but should you feel doubtful about attempting it, an alternative is offered along the Klammlweg (described in Route 67).

The Wilder-Kaiser-Steig will take two full days to walk, and an overnight is usually spent in the Grutten Hut, located roughly midway between Kirchdorf and Kufstein. Although refreshment facilities are available in a few isolated places along the route, it is essential to carry plenty of liquids with you, plus enough food to keep you going. Meals are provided, of course, at the Grutten Hut.

Day 1 The route begins near Litzlfelden, between St Johann in Tirol and Kirchdorf, and at once climbs the eastern end of the Wilder Kaiser range, known here as the Niederkaiser. It's an abrupt start, tackling the Gmailköpfl at 917m, then tracing the ridge westward over and around several minor summits before veering northwest from the 1279m Gscheuerkopf after about 3hrs.

The WKS regains a minor ridge south of the Maukspitze, the most easterly summit of the Wilder Kaiser proper, and

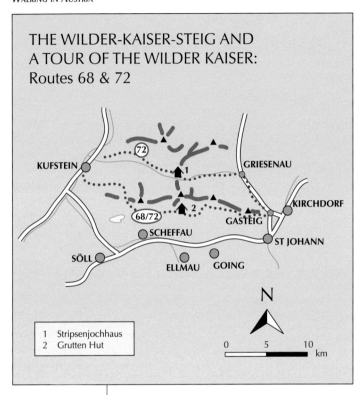

THE WILDER-KAISER-STEIG AND
A TOUR OF THE WILDER KAISER:
Routes 68 & 72

1 Stripsenjochhaus
2 Grutten Hut

N

0   5   10
                      km

comes to the ruins of the former Ackerl Hut (1720m) which
was destroyed by fire – a replacement was built nearly 300m
below. This is the highest point of the whole walk, and the
trail now contours below the Regalspitze before descending
a spur and turning northwestward into the great scree fan
below Ellmauer Tor and above the Gaudeamus Hut. It is this
section that leads to the Jubilaumssteig, but a lower alternative may be taken should you have doubts about tackling
the *klettersteig*. This alternative is the Klammlweg which also
ends at the **Grutten Hut**, about 8–8½hrs from the start.

Day 2 The route from the **Grutten Hut** to Kufstein is
ever-varied and undulating. It may not climb as high as the

first stage, nor have any *klettersteig* to confront, but it's quite demanding nonetheless. It begins with a broad trail sweeping across the lower flank of Ellmauer Halt, but it then narrows through forest and over the scree strips that hang below Tuxeck. From one of these screes a glimpse is afforded of the Hintersteiner See, almost encircled by forest and lying in the valley ahead. But this is nothing to the magnificent view of the lake that is gained on reaching Steiner Hochalm (1257m) about 2½hrs into the walk. On occasion it's possible to buy drinks at this *alm*, when the farmer is in residence.

From Steiner Hochalm to Walleralm the trail is almost entirely in forest, but Walleralm itself is open and sunny, and welcome refreshments can be had at the *gasthof* there, and also at the farm which lies a short distance below. It will have taken around 4–5hrs to walk this far, and another 2–2½hrs will be required to reach Kufstein, during which you travel through a succession of meadow and woodland, pass isolated farms, small groups of houses with fruit trees, and the charming little chapel of Locherer, before a track takes you down to the outskirts of **Kufstein** and the broad valley of the Inn. All in all, a delightful two-day expedition; highly recommended.

Wilder-Kaiser-Steig near the Grutten Hut

ROUTE 69

Griesenau (720m) – Griesner Alm (986m)

Location	Northwest of Kirchdorf
Grade	1
Distance	5km (one way)
Height gain	266m
Time	1½hrs (+ 1hr return)

The Kaiserbachtal slices into the eastern half of the Kaisergebirge mountains, forming a counter-balance to the Kaisertal on the other side of the Stripsenjoch's dividing ridge. But while the Kaisertal is largely wooded, the Kaiserbachtal is much more open, with the great upthrusting crags of the Wilder Kaiser looking dramatically impressive from the valley-bed trails. A toll road pushes into the valley as far as Griesner Alm, but this outing is so gentle, undemanding but rewarding, that to take a vehicle when you could walk seems almost sacriligeous. There's a large car park by the toll booths at the entrance to the valley, but the few buildings of Griesenau are served by public transport from St Johann, with a bus stop at Gasthof Griesenau where the walk begins.

Gasthof Griesenau is open both winter and summer, with 46 beds (☎ 05352 64180 gasthof-griesenau@aon.at; www.griesenau.com), and is conveniently placed for an exploration of the Kaiserbachtal, or for touring the neighbourhood.

The road into the Kaiserbachtal begins opposite Gasthof Griesenau northwest of Kirchdorf. Walk along the road between meadows for 5–10mins. When it crosses a bridge over the Kaiserbach shortly before reaching the large car park and toll booths, leave the road and walk ahead on a broad gravel path on the south bank of the stream. A large board advertising the Alpengasthof Griesner Alm suggests the walk will take 75mins.

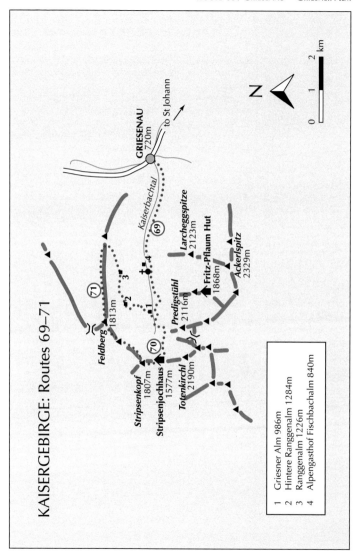

KAISERGEBIRGE: Routes 69–71

to St Johann

GRIESENAU
720m

Kaiserbachtal

69

Larcheggspitze
2123m

Fritz-Pflaum Hut
1868m

Ackerlspitz
2329m

Predigstühl
2116m

Feldberg
1813m

71

70

Stripsenkopf
1807m

Stripsenjochhaus
1577m

Totenkirchl
2190m

N

0 1 2 km

1 Griesner Alm 986m
2 Hintere Ranggenalm 1284m
3 Ranggenalm 1226m
4 Alpengasthof Fischbachalm 840m

No detailed description is necessary, since the path remains on the south bank (left side) of the Kaiserbach all the way to the head of the valley, either through or alongside luxuriant mixed woodland, but as you progress upvalley, views of the Wilder Kaiser peaks become more and more impressive.

About 10mins from the road bridge another route breaks to the left, climbing to Maukalm (in 4hrs) and Gasteig in 3½hrs. About 40mins later a bridge spanning the river provides an opportunity to cross to the 200 year-old **Alpengasthof Fischbachalm** (840m) for refreshments.

Alpengasthof Fischbachalm is an attractive, archetypal Tyrolean farmhouse with magnificent views to the head of the Kaiserbachtal. With 30 beds it is open winter and summer (☎ 05352 65526 fischbachalm@aon.at; www.fischbachalm.at).

The valley becomes wider and more open here, with pastures on the opposite side of the river rising gently to woodland under the north walling ridge.

◄ Just 1min beyond the bridge you pass a small chapel dedicated to climbers who lost their lives in the mountains, and from here you may be able to see the flag flying at the Stripsenjochhaus.

About 10mins later a narrow path cuts left to the Larcheneggspitze (3hrs) and the unmanned Fritz-Pflaum Hut, about 2½hrs from this point. Shortly after this junction the trail forks. Ignore the right branch and continue ahead, curving uphill and eventually coming to a signed junction. Cross the stream to **Griesner Alm** (986m) and the roadhead.

Alpengasthof Griesner Alm stands at the foot of the Stripsenjoch, with the Predigstuhl and Mitterkaiser bursting out of the woods just to the south. The *gasthof* is open in winter and summer, and has 38 beds (☎ 05352 64443 griesneralm@aon.at; www.griesneralm.com).

ROUTE 70
Griesenau (720m) – Stripsenjochhaus (1577m)

Location	West of Griesenau
Grade	2
Distance	7km (one way)
Height gain	857m
Time	3hrs

The large and ever-popular Stripsenjochhaus makes an obvious destination for a walk (see Route 63). Built upon a saddle in the ridge separating the Kaisertal from the Kaiserbachtal, it has remarkable close, full-on views of the major cliffs and summits of the Wilder Kaiser mountains. This approach walk is neither difficult nor overly demanding, and is highly recommended.

Note Should it be your intention to spend a night at the hut, you are strongly advised to telephone ahead to ensure a place (☎ 05372 62579).

Follow directions for Route 69 as far as **Griesner Alm** (1½hrs). At the path junction near the head of the valley, where you would otherwise cross the stream to reach Alpengasthof Griesner Alm, ignore that branch and, remaining left of the stream, keep ahead where the path rises through mostly deciduous woodland. About 25mins from the Griesner Alm junction another path breaks to the left for the Fritz-Pflaum Hut, but we continue ahead, climbing in and out of woodland, then above the trees with a wild scene of rock and scree to the left – the Steinerne Rinne, a massive stone chute between towering walls of limestone (see Route 64). With a few switchbacks the trail then comes onto the saddle with the **Stripsenjochhaus** (accommodation and refreshments) standing a few paces to the right.

ROUTE 71

*Griesner Alm (986m) – Stripsenkopf (1807m) –
Feldberg (1813m) – Griesner Alm*

Location	West of Gasteig
Grade	3
Distance	11km
Height gain	827m
Height loss	827m
Time	5½–6hrs

This is a very fine outing – a ridge walk on the north side of the Kaiserbachtal with outstanding views of the Wilder Kaiser mountains almost every step of the way. You'll need settled conditions as the ridge is no place to be caught in bad weather, and make sure you carry liquid refreshment and something to eat, for although the walk begins and ends at a *gasthaus* and visits a mountain hut (the Stripsenjochhaus), much of the route is well away from habitation.

Summit shelter on the Stripsenkopf

Begin at the Kaiserbachtal roadhead at the Alpengasthof **Griesner Alm**, cross the stream opposite and turn right at the footpath junction where a sign gives 1½hrs to the Stripsenjoch. This is described above as Route 70.

From the **Stripsenjochhaus** at 1577m, a signed path rises to the north, then forks about 15mins above the hut. Take the left branch for the Stripsenkopf (the right branch cuts across the east flank of the mountain on a more direct route to the Feldberg). In places the path calls for easy scrambling, aided by metal rungs and fixed cables, and above these you arrive at a minor saddle below the Hundskopf, whose summit is crowned by a metal cross. Turn left and continue to climb, reaching the ridge a little east of the **Stripsenkopf**. Again, turn left and walk up the final slope to the 1807m summit, on which there's a small shelter (about 35mins from the Stripsenjochhaus). ▸

Walk along the ridge heading northeast, but after a short distance the path leaves the crest and cuts down the steep right flank (caution when wet) to join the lower path which avoided the Stripsenkopf. Now the route rejoins the ridge crest and dodges from one side to the other; from the left side of the ridge you look directly down into the pastoral Weissenbach valley.

The lowest part of the ridge is reached at the Wiesensattel at 1627m, after which you climb again on the most scenic section of the route between the Stripsenkopf and Feldberg. There's one short fixed cable, otherwise the path is straight-forward, and it brings you onto a false summit (excellent views), after which you descend briefly, then up to a junction where a faint path breaks left to the Kohlalm. Ignore this path and keep ahead among dwarf pine which screens the views for a while. As you emerge from these, skirt a secondary high point and climb a final slope to gain the summit of **Feldberg** (1813m, 3½hrs).

A splendid panorama can be enjoyed from here, the most riveting scene being that to the south where Ellmauer Halt dominates a crowd of peaks jostling for attention.

Feldberg is a minor summit with the inevitable cross, and truly magnificent views across the Kaiserbachtal to the wonderful Wilder Kaiser peaks; north to the Walchsee and the flat country stretching into Germany, while Kufstein can be seen in the Inn Valley to the west.

Descend the ridge east of the summit, on a path weaving among more dwarf pine, and with another brief section of fixed cable. This takes you into several hollows before you descend to a grassy saddle and veer left ahead, then come to a more prominent saddle and a path junction (about 1465m, 45mins from the Feldberg summit).

Turn right and descend the steep south slope of the mountain, soon entering woodland. On emerging from the trees the way heads west on a descending traverse, and comes to another junction just above the building of **Ranggenalm** (1226m, refreshments sometimes available from the dairyman). One path drops past the hut on the way to Fischbachalm, but we contour westward, rising a little here and there and regaining another 100m or so before descending to the two *alm* buildings of **Hintere Ranggenalm** (also known as Ranggen Hochalm). Pass between the buildings to join the farm track which snakes its way down to **Griesner Alm**.

ROUTE 72
A Tour of the Wilder Kaiser

Location	East of Kufstein
Grade	3
Distance	58km
Highest point	Ackerl Hut ruins (1720m)
Start/Finish	Kufstein (499m)
Time	4 days
Map	See Route 68

Making a circular tour of the Wilder Kaiser mountains, this four-day walk reveals the full glory of this stunningly beautiful and scenically diverse region. It uses two mountain huts, and spends a third night in the small village of Gasteig, west of Kirchdorf. A brief outline only is given, although some individual sections of the route are treated to a more detailed description elsewhere in this guide. See map of Route 68 for an outline of this route.

*The Wilder Kaiser,
from Ellmau*

Day 1 From **Kufstein** to the Stripsenjochhaus, this initial stage of the walk explores the deep and enchanting Kaisertal. Route 60 above describes the route as far as the Hans-Berger-Haus, a short distance upvalley from Hinterbärenbad (3hrs), and from the TVN-owned hut the path continues, now climbing through woodland on the Nordalpenweg to gain the Stripsenjoch in another 1½–1¾hrs. Spend the night in the **Stripsenjochhaus**.

Day 2 The easiest stage of the tour, this day's route simply descends from the **Stripsenjoch** to Griesner Alm in the Kaiserbachtal, then takes the gentle path down the right bank of the Kaiserbach to **Griesenau** (Route 69 in reverse). The final section of this stage merely walks southeast through the Kohlenbach valley to **Gasteig**, a small village with at least 3 hotels (contact: kirchdorf@ferienregion.at; www.ferien region.at).

Day 3 Turning westward now, the first phase of the Wilder-Kaiser-Steig is followed as far as the **Grutten Hut** above Ellmau – see Route 68. In some ways this is the most demanding stage of the four-day tour, and the route reaches its highest point (1720m) about 5hrs into the walk. After this, there's the challenging *klettersteig* of the Jubilaumssteig which leads to the Grutten Hut.

Day 4 The circular tour of the district is completed by walking the second stage of the Wilder-Kaiser-Steig as outlined in Route 68. It takes an undulating course along the south flank of the Wilder Kaiser, in and out of forest, but with lovely views throughout, and finally descends to **Kufstein** where the tour began.

8 DACHSTEINGEBIRGE

Winter hoar frost in the Gosautal

Southeast of Salzburg, on the edge of the Salzkammergut lake district, the Dachstein group forms one of the most easterly massifs in the chain of the Northern Limestone Alps. The central core of the group is dominated by the 2995m Hoher Dachstein, the second highest of this limestone chain, whose south side is a precipitous wall of rock rising from a vast scree apron, and whose north flank contains several glaciers that drain down to forested lower hills and the mirror-like waters of the Gosausee and Hallstätter See. Encircled by roads, with a few cableways giving access to select high places, the district is liberally supplied with walkers' trails, mountain huts and alm restaurants.

ACCESS AND INFORMATION	
Location	Shared between the provinces of Salzburg, Upper Austria and Styria, the Dachstein group is bounded by the Ramsau terrace and Enns valley in the south, and the Gosaubach and Hallstätter See to the north. The Tennengebirge forms a buffer to the west, while the 2351m Grimming effectively closes the group in the east.
Maps	Alpenvereinskarte 14 *Dachstein* 1:25,000
	Kompass Wanderkarte 20 *Dachstein* 1:50,000

	Freytag & Berndt WK281 *Dachstein-Ausseer Land-Ramsau* and WK201 *Schladminger Tauern-Radstadt-Dachstein* 1:50,000
Bases	Filzmoos, Ramsau, Hallstatt
Information	Tourismusverband Filzmoos (e-mail: info@filzmoos.at; website: www.filzmoos.at)
	Tourismusverband Ramsau am Dachstein (e-mail: info@ramsau.com; website: www.ramsau.com)
	Tourismusverband Hallstatt (e-mail: hallstatt@inneres-salzkammergut.at; website: www.hallstatt.ent)
Access	By train to Radstädt or Schladming, then bus to Filzmoos or Ramsau. For Hallstatt, take the train from Salzburg via Bad Ischl. Hallstatt station is on the opposite shore of the lake, but there's a connecting ferry.
	By road take the A10 autobahn south of Salzburg to Eben, then via a minor road to Filzmoos and Ramsau.
	To reach Hallstatt by road, follow route 145 south of Bad Ischl to Bad Goisern, then minor road to Hallstatt.

At the western end of the Dachsteingebirge, the bewitchingly attractive group of the Gosaukamm is sometimes referred to as the Salzburg Dolomites. Six or seven major summits over 2000m, together with numerous other turrets and pinnacles bursting from scree or pasture, create a scene of jagged Dolomitic grandeur, around which a justifiably popular tour has been created.

By contrast, the Hoher Dachstein contains shrinking icefields and some exciting *klettersteig* routes, one of which takes an airy and spectacular journey eastward from the Dachsteinsüdwand cableway to the Guttenberghaus; an extravaganza of ladders, fixed cables and rungs, that lead to hours of scrambling among cliffs and towers with hundreds of metres of space beneath your boots.

There are limestone pavements and beautiful alpine meadows grazed by bell-clattering cows. There are larch groves and deep-shaded pinewoods, neat farmhouses hung about with flowers, icy lakes, and in Hallstatt, one of Europe's most beautiful villages. Seen from afar, the Dachsteingebirge seduces with a hint of mystery, but up close that mystery is replaced by a reality no less seductive or rewarding.

Main Bases
Filzmoos (1057m) This small but attractive resort village lies on the southern side of the Dachstein group below the 2459m Bischofsmütze, perhaps the most distinguished

DACHSTEINGEBIRGE

Mountain Huts
1 Gablonzer
2 Theodor-Körner
3 Hofpürgl
4 Adamek
5 Simony
6 Schlicherhaus
7 Seethaler
8 Dachstein-Südwand
9 Austria
10 Guttenberghaus
11 Brünner

to Linz

BAD ISC

to Salzburg

Hallstätter See

GOSAU

HALLSTATT

OBERTRAU

Gosausee

TENNENGEBIRGE

ANNABERG

DACH

1

Hochkesselkopf

Bischofsmütze

2   3

5

4

7

Hoher Dachstein

ST MARTIN

FILZMOOS

8   9   10

RAMSAU

RADSTADT

SCH

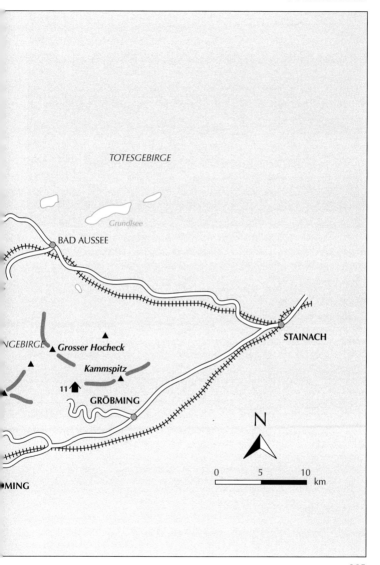

Hallstatt is one of Austria's finest villages

of the Gosaukamm's peaks. It has plenty of three- and four-star hotels, *gasthöfe*, *pensionen*, apartments and bed-and-breakfast accommodation. The village has modest facilities that include sports shops, a supermarket, post office, a helpful tourist office, and two banks with ATMs. The nearest campsite (Camping Dachstein) is located 8km further east on the way to Ramsau.

Ramsau am Dachstein (1135m) A seemingly uncoordinated string of hamlets scattered along a broad green terrace at the foot of the Dachstein's south face, Ramsau appears not to have one centre, but two; Kulm (1083m) and Ort (1135m), neither of which suggests much of a resort. Served by bus from Schladming, Ramsau is popular in winter for nordic skiing, in summer for gentle valley walking and with visitors eager to make the ascent of the Hoher Dachstein aided by the Dachsteinsüdwand cable car. There are cafés, restaurants, a few shops, a bank with ATM (in Ramsau Ort) and plenty of tourist accommodation.

Hallstatt (508m) Beautifully set on the western shore of the Hallstätter See, Hallstatt has an historical pedigree dating back to at least 800BC when salt was first mined there. With a precipitous cliff behind it, the village projects over and almost into the lake, and is understandably popular as one of Austria's major tourist attractions. Accommodation can be found in a few hotels, *gasthöfe*, private rooms and a youth hostel, and there's a campsite on the southern outskirts. The tourist office can provide full details.

Mountain Huts

Adamek Hut (2196m) Built in 1908 by the Austria section of the ÖAV below the now-receding Grosse Gosau glacier, this large Category I hut has 25 beds and 71 dormitory places, and is staffed from the end of May to the start of October (☎ 0664 5473481).

Austria Hut (1638m) Also owned by the Austria section of the ÖAV, this hut dates from 1880, and is easily reached from Ramsau Ort (just 20mins from a bus stop at the Türlwand Hut). It's a Category II building, staffed virtually all year except November, and has 35 beds and 25 dormitory places (☎ 03687 81522).

Dachstein-Südwand Hut (1871m) A privately owned hut built on a spur projecting from the south flank of the Dachstein, it can be reached in 30mins by an easy path cutting round the mountainside from the Türlwand Hut roadhead. It has 20 beds and 40 dormitory places, and is staffed from mid-May to the beginning of November (☎ 03687 81509).

Gablonzer Hut (1522m) Standing at the northern end of the Gosaukamm, just 300m from the top station of the Gosaukammbahn, the Category II Gablonzer Hut is owned by the ÖAV's Neugablonz section from Enns. Staffed most of the year, except May and November, it has 30 beds and 42 dormitory places (☎ 06136 8465).

Guttenberghaus (2147m) Built 1912–14 at the eastern end of the Dachstein massif, and reached by a walk of about 3½hrs from Ramsau Kulm, this Category I hut belongs to the Austria section of the ÖAV, has 25 beds and 45 dormitory places, and is manned from June to the end of September (☎ 03687 22753).

Hofpürgl Hut (1705m) From Filzmoos, this hut may be reached by a walk of about 2½hrs. Having a wonderful close view of the south face of the Bischofsmütze, good rock climbing nearby, and access for walkers to the circular tour of the Gosaukamm, it is understandably popular. Originally built in 1902, this Category I hut belongs to the Linz section of the ÖAV, has 40 beds and 70 dormitory places, and is fully staffed from the end of May to mid-October (☎ 06453 8304).

Schlicherhaus (1739m) A privately owned hut on the Gjaidalm south of the Hallstätter See, it is easily reached by cableway from Obertraun, so is very popular with day visitors as well as walkers exploring the limestone Dachstein plateau. It has 57 beds and 30 dormitory places, and is open most of the year except May and November (☎ 06131 596).

Seethaler Hut (2740m) This small Category I hut, located between the Hoher Dachstein and Dirndl, may only be used in an emergency. It was built by the Austria section of the ÖAV in 1929, has just 8 places in its dormitory, but is manned from June to mid-October (☎ 03687 81036).

Simony Hut (2203m) Standing at the foot of the Hallstätter glacier, the Simony Hut dates from 1878. With 30 beds and 90 dormitory places, it is fully staffed throughout the year, except for the period November to Christmas (☎ 0664 9184174). Owned by the ÖAV's Austria section, the Category I hut is reached by a walk of about 6hrs from Hallstatt, but 2½hrs from the Gjaidalm station of the cableway from Obertraun.

Theodor-Körner Hut (1466m) Nestling among trees below the Gosaukamm, this small, homely Category I hut was built in 1924 for the ÖAV's Academic section from Vienna. With 6 beds and 33 dormitory places, it is staffed from June to mid-October (☎ 0664 9166303).

WALKS FROM FILZMOOS

Filzmoos is arguably the finest base for a walking holiday on the south side of the Dachsteingebirge. The Hinterwinkl valley stretching behind the village gives access to the Gosaukamm, the Gosauer Stein and, via the Sulzenhals saddle, the great Dachsteinsüdwand (south face). A toll road, served by the Filzmooser Wanderbus, goes as far as Hofalm in the Hinterwinkl, and it is from there that some of the best walks begin.

ROUTE 73

Filzmoos (Hofalm: 1268m) –
Hofpürgl Hut (1705m) – Sulzenhals (1825m) –
Sulzenalm (1608m) – Filzmoos (1057m)

Location	North of Filzmoos
Grade	3
Distance	14km
Height gain	712m
Height loss	923m
Time	4½–5hrs

On this splendid near-circular walk both the Bischofsmütze and the impressive rock scenery at the head of the valley, north of Filzmoos, are seen at close quarters. It's a reasonably strenuous walk which visits a mountain hut and an attractive alm where refreshments can be had, and views are lovely throughout.

Take the bus, or drive upvalley from Filzmoos to **Hofalm**. Pass alongside the *alm* building, then cross two footbridges on the left which carry a footpath the short distance to **Unterhofalm**. Walk past the stables, then take path no 612 on the right, signed to the Hofpürgl Hut. After crossing

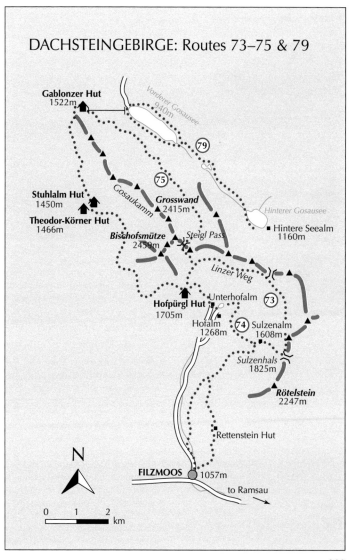

DACHSTEINGEBIRGE: Routes 73–75 & 79

Gablonzer Hut
1522m

Vorderer Gosausee
940m

(79)

(75)

Stuhlalm Hut
1450m

Gosaukamm

Grosswand
2415m

Theodor-Körner Hut
1466m

Bischofsmütze
2459m

Steigl Pass

Hinterer Gosausee

■ Hintere Seealm
1160m

Linzer Weg

Hofpürgl Hut
1705m

Unterhofalm

(73)

Hofalm
1268m

(74) Sulzenalm
1608m

Sulzenhals
1825m

▲ **Rötelstein**
2247m

Rettenstein Hut

N

FILZMOOS ● 1057m

to Ramsau

0   1   2
km

The Linzer Weg above Hofalm

a stony streambed, the way rises across grass slopes, then steepens, twisting uphill to dwarf pine and alpenroses. In 50mins or so it comes to a path junction a little north of the **Hofpürgl Hut** (1705m, accommodation and refreshments), a large building perched upon a grassy ridge.

Unless you need to visit the hut turn right along the Linzer Weg (now path no 601/612), which crosses the Kesselwand below the Bischofsmütze. The route takes you over screes, then up and over a spur with dwarf pine and more alpenroses leading to another path junction. The upper trail (612) climbs to the Steigl Pass, but we take the lower option curving right across the valley head; an interesting, ever-varied route with a persistant rise and fall.

About 1hr 50mins from the start arrive at another path junction (Untere Rinderfeld) where the right branch returns to Hofalm via the little Almsee tarn. Ignoring this option, cross the pasture before climbing to a higher pastureland. A signpost marks yet another junction (Rinderfeld), where the left branch climbs to the Reissgangscharte and, beyond it, to the Adamek Hut, while we veer right in the direction of the Rettenstein (Rötelstein) and Sulzenhof.

This is a lovely alm pasture, but with screes and a clutter of rocks and boulders lying below soaring limestone walls.

◄ Crossing the pasture the path then rises to a high point and a row of trees, beyond which you descend among rocks and alpenroses. Thereafter pick a way up and over a series of minor ridge spurs above a steep little hanging valley, eventually climbing to gain a major ridge spur, the Sulzenchied, in 3hrs. The path swings left, rises a little further to a shoulder at about 1975m (a cross can be seen to the left), then descends steeply to the saddle of **Sulzenhals** (1825m), which is almost completely covered with dwarf pine. On the south side rises the 2247m Rötelstein.

Turn right through a fence, and wander among dwarf pine, then down to a lovely stand of larches before easing across a pastureland slope, once again looking ahead to the majestic Bischofsmütze. **Sulzenalm** (also known as the Wallehen Hut, 1608m, accommodation and refreshments) is reached about 20mins from the Sulzenhals saddle, and makes a fine place to relax with a drink.

The **Wallehen Hut** is variously shown on maps as 1608m or 1590m, while some local literature gives the altitude as low as 1534m. It has 6 beds and 14 dormitory places, and is open both winter and summer (☎ 06453 8289).

From here a dirt road descends to the valley. At first a path drops below the road, then crosses to a second alm building. The way now cuts left of the road, and is signed to Filzmoos. Wander across more fine pastureland dotted with limestone rocks, then into forest where the path becomes a track. In a little over 4hrs, still in forest, take path no 638 which cuts to the right away from the track. Descending among trees come down to a dirt road, and after turning the first hairpin, take the continuing path down to the left, coming to another dirt road which you follow briefly to the left. Soon, with houses seen ahead, take the footpath alternative which breaks to the right alongside trees and through more forest to a metalled road. Shortly after this join the main valley road near the toll booth for traffic going to Hofalm, and follow this down to **Filzmoos**.

ROUTE 74

Filzmoos (Hofalm: 1268m) –
Sulzenalm (1608m) – Filzmoos (1057m)

Location	North of Filzmoos
Grade	2
Distance	9km
Height gain	340m
Height loss	551m
Time	2½–3hrs

This is a shorter variation of Route 73 which provides an attractive option for a gentle day's walk.

Begin at the **Hofalm** roadhead as for Route 73, and follow directions to Gasthof Unterhof. Immediately beyond the *gasthof* take the path/track on the right which rises easily to the little Almsee. Go through a gateway on the left into a meadow, where a faint path takes you in the direction of the Linzer Weg. Soon rising among trees you come to a crossing path by a little wooden bridge. Bear right, and when you arrive at a signed junction turn right on a broad path towards Oberhof (the left branch goes to the Linzer Weg and Hofpürgl Hut).

Descending a little, the path then forks and you branch left, rising towards the southeast. The way narrows and continues to climb, but much steeper now, heading up the hillside with a few zigzags to ease the gradient. Eventually the slope slackens, and an alm building is seen ahead. A sign now directs the path to the right, across a meadow and on to a farm road. Turn left and wander up this to **Sulzenalm** (the Wallehen Hut, 1608m, accommodation and refreshments) with its lovely view up to the Bischofsmütze.

The descent to Filzmoos begins as for Route 73, as far as the point where path no 638 leaves the forest track. Do not

follow this path, but continue down the track which eventually brings you out of the forest near a farm. Ignore the narrow road cutting right (signed *Fussweg nach Filzmoos*) and remain on the track which soon passes through another belt of forest and leads to the **Rettenstein Hut** (a ski hut, not open in summer). By now you're on a narrow tarmac road with views down to Filzmoos. Keep alert for a footpath shortcut that descends steeply through trees and rejoins the road lower down by a *gasthof*. Wander down the road into **Filzmoos**.

Sulzenalm and the Bischofsmütze

ROUTE 75
The Gosaukamm Circuit

Location	A counter-clockwise tour of the Gosaukamm north of Filzmoos
Grade	3
Distance	23km
Highest point	Steigl Pass (2016m)
Start/Finish	Filzmoos (Hofalm: 1268m)
Time	2 days

This understandably popular two-day tour of the Gosaukamm (the so-called Salzburg Dolomites) is the most celebrated route in the Dachsteingebirge. Although not unduly arduous, the crossing of the Steigl Pass involves some scrambling aided by fixed cables, and with a modest amount of exposure. In his *Mountain Walking in Austria*, Cecil Davies described the route beginning with a ride on the Gosaukammbahn cable car above the Gosausee on the northern side of the range, and that, of course, will be the choice of those based on that side of the mountain. In which case, you should join the following description at the Gablonzer Hut at the start of Day 2.

Day 1 From the **Hofalm** roadhead cross two footbridges to reach the *alm* restaurant of **Unterhofalm**, from where you join path no 612 signed to the Hofpürgl Hut. Across a stony streambed the path rises over grass slopes, before the gradient steepens with the trail twisting up to dwarf pine and alpenroses. A path junction about 200m from the **Hofpürgl Hut** is gained in 50mins or so from the roadhead.

Turn right on the Linzer Weg which heads towards the shapely Bischofsmütze, negotiates screes and a spur with more dwarf pine and alpenroses, and comes to another path junction at about 1720m. Take the upper branch (path no 612) which zigzags up the stony slope towards the Gosaukamm's crags, where the way continues over ledges and up steps (fixed cables) with modest exposure to gain the **Steigl Pass** (2016m, 1¾–2hrs) with its wonderful views to north and south, while the Bischofsmütze rises to the west, and the Steiglkogel to the east.

On the northern side of the pass the trail makes an initial gentle descent over sections of limestone pavement, then down steps and a brief gully before curving northwest to pass below the Gabelkogel. The route exchanges rock for pinewoods, then, standing on what was once an alm, you'll see a memorial chapel recalling those who have lost their lives in the mountains. After this wander past two or three huts and gain a view of the Gosausee about 400m below. The path goes down in zigzags, but as you descend keep alert for a junction where you leave path no 612 (which descends to the Gosautal) and take the left branch, a faint trail contouring across the slope to reach path no 620 – the main linking route between the Gosausee and the Gablonzer Hut. Here you turn left and climb steeply at first, then on a track which brings you to the **Gablonzer Hut** (1522m, 5½hrs) and the end of the first stage of the tour.

Day 2 Leaving the hut, the way follows the Austriaweg, climbing briefly to the Obere Törlecksattel, just 72m above the hut, then on to a second, lower, saddle at 1575m (the Untere Torlecksattel) where there's a junction offering an uncomplicated route to the Grosse Donnerkogel, a noted

The Gosaukamm peaks, viewed from near Sulzenchied

viewpoint at 2054m. However, the Gosaukamm tour ignores this and descends to the **Stuhlalm** where there's a privately-owned hut.

The **Stuhlalm Hut** (1450m) has 4 beds and 40 dormitory places, and is open from mid-May to the end of October (☎ 06463 8416).

Now on a broad track you shortly arrive at the idyllic **Theodor-Körner Hut** (1466m, 1½hrs, accommodation and refreshments). Unless you need accommodation or refreshment it's not essential to go this far, for about 100m short of the hut the Austriaweg trail breaks away, heading southeast towards the Bischofsmütze and signed to the Hofpürgl Hut.

After making a short descent, the way then climbs a gully with fixed cable safeguards, among impressive (if slightly intimidating) rock scenery to gain the Jöchl, a little pass at 1610m. This marks the end of any perceived difficulties, for you now cross several meadows on an undulating course at the base of the Gosaukamm cliffs and with expanding views to less dramatic, but no less beautiful country spreading south. Curving below the Bischofsmütze you cross a shoulder to see the **Hofpürgl Hut** perched on a ridge ahead. The path goes directly to it, arriving about 4hrs after you set out from the Gablonzer Hut.

To return to Filzmoos, simply reverse the first part of the route taken on Day 1.

WALKS FROM THE BACHLALM

Six kilometres east of Filzmoos, the road leading to Ramsau am Dachstein makes a sharp right-hand hairpin at the entrance to a charming valley immediately below the Dachstein's south face. This valley is wooded in its lower regions, but rough pastures spread from the upper tree level to the vast scree fans that spill from the face of the mountains. A private road (partly unsurfaced) winds up into this valley, and 4km from its entrance, ends at the Bachlalm. In summer the Filzmooser Wanderbus runs a direct service here about three times a day, but a much more frequent shuttle minibus service operates along the private road to Bachlalm every 30mins from 8am to 4.30pm. For visitors with their own transport, there's plenty of parking space near the start of this road.

Useful as a base for a variety of walks and climbs, **Bachlalm** has 16 beds and 32 dormitory places, and is open from May to October (☎ 03687 81439).

ROUTE 76
Bachlalm (1495m) – Tor (2033m) –
Dachstein-Südwand Hut (1871m) – Bachlalm

Location	North of Bachlalm
Grade	3
Distance	12km
Height gain	915m
Height loss	915m
Time	4½–5hrs

This scenically varied and rewarding walk makes an elongated circuit among woodland, pasture and scree. In places it's rough underfoot and shadeless, and on a bright summer's day the sun often reflects its heat from the bleached limestone to create a furnace-like atmosphere – make sure you carry plenty of liquids with you. Although much of the route leads across what might at first seem to be barren rock and scree, there's a surprising amount of vegetation, with many alpine flowers to brighten the way. Refreshments are available at the Dachstein-Südwand Hut, about 3hrs after setting out.

Descend a short distance down the track from **Bachlalm**, then branch left when it forks. Rising gently the now stony track is flanked for a while by larches, but in 30mins you emerge from these into the valley's upper pastures where there's a signed junction. Fork right on a narrow path which soon twists among dwarf pine through which you come to the base of a large scree tumbling from the Windleger Spitze.

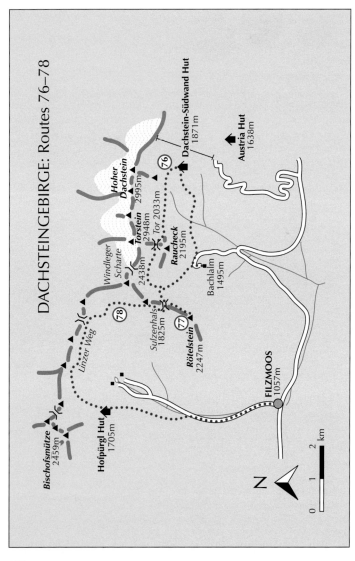

DACHSTEINGEBIRGE: Routes 76–78

Hoher Dachstein

Torstein 2948m

2995m

Tor 2033m

Windleger Scharte

2438m

Raucheck 2195m

Dachstein-Südwand Hut 1871m

Austria Hut 1638m

Bachlalm 1495m

Linzer Weg

78

Sulzenhals 1825m

77

Rötelstein 2247m

Bischofsmütze 2459m

Hofpürgl Hut 1705m

FILZMOOS 1057m

76

N

0 1 2 km

At first you go up the left-hand side of this scree, before picking a way up the centre to gain another belt of dwarf pine that effectively divides the scree into two sections. On the edge of this dwarf pine there's another path junction where you continue ahead for another 10mins across the next scree, to yet another junction marked this time on rocks. It is here that a route to the Adamek Hut via the Windleger Scharte breaks away to the left. Ignore this option and keep ahead to rise through a rocky cauldron of a hanging valley between the Torstein on the left and Raucheck on the right. At its head the U-shaped col of **Tor** (2033m) is gained about 1½hrs from Bachlalm.

Descend steeply on the eastern side, at first down rocks, then scree, at the foot of which you come to a rocky basin with a small 'island' of grass. Abundant waymarks guide a way through a wilderness of stone, on the far side of which you cross a low ridge of grass and dwarf pine to gain a view of the Dachstein-Südwand Hut ahead, set upon a spur reached by a trail rising across yet more screes.

The way descends again, then rises in a long slant to be joined about 10mins below the hut by a path which will be used on the return to Bachlalm. The privately owned **Dachstein-Südwand Hut** (1871m, accommodation and

The Bachlalm trail below the Dachstein south face

refreshments) is reached about 3hrs from Bachlalm. Since it can be reached in just 30mins from the Türlwand roadhead, it is invariably busy on fine summer days, but it makes a perfect lunch stop, with tremendous views from the terrace.

Descend the same path used on the approach as far as the junction where a sign indicates the way to Bachlalm in 1hr 45mins. Take this left branch which goes steeply down to pastureland, then steep larch-clad slopes that eventually bring you into an idyllic pasture, about 50mins from the hut, where a track cuts left to the Austria Hut.

This pasture at the foot of the Dachstein's bold south face, is almost like a small parkland, with rocks and stands of larch, flowers in the grass, and a clear stream easing through a bed of white stones. Perfection!

Ignore the track and continue ahead on the left bank of the stream, soon arriving at a footbridge (Martinsbrücke) at a confluence of streams. Over the bridge follow a track down-valley, eventually coming to the dirt road below Scharlalm. Turn right and wander up the road for another 10mins or so to arrive back where you began at **Bachlalm**.

Pastureland trail junction below the Sulzenhals (Route 77)

ROUTE 77

Bachlalm (1495m) –
Sulzenhals (1825m) – Rötelstein (2247m)

Location	Northwest of Bachlalm
Grade	3
Distance	4km (one way)
Height gain	782m
Time	2½hrs (+ 1¾hrs return)

Often visited from Filzmoos, the summit of the Rötelstein is another noted vantage point with a splendid panorama. Standing south of the main Dachstein massif, it commands a wide vista, not only of the Dachstein, but the continuing line of the Northern Limestone Alps in the west, and southwest to the Grossglockner and Venediger groups.

Follow directions for Route 76 as far as the path junction in the valley's upper pastures at the head of the stony track (30mins). Take the path signed for the Sulzenhals. This continues ahead across the pasture, then swings left up an easy slope to reach the 1825m saddle of **Sulzenhals** in another 30mins. This saddle, visited on Route 73, is on the ridge which divides the Bachlalm valley from the Hinterwinkl above Filzmoos.

Turn left (south) here and climb the steepening ridge (caution) to gain the 2247m summit of the **Rötelstein** with its large cross and remarkable panoramic views.

Note While the suggestion here is to return to Bachlalm by the path used on the approach, an alternative continuing route crosses the summit and descends to Filzmoos via the Ahorneggalm and Rettenstein Hut.

ROUTE 78

Bachlalm (1495m) – Sulzenhals (1825m) –
Hofpürgl Hut (1705m) – Filzmoos (1057m)

Location	Northwest and west of Bachlalm
Grade	3
Distance	14km
Height gain	510m
Height loss	938m
Time	5½–6hrs

Although there are easier, shorter and more direct routes between Filzmoos and Bachlalm, this moderately strenuous walk explores the wild and rugged beauty of the mountains on a tour which crosses the Sulzenhals saddle, then curves below the headwall of the Hinterwinkl valley before descending from the Hofpürgl Hut through woodland and pasture. Since there's no opportunity for refreshment between Bachlalm and the Hofpürgl Hut (4hrs), it is essential to carry plenty of liquids with you.

Follow directions for Route 77 as far as the saddle of **Sulzenhals** (1825m, 1hr), then bear right, heading north on a steepish climb to gain the ridge spur of the Sulzenchied at about 1975m. Over this you cross a series of minor spurs above a little hanging valley, before rising among rocks and alpenroses to gain a crest bearing a row of trees. The way then takes you into a lovely *alm* pasture and comes to the junction of Rinderfeld (1760m), where the right branch climbs steeply to the Reissgangscharte on the way to the Adamek Hut. Ignore this option and continue ahead, losing height on the way to a second pasture with yet another path junction. This is Untere Rinderfeld, and should you feel the need for a quick descent to Filzmoos, you could take the left branch to Hofalm. For the full tour, however, keep ahead.

Tucked beneath the crags of the Gosauer Stein, the path (the Linzer Weg) heads northwest towards the Bischofsmütze, then curves left above the Kesselwand to a junction with a

path used on the Gosaukamm Circuit (see Route 75). The **Hofpürgl Hut** is now seen ahead, and the path goes directly to it, about 4hrs from Bachlalm.

Dachstein outliers above Filzmoos

The quickest way down to Filzmoos takes a path about 200m north of the hut, which descends the east side of the ridge to Hofalm, from where the *Filzmooser Wanderbus* ferries passengers through the valley to the village. But for our continuing walk, it is better to take path no 634 from the hut. Heading due south, this makes a long slanting descent through forest, and joins the quiet valley road about 3km north of **Filzmoos**.

OTHER ROUTES FROM BACHLALM

The whole area spreading out from Bachlalm promises plenty of good walking. There are various tracks cutting through forests that lead to secluded *alm* pastures unmarked on the maps, and no shortage of marked trails too. The following list offers a small sample.

- From the Bachlalm Gasthof at least two routes (paths no 614 and 671) go directly to **Filzmoos** in 2hrs or so.

- Heading north across the Dachstein massif, the **Adamek Hut** can be reached in 4hrs via the 2438m Windleger Scharte. This is a demanding route for experienced mountain walkers only.

- A less demanding, but somewhat complicated route takes walkers to **Ramsau Ort** in 3½hrs, while rock climbers have a vast playground on which to practise their sport.

WALKS FROM RAMSAU
AM DACHSTEIN

As mentioned above, Ramsau is well-known to nordic skiers, for the broad green terrace on which the village is scattered is ideal for cross-country skiing, and in the summer for gentle valley walks. But being situated at the foot of the Dachstein gives it something extra, for the great limestone walls are on show at almost every turn. Apart from the obvious appeal of the Dachsteinsüdwand cable car which lifts visitors to the ridge overlooking the Schladminger glacier, there are hut walks to consider, exciting *klettersteig* routes, and a multi-day tour of the Dachsteingebirge that would satisfy any hut-to-hut enthusiast.

- The **Dachstein-Südwand Hut** is understandably popular with visitors to Ramsau, for it can be reached in little more than 30–40mins from the Türlwand roadhead (bus services and large car park) at the foot of the cableway. Its location is very fine, being set on a spur thrust forward from the Dachstein's south face.

- The **Austria Hut** is also popular for the same reason as the Südwand Hut – ease of access from the roadhead.

- Tucked on the Dachstein's ridge at 2740m, the **Seethaler Hut** is visited by plenty of walkers in summer; after riding the cable car, the hut can be reached in 40–45mins. Spectacular views add to its appeal.

- North of Ramsau Kulm, the **Guttenberghaus** sits at 2147m at the base of the Eselstein towards the eastern end of the Dachstein massif. A lovely walk of 3½–4hrs along the Anton-Baum Weg takes you there from the outskirts of Kulm.

- The 2553m **Eselstein** has a *klettersteig* route which begins at the Guttenberghaus, and this is linked with the classic, much longer *klettersteig* created along the main spine of the Dachstein. Adepts only need consider.

GOSAUTAL AND HALLSTÄTTER SEE

Linked by a common road the Gosautal and Hallstätter See rather dominate the northern side of the Dachsteingebirge. The first leads to a string of lakes under the cliffs of the Gosaukamm, the second lies in a deep trench, an 8km-long gem of a lake that is one of the undisputed jewels of the Salzkammergut Lake District. No, it's more than that, it's one of the jewels of the Alps. Two undemanding walks are suggested here. Both are romantic and rewarding.

Vorderer Gosausee and the Dachstein in winter

ROUTE 79

Vorderer Gosausee (940m) –
Hintere Seealm (1160m)

Location	South of Gosau
Grade	1–2
Distance	7km (one way)
Height gain	220m
Time	2hrs (+ 1½hrs return)
Map	See Route 73

Famed for its views of the ice-draped Dachstein, the Vorderer Gosausee is justifiably popular. Reached by bus from Bad Ischl, there's a *gasthof* and a large car park below the northwestern end of the lake, and a cable car rising to the west, its top station located about 300m from the Gablonzer Hut. The majority of visitors go no farther than the first lake, but this walk links all three lakes (the second is a modest, shallow tarn) to enjoy some truly spectacular views.

From the top car park or bus stop, go up to the lake and wander along the left-hand (northern) shore on a broad track. A footpath traces the southern shore, and this should be taken on the return walk, but the north shore provides spectacular views of the mighty Dachstein mirrored in the water, with the crags of the Gosaukamm towering over the south side of the valley.

The track continues beyond the first lake, then enters forest to pass a small tarn (the Gosaulacke) below on the right, and shortly after, the Launigg Wasserfall on the left. Rising steeply you come to a viewpoint from which the **Hinterer Gosausee** is suddenly revealed; a serene pearl of a lake lying at the foot of the Dachstein. Take the path round the south shore to reach the **Hintere Seealm** (1160m, 2hrs, accommodation and refreshments), an idyllic place to relax and enjoy lunch.

Return by the same path and track as far as the **Vorderer Gosausee**, then take the footpath along the south side of the lake; a walk of about 1½hrs.

Note The path taken round the southern shore of the Hinterer Gosausee continues to the Adamek Hut at 2196m in another 2hrs, but on the north side of the lake a more challenging trail (path no:613) crosses lightly wooded limestone country to Hallstatt.

ROUTE 80
Steeg-Gosau (520m) –
Hallstatt (508m) – Steeg-Gosau

Location	North of Hallstatt
Grade	2
Distance	16km
Height gain	335m
Height loss	335m
Time	4hrs (+ ferry)

This is a walk of two parts. The first journeys along the eastern shore of the lovely Hallstätter See, the second returns along an historic trail (the Soleleitungsweg) created in 1607 to transport salt from the mine above Hallstatt to a refinery at Ebensee, 40km away. The two sections of the walk are linked by a romantic ferry ride across the lake to Hallstatt itself, and you should allow plenty of time to explore this remarkable little town which makes such an appealing halfway point.

Steeg-Gosau is the name of the railway station at the northern end of the Hallstätter See. It is served by trains from Bad Ischl and Bad Aussee. A regular *postbus* service also visits Steeg.

From the station walk down to the main road, bear left to cross the railway line, then turn right on a path signed to the *Hallstätter See Ostuferweg*. Curving round the edge of a meadow you reach a minor road where you turn right, soon gaining a first view of the lake, and walk into **Untersee**. Cross

DACHSTEINGEBIRGE: Route 80

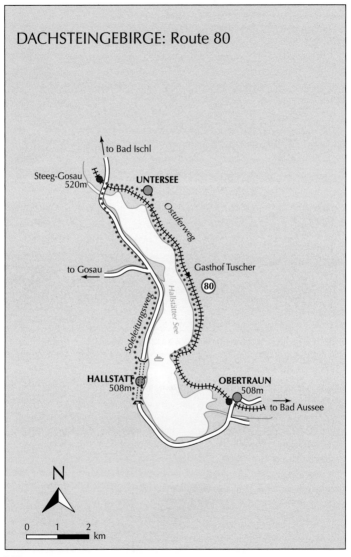

a stream and bear right, then left along a lane. Passing a few houses on the outskirts of the village, you then duck beneath the railway and wander alongside open meadows with the lake, its far end crowded with mountains.

When the lane ends, a footpath continues along the lakeside. Shortly after passing the Gosaumühle-Obersee railway halt, the path comes to **Gasthof Tuscher** (refreshments). Soon the path is directed away from the shoreline and up the slope to pass behind houses before returning to the lakeside.

At the point where the mountainside becomes too steep to allow a natural line for a footpath, a boardwalk overhanging the water has been created. This leads directly to the Hallstatt railway halt (1½–2hrs), where you walk along the platform, then down a tarmac path to a jetty for the hourly ferry to **Hallstatt**. (Buy a one-way ticket – *einfach*.)

When you are able to tear yourself away, wander along the waterfront to the bus park at Lahn, then turn right along a narrow road signed to the Salzbergwerk. Pass along the right-hand side of the funicular and walk up a narrow lane which climbs quite steeply, with views across the lake. After passing a wooden shelter and a path for the salt mine, you soon come to a fine waterfall.

On coming to a crossing path (with stairs leading from Hallstatt), climb a long flight of steps on the left leading into beechwoods. At the top of the steps bear right on a crossing path; this is the **Soleleitungsweg** which takes you almost all the way back to Steeg. In places the path has been carved from the rockface with a low, overhanging roof. Mind your head! Still among trees, the trail takes you high above Gosaumühle, then slopes downhill to cross a footbridge over the Gosaubach, and the road to Gosau. Eventually emerge from the beechwoods where the path becomes a track. Soon after, take a path cutting ahead just to the left of the track, and return to woodland. When the path forks, take the right branch and in another 2mins you arrive in the village of **Steeg**.

9 HOHE TAUERN

Lying south of the Kitzbüheler Alps, this extensive area of high mountains, numerous glaciers, spectacular waterfalls and deep valleys contains Austria's largest National Park. The Hohe Tauern is made up of several individual mountain groups, notably the Glockner, Venediger, Lasörling, Schoberg and Granatspitz, and is shared by no less than three provinces: Salzburg, Carinthia and Osttirol. Of the three major roads that cross the Hohe Tauern from north to south, only one – the Grossglockner Hochalpenstrasse – has been made over a high pass. In the west the highway running from Mittersill to Matrei penetrates the mountains via the 5km-long Felbertauern tunnel, while the easternmost road through the Gasteinertal uses a rail tunnel to transport vehicles from Bockstein to Mallnitz in the Ankogel group.

ACCESS AND INFORMATION	
Location	South of the Salzach river and north of the Gailtal and Lesachtal. The western boundary is the Austro–Italian border, while at the eastern end the mountains butt against the various groups of the Niedere Tauern.
Maps	Alpenvereinskarte 36 *Venedigergruppe*; 40 *Glocknergruppe*; 41 *Schobergruppe;* 42 *Sonnblick*; and 44 *Ankogel-Hochalmspitze* 1:25,000
	Freytag & Berndt *Nationalpark Hohe Tauern Wanderkarte*; WK191
	Gasteinertal, Wagrain, Grossarltarl; WK382 *Zell am See, Kaprun, Saalbach*; WK121 *Grossvenediger, Oberpinzgau*; WK122 *Grossglockner, Kaprun, Zell am See*; and WK193 *Sonnblick, Grossglocknerstrasse, Unterpinzgau* 1:50,000
	Kompass Wanderkarte 38 *Venedigergrupper, Oberpinzgau*; 39 *Glocknergruppe, Zell am See*; 40 *Gasteiner Tal, Goldberggruppe*; 46 *Matrei in Osttirol, Venedigergruppe*; 47 *Lienzer Dolomiten, Lesachtal*; 48 *Kals am Grossglockner*; 49 *Mallnitz, Obervellach*; and 50 *Heiligenblut, Grosskirchheim* 1:50,000
Bases	Badgastein, Kaprun, Matrei in Osttirol, Kals am Grossglockner
Information	Badgastein Spa & Tourism Association (e-mail: bad@gastein. com; website: www.badgastein.at)

Zell am See Tourismus (e-mail: welcome@zellamsee-kaprun. com; website: www.zellamsee-kaprun.com)

Infobüro Matrei in Osttirol (e-mail: matrei@hohetauern-osttirol. at; website: www.matreiinosttirol.at)

Infobüro Kals am Grossglockner (e-mail: kals@hohetauern-osttirol.at; website: www.kals.at)

National Park Region Carinthia, 9843 Grosskirchheim (website: www.tauernalpin.at)

National Park Region Osttirol, 9971 Matrei in Osttirol (website: www.hohetauern-osttirol.at)

Fereinregion National Park Hohe Tauern, 5730 Mittersill (website: www.nationalpark.at)

Access   Mainline rail services to Badgastein, and to Zell am See (for Kaprun). The nearest mainline train station for Matrei and Kals is Lienz. A regular bus service runs from Mittersill through the Felbertauern tunnel to Matrei. Good roads feed many side valleys, but note that the three routes that cross the range from north to south are all toll roads.

The Glockner group may be seen from the hills above Kaprun (Route 85)

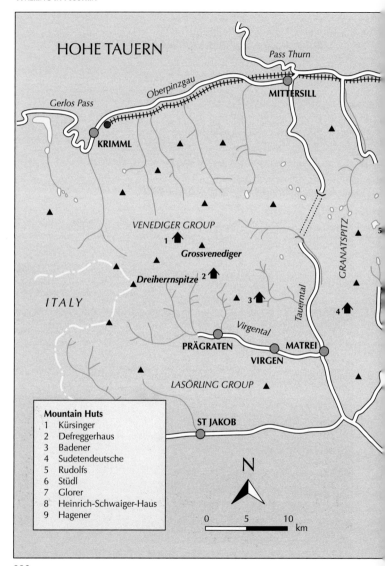

HOHE TAUERN

Pass Thurn

Gerlos Pass

Oberpinzgau

MITTERSILL

KRIMML

VENEDIGER GROUP

1

Grossvenediger

Dreiherrnspitze 2

3

ITALY

GRANATSPITZ

Tauerntal

5

4

Virgental

PRÄGRATEN

VIRGEN

MATREI

LASÖRLING GROUP

Mountain Huts
1 Kürsinger
2 Defreggerhaus
3 Badener
4 Sudetendeutsche
5 Rudolfs
6 Stüdl
7 Glorer
8 Heinrich-Schwaiger-Haus
9 Hagener

ST JAKOB

N

0   5   10
                    km

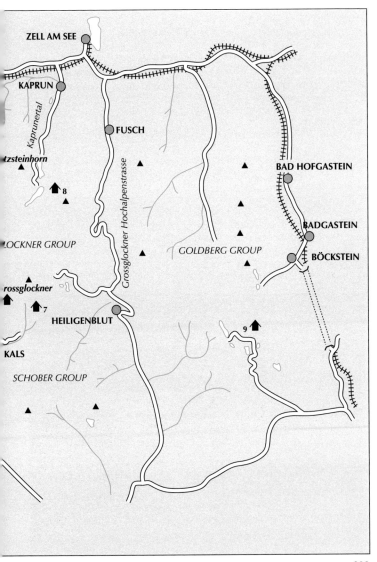

Forming the most westerly section of the Hohe Tauern range, the Venediger group contains Austria's largest area of glaciers after the Ötztal range, its highest peak being the 3674m Grossvenediger, standing head and shoulders above its neighbours. A series of comparatively short but deeply cut valleys flow northward from the Venediger in parallel lines to the Salzach. The best-known of these is that of the Krimmler Ache, with the celebrated Krimml Falls plunging 380m in three cascades, famed as one of the grandest waterfalls in the Eastern Alps.

On the south slope of the Venediger group the Virgental takes the snowmelt from the high mountains down to the Iseltal at Matrei. Matrei in Osttirol is arguably the best centre for mountain activities on this side of the Hohe Tauern, for it also has access to the Granatspitz, Glockner, Schober and Lasörling groups. The Granatspitz group is small and compact, a narrow group of peaks wedged between the Tauerntal and Dorfertal. Surprisingly its highest summit is not the mountain after which it takes its name, but the 3232m Grosser Muntanitz which stands almost due west of the Grossglockner, and is separated from it by the sparsely inhabited Dorfertal.

At 3798m the Grossglockner is Austria's crowning pinnacle, a graceful peak first climbed in 1800, and now a major attraction for hundreds of mountaineers every summer, and a focal point for the thousands of car and coach passengers who gaze at it from the Hochalpenstrasse several kilometres away to the east. Although the Grossglockner may be the loftiest peak in Austria, it is matched for grace and beauty by the 3203m Kitzsteinhorn – another sharply pinnacled summit rising from glaciers above Kaprun.

Badgastein

Kaprun is linked with Zell am See across the Salzach river valley, but while Zell is one of the major resorts of the Kitzbüheler Alps, the Kaprunertal is very much part of the Hohe Tauern's drainage system, and in its upper reaches two large reservoirs gather melt water from the Pasterze glacier on the Grossglockner, which helps generate electricity at a power plant above Kaprun. A trail alongside the topmost reservoir (the Mooserboden) continues across the 2639m Kapruner Törl to the huge Rudolfs Hut, used as an Alpine centre for training courses run by the ÖAV.

East of the Kaprunertal, the Fuschertal has been invaded by the Grossglockner Hochalpenstrasse, but the next valley (the Rauristal) which pushes into the Sonnblick group, has no traffic congestion, and the Gasteinertal towards the eastern end of the Hohe Tauern is green and pleasant and with good walking country above Badgastein on the edge of the Ankogel group.

But there's good walking to be had almost everywhere in the Hohe Tauern, while the National Park gives the district additional status and much-needed protection.

Main Bases

Badgastein (1002m) As its name suggests, Badgastein is a spa town that developed as one of Austria's best-known health resorts, and this reputation makes it the more surprising, perhaps, to discover that it has some fine walking country close by. Built on a series of terraces overlooking the low meadows of the Gasteinertal, the palatial hotels, spa buildings and shops give way to a thunderous waterfall that cascades in a burst of spray through the town. As well as the rather grand-looking hotels with their saunas and swimming pools, Badgastein also has more modest accommodation with *pensionen*, bed-and-breakfast establishments and private rooms to let; there are campsites in the lower valley near Bad Hofgastein. With a variety of shops, banks, restaurants and bars, the town also has chairlifts and gondolas on hillsides to the west and south, a railway station (trains from Salzburg), post office and a tourist office.

Kaprun (786m) A small resort village at the foot of the Kitzsteinhorn, and overlooked by a 12th-century castle, Kaprun is at its busiest in the ski season, although it developed in the 19th century as a mountaineering centre, boasting more than 100 local guides. It has a choice of hotels and *pensionen* (list available from the tourist office), a few shops and restaurants, but most facilities are to be found at Zell am See, 5km away across the Salzach valley.

Matrei in Osttirol (975m) Conveniently bypassed by the main north–south Felbertauern highway (buses from Mittersill in the north, and Lienz in the south), Matrei stands astride the Isel at the entrance to the Virgental. A neat and attractive little resort with plenty of accommodation of all standards, including a campsite (the Edengarten ☎ 4875 5111) just to the south, there's a variety of shops, banks with ATM, a Nationalparkhaus, post office and a tourist office in the village square.

Kals am Grossglockner (1325m) Nestling in the Kalsertal/Dorfertal, a tributary of the Iseltal which it joins below Matrei, Kals am Grossglockner comprises the neighbouring hamlets of Kals Lesach, Lana, Ködnitz, Berg and Grossdorf, and is an important

Kals am Grossglockner

centre for Grossglockner-based activity. Reached by bus from Matrei and Lienz, it has a reasonable amount of accommodation, including 4-star hotels, *gasthäuser*, apartments, private rooms and romantic *alm* huts to rent. The village has cafés, restaurants, a bank with ATM, a post office and tourist office. The nearest campsite is located upvalley at Taurer below the junction with the Teischnitz Tal.

Mountain Huts

Since there are more than 100 huts in the various groups that make up the Hohe Tauern district, the following list only includes those that are located in or near areas described in this chapter. Details of the remaining Tauern huts can be found in the 'green book' published in Munich by Rother, *Alpenvereins Hütten 1: Ostalpen*.

Badener Hut (2608m) Standing below the Frossnitzkees glacier high in the remote Frossnitztal, this Category I hut is visited by walkers tackling the Venediger Höhenweg. It has 17 beds and 31 dormitory places, but is staffed only from July until mid-September (☎ 0664 9155666).

Badgasteiner Hut (2465m) Also known as the Gamskarkogel Hut after the peak on which it stands above Bad Hofgastein, this small Category I hut has 7 beds and 19 places in its dormitory, and is manned from mid-June to mid-September (☎ 0664 3566707). It is gained by a walk of 4½hrs from Bad Hofgastein via the Rastötzenalm.

Bonn-Matreier Hut (2745m) Jointly owned by the DAV's Bonn section, and the Matrei section of the ÖAV, this comfortable Category I hut stands on the north flank of the Virgental and is reached by a walk of about 3½hrs from Virgen. With 13 beds and

40 dormitory places, it is fully staffed from the end of June until the end of September (☎ 04874 5577).

Clara Hut (2036m) A small, single-storey Category I hut with just 16 dormitory places, it stands below the Malham Spitzen in the Umbaltal, the upper reaches of the Virgental accessed from Matrei. It is manned from June to mid-October (☎ 0664 9758893).

Defreggerhaus (2962m) Owned by the ÖTK and located on the edge of the Rainer Kees south of the Grossvenediger, about 4½hrs from Hinterbichl, it has 30 beds and 42 places in its dormitories, and is fully staffed between Easter and Whitsun, and from July until the end of September (☎ 0676 9439145).

Eissee Hut (2520m) Standing near the head of the Timmeltal north of Prägraten, from which it is reached by a walk of 3½hrs, this small, privately owned hut is on the route of the Venediger Höhenweg. It has 14 beds and 31 dormitory places, and is manned from June to the end of September (☎ 0664 4606459).

Erzherzog-Johann Hut (3451m) The highest mountain hut in the Eastern Alps, it's perched on the Adlersruhe (Eagle's Rest) less than 350m below the summit of the Grossglockner. Despite its lofty position, and the fact that it has 10 beds and 120 dormitory places, the hut is invariably crowded with climbers in the high season. Gained in about 5hrs from the Lucknerhaus roadhead above Kals, it is manned from July to the end of September (☎ 04876 8500).

Essener Rostocker Hut (2207m) Large adjoining buildings with a total of 50 beds and 50 dormitory places, the huts belong to two different sections of the DAV and stand on the west flank of the Maurertal, about 2½–3hrs from Ströden in the Virgental; staffed from March until mid-May, and from mid-June until early October (☎ 04877 5101).

Glorer Hut (2651m) Standing on the windy saddle of the Bergertörl northeast of the Lucknerhaus roadhead above Kals am Grossglockner, the Glorer Hut was built by the DAV's Eichstätt section in 1887. A Category I hut, it has 50 dormitory places, and is staffed from June until October (☎ 0664 3032200).

Grünsee Hut (2235m) A small, timber-built Category I hut, it overlooks the tarn from which it takes its name, about 2½hrs northeast of the Matreier Tauernhaus, and is useful for walkers tackling the St Pöltner Ostweg. Owned by the ÖAV's Matrei section, the hut has just 20 dormitory spaces, but is unmanned (for the key, ☎ 04875 6169).

Hagener Hut (2448m) Reached by a walk of 4½hrs from Bockstein above Badgastein, this Category I hut is located on the Mallnitzer Tauern where the Goldberg group gives way to the Ankogel group. Built in 1912 by the Hagen section of the DAV, it has 14 beds and 27 dormitory places, and is staffed from July to mid-October (☎ 0664 4036697).

Hannoverhaus (2720m) Built on a ridge west of the 3252m Ankogel, on the National Park boundary about 6hrs from Bockstein, this Category II hut belongs to the DAV's Hanover section. With 35 beds and 35 dormitory places, it is fully staffed from July to the end of September (☎ 0664 1619367).

Hohe Tauern view on the way to the Palfnersee (Route 81)

Heinrich-Schwaiger-Haus (2802m) Standing almost 800m above the Mooserboden reservoir in the upper Kaprunertal, this Category I hut belongs to the Munich section of the DAV. With 14 beds and 64 dormitory places it is fully staffed from mid-June to the end of September, and may be reached by a steeply climbing path in 2½hrs from the reservoir (☎ 06547 8662).

Johannis Hut (2116m) This popular Category I hut stands on the east bank of the Dorferbach below the Grossvenediger, and is used by walkers on the Venediger Höhenweg, and by day visitors travelling through the valley from Hinterbichl. Owned by the DAV's Oberland section from Munich, it has 50 dormitory places, and is staffed from mid-March until mid-May, and from mid-June until the end of September (☎ 04877 5150).

Kalser Tauernhaus (1754m) Standing in the upper Dorfertal north of Kals am Grossglockner, this stone-built Category I hut belongs to the DAV's Mönchengladbach section. It has 22 beds and 21 dormitory places, and is manned from mid-June to the end of October (☎ 0664 9857090).

Kals-Matreier-Törlhaus (2207m) As its name suggests, the Kals-Matreier-Törl is a saddle on a ridge linking Kals am Grossglockner and Matrei in Osttirol. With use of the two-stage Goldried cableway from Matrei, this privately owned hut is reached without much effort in less than 1hr. It has just 14 beds and 9 dormitory places, but is very busy with day-visitors. It is fully staffed from July to the end of September (☎ 0664 9256806).

Karl-Fürst Hut (2629m) This small unmanned hut was built in 1936 at the head of the seemingly remote Landecktal west of the Sonnblick. It has spaces for 12 in its dormitory, and may be reached in about 5hrs from the Felbertauern highway, midway between the tunnel and Matrei.

Kleine Philipp-Reuter Hut (2677m) Built below the Austro–Italian border ridge at the head of the Umbaltal, 2½hrs from the Clara Hut, this unmanned hut has just 8 places and is permanently open.

Krefelder Hut (2293m) A large Category II hut, built in 1907 by the DAV's Krefeld section, it sits directly below the Kitzsteinhorn, just 30mins from the second station of the Glacierbahn gondola from Kaprun, and is popular with skiers. With 32 beds and 24 dormitory places, it is staffed all year round except in June and from mid-September to the beginning of November (☎ 06547 7780).

Krimmler Tauernhaus (1622m) Approached by a 3hr walk from Krimml, this privately owned hut stands in the valley of the Krimmler Ache, has 23 beds and 38 dormitory places and is staffed throughout the year (☎ 06564 8327).

Kürsinger Hut (2558m) Perfectly placed near the Obersulzbach glacier for the ascent of the Grossvenediger, this large Category I hut has 50 beds and 100 dormitory places, and is staffed from Easter until the end of September (☎ 06565 6450). Approached from Neukirchen in the Salzachtal by a long walk of 6–7hrs.

Luckner Hut (2241m) Privately owned, the Luckner Hut is set below the Grossglockner, an hour's easy walk from the roadhead at the Lucknerhaus. With 12 beds and 23 dormitory places, it is manned from June to mid-October (☎ 04876 8455).

Mindener Hut (2431m) This small unmanned hut with 12 dormitory places, is only open from mid-June to mid-September. It is located above Mallnitz, midway between the Hannoverhaus and Hagener Hut on the route of the Tauernhöhenweg.

Neue Prager Hut (2782m) Standing 300m above the unmanned Alte Prager Hut close to the Schlatenkees glacier on the eastern side of the Grossvenediger, this climbers' hut was built in 1904 by the DAV's Munich-based Oberland section. Reached by a trail from Innergschloss in 4hrs, it has 62 beds and 36 dormitory places, and is staffed from mid-March until mid-May, and from Whitsun until the end of September (☎ 04875 8840).

Niedersachsenhaus (2472m) Most conveniently reached from Sportgastein (about 6km from Bockstein) the Niedersachsenhaus lies midway between the upper Gasteinertal and the Hüttwinkltal. Originally built by the DAV's Hanover section in 1926, and rebuilt in 1987, it has 12 beds and 46 dormitory places, and is staffed from July to the end of September (☎ 0664 9143440).

Rudolfs Hut (2315m) This massive Berghotel standing by the Weissee northeast of the Granatspitze, is the Alpine centre used by the ÖAV for training courses. Despite the large number of places (200 beds and 53 dormitory places), accommodation is often at a premium in the summer, and advanced booking is essential (☎ 06563 8221). It is fully staffed throughout the year, except in May and from October to Christmas.

St Pöltner Hut (2481m) At the head of the Tauernbach tributary valley north of the Matreier Tauernhaus, this Category I hut was built in 1922 by the ÖAV's St Pölten section. It has 18 beds and 59 dormitory places, is staffed from the end of June until the end of September (☎ 06562 6265), and may be reached by a walk of about 3hrs from the Matreier Tauernhaus.

Sajat Hut (2600m) This privately owned hut stands on the north flank of the Virgental on the Prägraten Höhenweg. With 43 beds and 15 spaces in its dormitory, it's staffed from mid-May until the end of October (☎ 0664 5454460).

Salm Hut (2638m) Approached from the Stüdl Hut along the Stüdl-Weg, this hut lies on the south side of the Grossglockner above the Leitertal. Owned by the Vienna section of the ÖAV, it has 30 beds and 31 dormitory places, and is staffed from mid-June until the end of September (☎ 04824 2089).

Salzburger Hut (1860m) Owned by the ÖTK (the Austrian Touring Club), and standing on a very pleasant hillside below the Kitzsteinhorn, this small hut has only 5 dormitory places, but makes a useful refreshment stop for Kaprun-based walkers. It's manned from mid-June until the end of September.

Stüdl Hut (2802m) Originally built in 1868 by Johann Stüdl, one of the co-founders of the DAV, and rebuilt to a modern, half-dome design in 1996, this Category I hut is used as a base by climbers tackling the Grossglockner. Reached by a walk of about 3hrs from the Lucknerhaus roadhead above Kals, it stands on the Fanatscharte southsouthwest of the Glockner, has an indoor climbing wall, 114 dormitory places and is staffed from March until mid-May, then from the end of June until early October (☎ 04876 8209).

Sudetendeutsche Hut (2656m) Set beside a small tarn high above the Tauerntal in the Granatspitz group, this Category I hut is used by walkers tackling the splendid *höhenweg* which bears the name of the hut (about 4½hrs from the Matrei-Goldried cableway). Fully staffed from the end of June until the end of September, it has 23 beds and 32 dormitory places (☎ 04875 6466).

Warnsdorfer Hut (2336m) Standing below the Krimmler Kees at the head of the valley of the Krimmler Ache, about 2½hrs above the Krimmler Tauernhaus, this Category I hut has 13 beds and 61 dormitory places, and is fully staffed from mid-June to the end of September (☎ 06564 8241). It's well situated for climbs on the Dreiherrnspitze and Simony Spitzen, among others.

HOHE TAUERN NATIONAL PARK

Established in 1981, the Hohe Tauern National Park now covers an area of more than 1800 km², making it the largest nature reserve in Central Europe. A landscape of high mountains, deep valleys and scores of lakes and smaller tarns, its crowning glory is the 3798m Grossglockner,

National Park sign above Badgastein

but in addition there are over 300 summits in excess of 3000m within, or along, the park's boundaries, which embrace sections of three provinces: Carinthia, Salzburg and Osttirol. The heart of the park is still heavily glaciated, but as with every other Alpine region, the glaciers are in retreat. Yet they, and the gleaming snowfields, add an undoubted allure to the region's scenic qualities.

Though it has its wild and seemingly remote corners, the National Park is not a wilderness, for the valleys of the Hohe Tauern have been settled and worked for 5000 years, creating the neat mountain pastures and areas of cultivation that add a human dimension. One third of all Austrian plant species are found here, along with an abundant wildlife; according to park literature, approximately 10,000 species, which include the golden eagle, bearded vulture, ibex, chamois and marmot.

More than a dozen Information Centres and National Park Houses will be found in and around the park, with displays, information panels and plenty of literature available.

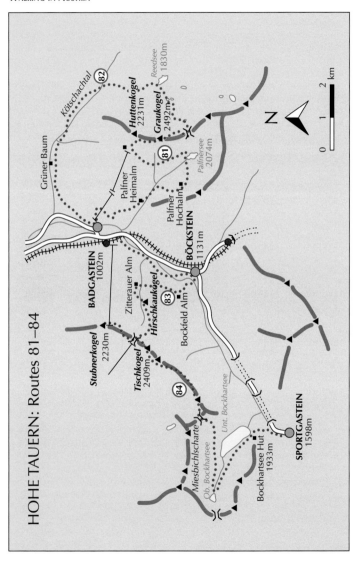

HOHE TAUERN: Routes 81–84

WALKS FROM BADGASTEIN

Located just outside the borders of the Hohe Tauern National Park, Badgastein overlooks the flat-bottomed Gasteinertal stretching to the north, while having easy access to both the upper valley stretching southwest to Böckstein and Sportgastein, and the lovely tributary valley of the Kötschachtal digging into the mountains southeast of the town. Easy walking can be found in each of these valleys, but more demanding routes venture onto the slopes of the surrounding mountains. A sample of four such routes is given below. To access these, the two-stage Graukogel chairlift and Stubnerkogel gondola are usefully employed. The first rises immediately above the town, the second rises to the west of Badgastein.

ROUTE 81

Badgastein (Graukokel lift: 1950m) –
Palfnersee (2074m) – Badgastein (1002m)

Location	Southeast of Badgastein
Grade	2
Distance	8km
Height gain	180m
Height loss	1088m
Time	4–4½hrs

The Graukogel chairlift removes the need for a steep woodland walk to begin this route, thereby making it acceptable to most active visitors to the Gasteinertal. Densely vegetated hillsides on the way to the Palfnersee are a riot of colour in the early summer when alpenroses are in flower, but later in the season, masses of bilberries threaten to delay the walk. Note that the descent from the Palfnersee is very steep in places.

On the way to the Palfnersee

From the top station of the Graukogel lift, make your way uphill along the right-hand side of a restaurant, to a ski hut 4mins beyond it where there's a path junction. Here you take the lower option to contour across the hillside heading southwest among masses of alpenrose and bilberry below the Graukogel. ◄

Ahead rise the snowy Tauern mountains, while in the north the view is of the Gasteinertal stretching far off.

After an initial steady traverse, the trail descends to cross a narrow stream, then rises to follow an undulating course curving left to gain a view into a hanging valley, before sloping downhill again to a trail junction at 1935m (40mins). Although the right branch goes to Badgastein via the Palfner Hochalm, we take the left fork to climb the stony, flower-starred hillside. On topping a rise from which you gain a view down to the Palfnersee, come to another junction and turn right.

This path cuts across rocky terrain along the northern edge of the **Palfnersee** (2074m, 1hr 20mins) to a second, much smaller tarn. Cross the outlet stream from this and continue across open countryside with Badgastein seen 1000m below. Over a grassy bluff descend to the ruins of **Palfner Hochalm** (1880m) which you reach about 40mins from the lake.

Go through a gate left of the hut ruins, and descend on a steep and narrow path over a heavily vegetated hillside, then into forest. About 1½hrs from the lake cross a stream on step-ping stones below a waterfall. The gradient now eases and the path shortly becomes a track leading to **Palfner Heimalm** (1473m). Beyond the *alm* the track goes through forest, and in another 10mins you bear left at a junction, and wind down-hill. The track becomes a surfaced road above a large farm, and shortly after passing the farm you come to another junc-tion and bear right towards Café Windischgrätzhöhe (1230m).

Opposite the café take an insignificant-looking path which descends left through a meadow and into forest. The way then twists easily down among trees to a road. Bear left, turn a corner, then descend the steps of the *Wasserfallweg* to reach the centre of **Badgastein**.

ROUTE 82
*Badgastein (Graukogel lift: 1950m) –
Graukogel (2492m) – Reedsee (1830m) –
Badgastein (1002m)*

Location	Southeast and east of Badgastein
Grade	3
Distance	12km
Height gain	547m
Height loss	1487m
Time	5½hrs

This very fine circular walk crosses two summits, visits a mountain lake and some tiny pools, and descends back to Badgastein through the Kötschachtal. It's quite a demanding route that calls for sure-footedness and a good head for heights – a slip from the Graukogel ridge could have serious consequences – and the need for settled weather is essential. Since the descent from the Graukogel summit to the Palfnerscharte should only be attempted by experienced mountain scramblers, an alternative route is described in the box below. Views are far-reaching and varied, and in early summer the alpine flowers are magnificent. Keep alert for a sight of chamois.

Walkers on the Huttenkogel

Leaving the Graukogel lift at its upper station, pass along the right-hand side of the restaurant, and 4mins later reach a ski hut. Two paths will be found to the right of this hut. While the route to the Graukogel takes the upper path (no 525), the lower option (no 527) is an easier alternative route which is described below.

Taking the upper path, this is shortly joined by another trail known as the *Dr Alfred Schwarz Weg*. Twisting steeply up the hillside you gain the 2231m summit of the **Hüttenkogel** about 40mins from the chairlift. To the south rises the impressive Graukogel which, like the Hüttenkogel, is topped by a large cross.

The route to the Graukogel slants along the right-hand (western) side of the ridge crest. Rarely does it venture onto the actual crest, and it is only on the final steep ascent that exposure is such that a fixed cable safeguard is required. The 2492m **Graukogel** summit is reached about 50mins from the Hüttenkogel, and the panoramic view is worth savouring. The Hohe Tauern National Park boundary crosses the summit, and a sea of peaks fills the southern horizon, while the Kötschachtal lies enticingly below to the east.

The descent to the Palfnerscharte is exposed for much of the way (caution), going along the ridge crest, or close to it, often guided by waymarks with no other sign of a path. After about 40mins the route cuts down the left side of the ridge and soon improves. Finally, wander over broad slopes to gain the saddle of the **Palfnerscharte** (2321m) about 2hrs 45mins from the chairlift.

ALTERNATIVE ROUTE TO THE PALFNERSCHARTE

From the ski hut path junction, take the lower option (no 527) which takes you across a hillside carpeted with alpenrose and bilberry and pitted with tiny pools. After an initial contour you then descend about 20m among dwarf pine, after which there's a change in vegetation with alder scrub dominating. In 40mins the path forks at 1935m. Take the upper trail, climbing steeply at times among dwarf pine and alpenrose, then top a rise at about 2090m where there's another path junction by a large boulder. Bear left and resume the ascent to the **Palfnerscharte** which you gain about 1hr 45mins from the Graukogel chairlift.

On the east side of the saddle, slant leftwards to pass round the western end of the tiny **Windschursee** tarn, then cross a grassy bluff to find the green Reedsee lying about 400m below. ▸ About 45mins below the pass you come to an idyllic shallow groove in which there's a stream flowing from two small pools, unseen from here. The stream is crossed on stepping stones, then you bear left (should you wish to visit the pools, turn right for about 2mins), and descend steeply to the **Reedsee** (1830m). This is reached about 45mins after leaving the Palfnerscharte.

The way to the lake twists down from one level to the next, with alpine flowers becoming more prolific as you lose height.

Backed by the Tischlerkarkogel ridge, the **Reedsee** is set in a beautiful pine-rimmed hollow. A timber-built hut stands on its southeastern shore.

Bear left just above the lake, and soon after descend into forest. At times the path is steep, and after a while you can see the **Kötschachtal** track below. The way becomes even steeper, but eventually you reach the floor of the valley where you then wander downstream on the left bank of the Kötschachbach. Before long a bridge takes you over to the right bank (1½hrs from the Reedsee) where you walk down the dirt road to Jausenstation Himmelwand (refreshments) and continue to the hamlet of **Grüner Baum** (1066m, 4hrs 45mins, accommodation and refreshments).

Continue downvalley on a footpath which crosses to the left of the road by Hotel Stubnerhof. This path is the Kaiser Wilhelm Promenade, and it leads all the way to the centre of **Badgastein** in about 40mins from Grüner Baum.

ROUTE 83

Badgastein (Stubnerkogel: 2230m) –
Böckstein (1131m) – Badgastein (1002m)

Location	Southwest of Badgastein
Grade	2–3
Distance	9km
Height loss	1225m
Time	3hrs

A ridge walk, gained by gondola lift, followed by a long and sometimes steep descent over pastures and through forest, brings this route to the one-time gold mining village of Böckstein.

Ride the gondola lift to the **Stubnerkogel**, a 16min ride which delivers you a short distance below the summit. On leaving the top station there are two tracks and a footpath. The upper track cuts just below the ridge and leads to a ski lift; the lower track descends to the middle station, while the footpath, which we take, goes along the ridge crest to a viewpoint with an orientation table. Among the many mountains in view the Grossglockner can be seen to the west.

From the orientation table the path then descends to join the upper track where you bear right and wander along the west side of the ridge. Take a path which breaks from the track to climb along the ridge itself, and in 15mins come to a path junction just above the top of a ski tow at the Zitterauer Scharte.

The Stubnerkogel gondola

LONGER WALK VIA THE TISCHKOGEL AND ZITTERAUER TISCH

Continue along the ridge, ignoring another path (Dr Reichert-Weg) which breaks to the right. After a while the ridge path goes along the left flank, then crosses to the right side of the ridge before rising steeply to the cross-marked summit of the **Tischkogel** (2409m, 1hr). The 2461m **Zitterauer Tisch** is gained in a further 20mins. Return to the Tischkogel and take a steep path which descends a grassy spur on the east slope (**caution on this descent**) to join the main walk at the **Zitterauer Alm**.

Branch left on the trail signed to Böckfeld Alm and Zitterauer Alm. The main path crosses rough grass slopes below the east face of the Tischkogel, then rises to cross a narrow spur at 2215m. Bear left and descend this grassy spur which plunges steeply on either side. Across the valley the deep cleft of the Aulauftal, headed by the Ankogel, looks very impressive. To the right the headwall of the Nassfelder Tal is splashed with snow and ice, while the rooftops of Böckstein lie more than 1000m below.

On reaching an avalanche fence continue down the right-hand side, and just before a bluff covered with dwarf pine and marked by a large wooden cross (**Hirschkaukogel**: 2002m), descend left into a vegetated basin.

The **Hirschkaukogel** cross was erected in memory of a mountaineer killed in the Pamirs while climbing Pik Communism.

At the foot of the slope bear right on a path which shortly descends to the **Zitterauer Alm** (1872m, 50mins, refreshments) standing beside a track coming from the middle station of the gondola. Immediately to the right of the *alm* building take the path of the Böcksteiner Höhenweg which soon enters forest. After an initial contour, the forest path begins its descent; at first gently, then more steeply through alder scrub and over meadows, then back into forest again. In 1hr 45mins come to **Böckfeld Alm** (1536m, refreshments) and a broader path.

Bear left and swing down through more forest, less steeply than before, to arrive in **Böckstein** about 2hrs from the start of the walk. This is an attractive place with pleasant buildings around a garden square in the middle of which there's a fountain. Turn left at the far end of Hotel Rader, then left again on the Kaiserin Elisabeth Panoramaweg below a circular church. The service road eventually gives way to a broad gravel path on the left bank of the Gasteiner Ache, which leads back to **Badgastein**.

ROUTE 84

Badgastein (Stubnerkogel: 2230m) – Oberer
Bockhartsee (2070m) – Sportgastein (1598m)

Location	Southwest of Badgastein
Grade	3
Distance	12km
Height gain	122m
Height loss	754m
Time	5hrs (+ bus from Sportgastein)

A high route which leads to two mountain lakes, giving lovely views to big snow-capped mountains and charming valleys. It's reasonably demanding, and should only be attempted in settled conditions. Please note that currently there's only one bus in the afternoon from Sportgastein (Nassfeld) to Badgastein, so you are advised to check the timetable before setting out. Miss it, and you'll have another 8km or so to walk!

Take an early lift on the Stubnerkogelbahn gondola to the start of the walk. Out of the gondola station follow directions given for Route 83 as far as the path junction at the Zitterauer Scharte where the Dr Reichart-Weg breaks to the right in the 'longer walk' option (25–30mins). Bear right on this path to traverse the north and west flanks of the Zitterauer Tisch.
▶ Reach a rocky spur, then twist up it to a high point at 2285m marked by a cairn (55mins). Although narrow, the path is well waymarked across rocks.

About 1hr 15mins from the start come onto the Ortbergschartl, a 2273m saddle on the ridge coming from the Zitterauer Tisch. The path now cuts round the north side of the craggy Ortberg, then curves leftward with the **Miesbichlscharte** saddle ahead. Rocks are traded for grass slopes on the brief climb to this pass at 2237m. Ahead stands a long wall of snow-draped mountains of the Goldberg group.

With the Unterer Bockhartsee coming into view, descend to a fork in the path (3mins from the Miesbichlscharte) and

Rich in alpine flowers growing among the shale and rocks, the trail is slightly exposed in places, but fixed cables safeguard the way.

Peaks of the Goldberg group, seen from the Zimburgweg

branch right along the Zimburgweg which makes a traverse across the steep headwall of the hanging valley. Narrow and exposed, the path is flanked by lovely alpine flowers, and with views down the length of the lake to the Weissenbachtal, a gentle pastoral valley southeast of Sportgastein.

Continue heading west on an undulating trail, mostly on grass slopes, but later over rocks. In 2hrs 15mins come to a high point of 2215m and continue the traverse among alpenroses before sloping downhill towards the valley's upper basin in which lies the Oberer Bockhartsee. Come to a path junction in 2hrs 45mins. While the left branch goes down to the lower lake, we continue upvalley for another 15mins to reach the **Oberer Bockhartsee** which lies at 2070m. The Bockhartscharte saddle is seen about 150m above the lake, while both above and below the lake there are various signs of past mining work.

The way soon improves and becomes a delightful trail accompanying the stream until it cascades to the lower lake.

Cross the lake's outlet stream and descend on its right-hand side. ◄ The path then keeps several metres above the shoreline of the **Unterer Bockhartsee**, at the far end of which you come onto a track (4hrs). Just 2mins away to the right stands the **Bockhartsee Hut** (1933m, refreshments). Unless you need refreshments, walk ahead along the path which passes just below the hut, and zigzags downhill, becoming more narrow and steep as height is lost. This brings you onto a track which leads directly to Alpengasthaus Valerie at **Sportgastein**. The bus stop for Badgastein is located by the Goldbergbahn.

OTHER ROUTES FROM BADGASTEIN

There's no shortage of walking possibilities in the countryside around Badgastein, ranging from short valley routes suitable for families with young children, to longer and more challenging routes that cross high passes or reach non-technical summits. The following is a small sample, but careful study of the local maps will reveal many more.

- A gentle 2½hr walk to **Bad Hofgastein** along the Martin Lodinger Höhenweg, also known as the Gasteiner Höhenweg, leads through meadows on the east side of the valley, and makes a pleasant half-day outing.

- The **Kötschachtal** is definitely worth exploring (it was visited on Route 82), and the most obvious route to take is the Kaiser Wilhelm Promenade which begins in Badgastein and goes as far as the hotel hamlet of Grüner Baum. From there a continuing route (track/dirt road) leads to the **Alpenhaus Prossau** at 1278m under the valley's headwall (2½hrs from Badgastein).

- From the top of the Stubnerkogel gondola a 5½–6hr trek extends Route 84 beyond the Oberer Bockhartsee to the Bockhartscharte, then heads south on the Senator-Beindorf-Weg to the **Niedersachsenhaus**. A route for strong walkers only.

- A further option from the Niedersachsenhaus is to make the 4hr ascent of the 3106m **Hoher Sonnblick** which rises to the west in the Goldberg group. There's a hut, the **Zittelhaus**, built in a stunning position on the summit ridge, which is manned from the end of June to the end of September, with 26 beds and 57 dormitory places (☎ 06544 6412).

- Reached in about 6hrs from Böckstein via the 2459m Korntauern (Hoher Tauern) pass, the **Hannoverhaus** makes a worthwhile destination. From it the **Ankogel** (3252m) may be climbed in 3hrs.

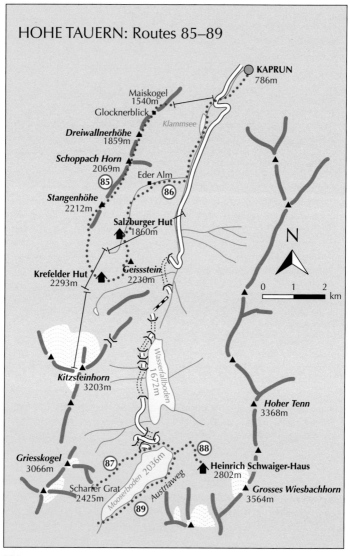

HOHE TAUERN: Routes 85–89

KAPRUN
786m

Maiskogel
1540m
Glocknerblick
Klammsee

Dreiwallnerhöhe
1859m

Schoppach Horn
2069m

(85)

Eder Alm

(86)

Stangenhöhe
2212m

Salzburger Hut
1860m

Geissstein
2230m

Krefelder Hut
2293m

N

0   1   2
km

Wasserfallboden
1672m

Kitzsteinhorn
3203m

Hoher Tenn
3368m

(88)

Griesskogel
3066m

(87)

Heinrich Schwaiger-Haus
2802m

Mooserboden 2036m

Scharfer Grat
2425m

Austriaweg

Grosses Wiesbachhorn
3564m

(89)

WALKS FROM KAPRUN

Wasserfallboden reservoir, seen from the Sedlgrat trail (Route 87)

Modest in size and facilities, Kaprun can nonetheless reward visiting walkers with a few truly worthwhile outings. Together with Zell am See across the Salzach valley at the foot of the Kitzbüheler Alps, the village forms part of the so-called 'Europa-Sport-Region'. The Kaprunertal which stretches to the south digs into the Hohe Tauern range in spectacular fashion, its upper reaches containing two large reservoirs flanked by lofty, steep-walled 3000m mountains. An undemanding walk entices alongside the higher of the two lakes; others venture onto hillsides above it, while a very fine ridge walk makes the most of the lower hills between Kaprun and the Kitzsteinhorn. To access some of the higher walks cable cars swing visitors out of the valley to the Maiskogel above Kaprun, and onto the slopes of the Kitzsteinhorn further upvalley, where skiing takes place throughout the year. Buses run frequently through the valley, with a special service operating between the Kesselfall Alpenhaus and the Mooserboden dam via two buses and an open lift platform.

ROUTE 85

*Kaprun (Maiskogel: 1540m) –
Krefelder Hut (2293m)*

Location	Southwest of Kaprun
Grade	2–3
Distance	10km
Height gain	892m
Height loss	45m
Time	4hrs

By using the Maiskogel cable car at the start of the day, plenty of time is then allowed to enjoy to the full this airy ridge walk along the Alexander-Enzinger-Weg, which is one of the classic routes of the Kaprunertal. Major summits of the Hohe Tauern are on show for much of the way, including the Grossglockner, and the walk ends at a mountain hut at the foot of the shapely Kitzsteinhorn. Options for a return to Kaprun are given at the end of the route description.

From the top station of the **Maiskogel** cable car, wander along a broad track signed to the Glocknerblick. It winds along the forested hillside and brings you to the **Alpengasthaus Glocknerblick** (1670m, refreshments) in just 20mins. As the name implies, you can see the top of the Grossglockner which is due south from here. Now follow the footpath which strikes ahead uphill among trees. When it forks 3mins later, take the left branch and rise steadily through forest, then come onto a grass crest by a ski tow. The way now skirts round the left side of the ridge, then returns to the crest to gain the top of the 1859m **Dreiwallnerhöhe** on which there's a small wooden cross.

Descend about 15m to a grass saddle, then climb towards another grass-covered crown of the ridge with snow-peaks of the Glockner group on show at the head of the Kaprunertal. The **Schoppach Horn** (2069m, 1hr 45mins) is gained about 50mins from the Dreiwallnerhöhe, and this too is topped by a wooden cross.

▸ The path avoids a few minor tops by cutting along the left-hand side of the ridge, then slopes down to a saddle at 2055m. Climbing from this saddle brings you onto the highest part of the ridge at the 2212m **Stangenhöhe**. This is not so much a summit as a very narrow section of ridge with fixed cable safeguard. Beyond this the path abandons the ridge crest and slants down the left flank, and goes from grass slopes into a more stony landscape in which old slips of snow sometimes remain into late summer, and there are several streams to cross.

Along the next stretch of ridge, the crest narrows, and is rich in alpine flowers.

In a little over 3hrs come to a large cairn beside the trail marking a junction. The left branch cuts down to the Salzburger Hut, unseen from here, but we continue ahead, now with the Krefelder Hut on show to the south. Crossing more streams and snow patches, in another 40–45mins the well-defined path brings you to the large **Krefelder Hut** (2293m, accommodation and refreshments), with the Kitzsteinhorn soaring above, but with more than a dozen assorted cableways and ski tows sadly disfiguring the landscape.

Major peaks of the Hohe Tauern are on show from the ridge leading to the Krefelder Hut

To return to Kaprun you have three main options:

• walk up to the Alpincenter (40mins) and ride the Gletscherbahn gondola down to the valley;

• walk down to the Gletscherbahn's middle station, located close to the Salzburger Hut in 1hr, and take a gondola from there;

• descend all the way to Kaprun by following Route 86 below (4hrs).

ROUTE 86
Krefelder Hut (2293m) –
Salzburger Hut (1860m) – Kaprun (786m)

Location	Southwest of Kaprun
Grade	2–3
Distance	10km
Height loss	1507m
Time	4hrs

A long and steady descent, with some steep sections, makes this a fitting conclusion to Route 85. But it's also a fine walk in its own right, and one to commend to walkers who might have ridden the Gletscherbahn gondola to sample the Kitzsteinhorn at close quarters, or who have made a visit to the Alpincenter.

From the **Krefelder Hut** descend on path no 711 from which you have views of Kaprun, Zell am See and the distant group of the Steinernes Meer which carries the Austro–Bavarian border. Heading towards the shark's fin of the Geissstein a sudden direct view is gained of high mountains walling the upper reaches of the Kaprunertal, but you then cut round the **Geissstein**'s left (west) flank among alpenroses before

descending in zigzags to reach the **Salzburger Hut** (1860m, 1hr, accommodation and refreshments).

The path to the Salzburger Hut skirts round the Geissstein

Note An alternative path cuts away from the main route to make the non-technical ascent of the 2230m Geissstein. Waymarked blue and white, the trail leads to the summit in about 20mins.

Pass along the left-hand side of the hut into the charming valley of the Grubbach, among alpenrose and bilberry, with a lovely stream cascading in a series of brief steps – and a waterfall spraying from the western slope. The path deserts the stream to descend steeply into a level area with magnificent views, and the remains of an old barn. Beyond this the path resumes its steep descent, comes to a shingle-walled hut perched on a spur, then down to the **Eder Alm** (1420m, 1hr 50mins, refreshments).

Below the *alm* the way twists steeply down through forest, but then the gradient is eased with long switchbacks. At the foot of the descent you emerge from the forest among pastures. The path takes you to a farm where you turn left along a track which leads to a bridge over the Kapruner Ache (3hrs). Immediately before the bridge, cross a stile on the

359

left and follow the river downstream for about 1hr to reach **Kaprun** via the attractive green Klammsee.

Note Instead of following the river all the way to Kaprun, an alternative option is to cross the bridge to **Gasthof Wüstlau** where there's a bus stop for Kaprun-bound buses.

ROUTE 87

Kaprun (Mooserboden: 2036m) –
Scharfer Grat (2425m)

Location	South of Kaprun
Grade	2
Distance	2.5km (one way)
Height gain	389m
Time	2hrs (+1–1½hrs return)

South of Kaprun, at the upper end of the Kaprunertal on the edge of the National Park, lie two large reservoirs, the Wasserfallboden at 1672m, and the higher Mooserboden. Both are flanked by high mountains, but the Mooserboden's backdrop is truly spectacular. No wonder it's such a magnet for tourists. A number of short walks are accessible from the bus terminal at the Mooserboden dam; arguably the best of the bunch is that which climbs to the Scharfer Grat viewpoint. Although short, it would be worth taking a picnic lunch and making a day of it, for it would be so easy to spend several hours simply enjoying the views!

Public buses make the 6km journey from Kaprun to the Kesselfall Alpenhaus roadhead, where there's plenty of free parking for visitors with their own transport. From there buses continue through a tunnel to the bottom station of the Lärchwand funicular, a huge lift platform capable of transporting 185 passengers up a slope to gain 430m. A second bus then takes you through more tunnels alongside and above the Wasserfallboden reservoir, eventually arriving at the Mooserboden dam where there's a restaurant, the Heidnische Kirche, and an information centre telling the history of the Tauernkraft pumped storage scheme.

The path to take is a broad one which starts at the western side of the bus terminal, and is signed as the *Panoramaweg Sedlgrat*. Several other paths soon break from it, and as you gain height the trail becomes narrower, while the gradient steepens as it twists up a flower-rich hillside from where views grow increasingly dramatic.

Having gained almost 300m, about 1hr from the reservoir you come to a sign announcing the Hohe Tauern National Park boundary. Just beyond this there's a trail junction where you ignore the right-hand option and continue ahead, the slope less steep now. The way is obvious, although care needs to be exercised if there is snow still lying. The **Scharfer Grat** viewpoint is reached in a little under 1hr from the National Park's boundary. At 2425m this is the culminating point of the Sedlgrat. From it you have a splendid grandstand view of the Kaprunertal's headwall where the Karlinger Kees glacier hangs against the flank of the Hohe Riffl, while across the valley to the east the imposing Grosses Wiesbachhorn (3564m) dominates. Climbed in the late 18th century, this was the first major summit in the Eastern Alps to be won.

Allow a little over an hour for a return to the reservoir.

Snowpeaks capture your attention throughout the walk along the Sedlgrat

Note The right-hand path breaking away beyond the National Park's boundary offers an uncomplicated ascent up a broad ridge to the 2669m **Kleiner Griesskogel** in 1hr 15mins. A second summit may also be gained from the Scharfer Grat. This is the 3066m **Griesskogel** (sometimes known as the Grosses Griesskogel to avoid confusion with the lower summit). The route for this turns sharply to the right at the Scharfer Grat to climb the narrowing grat or ridge, with some scrambling in the upper section, before coming onto the summit, a satellite peak of the great pyramid of the Hocheiser which rises in the southwest.

ROUTE 88

Kaprun (Mooserboden: 2036m) –
Heinrich-Schwaiger-Haus (2802m)

Location	South of Kaprun, east of the Mooserboden reservoir
Grade	2–3
Distance	2.5km (one way)
Height gain	766m
Time	2½hrs (+1½–2hrs return)

Standing on a little terrace below the Grosses Wiesbachhorn with spectacular views, the Heinrich-Schwaiger-Haus is understandably popular with day visitors, despite the steepness of the approach. It was built in 1902 by the Munich section of the DAV, and makes an obvious goal for a walk.

Cross the Mooserboden dam, which is in two sections, and at the eastern end of the second of these, the Drossen dam, branch left. Moments later fork right at a path junction. (The left branch here is the Max-Hirschel-Weg, no 723, which makes a long and sometimes exposed route to the Gleiwitzer Hut.) The Schwaiger Haus route is clearly marked and is no 718.

Very shortly it twists left and makes a rising traverse heading northeast, before swinging right to climb in switchbacks to the southeast. There are no alternatives, and it brings you directly to the **Heinrich-Schwaiger-Haus** in a little under 2½hrs.

ROUTE 89

Kaprun (Mooserboden: 2036m) –
Austriaweg (2040m)

Location	South of Kaprun
Grade	1
Distance	5km (one way)
Height gain	39m
Time	1½hrs (+1½hrs return)

The Austriaweg is an easy and very popular trail which goes along the east side of the Mooserboden reservoir, eventually crossing the Kapruner Törl col in the valley's headwall and continuing to the Rudolfs Hut. So far as this walk is concerned, though, we will go only as far as the southern end of the lake. It's an undemanding but scenically rewarding outing, especially for flower lovers.

From the bus terminal by the Heidnische Kirch restaurant, cross the two-section Mooserboden dam, and at the eastern end keep to the main path which aims south below cliffs and soon brings you to the mouth of a hanging valley topped by the 3419m Klockerin, a peak formerly known as the Glockerin for its distinctive bell-shaped summit. Old snow patches often cover the path at this point, but the way soon begins to rise in order to cross an alder-covered bluff at 2075m; the highest part of the walk.

On the other side of the bluff a fixed cable offers support on a brief section then, skirting above the lake, you cross several glacial streams either on stepping stones or simple plank footbridges, while ice cliffs of the Bärenkopfkees and Schwarzköpflkees glaciers can be seen above to the left. ▶

At the head of the valley, the Hocheiser, Kleine Eiser and Hohe Riffl call for your attention.

Headwall of the Kaprunertal, seen from the Mooserboden dam

In a little under 1½hrs from the start, path no 717 breaks away to the left, heading for the Riffeltor, a high glacier pass over which climbers make their way to the Oberwalder Hut by the Pasterzen Kees. And shortly after passing this junction the hanging Karlinger Kees glacier appears directly ahead. The path then slopes down to a footbridge spanning the glacial torrent, on the far side of which an area of grassland, with alder scrub and scattered rocks, makes this as good a place as any to stop and absorb the wild beauty of the scene. If you sit quietly it's quite possible that you could see marmot and chamois here.

ROUTE 90

Hut to Hut across the Glockner Group

Location	North to south, from Kaprun to Heiligenblut
Grade	3
Distance	68km
Highest point	Stüdl Hut (2802m)
Start	Kaprun (Maiskogel: 1540m)
Finish	Heiligenblut (1288m)
Time	6–7 days

This is not an officially recognised tour, but it follows an obvious north–south line across the central and highest part of the Hohe Tauern. Apart from a few fairly short stretches where the route calls for steady hand- and footwork and a good head for heights, the demands are not great. But the scenery is first-class.

Day 1 The tour begins by riding the Maiskogelbahn cable car from the south side of Kaprun up to the Maiskogel Alm, thereby saving an initial climb (mostly on service roads) of more than 750m. ▸ Fully described above as Route 85, the 4hr trek ends at the **Krefelder Hut** (2293m) below the ice-plastered **Kitzsteinhorn**.

    Day 2 On this stage, the route makes an airy descending traverse of the Kitzsteinhorn's east flank on the way to the Mooserboden reservoir. But first, on leaving the **Krefelder Hut**, you need to climb for 40mins to the Alpincenter cableway station, where path no 726 is joined. This continues to gain height in order to cross the 2689m Kammer Scharte, after which the trail teeters across the steep mountainside hundreds of metres above the Wasserfallboden reservoir. Making the descending traverse mentioned above, the way eventually comes to the Fürthermoar Alm where refreshments can be had. The alm is situated close to the road, but our path ignores this and eases through a flower-filled meadow before climbing steeply and eventually arriving at the Mooserboden dam, about 3½hrs from the Krefelder Hut.

The route then heads roughly southward along the Alexander-Enzinger-Weg, a ridge walk that takes in several minor summits and enjoys excellent high mountain views almost every step of the way.

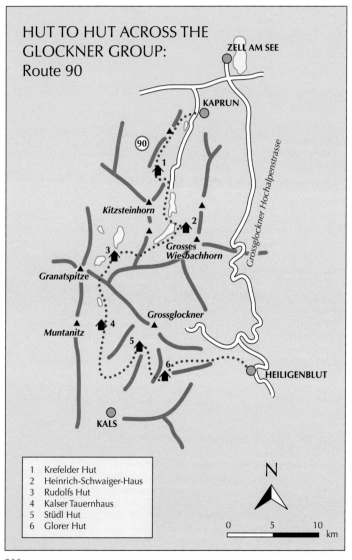

HUT TO HUT ACROSS THE GLOCKNER GROUP:
Route 90

ZELL AM SEE

KAPRUN

(90)

Kitzsteinhorn

1

2

Grosses Wiesbachhorn

3

Granatspitze

Grossglocker

Grossglockner Hochalpenstrasse

4

Muntanitz

5

6

HEILIGENBLUT

KALS

1	Krefelder Hut
2	Heinrich-Schwaiger-Haus
3	Rudolfs Hut
4	Kalser Tauernhaus
5	Stüdl Hut
6	Glorer Hut

N

0   5   10
km

Kapruner Törl, from the Austriaweg

From here a 2½hr climb leads to the **Heinrich-Schwaiger-Haus**, built on a terrace of hillside at 2802m, and described in Route 88.

Day 3 A steep return back down to the Mooserboden reservoir starts the day, but from the Drossen dam you join the Austriaweg (Route 89) along the east shore of the lake, and at its southern end continue up through the Wintergasse's hanging valley to reach the col at its head. This is the 2639m Kapruner Törl on the ridge linking the Kleine Eiser in the north, with the Torkopf to the southeast. On the far side the Austriaweg makes an anti-clockwise curve round the Übelkar, then descends for 250m to the southern end of another reservoir, the Tauernmoossee. The way now cuts sharply back to the southwest, and climbs to the large and busy **Rudolfs Hut** (2315m), reached about 6hrs after setting out from the Schwaiger Haus.

Day 4 Although this is the shortest stage so far, it has a reputation for being somewhat difficult in poor visibility, especially on the initial descent from the Kalser Tauern col. With the Weisssee below to the right (west) make your way from the Rudolfs Hut to the bottom of the Medelz chairlift, and across a small bridge join path no 711 which leads to the Kalser Tauern, soon breaking away from the path which makes a circular tour of the lake. On the way up into the little hanging valley with the pass at its head, ignore another trail cutting to the right, and continue up the western side of the valley to gain the 2518m Kalser Tauern (1hr), where you re-enter the Hohe Tauern National Park. (Given good conditions, the ascent of the 2760m Medelzkopf which rises to the southeast, could be worth considering – 1hr from the pass.) On the south side of the pass descend through rocky outcrops, twisting southwest down to a junction at Erdiges Eck, about 240m below. Take the left branch and follow a stream flowing down to the little Dorfer See, and beyond the lake continue downhill until you reach the **Kalser Tauernhaus** (1754m), about 3½hrs from the Rudolfs Hut. Set among meadows and trees of the Beheimeben Alm in the upper reaches of the Dorfertal, the Tauernhaus is a complete contrast to the Rudolfs Hut, but such contrasts are the very essence of hut touring.

Day 5 Leaving the **Tauernhaus** head downvalley along the track on the east side of the Seebach stream. Mountains walling the west side of the valley belong to the Granatspitz group, while the Glockner group spreads off to the east. After about 1hr the way forks. The right branch (straight ahead) goes down through the gorge of the Dabaklamm, while the left fork is perhaps better suited for our purposes, for it soon comes onto a road at a small parking area, a short distance from which you come to the Gasthof Moa-Alm. Below this, after going round two hairpins, the road digs into the mouth of the Teischnitztal. At the next hairpin, leave the road on a footpath signed to the Stüdl Hut. A long and fairly arduous walk now leads up through this tributary valley and finally reaches the **Stüdl Hut**, perched upon the Fanatscharte at 2802m, about 3½hrs from the road. The Grossglockner rises to the northeast.

Day 6 Since it takes only 2½hrs or so to trek from the Stüdl Hut to the Glorer Hut, it should be feasible to continue as far as Heiligenblut (6½hrs) in the Mölltal, where the tour ends. However, the scenery is so spectacular here, with the Grossglockner towering over everything, that a short morning's walk could so easily stretch into a full day of pleasure – if you have the time to spare, that is. Out of the **Stüdl Hut** descend southeastwards for about 250m below the Grossglockner into the head of the Ködnitztal, until you come to a marked junction at 2550m. Here you leave the descending path and branch left for the Salm and Glorer Huts. The way now crosses a stream and climbs steeply to a minor ridge and a second path junction with another fine view of the Glockner to the north. From here the path is easy-angled for a while, but later the route becomes more tricky and demanding; especially after contouring across a steep slope of shale and slate below the Pfortscharte where the route to the Salm Hut parts company with ours. A long section of narrow ledges, tight gullies and rock scrambling with considerable exposure is safeguarded with fixed cables and a wooden ladder, before you climb to the easy Medlscharte, from which you can see the **Glorer Hut** (2651m) for the first time. A 15min stroll takes you to it.

Day 7 On this final stage of the tour, the route is downhill almost every step of the way, with a difference in altitude between the Glorer Hut and Heiligenblut of around 1350m. Out of the hut turn right and follow path no 714 away from the Berger Törl, descending the right flank of the little tributary valley of the Glatzbach which drains into the Leitertal. Just below the confluence of these two valleys, the path crosses to the north bank of the Leiterbach, goes up the slope a short way to join path no 919 from the Salm Hut, then continues downvalley, on the left bank almost all the way to the Mölltal. In the mouth of the Leitertal, recross the stream to the right bank, then cut round the hillside to the mouth of the Gössnitztal, where you then descend to **Heiligenblut** (1288m) at the foot of the Grossglockner Hochalpenstrasse.

Note The village has hotel, pension and bed-and-breakfast accommodation, and 3 buses run daily to Lienz.

OTHER ROUTES FROM KAPRUN

The few routes described above are arguably the best of the bunch, but that's not to say they are the only walks worth considering.

- In the Kaprunertal itself a short, pleasant and undemanding route accompanies the Kapruner Ache upstream, explores the gorge of the **Sigmund Thun Klamm** (fee payable) and makes a circuit of the **Klammsee**, a tranquil green lake. Or you could continue upvalley beyond the Klammsee on footpaths or tracks as far as the **Kesselfall Alpenhaus** roadhead (2hrs 15mins from Kaprun), where you can catch a bus back again.

- Although a cable car offers an effortless ascent of the **Maiskogel**, southwest of Kaprun, a series of service roads, tracks and footpaths provides an alternative 2½hr walk from the village.

- After ascending the Maiskogel, an interesting return to Kaprun visits the **Unterberg Alm** and **Schaufelberg forest** in 2½–3hrs.

- Another descent from the Maiskogel (in 2hrs) goes steeply down the east flank to the **Klammsee**, then back to Kaprun alongside the Kapruner Ache.

- The ascent of the majestic **Kitzsteinhorn** (3203m) by its steep and narrow northwest ridge has been made possible for walkers via the third section of the cableway above the Alpincenter. From the top station a very short effort (30mins) with lots of cable support leads to the summit. While the mountain's glaciers have been vandalised by an excess of ski machinery, the summit panorama is outstanding.

WALKS FROM MATREI IN OSTTIROL

Matrei is centrally placed for a wide range of walks in the Venediger and Granatspitz groups, as well as routes among the Lasörling group south of the Venediger range. Buses serve all the main valleys, and there's a fair number of car parks for visitors with their own transport. A very small number of walks (out of the huge number possible) are fully described below. These take place in the Gschlösstal, Virgental and on the east flank of the Tauerntal.

THE GSCHLÖSSTAL

The Gschlösstal drains the eastern side of the Grossvenediger, and feeds into the upper Tauerntal near the Felbertauern Tunnel. To get there from Matrei either take a taxi, a bus (ask for the Matreier Tauernhaus; there's a bus stop on the main road 2km from it) or drive 14km upvalley towards the Felbertauern Tunnel, then take a signed minor road on the left which leads to a large car park. Just beyond this stands a small chapel opposite the Matreier Tauernhaus, a large and locally famous building with 60 beds, open all year (☎ 04875 881) and a popular base for numerous excursions.

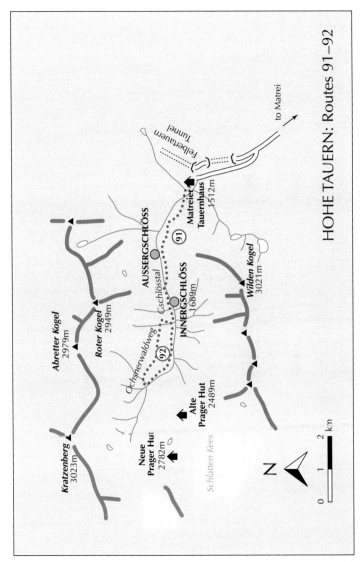

HOHE TAUERN: Routes 91–92

ROUTE 91

Matreier Tauernhaus (1512m) –
Innergschlöss (1689m)

Location	North of Matrei
Grade	1
Distance	4km (one way)
Height gain	189m
Time	1hr 15mins (+1hr return)

Although this is a short and fairly undemanding valley walk, it's rewarding for the quality of the views and the gentle charm of the Gschlösstal, a beautiful, sparsely-inhabited valley headed by the Grossvenediger.

Walk upvalley past the **Matreier Tauernhaus** along the continuing road for about 5mins, then take a footpath on the left. Crossing a bridge, follow the river upstream for a short distance before going between fences to a broad crossing path where you turn right. Apart from the intrusion of high-voltage power cables, this section of the valley is very attractive, with hay meadows and forested slopes, and waterfalls that streak the bare rock of the upper hillsides.

Leave the broad path about 15mins from the Tauernhaus, and take a narrower trail cutting left, signed to the Venedigerhaus and Innergschlöss. At first skirting the forest edge, the path then rises among trees, steeply in places, to gain 100m or so, before contouring in and out of trees, with wild raspberry canes bordering the trail. The way climbs again, now using several timber-braced steps, to reach an open grassy bluff at 1701m, from where you gain a brief view of the Grossvenediger.

Now losing height the group of time-worn buildings of **Aussergschlöss** appear below on the opposite bank of the river. As you emerge from the trees, a magnificent view is gained to the head of the valley where the Grossvenediger, adorned by the broad ice-sheet of the Schlatenkees glacier, captures your attention.

Note It would be worth descending to a footbridge spanning the river in order to visit the pretty huddle of buildings that comprise **Aussergschlöss** (55mins), one of which is a berghaus restaurant (refreshments).

The continuing walk to Innergschlöss remains on the south bank of the river where the path crosses pastures and goes through lightly wooded areas of larch, pine and fir, with juniper and bilberries growing among the rocks. Ten minutes from the Aussergschlöss footbridge junction, come to another timber footbridge that takes you across to the north bank, where you then bear left and walk along the dirt road to **Innergschlöss** (1689m, 1hr 15mins, accommodation and refreshments).

Innergschlöss is not so much a village as two rows of one-time farm buildings facing each other across the river. The last building on the left is the large, privately-owned **Alpengasthof Venedigerhaus** which has 24 beds and 8 dormitory places, and is open from mid-May until the end of October (☎ 04875 8820). Not only does the Venedigerhaus make a popular valley base for walks and climbs, it also has a restaurant invariably busy with day visitors. Taxis (motorised and horse-drawn) run a regular service between here and the Matreier Tauernhaus.

Innergschlöss

LONGER WALKS FROM INNERGSCHLÖSS

- The **Talschluss Rundweg** is a 45min circular walk which continues upvalley from Innergschlöss for a further 25mins along the dirt road, as far as a bridge at 1720m. From here you gain an excellent view of a waterfall crashing down from the Venediger's glaciers. Cross the river and return to Innergschlöss through pastures on the right bank.

- A locally publicised walk in the upper valley is the so-called **Gletscherweg Innergschlöss** (grade 3) which takes about 4–4½hrs from the Venedigerhaus. It heads upvalley to the bridge mentioned in the previous outline (25mins), then crosses the river and goes up to the impressive waterfall that drains the Schlatenkees glacier. The way then crosses a big moraine, edges the glacier and skirts below the unmanned Alte Prager Hut (30mins diversion to reach it) before descending back to Innergschlöss.

- The **Neue Prager Hut** stands at 2782m (1100m higher than Innergschlöss) on the northeast flank of the Grossvenediger, close to the Schlatenkees glacier, and is reached by a signed trail from the roadhead in a steep walk of about 4hrs from Innergschlöss. Being used by climbers attempting the Grossvenediger, it has a reputation for being very busy in the summer, so advanced booking is advised if you plan to spend a night there.

ROUTE 92

Innergschlöss (1689m) –
Ochsnerwaldweg (2030m) – Innergschlöss

Location	Northwest of Innergschlöss
Grade	3
Distance	6km
Height gain	341m
Height loss	341m
Time	2½hrs

While views of the Grossvenediger are splendid from the bed of the Gschlösstal, the high path of the Ochsnerwaldweg, which runs at mid-height level on the north flank of the upper valley, gives more views of mountains and glaciers and a different perspective of the Venediger. The path itself is a delight of alpenrose, bilberry and juniper, and has a surprise round every corner.

From **Innergschlöss** walk upvalley through pastures along the dirt road to the bridge at 1720m (25mins). About 3mins beyond this the trail to the Alte and Neue Prager Huts cuts off left ahead, while the road/track branches right and rises steadily for another 10mins before ending at the huts' goods lift. A path continues along the right-hand side of the river where the valley narrows. When it broadens a little, the trail climbs in zigzags beside a stream, and brings you to a junction at about 1910m. The left branch offers an alternative route through a wild landscape to the Prager Huts, but we take the right fork which is the **Ochsnerwaldweg**.

The way loops up a hillside growing more and more lush with bilberry and alpenrose as you gain height, and offers a welcome contrast to the rocky scene of the hanging valley in the northwest. ▶ The panoramic view to the south, west and northwest also becomes more impressive on the way to a high point of about 2030m. After this the trail contours before sloping down across a more open hillside which presents wonderful views of the Grossvenediger and

The south-facing slope traversed by the Ochsnerwaldweg is truly luxurious with vegetation, for great mattresses of bilberry and juniper cover the rocks and boulders.

The Grossvenediger can be seen from the Ochsnerwaldweg

its glaciers, and also to the Granatspitz group of mountains above the Tauerntal in the east and southeast.

As you cross little boggy areas fluffed with cotton grass, and dodge in and out of trees, the views are rearranged every few minutes. Eventually come down to a heavily wooded section where the path makes long sweeping switchbacks to lose height. When you come out of the trees, descend a last open slope, cross a pasture and rejoin the valley's dirt road Turn left and wander down to **Innergschlöss**.

THE VIRGENTAL

Dividing the glaciated Venediger group from the shaly Lasörling group west of Matrei, the Virgental is an extremely pleasant valley giving access to numerous huts lodged at the head of tributary glens to north and south. Several small villages and hamlets nestle in it. The first is **Mitteldorf** at 1091m. Then comes **Virgen** (1194m), with fine mountain views, tourist information, a few shops, and a choice of accommodation including a campsite. Beyond Virgen the road bypasses **Obermauer** and **Niedermauer**, goes through snow galleries and a tunnel and emerges at the tiny village of **Bobojach** at 1268m. **Prägraten** (1310m) lies at the entrance to the Timmeltal, has a supermarket, a bank (with ATM), tourist information and various types of accommodation. And finally there's **Hinterbichl** (1329m) at a confluence of valleys below the Grossvenediger. With a campsite, and a limited amount of accommodation, it is from here that many visitors journey up the Dorfer Tal road to spend a day at the Johannis Hut. There's a summer bus service to Hinterbichl and beyond as far as Ströden (about 4 buses per day), and car parks can be found in or near most villages.

ROUTE 93
Ströden (1403m) –
Essener-Rostocker Hut (2207m)

Location	Northwest of Ströden
Grade	2–3
Distance	6km (one way)
Height gain	804m
Time	2½–3hrs (+1½-2hrs return)

Ströden (Streden) lies deep in the Virgental at the mouth of the Maurer Tal about 18km from Matrei. There is no village, but this is as far as private vehicles are allowed in the valley. The route from here to the Essener-Rostocker huts is an uncomplicated one which leads through the beautiful Maurer Tal, from its lower reaches to an ancient moraine flanking a small tributary valley where the adjoining huts stand on a spur below the Rostock Eck. The backdrop is spectacular.

Follow the broad track up the left-hand (west) side of the Maurerbach. This crosses to the east bank to reach **Stoanalm** (1459m, refreshments), and continues rising steadily through the valley as far as the hut's goods lift. The track ends here, but a path (no 912) goes ahead, climbing above a ravine

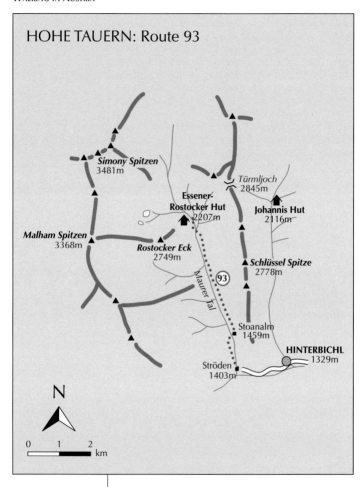

HOHE TAUERN: Route 93

Simony Spitzen
3481m

Malham Spitzen
3368m

**Essener-
Rostocker Hut**
2207m

Rostocker Eck
2749m

Türmljoch
2845m

Johannis Hut
2116m

Schlüssel Spitze
2778m

Maurer Tal

(93)

Stoanalm
1459m

HINTERBICHL
1329m

Ströden
1403m

N

0   1   2
km

across the lower flank of the Schlüssel Spitze. Passing a hut
at 1950m the gradient eases, and at 2068m you recross to
the west bank, continue alongside the stream, then make a
sharp left-hand kink to climb in zigzags to reach the **Essener-
Rostocker Hut** (2207m).

The original Essener Hut was built by the Essen section of the DAV in the Passiertal in South Tyrol, but was destroyed by avalanche in 1935. The re-sited Neue Essener Hut met a similar fate in 1958. The present building dates from 1962–64, as an adjunct to the Rostocker Hut; a traditional hut built in 1912 by the DAV's Main-Spessart section. A magnificent vantage point can be reached by continuing up the moraine beyond the buildings, while a recommended circular walk taking in the 2749m summit of the **Rostocker Eck**, will take about 2½hrs.

ROUTE 94

The Venediger Höhenweg

Location	Northwest of Matrei
Grade	3
Distance	48km
Highest point	Zopetscharte (2958m)
Start	Ströden (1403m)
Finish	Matreier Tauernhaus (1512m)
Time	6–7 days

The Venediger Höhenweg is understandably one of Austria's classic hut-to-hut routes. Making a counter-clockwise loop round the south and eastern limits of the Venediger group, the tour is a scenically dramatic one, with some high passes to cross and a diverse range of huts in which to stay overnight. Since it is not a circular tour it is advisable to take a bus as far as Ströden for the start of the route, and either taxi or bus from the Matreier Tauernhaus down to Matrei at the end of the tour.

Day 1 Taking into account time needed to travel from Matrei to Ströden, it's as well that this first stage is a short one. Wandering north of Ströden through the Maurer Tal, you reach the **Essener-Rostocker Hut** at 2207m in 2½–3hrs, as described above in Route 94. Although it is only a short stretch, the valley is attractive, and the backdrop to the hut uplifting, and given sufficient time on arrival, there are some

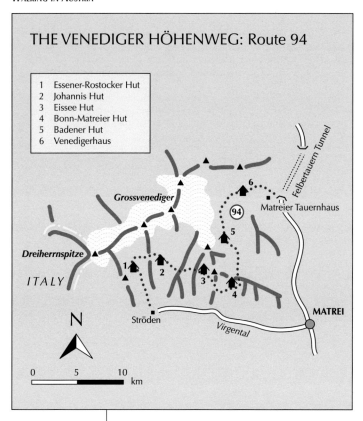

THE VENEDIGER HÖHENWEG: Route 94

1   Essener-Rostocker Hut
2   Johannis Hut
3   Eissee Hut
4   Bonn-Matreier Hut
5   Badener Hut
6   Venedigerhaus

Grossvenediger

Dreiherrnspitze

ITALY

Felbertauern Tunnel

Matreier Tauernhaus

94

MATREI

Ströden

Virgental

N

0   5   10

km

exciting landscapes to study from a path which extends along the moraine wall.

Day 2 This and the subsequent two stages move the route eastward across a series of tributary glens gouged out by long-vanished glaciers. Dividing these glens, projecting ridges or spurs have to be crossed or skirted, thereby giving the route a helter-skelter profile. On this second day, a trail is taken initially towards the wild head of the Maurer Tal before turning eastward on the Schweriner Weg. This climbs the boulder-strewn east flank of the valley, crosses a couple of streams and zigzags up grass then rocks to gain the Türmljoch (2845m) on the dividing ridge between the Maurer Tal and Dorfer Tal. Descend to the east over rocks, then swing northeast along the crags of the Aderkamm before cutting down below them heading south. Cross the Dorferbach by footbridge, and wander across meadows to reach the DAV's **Johannis Hut** at 2116m, about 3½hrs after setting out from the Essener-Rostocker Hut.

Day 3 The highest point of the Venediger tour is crossed on this stage, on the way to the Eissee Hut. Leaving the Johannis Hut a very steep zigzag path climbs southeastward up grass slopes, then forks. The right branch is the Sajat Höhenweg which leads to the privately owned Sajat Hut, while the left-hand path is the continuing route of the Venediger Höhenweg which turns north, then east through a stony corrie, still climbing with magnificent high mountain views, to reach the 2958m Zopetscharte. Given settled weather, this narrow pass is a splendid place on which to sit and absorb the untamed nature of the mountains, before descending steeply (some cable safeguards) down to boulder slopes into the Timmeltal with the 3300m Weissspitze at its head, and Hexenkopf and Hoher Eichham opposite. The **Eissee Hut** (2520m) is privately owned, with 14 beds and 31 dormitory places, and is reached about 4hrs or so from the Johannis Hut.

Day 4 A gentle start to this 3½–4hr day takes path no 923 on an easy contour heading southeast below the Hoher Eichham, and round a minor spur of the Wun Spitze to be joined by another path climbing from the Timmeltal. Rounding the southwest spur of the Wun Spitze the *höhenweg* heads east then northeast, before making a sudden short climb. The way eases, then climbs again, this time to mount the ridge of the Esels Rücken. A sharp little gully has to be descended on the east side of the ridge, below which you go down to a boulder field, then curve round the head of the Nilltal over rocks and boulders on the way to the **Bonn-Matreier Hut** at 2745m. Given sufficient energy, it might be tempting to make the 1½–2hr ascent of the 3209m Sailkopf, northwest of the hut. From it, there's said to be a wonderful view of the Grossglockner.

Day 5 This is the longest (6hrs) and most challenging stage of the Venediger Höhenweg, with the crossing of the

2882m Galten Scharte being marked as *Nur für Geübte* – 'only for the experienced'. In truth the route is not especially difficult in reasonable conditions, but the rock is very poor, loose and potentially dangerous on the descent from the pass after rain or recent snowfall. Caution is advised. From the hut, the path to take initially heads north before swinging to the right to cross the narrow Kälber Scharte (2791m) below the Raukopf. Below the pass you descend into another boulder field, then curve round to the left to make a rocky zigzag approach to the Galten Scharte between the Maurer Röte and Galten Kogel. The descent from here demands caution, for it's exposed (fixed cables), the shale is unstable and the path has countless twists. Cecil Davies gleefully recalls the comment made to him by a Dutch climber who complained that there was 'no proper rock' on this side of the pass. Now the route works its way down into a small tributary valley, crosses its stream, then heads north along the west flank of the Frossnitztal to the tiny Achsel tarn and a path junction. Fork left and rise steadily to another junction where you turn left for the final steep climb to the **Badener Hut**, which stands at 2608m below the Frossnitzkees glacier on the east flank of the Weissspitze.

Grossvenediger, seen from the Gschlösstal

Day 6 Four hours should be sufficient (in reasonable conditions) to reach Innergschlöss in the Gschlösstal, with another 1–1½ hrs of easy walking downvalley to Matreier Tauernhaus and the end of the tour. ▸ This is a landscape to absorb; to drift slowly through. So perhaps it is better to make this a two-day stage. Dreaming is fine, but not when you're moving, so keep your concentration as you leave the **Badener Hut** and work a way northwest across rocky slopes, pass below the shrinking Kristallwand Kees glacier, where an alternative path cuts to the right for the Wilden Kogel, and begin the climb to the 2770m Löbben Törl, the crux of the day's route. From the pass you gain a fabulous view across and up the Schlatenkees glacier to the Grossvenediger, then make your way down below the glacier to a moraine rib, and down this to post-glacial pools and streams, and the last steep drop into the Gschlösstal, leaving a short, pleasant walk through meadows to the **Venedigerhaus** at Innergschlöss, as delightful as any valley base in which to spend a last night among the mountains.

Day 7 Unless you had a good reason to continue down to the **Matreier Tauernhaus** at the end of yesterday's stage, the hour-long ramble downvalley could be extended by visiting a tiny chapel built into the rocks beside the dirt road on the way to Aussergschlöss, and having refreshment at Aussergschlöss itself before crossing to the right bank of the river and following a good footpath to the Tauernhaus road for a bus (or taxi) down to Matrei.

But the route to Innergschlöss is so spectacular, with its glacier views and the graceful Grossvenediger rising over everything, that it's tempting to spend time perched upon a rock dreaming.

THE TAUERNTAL

This major valley separates the Venediger and Granatspitz groups north of Matrei. Between Matrei and its head near the Matreier Tauernhaus, it's a narrow, steeply walled valley, fed by only a few tributaries: the Frossnitztal being the most important on the west side; the Landecktal and valley of the Steinerbach on the east. Although there are paths working along the Tauerntal, both in its bed and on the east flank, the following routes are concentrated on the ridges of the lower Granatspitz, being accessible from Matrei via the Goldried Bergbahn, whose top station is at 2156m.

ROUTE 95

Europa Panoramaweg
Goldried (2156m) – Kals-Matreier-Törlhaus
(2207m) – Kalser Höhe (2434m) –
Goldried (2156m)

Location	East of Matrei
Grade	1–2
Distance	9km
Height gain	278m
Height loss	278m
Time	3hrs

Don't expect to have this walk to yourself, for the Europa Panoramaweg is one of the most popular in the Hohe Tauern region. With cableway access, good refreshment facilities and a famed 360° panoramic view that is supposed to include 63 summits of 3000m or more, it's no wonder it should be high on the list of visitors to Matrei or Kals (there's also cableway access from Grossdorf near Kals am Grossglockner).

Leaving the top station of the **Goldried** cableway head to the right on a broad and easily-graded track which curves round the hillside, and in a little under 1hr brings you to a saddle and the privately owned **Kals-Matreier-Törlhaus** (2207m, accommodation and refreshments) at a junction of paths.

Take the path on the right-hand side of the hut which heads north and is signed for the Sudetendeutscher Höhenweg. It climbs the ridge above the hut, continues over the 2387m **Pfarrerbüchel** and reaches the high point of the walk at the 2434m **Kalser Höhe**. Along the ridge views grow in extent, but if you're lucky with clear visibility when you summit the Kalser Höhe, the panorama will reward with a wealth of mountains (if not the full 63 summits) stretching in every direction. Both Grossglockner to the northeast, and Grossvenediger to the northwest rise above their neighbours and capture your attention with their glacial armoury.

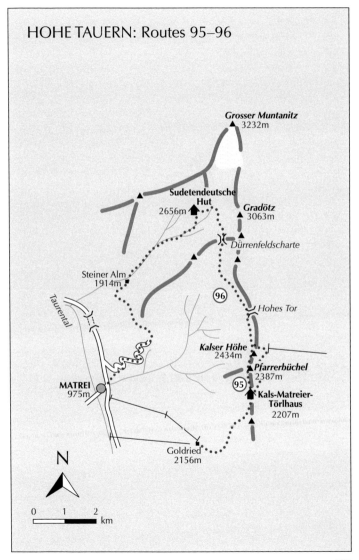

HOHE TAUERN: Routes 95–96

Grosser Muntanitz
3232m

Sudetendeutsche
Hut
2656m

Gradötz
3063m

Dürrenfeldscharte

Steiner Alm
1914m

Taurental

96

Hohes Tor

Kalser Höhe
2434m

Pfarrerbüchel
2387m

MATREI
975m

95

Kals-Matreier-
Törlhaus
2207m

Goldried
2156m

N

0   1   2 km

On the Europa Panoramaweg

The way now descends to a path junction where you leave the Sudetendeutscher route by veering right down a steep trail to another junction near the top station of the cableway from Grossdorf. Once again, turn right and wander along the broad path which leads back to the Kals-Matreier-Törlhaus, where you then retrace your earlier route along the track back to the **Goldried Bergbahn**.

ROUTE 96

Matrei (Goldried: 2156m) –
Sudetendeutsche Hut (2656m) – Matrei (975m)

Location	East and northeast of Matrei
Grade	3
Distance	21km
Height gain	720m
Height loss	1890m
Time	2 days

The Sudetendeutscher Höhenweg is another of the classic, much-loved routes of the Hohe Tauern region, and one that rewards with many memorable views. The first stage journeys northward along the mountain spine separating the Tauerntal from the Dorfertal, while the second day takes the route from the Sudetendeutsche Hut down the east flank of the Tauerntal to Matrei.

Day 1 Begin by taking the **Goldried** cableway to its top station, then follow directions given for Route 95 to the Kals-Matreier-Törlhaus and along the ridge above it as far as the junction north of the Kalser Höhe. While the Europa Panoramaweg branches right, we take the left fork and skirt the 2593m Blauer Knopf, and rejoin the ridge at another junction at the col of **Hohes Tor**. The right-hand path here descends to Taurer in the Dorfertal, across whose depth can be seen the Grossglockner in a surprise view.

Branch left at the col to cross steep grass slopes that become more rocky with slips of scree as you progress below the Kendlspitze. Then you zigzag up the side of a scree basin to gain the highest part of the *höhenweg* at the rocky col of the 2823m **Dürrenfeldscharte**, with the highest peak of the Granatspitz group, the Grosser Muntanitz, seen ahead to the north.

Fixed cables give physical as well as psychological support on the steep descent on broken and rather unstable rock, below which you cross old moraines and streams that drain

Kals-Matreier-Törlhaus (Route 95)

the melt from the Gradötzkees glacier on the final approach to the **Sudetendeutsche Hut**, reached in about 4½hrs from the Goldried cableway.

Day 2 With something like 1700m of descent on this second stage of the route, it's clear that this is likely to be more tiring than yesterday's trek. A sign at the hut directs the way down into the valley of the Steinerbach over meadows and streams, then along a track leading to the **Steiner Alm** (1914m, 1½hrs, accommodation and refreshments) and a choice of routes. Go through a gate and turn left along a path in the direction of Glanz. This trail is known as the *Edelweisswiese*, and it takes you through pinewoods and across meadows, leaves the National Park and comes to a dirt road. Follow this down to a parking area.

The road now twists down to Matrei, but there are footpath options with several shortcuts where the road loops round hairpins, but at last you run out of options and follow the road to its junction with the main valley highway. Turn left, and shortly after turn right into **Matrei in Osttirol**.

WALKS FROM
KALS AM GROSSGLOCKNER

South of Kals its valley is known as the Kalsertal. It climbs out of the Iseltal between the lower Granatspitz group on the west and the Schober group to the east, and on the journey up to Kals a highlight is the glorious Schlier waterfall which bursts from the eastern mountains. At this point you also gain an exciting view of the Grossglockner. From Kals on, the valley is the Dorfertal (not to be confused with the Dorfer Tal tributary of the Virgental) which divides the Granatspitz from the Glockner group. A major tributary of the Dorfertal cuts into the mountains at Kals. This, the Ködnitztal, is made accessible by the Kalser Glocknerstrasse toll road, built between 1976 and 1980, which rises almost 600m in 7km. From the roadhead at the Lucknerhaus the Grossglockner announces its supremacy; there are some great walks to be had in its shadow, and several huts to visit. An infrequent bus service from Kals journeys up the Glocknerstrasse, while for those with their own transport, there's a large car park

at the roadhead. The **Lucknerhaus** hotel by the car park has
39 beds and 16 dormitory places, and is fully open from
February until the end of October (☎ 04876 8555).

ROUTE 97

Kals (Lucknerhaus: 1918m) – Stüdl Hut (2802m)

Location	North of the Lucknerhaus
Grade	2–3
Distance	5km (one way)
Height gain	884m
Time	2½–3hrs (+2hrs return)

Although the Stüdl Hut is primarily used by climbers as a base from which to
tackle the Grossglockner and routes on the Glocknerwand, its situation on the
Fanatscharte in view of Austria's highest peak, makes it an obvious goal for
walkers, either as a there-and-back trek, or on a circular walk with a return to
Matrei via the Teischnitztal.

From the car park opposite the **Lucknerhaus**, either take the
track on the left (west) side of the river, or the footpath on the
east bank. Heading north, the track cuts between meadows
and, rising steadily, crosses the Ködnitzbach to be joined by
the footpath. It then climbs to the privately owned **Luckner
Hut** (2241m, accommodation and refreshments) about 1hr
from the roadhead.

The track ends at the hut's goods lift, with a footpath
continuing from it. About 15mins later, the Glorer Hut path
breaks to the right (see Route 98), but we keep ahead and
soon recross the Ködnitzbach. The way now climbs above
the stream and comes to a path junction at 2550m, where the
right branch is the Johann Stüdl Weg, linking the Stüdl and
Salm Huts. Keep left and zigzag northwest below the Blaue
Wand crags, then suddenly emerge onto the Fanatscharte
saddle where the **Stüdl Hut** occupies a prime position.

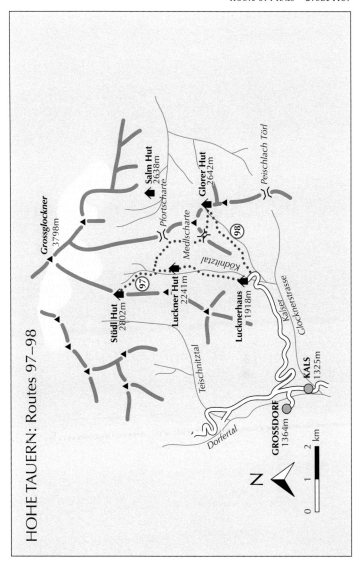

HOHE TAUERN: Routes 97–98

The Grossglockner dominates the upper Ködnitz Tal

Note If you took the bus to the Lucknerhaus, a return to Matrei via the Teischnitztal (the valley which lies below the Fanatscharte on the west) makes a good alternative option. Path no 712 descends the east flank of the Teischnitztal, and eventually joins a road a little south of the Moa-Alm. Either walk down the road to Kals, or descend to the bed of the valley where a trail can be followed downstream alongside the Kalserbach as far as Grossdorf, then road from there to Kals (about 3½hrs from the Stüdl Hut).

ROUTE 98

Kals (Lucknerhaus: 1918m) –
Glorer Hut (2642m) – Lucknerhaus

Location	Northeast of the Lucknerhaus
Grade	3
Distance	10km
Height gain	724m
Height loss	724m
Time	3½–4hrs

This walk has something of everything. For a start it has impressive views of the Grossglockner. It visits two huts, tackles long sections of *klettersteig* (via ferrata), crosses grassy hillsides, and in early summer is brightened by countless alpine flowers. Since the *klettersteig* is quite challenging, with considerable exposure, it is a route that cannot be recommended to anyone with a tendency towards vertigo.

The walk begins by following directions for Route 97 as far as the path junction 15mins beyond the **Luckner Hut**. While the Stüdl Hut path continues ahead, we fork right (sign for the Glorer and Salm Huts). Rising up and across the hillside away from the Grossglockner, the path then cuts back and climbs in a long north-bound slant to another junction on a high point (1½hrs), from which the Grossglockner can be studied rising as an elegant pyramid just ahead.

Bear right and contour southeastward for a while, until you reach a rocky area with a fixed cable safeguarding an easy scramble, at the top of which the Grossglockner once more hoves into view. The trail now crosses a hillside starred with flowers, and comes to yet another path junction. Take the right fork. This leads to another rocky section aided by more fixed cable. Turn a spur, descend briefly, then contour across to a slope of shale and slate below the **Pfortscharte**. Another path breaks away here to climb to the *scharte* en route to the Salm Hut, while we cut straight across the slope and begin a lengthy section of *klettersteig* (**caution**).

Using plenty of fixed cable as support, the way negotiates a rocky region of narrow ledges, shelves, little gullies, scrambling pitches, and even a wooden ladder to climb. In many places there's considerable exposure, but invariably in such places you will find adequate cable support.

At the end of the *klettersteig* there follows an undemanding traverse of a grass slope, before you stomp your way up a short but steep slope of shale to gain a minor spur. Up this spur you soon come onto the **Medlscharte** (2676m, 2½hrs), from which you should be able to see the **Glorer Hut** on the Berger Törl saddle to the east. It will only take 15mins to reach it by the continuing path which contours round the head of a grassy basin.

The **Glorer Hut** (2651m, 2¾hrs, accommodation and refreshments) stands on the windy Berger Törl at the foot of the 2821m Kasteneck; a path strikes south from the hut to the summit of this minor peak in 1hr. Another path goes in the opposite direction to the Salm Hut in 1½hrs; yet another descends through the Leitertal to Heiligenblut in 3½–4hrs.

There are two ways to return to the Lucknerhaus roadhead from the Glorer Hut. The first takes path no 713 (the Wiener Höhenweg) cutting southsouthwest then east to the 2484m Peischlach Törl, and descends steeply from there down the valley of the Peischlachbach to the Lucknerhaus, while a more direct route is that which is described below.

Curling its way round the hillside, the track goes through several gates and pleasant light woodland.

Path no 714 descends southwestward below the hut, cutting down an extensive grass hillside, then in switchbacks to a track where the gradient eases. ◀ After turning a corner,

Above the Luckner Hut, the trail is used by walkers approaching both the Stüdl and Glorer Huts

the Grossglockner can once more be seen in the north. When you go through another gate just above a dark timber farmhouse, leave the track for a narrow footpath on the right. This goes down among trees and leads directly to the car park opposite the **Lucknerhaus**.

OTHER ROUTES FROM KALS

- From the parking area at **Taurer**, upvalley from Kals, a walk of 1½–2hrs goes through the gorge of the Dabaklamm, and continues through meadows along the east bank of the Seebach to the **Kalser Tauernhaus** at 1754m, and from there, a further hour's walk leads to the **Dorfersee** tarn at 1935m. Either overnight at the Tauernhaus, or return downvalley to Taurer, for which you should allow at least 2hrs.

- A 4½hr link with the **Sudetendeutsche Hut** in the Granatspitz can be made from the **Kalser Tauernhaus** by a trail which climbs the east flank of the Grosser Muntanitz to the 2684m Plojwand, and crossing the dividing ridge north of Gradötz at 2848m. With 1100m to climb from the Tauernhaus, it's a strenuous but rewarding route.

- A much more gentle 1½hr walk can be had by first taking the cableway from Grossdorf to the **Europa Panoramaweg**, then following this easy trail southwestward to the **Kals-Matreier Törlhaus** and continuing to the Goldried Bergbahn where you then ride down to Matrei.

THE GROSSGLOCKNER

At 3798m the Grossglockner is not only Austria's highest mountain, but it ranks among the most elegant peaks in the Eastern Alps. Seen from the south it appears as a rock pyramid daubed with ice and snow high above the Ködnitztal, but from the east, or almost anywhere above the Pasterze glacier, it soars to a graceful, tapering pinnacle to delight any mountain lover. As John Ball, the Victorian mountaineer and first president of the Alpine Club, wrote in the original English-language climbing guide to the Central Tyrol in 1873: 'The exquisitely sharp cone … rising in an unbroken slope of 5000ft above the Pasterze glacier, is not surpassed for grace and elegance by any in the Alps … No true mountaineer can behold that beautiful peak without longing to attain its summit.'

Count Franz von Salm-Reifferscheid, Prince-Bishop of Gurk and a future Cardinal, was both rich and powerful, and shared that longing. On his behalf,

two Heiligenblut carpenter brothers, J and M Klotz, set out in June 1799 to recon-
noitre a route, but were forced by storm to make their retreat from below the
Kleinglockner. A week later they tried again by way of the Leiterkees glacier and
the Adlersruhe, and managed to secure the route on the steep upper slopes with
140m of rope, before again being forced down by bad weather.

After this, von Salm gave instructions for a shelter to be built below the
Leiterkees (the forerunner of the hut which now bears his name) to aid future
attempts. The next of these was made on 18 August by a party of no less than 30
– all of whom were turned back by a snowstorm. Six days later, the Klotz brothers, with two other local carpenters, tried yet again, and once more were beaten
by the weather. However, the next day all four returned, along with von Salm's
curate-in-chief, Sigmund von Hohenwart, and this time they actually gained the
secondary summit of the Kleinglockner, which is just 15m lower than the main
peak.

With the winning of the Grossglockner now virtually guaranteed, von Salm
was willing to finance another major expedition the following year, for which a
second hut was erected higher up the mountain, just below the Hohenwartkopf,
and the original Leitertal cabin enlarged to house the 62 people who gathered
there on 27 July 1800.

Next morning von Salm accompanied the 11 chosen climbers and their 19
guides to the upper hut, and waited there while the Klotz brothers and two other
carpenter-guides, plus two local priests, a botanist and von Hohenwart, continued to the Kleinglockner. With the aid of a tree trunk, Father Horasch and the four
guides then crossed the exposed gap now known as the Obere Glocknerscharte,
and stood upon the true summit for the first time, their achievement effectively
marking the birth of alpinism in the Eastern Alps.

Today the Grossglockner boasts some 30 routes and variations of routes to
the summit, the variety of which exceeds that of any other mountain in Austria.
Of these, the most popular by far are the Ordinary Route via the Adlersruhe and
Kleinglockner; and the Stüdlgrat, a rock route on the Southwest Ridge approached
from the Stüdl Hut. In recent years glacier retreat has led to an increase in stone
fall, a danger exacerbated by the large number of climbers forming bottlenecks
on exposed places. But experienced walkers eager to make the ascent are advised
to contact the mountain guides in either Kals am Grossglockner (☎ 04876 263),
or Heiligenblut (☎ 04824 2700).

10 KARAWANKEN

Shared with neighbouring Slovenia, Austria's most southerly mountains are largely hidden from view by wooded foothills that rise from the Rosental valley. Narrow roads thread their way through gorges in the hills, emerging to alpine meadows interrupted by tiny villages and hamlets that bear little resemblance to the more 'traditional' picture-postcard communities found in Tyrol or Salzburg Land. Here in deepest Carinthia the Slav influence remains in both architecture and language, for villages and mountains often have two names, while the sun-bleached limestone crags, slabs and finely shaped summits provide a backdrop to trails seldom visited by British walkers, despite the close proximity of Klagenfurt's airport making it one of the easiest groups in all the Alps to reach from the UK.

ACCESS AND INFORMATION

Location	In southern Carinthia, east of the Carnic Alps, from the Wurzen Pass south of Villach, to where the Drau enters Slovenia east of Klagenfurt. The mountains carry the Austro–Slovenian frontier.
Maps	Kompass Wanderkarte 61 *Wörthersee, Karawanken West* and 65 *Klopeiner See, Karawanken* 1:50,000
	Freytag & Berndt WK232 *Volkermarkt, Klopeiner See, Turner See*; WK233 *Kärntner Seen, Villach, Klagenfurt*; and WK234 *Klopeiner See, Rosental, Klagenfurt* 1:50,000
	Planinska zveza Slovenije *Karavanke* and *Kamnisko-Savinjske Alpe* 1:50,000
Bases	Ferlach, Bad Eisenkappel
Information	Ferlach Tourismus, 9170 Ferlach (e-mail: office@carnica-rosental.at; website: www.ferlach.at)
	Turismusverein Bad Eisenkappel, 9135 Bad Eisenkappel (e-mail: bad.eisenkappel@netway.at; website: www.tiscover.com/bad-eisenkappel)
Access	By road from Klagenfurt (17km) to Ferlach; and via Volkermarkt to Bad Eisenkappel. Minor roads stretch into the wooded hills from both valley bases; infrequent bus services from Ferlach and Bad Eisenkappel link outlying villages.

Karawanken wall at the head of the Bodental

Persistence is required to discover the best of the Karawanken beyond the forests, but once found, the unique beauty of the region is hard to forget. With Feistritz at its mouth, the narrow, steep-walled and heavily wooded Bärental is typical, for as you journey south through it, only the briefest of hints are given that the narrow line of abrupt frontier mountains are waiting ahead. The highest in the range erupts from a wasteland of screes, spreading its influence in four directions. At just 2237m, Hochstuhl cannot compete with major peaks of other regions included in this guide, but altitude is not everything. Hochstuhl, with its popular north-facing *klettersteig* and easy trail from the south, has its own undeniable appeal and some glorious summit views. The Klagenfurter Hut is one of very few huts in the Karawanken, but it makes an almost perfect base, not only for climbs on Hochstuhl, but for the 1959m Bielschitza above it, and for cross-border treks. It's in a well-chosen position, for it can be reached from two very different valleys; that of the Bärental, the other being the glorious Bodental.

The Bodental is approached by a spur off the Ferlach to Loiblpass road, with a bus service from Ferlach terminating at a large *gasthof* surrounded by meadows. Trails and tracks cut through the meadows, edging ever closer to the main crest of the Karawanken. At the head of one single-track road, a beautiful old farm-cum-*gasthof*, shaded by linden trees, has a distinctly Slovenian atmosphere and a tranquil outlook across gently rising meadows to the frontier crest.

The Loibltal, between Ferlach and the pass, boasts the wildly romantic Tscheppaschlucht gorge (fee to walk through) and the nearby Tschauko waterfall, but a less-travelled road southeast of town pushes through the valley of the Waidischbach for a little over 10km before twisting up into a high pastoral valley running parallel with the main mountain ridge. Zell-Pfarre nestles among the pastures, but above it to the south the few buildings of Zell-Koschuta stand either side of a minor toll road

399

KARAWANKEN

VILLACH

Drau

Faaker See

ARNOLDSTEIN

Berta Hut

Wurzen Pass

Mittagskogel

Rosenbergsattel

SLOVENIA

N

0   5   10
km

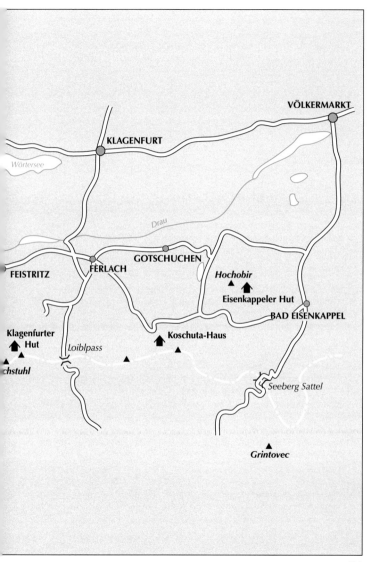

which becomes a track leading to the Koschuta-Haus, at the foot of challenging crags and peaks.

The Zell road continues eastward, but then forks at Zell-Schaida. One now descends northward and eventually runs alongside the dammed Freibach lake, while the eastward option climbs to the Schaidasattel at 1068m. From here a recommended trail sets out to make the ascent of the Hochobir, a tremendous vantage point from which to study not only the Karawanken on both sides of the border, but the low-lying country to the north, lit by the Drau. Over the Schaidasattel the road snakes down into more gorge-like wooded narrows before coming to Bad Eisenkappel on the Volkermarkt to Seebergsattel road.

Main Bases

Ferlach (466m) This small town lies south of Klagenfurt above the Drau, and is at the hub of several roads. Despite being the largest base in the Karawanken mountain district, it has only modest facilities; among them a few shops and restaurants, a supermarket, tourist information, a post office, banks with ATMs and a limited amount of accommodation. The nearest campsite is at Gotschuchen, about 8km to the east.

Bad Eisenkappel (556m) A modest-sized village with spa facilities astride the Seebergsattel road which crosses the mountains into Slovenia, it is not immediately obvious as a base for a mountain walking holiday, but with your own transport a lot of options become possible. It has *gasthaus*, *pension* and hotel accommodation, several restaurants, banks with ATM, a post office, tourist information and basic shops.

Mountain Huts

Berta Hut (1527m) The westernmost hut in the Karawanken, it sits below the Mittagskogel southeast of the Faaker See. Owned by the Villach section of the ÖAV, this timber-clad Category I hut was built in 1963. It has 34 dormitory places, and is staffed from June until the end of September (☎ 0699 10502184).

Eisenkappeler Hut (1553m) Accessible by road all the way to the hut, it is perfectly placed for an easy ascent of Bad Eisenkappel's 'house mountain' Hochobir, northwest of the village. The hut has 15 beds and 12 dormitory places, is owned by the ÖTK, and is fully staffed from May to mid-October, and weekends the rest of the year (weather permitting). For bookings ☎ 04238 8170.

Klagenfurter Hut (1664m) Standing on the Matschacher Alm near the head of both the Bärental and Bodental, this Category I hut belongs to the Klagenfurt section of the ÖAV, and has a direct view of the Bielschitza and Hochstuhl on the frontier ridge. With 24 beds and 38 dormitory places, it is fully staffed from Whitsun to the end of October, Christmas and the New Year, and then at weekends (☎ 04253 8556).

Koschuta-Haus (1279m) Owned by the TVN (Friends of Nature), this hut is approached via toll road from Zell-Pfarre, and looks onto the Hohe Spitze, Larchenberg and Koschutnikturm. It has 24 beds and 24 dormitory places, and is staffed from May until early November (☎ 04227 7110).

ROUTE 99

Bärental (Parking: 1152m) –
Klagenfurter Hut (1664m)

Location	South of Feistritz
Grade	1–2
Distance	3km (one way)
Height gain	512m
Time	1½hrs (+1hr return)
Valley base	Ferlach

Although this is only a very short walk, it gives a good introduction to the area. But you will either need your own transport to get there, hitch a lift, or take a taxi. Alternatively you could walk all the way from Feistritz.

The narrow road south of Feistritz through the Bärental leads to a small parking area at a junction marked Stouhütte (960m). This is about 6.5km from the village and a sign there

The Klagenfurter Hut

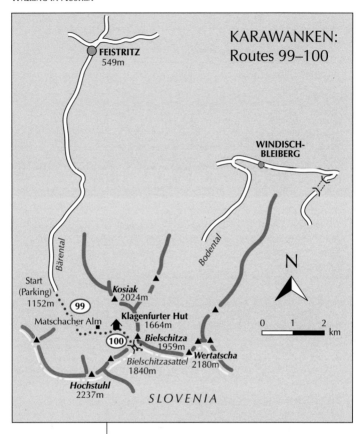

KARAWANKEN:
Routes 99–100

FEISTRITZ
549m

WINDISCH-
BLEIBERG

Bärental

Bodental

N

Start
(Parking)
1152m

99

Kosiak
2024m

Klagenfurter Hut
1664m

Matschacher Alm

100

Bielschitza
1959m

Bielschitzasattel
1840m

Wertatscha
2180m

0   1   2
km

Hochstuhl
2237m

SLOVENIA

suggests it will take 2hrs to walk to the Klagenfurter Hut.
Continue heading south, and the paved road deteriorates to
a stony track before coming to a larger parking area shortly
before a barrier closes the track to public use. This is where
the walk begins.

Since the continuing track goes all the way to the hut,
detailed description is unnecessary, except where a recommended alternative path is offered. At first rising and winding through mixed woodland, mountain views appear about

15mins from the car park. In another 35mins you come to a signed junction at about 1425m, where a path breaks away across screes to the south. This leads to the Hochstuhl *klettersteig* (3hrs to the summit from here).

Leave the track at this point and take a footpath ahead, edging the screes. This soon climbs steeply through woodland to regain the track at a bend. Almost immediately leave the track again where the path resumes steeply up the wooded hillside, returning to the track at a much higher point. Walk along the track for another 4mins, then take an unmarked path which rises above it, cuts across pastures with lovely open views of the wall of frontier peaks off to the right, and rejoins the track once more for the final few metres to the **Klagenfurter Hut**.

The hut commands a panoramic view of frontier peaks sweeping to the south, from nearby Bielschitza to the Hochstuhl and beyond to the west – abrupt white limestone peaks erupting from great fans of scree.

Hochstuhl, seen in profile across the screes from the trail to Bielschitzasattel

ROUTE 100
Klagenfurter Hut (1664m) – Bielschitza (1959m)

Location	Southeast of the Klagenfurter Hut
Grade	3
Distance	1.5km (one way)
Height gain	295m
Time	1hr (+1hr return)
Valley base	Ferlach

A short, steep but undemanding ascent of an appealing rock peak, this route takes us onto the Slovenian side of the mountains by way of a long scree ramp and a narrow col. Whilst the ascent from the col is straightforward, there's a very brief section of exposed ridge immediately before the summit is reached, and the descent back to the hut is more taxing than the ascent

The path to the Bielschitzasattel is clearly seen from the hut, slanting across the screes at a steady angle below the Bielschitza peak. From the hut descend a little to a stand of larch trees, below which the ubiquitous dwarf pine is slowly invading the scree slopes. The way squeezes between rocks and boulders and dwarf pine, then angles across the lower screes to gain a fine profile of Hochstuhl to the right. Over the first scree, you then climb rock ledges with fixed cable safeguards, before resuming up and across the mountainside on another scree path to reach the **Bielschitzasattel** (1840m) in 30mins from the hut. There are in fact two cols, separated by a minor rock lump below which the path forks. The more obvious choice is the right branch.

Emerging at the Slovenian border it is a surprise to find that on the south side there's a curious hollow of grass and more dwarf pine, almost completely ringed by limestone crags and ridges. Although the route to the Bielschitza turns left, it's worth taking the path along the right-hand side of the hollow for a couple of minutes to gain a wild view of the south side of the frontier ridge.

Return to the col and bear right (east) to pass below the Bielschitza and enjoy another fine view from a saddle which looks onto the impressive Wertatscha and Selenitza carrying the frontier eastward, their north flanks plunging into the head of the Bodental.

There are two options for climbing Bielschitza. One climbs steeply by way of a series of natural rock steps up the ridge immediately above the Bielschitzasattel's twin col; the other strikes up the peak through a covering of dwarf pine above the grass saddle from which you gained views of Wertatscha. The two routes eventually come together and continue up the ridge to a narrow and exposed rocky crest. This is crossed (**caution**) to the actual 1959m summit of the **Bielschitza** whose panoramic view is immense. It includes Klagenfurt beyond the Drau, while the Karawanken ridge stretches to east and west. ▶

Bielschitzasattel on the Austro-Slovenian border

Note Take care on the descent – especially on the scree path above the fixed cables.

OTHER ROUTES FROM THE KLAGENFURTER HUT

- A short stroll across the pastures west of the hut leads to the group of chalets and a cattle byre at the **Matschacher Alm**. This has an idyllic pastureland setting facing the limestone wall of the highest Karawanken mountains.
- The **Hochstuhl klettersteig** is reached in 20mins from the hut, and the route then takes another 3hrs to gain the summit.

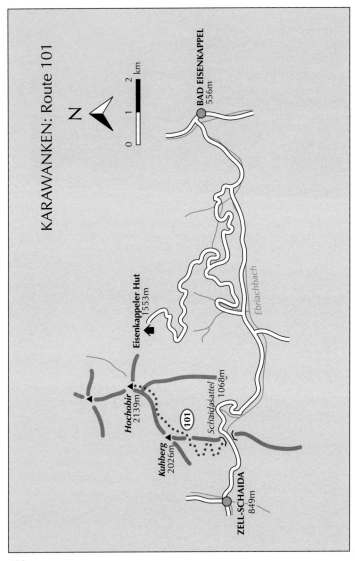

KARAWANKEN: Route 101

- Another route to the summit of the 2237m **Hochstuhl** goes by way of the Bielschitzasattel (see Route 100) and a contouring path along the south flank, leaving a short final ascent – about 2–2½hrs from the hut.

- Immediately above the hut to the north, the 2024m **Kosiak** (Geisberg) is gained in 1hr via the Franz-Zoop-Weg.

- And finally, a 2½hr walk follows a marked path down to **Gasthof Sereinig** in the lovely **Bodental**, where you can catch a bus to Ferlach.

ROUTE 101
Schaidasattel (1068m) – Hochobir (2139m)

Location	West of Bad Eisenkappel
Grade	2
Distance	5km (one way)
Height gain	1071m
Time	3hrs (+ 2hrs return)
Valley base	Bad Eisenkappel

Standing north of the main Karawanken ridge, Hochobir is the fourth highest in the range and has long been adopted as the local 'house mountain' of Bad Eisenkappel. The Bad Eisenkappeler Hut sits at the head of a road 580m below and to the east of the peak, and it is from this hut that the ascent is usually made. Our route, however, is rather more varied and interesting.

The Schaidasattel, where our route begins, is a road pass linking Bad Eisenkappel with the Zell communities. The road to take is clearly signed from the northern end of the village, plunging at once into the narrow, wooded Ebriach valley. A little over 2km later, you may notice a side road which branches off to the Bad Eisenkappeler Hut. In another 4km a second road branches off. The so-called Hochobir Hochalpenstrasse, this too goes to the Bad Eisenkappeler Hut, while the Schaidasattel road becomes more sinuous on the final climb to the pass. A few parking spaces are found here, with very fine views over the Zell valley and the frontier mountains.

Limestone ridge below Hochobir

On the north side of the road at the **Schaidasattel** walk up a broad path/track leading into forest. Very shortly a sign directs you onto a footpath (the Simon-Rieger-Weg) climbing roughly northeast, crossing and recrossing a forest track until you emerge from the trees near the subsidiary peak of the Kuhberg, to gain lovely views south.

Come to a saddle below the **Kuhberg**, from where you should be able to see the Freibach reservoir below to the northwest, beyond that to the Drau, and even farther away to Klagenfurt in the low-lying country north of the Drau.

The path now skirts the east side of the ridge linking Hochobir with the Kuhberg, and works its way up flowery slopes to gain a point where you look down on some rugged limestone formations. Here the ridge plunges into a seemingly bottomless valley on its west side. Join a broad path coming from the right. This is the standard route of ascent from the Bad Eisenkappeler Hut, and you now head north along it for the final climb to the summit of **Hochobir** (2139m), which is topped by a large cross.

Note A longer alternative route back to the Schaidasattel descends to the Bad Eisenkappeler Hut in 45mins or so, then takes a varied route along footpaths and tracks used by the Karawanken Wanderweg. The route is well signed and way-marked, and it brings you onto the road a few paces from the **Schaidasattel** in a little under 2½hrs from the hut – allow 3hrs from the Hochobir summit.

In the late 19th century an observatory and meteorological station stood on the summit of **Hochobir**, and a few remains can still be found there. It has a wonderful panoramic view which encompasses a vast sweep of country to the north, the final modest heights of the Karawanken to the east, the Carnic Alps away to the west, the impressive frontier wall to the south, and beyond that the mountains of Slovenia culminating in the summit of Triglav, highest in the Julian Alps, peering above ridges to the westsouthwest.

OTHER ROUTES FROM BAD EISENKAPPEL

- Upvalley from Bad Eisenkappel, 5km below the Seebergsattel on the Austro–Slovenia border, a side road branches east, signed to the **Vellacher Kotschna Naturschutzgebiet** (nature reserve). At a hairpin bend a short way down this road, take a footpath directly ahead. This leads through the lovely Kotschnatal, at the head of which the trail climbs to the 1999m **Sanntaler Sattel** on the frontier ridge – a wonderfully wild and rocky landscape, and close to Austria's southernmost point (about 4½hrs from the main road). The path continues on the Slovene side of the mountains and descends to the Frischautov mountain hut above the Logartal (Logarska Dolina).

- North of the Seebergsattel, but standing a short distance away from the frontier ridge, the 1759m summit of the **Kärntner Storschitz** makes a splendid lookout from which some of the loveliest of Slovene mountains can be studied – in particular Grintovec (2558m) to the south. From the Seebergsattel the summit can be reached in about 1½hrs.

APPENDIX A
Useful Addresses

**Tourist Information and
Austrian Alpine Club**
Holiday Service of the Austrian National
Tourist Office
☎ 0845 101 1818
(calls charged at local rate)
e-mail: holiday@austria.info
website: www.austria.info

Austrian Alpine Club (UK)
12a North Street
Wareham
Dorset BH20 4AG
☎ 01929 556870
e-mail: aac.office@aacuk.org.uk
website: www.aacuk.org.uk

Oesterreichischer Alpenverein
Olympiastrasse 37
A-6020 Innsbruck
website: www.alpenverein.at

Map Suppliers
Cordee Ltd
11 Jacknell Road
Dodwells Bridge Industrial Estate
Hinckley, Leics LE10 3BS
☎ 0116 254 3579
e-mail: sales@cordee.co.uk
website: www.cordee.co.uk

The Map Shop
15 High Street
Upton-upon-Severn
Worcs WR8 0HJ
e-mail: themapshop@btinternet.com
website: www.themapshop.co.uk

Edward Stanford Ltd
12–14 Long Acre
London WC2E 9LP
☎ 020 7836 1321
e-mail: sales@stanfords.co.uk
website: www.stanfords.co.uk

Specialist Mountain Activity Insurers
Austrian Alpine Club (see above)
*(membership carries automatic accident
and rescue insurance)*

British Mountaineering Council
177–179 Burton Road
West Didsbury
Manchester M20 2BB
☎ 0161 445 6111
e-mail: office@thebmc.co.uk
website: www.thebmc.co.uk

APPENDIX B
Bibliography

General Tourist Guides

Austria – the Rough Guide by Jonathan Bousfield and Rob Humphreys (Rough Guides, 1998) – One of the best general guides to the country available.

Baedeker's Austria (AA; 2nd edition 1992) – A gazeteer-style guide with concise paragraphs of useful background information.

Mountains and Mountaineering

Nanga Parbat Pilgrimage by Hermann Buhl (latest English edition, Bâton Wicks, 1998) – The autobiography of one of Austria's finest climbers who made the first ascent of Nanga Parbat in 1953, but died in 1957 after falling through a cornice on Chogolisa. This book contains the account of many of his early climbs in the Eastern Alps.

Climbs and Ski-Runs by FS Smythe (Blackwood, 1929) – The first (and some say the best) book by the most prolific and widely-read mountaineer of the inter-war years.

Eastern Alps: the Classic Routes on the Highest Peaks by Dieter Seibert (Diadem, 1992) – As the title suggests, it includes routes for climbers in the Ötztal, Stubai, Zillertal and Hohe Tauern.

Over Tyrolese Hills by FS Smythe (Hodder & Stoughton, 1936) – Despite the title, this is an account of his climbs in many parts of Austria.

Glockner Region by Eric Roberts (West Col, 1976) – A climbers' guide to Austria's highest mountain and other neighbouring peaks. Some of the information is inevitably out of date, especially in regard to the size and condition of glaciers and snowfields, but still the only such guide in the English language.

Oetztaler Alps by Jeff Williams (West Col, 2000) – One of three climbers' guides to Austrian mountains by Jeff Williams, it includes several summits that would be accessible to experienced mountain walkers with scrambling ability.

Silvretta Alps by Jeff Williams (West Col, 1995) – An excellent guide to these mountains for the peak-bagger.

Stubai Alps & South Tirol by Jeff Williams (West Col, 1991) – Another very fine climber's guide with routes described on both sides of the international border.

Zillertal Alps by Eric Roberts and Robin Collomb (West Col, 1980) – All the major Zillertal peaks, plus numerous others, are given the West Col treatment in this climbers' guide.

Mountain Walking

Walking in the Alps by J Hubert Walker (Oliver & Boyd, 1951) – In this classic of mountain literature, Walker describes the Ötztal and Stubai Alps for the walker and climber, in an inspirational manner. The book actually covers 12 Alpine districts, only two of which are in Austria.

Walking in the Alps by Kev Reynolds (Cicerone Press; 2nd edition, 2005) – Based on Walker's book (see above), this 495 page all-colour volume covers 19 regions of the Alps, from the Alpes Maritimes to the Julians of Slovenia, and includes almost all of Austria's mountains.

Walking in the Alps by Helen Fairbairn *et al* (Lonely Planet, 2004) – In recognisable Lonely Planet style, this book describes a handful of routes among Austria's Alps.

Klettersteig: Scrambles in the Northern Limestone Alps by Paul Werner (Cicerone Press, 1987) – Translated from the German by Dieter Pevsner, this is a guide to more than 40 *Via Ferrata* protected routes in Austria and Bavaria.

Walking Austria's Alps Hut to Hut by Jonathan Hurdle (The Mountaineers/Cordee, 2nd edition,1999) – A selection of multi-day hut-to-hut routes by a variety of authors.

Trekking in the Alps edited by Kev Reynolds (Cicerone Press, 2011) – A collection of 20 of the best multi-day Alpine treks, including descriptions of the Rätikon Höhenweg, Stubai and Zillertal hut to hut routes, and the European E5 trail across the Eastern Alps.

Trekking in the Silvretta and Rätikon Alps by Kev Reynolds (Cicerone Press, 2014) – A collection of hut-to-hut routes in these neighbouring districts of western Austria.

Trekking in the Stubai Alps by Allan Hartley (Cicerone Press, 2003) – A guide to two excellent hut tours in the Stubai Alps.

Trekking in the Zillertal Alps by Allan Hartley (Cicerone Press, 2003) – By the same author as the Stubai guide (above), this book describes the 10–12 day hut tour of the Zillertal region.

Trekking in Austria's Hohe Tauern by Allan Hartley (Cicerone Press, 2010) – Four treks and a 10-day traverse of this scenically dramatic region, described by the author of the Stubai and Zillertal guides.

Walking in the Salzkammergut by Fleur and Colin Speakman (Cicerone Press, 1989) – Mostly gentle walks in the ever-popular Salzburg 'Lake District' which edges the Dachsteingebirge.

The Adlerweg by Mike Wells (Cicerone Press, 2012) – This 300km long-distance route, from St Johann to St Anton, is described in 23 main stages.

APPENDIX C
Menu items

Austrian	English
Almdudler	soft drink flavoured with herbs
Apfelsaft	apple juice
Apfelstrudel	cooked apple wrapped in pastry
Aprikose	apricot
Augsburger	type of sausage
Bacherbsensuppe	clear soup with croutons
Bauernspeckplatte	home-cured bacon, served with bread and horseradish
Bergsteigeressen	high calorie, economy 'mountaineer's meal' for AV members
Bier	beer
Birnen	pears
Bratwurst	fried sausage
Brot/Brötchen	bread/rolls
Burner Würstl	sausage stuffed with cheese and wrapped in bacon
Butterbrot	bread and butter
Ei(er)	egg(s)
Eierkuchen	omelette
Erdbeer	strawberry
Erbsensuppe	thick pea soup
Frühlingsuppe	spring vegetable soup

Austrian	English
Frühstück	breakfast
Gemüse	vegetables
Gemüsesuppe	vegetable soup
Germknödel	dumpling with jam
Gespritz	soda water addition (to a drink)
Glühwein	hot spicy red wine
Grünersalat	green salad
Gulasch	cubed meat in a rich sauce
Gulaschsuppe	spicy stewlike soup
Himbeer	raspberry
Jägerschnitzel	beef schnitzel with mushrooms
Kaffee	coffee
Kaiserschmarren	sugar-coated pancake with sultanas
Kalbsbraten	roast veal
Kartoffeln	potatoes
Käse	cheese
Käsebrot	bread and cheese
Knödel	large dumpling
Knödelsuppe	soup with dumplings
Kompott	stewed fruit
Kohl	cabbage
Leber	liver
Leberkäse	spam-like meat

Austrian	English
Marmelade	jam
Milch	milk
Milchrahmstrudel	pastry with creamy filling, served with vanilla sauce
Nudeln	noodles or macaroni
Palatschinken	large sweet pancake
Pflaume	plum
Pilz	mushroom
Preiselbeere	cranberry
Radler	shandy
Reis	rice
Rindfleisch	beef
Saft	fruit juice
Salat	salad
Salz	salt
Schinken	ham
Schinkenbrötchen	ham sandwich
Schnitzel	thin veal or pork cutlet

Austrian	English
Schweinebraten	roast pork
Senf	mustard
Speck	bacon
Spiegeleier	fried eggs
Spiesekarte	menu
Stück	piece or slice
Tagesuppe	soup of the day
Tee	tea
Torte	fancy cake, tart or pie
Tiroler Gröstl	fried potato mixed with sausage or bacon
Wein	wine
Wurst	sausage
Zitrone	lemon
Zucker	sugar
Zwiebelfleisch	minced steak with onion
Zwiebelrostbraten	fried or broiled beef with onions

APPENDIX D
German–English Glossary

German	English
Abfahrt	departure
Abhang	slope
Absteige	descent
Absteigen	to descend
Ache	river or stream
Alm	high alpine pasture where farmers spend the summer
Alpenverein	alpine club
Alpenvereinsführer	alpine club guidebook
Alpenvereinskarten	alpine club maps
Ankunft	arrival
Arzt	doctor
Aufsteig	ascent
Auskunft	information
Aussichtspunkt	viewpoint
Bach	stream or river
Bäckerei	bakery
Bahnhof	railway station
Bahnsteig	railway platform
Berg	mountain
Bergführer	mountain guide
Berggasthof	mountain inn
Bergschrund	crevasse between glacier and mountain wall
Bergsteiger	mountaineer

German	English
Bergsteigeressen	mountaineer's meal – see Appendix C
Bergwanderer	mountain walker
Bergweg	mountain path
Blatt	map sheet
Briefmarke	postage stamp
Brücke	bridge
Dorf	village
Drahtseilbahn	cable car
Eisenbahn	railway
Feiertag	public holiday
Fels	rock
Ferienwohnung	holiday apartment
Ferner	glacier (eastern Alps)
Fernsprecher	telephone
Firn	snowfield
Fliesswasser	running water
Flughafen	airport
Funktelefon	radio telephone
Fussweg	footpath
Ganzjährig	all-year
Garni	hotel with breakfast only
Gasthof	hotel
Gästehaus	bed-and-breakfast hotel
Gasthaus	restaurant, inn

German	English
Gaststube	common room
Gebirge	mountain group
Gefährlich	dangerous
Gemse	chamois
Geröllhalde	scree
Geschlossen	closed
Gipfel	summit, peak
Gletscher	glacier (western Alps)
Gletscherspalte	crevasse
Gondelbahn	gondola lift
Grat	ridge
Haltestelle	bus stop
Heilbad	spa
Hoch	high
Höhe	altitude, height
Höhenweg	high route or path
Hilfe	help
Hirsch	red deer
Hütte	mountain hut
Hüttenwirt	hut warden
Joch	pass or col
Jugendherberge	youth hostel
Kamm	crest or ridge
Kopf	peak
Kumme	combe or small valley
Landgrenze	boundary
Landkarte	map
Landschaft	landscape
Lawine	avalanche
Lebensmittel	grocery, foodstuffs

German	English
Leicht	easy
Links	left (direction)
Materialseilbahn	goods lift
Matratzenlager	dormitory
Moräne	moraine
Nebel	low cloud, mist
Nord	north
Nur für Geübte	only for the experienced
Ober	upper
Ost	east
Pfad	path
Pickel	ice axe
Postamt	post office
Rechts	right (direction)
Regen	rain
Reh	roe deer
Sattel	saddle or pass
Scharte	narrow gap or pass
Schlafraum	bedroom, dormitory
Schlepplift	Ski lift/drag lift
Schlucht	gorge
Schlüssel	key
Schnee	snow
Schnell	quick
Schwierig	difficult
See	lake
Seil	rope
Seilbahn	cable car
Selbstversorger	self-catering only
Selbstversorgerraum	self-catering room

German	English
Sesselbahn	chairlift
Sessellift	chairlift
Speisekarte	menu
Spitze	summit or peak
Stausee	reservoir
Steig	steep path, climb
Steigeisen	crampons
Steil	steep
Steinmann	cairn
Steinschlag	rockfall
Stunde(n)	hour(s)
Sud	south
Tal	valley
Tauern	pass
Teewasser	hot water for drinks
Telefon	telephone
Trockenraum	drying room

German	English
Über	via or over
Unfall	accident
Unterkunft	accommodation
Verkehrsverein	tourist office
Wald	forest, woodland
Wanderweg	footpath
Wasser	water
Weit	far
Weiter	farther
Wetter	weather
Wildbach	torrent
Zahnradbahn	rack railway
Zelt	tent
Zeltplatz	campsite
Zimmer	room
Zimmerfrei	vacancies

APPENDIX E
Index of Routes

	Rätikon Alps	Grade	Time	Page
1	Douglass Hut – Lünersee Circuit – Douglass Hut	1	1¾hrs	49
2	Douglass Hut – Totalp Hut – Douglass Hut	3	3hrs	50
3	Douglass Hut – Schesaplana	3	3hrs	52
4	Douglass Hut – Cavelljoch – Douglass Hut	2	3hrs	53
5	Rätikon Höhenweg Nord	3	3 days	55
6	Tschagguns (Latschun) – Lindauer Hut	2	2½hrs	61
7	Tilisuna Hut – Sulzfluh	3	2hrs	63
	Silvretta Alps	**Grade**	**Time**	**Page**
8	Gaschurn – Tübinger Hut	2–3	4–4½hrs	73
9	Tübinger Hut – Hochmaderer Joch – Bielerhöhe	3	4–4¼hrs	74
10	Bielerhöhe – Saarbrucker Hut	2	3hrs	77
11	Wiesbadener Hut – Litzner Sattel – Saarburcker Hut	3	4½hrs	79
12	Bielerhöhe – Wiesbadener Hut – Bielerhöhe	2–3	5–6hrs	80
13	Galtür – Jamtal Hut	1–2	3hrs	85
14	Hut to Hut Across the Silvretta Alps	3	5 days	89
	Ötztal Alps	**Grade**	**Time**	**Page**
15	Hut to Hut Across the Ötztal Alps	3	3 days	103
16	Obergurgl – Schönwies Hut – Rotmoostal	2–3	3hrs	111
17	Obergurgl – Langtalereck Hut	2–3	2½hrs	114
18	Langtalereck Hut – Hochwilde Haus	3	2hrs	116
	Stubai Alps	**Grade**	**Time**	**Page**
19	Circular Walk from Gries-im-Sulztal	1	1½hrs	131
20	Gries-im-Sulztal – Winnebachsee Hut	3	2½hrs	132
21	Gries-im-Sulztal – Amberger Hut	2	2hrs	134
22	Hut to Hut in the Northwest Stubai Alps	3	4 days	139

23	Neder – Innsbrucker Hut	2	4–4½hrs	143
24	Ranalt – Nürnberger Hut	2–3	2½hrs	147
25	Nürnberger Hut – Grünausee	3	1¾–2hrs	148
26	Oberiss – Franz Senn Hut	1	1½hrs	151
27	Franz Senn Hut – Rinnensee	2–3	1½hrs	152
28	The Stubaier Höhenweg	3	7–9 days	155

Zillertal Alps		Grade	Time	Page
29	Ramsau (Sonnalm) – Mayrhofen	2	3–4hrs	169
30	Mayrhofen – Finkenberg – Mayrhofen	1–2	3–3½hrs	170
31	Penkenalm – Niedermoor – Penkenalm	1–2	2½hrs	173
32	Zillergrund Reservoir – Plauener Hut	2–3	1½hrs	175
33	Madseit – Höllenstein Hut – Lanersbach	2	3hrs	178
34	Breitlahner – Berliner Hut	2	3hrs	181
35	Schlegeis Reservoir – Pfitscher-Joch-Haus	2	1¾–2hrs	185
36	The Berliner Höhenweg	3	3–4 days	187
37	The Zillertal Höhenweg	3	8–9 days	191

Kitzbüheler Alps		Grade	Time	Page
38	Söll – Scheffau	1	2hrs	203
39	Ellmau (Hartkaiser) – Hochsöll	1–2	4hrs	206
40	Ellmau (Hartkaiser) – Rahnhartalm – Ellmau	1	3hrs	208
41	Westendorf – Brixen im Thale – Westendorf	1	3hrs	210
42	Westendorf – Einködlscharte – Westendorf	3	6½–7hrs	214
43	Talkaser – Brechhornhaus – Talkaser	1	2–2½hrs	217
44	Talkaser – Gampenkogel – Talkaser	3	3–3½hrs	219
45	Talkaser – Brixenbachgraben Valley – Brixen	2–3	2½–3hrs	220
46	Brixen – Hochbrixen – Söll	3	3½hrs	222
47	Kitzbühel (Hahnenkamm) – Schwarzkogel	2	3½hrs	225
48	Hechenmoos – Bochumer Hut	2	1½hrs	228
49	Hechenmoos – Tristkogel – Hechenmoos	3	6–6½hrs	230
50	Saalbach – Hinterglemm – Lindlingalm	1	3hrs	234

Kitzbüheler Alps (continued)	Grade	Time	Page
51 Mitterlengau – Tristkogel – Hochtorsee	2–3	3–3½hrs	239
52 Saalbach – Spielberghaus – Burgeralm	1–2	1½hrs	241
53 Saalbach – Spielberghaus – Kleberkopf	2–3	3hrs	243
54 Kohlmaiskopf – Spielberghorn – Saalbach	2–3	5½hrs	245
55 Kohlmaiskopf – Geierkogel – Viehhofen	2–3	4½–5hrs	248
56 Schattberg – Klinglertörl – Zell am See	3	5–6hrs	250
57 Zell am See – Thumersbach – Zell am See	1	2½–3hrs	255
58 Schmittenhöhe – Viehhofen	2–3	2½hrs	258
59 Schmittenhöhe – Maurerkogel – Schmittenhöhe	2–3	4–4½hrs	260
Kaisergebirge	**Grade**	**Time**	**Page**
60 Kufstein – Hinterbärenbad – Hans-Berger-Haus	2	3hrs	269
61 Kufstein – Vorderkaiserfelden Hut	2	2½hrs	273
62 Vorderkaiserfelden Hut – Pyramidenspitze	3	2½hrs	274
63 Kufstein – Stripsenjochhaus	3	5½–6hrs	275
64 Stripsenjochhaus – Ellmauer Tor – Grutten Hut	3	3½–4hrs	278
65 Söll – Hintersteiner See – Söll	2	6½–7hrs	281
66 Scheffau – Riedl Hut – Ellmau	3	5hrs	285
67 Ellmau – Grutten Hut – Ellmau	3	4–4½hrs	288
68 The Wilder-Kaiser-Steig	3	2 days	291
69 Griesenau – Griesner Alm	1	1½hrs	294
70 Griesenau – Stripsenjochhaus	2	3hrs	297
71 Griesner Alm – Feldberg – Griesner Alm	3	5½–6hrs	298
72 A Tour of the Wilder Kaiser	3	4 days	300
Dachsteingebirge	**Grade**	**Time**	**Page**
73 Filzmoos – Hofpürgl Hut – Sulzenalm – Filzmoos	3	4½–5hrs	308
74 Filzmoos – Sulzenalm – Filzmoos	2	2½–3hrs	312
75 The Gosaukamm Circuit	3	2 days	314
76 Bachlalm – Dachstein-Südwand Hut – Bachlalm	3	4½–5hrs	317
77 Bachlalm – Sulzenhals – Rötelstein	3	2½hrs	321

78	Bachlalm – Hofpürgl Hut – Filzmoos	3	5½–6hrs	322
79	Vorderer Gosausee – Hintere Seealm	1–2	2hrs	326
80	Steeg-Gosau – Hallstatt – Steeg-Gosau	2	4hrs	327

Hohe Tauern		**Grade**	**Time**	**Page**
81	Badgastein – Palfnersee – Badgastein	2	4–4½hrs	343
82	Badgastein – Graukogel – Badgastein	3	5½hrs	345
83	Badgastein – Böckstein – Badgastein	2–3	3hrs	348
84	Badgastein – Oberer Bockhartsee – Sportgastein	3	5hrs	351
85	Kaprun – Krefelder Hut	2–3	4hrs	356
86	Krefelder Hut – Salzburger Hut – Kaprun	2–3	4hrs	358
87	Mooserboden – Scharfer Grat	2	2hrs	360
88	Mooserboden – Heinrich-Schwaiger-Haus	2–3	2½hrs	362
89	Mooserboden – Austriaweg	1	1½hrs	363
90	Hut to Hut Across the Glockner Group	3	6–7 days	365
91	Matreier Tauernhaus – Innergschlöss	1	1¼hrs	372
92	Innergschlöss – Ochsnerwaldweg – Innergschlöss	3	2½hrs	375
93	Ströden – Essener-Rostocker Hut	2–3	2½–3hrs	377
94	The Venediger Höhenweg	3	6–7 days	379
95	Europa Panoramaweg	1–2	3hrs	384
96	Matrei – Sudetendeutsche Hut – Matrei	3	2 days	387
97	Lucknerhaus – Stüdl Hut	2–3	2½–3hrs	390
98	Lucknerhaus – Glorer Hut – Lucknerhaus	3	3½–4hrs	393

Karawanken		**Grade**	**Time**	**Page**
99	Barental – Klagenfurter Hut	1–2	1½hrs	403
100	Klagenfurter Hut – Bielschitza	3	1hr	406
101	Schaidasattel – Hochobir	2	3hrs	409

NOTES

NOTES

NOTES

NOTES

LISTING OF CICERONE GUIDES

BRITISH ISLES CHALLENGES, COLLECTIONS AND ACTIVITIES

The End to End Trail
The Mountains of England and Wales
  1 Wales & 2 England
The National Trails
The Relative Hills of Britain
The Ridges of England, Wales and Ireland
The UK Trailwalker's Handbook
The UK's County Tops
Three Peaks, Ten Tors

UK CYCLING

Border Country Cycle Routes
Cycling in the Hebrides
Cycling in the Peak District
Cycling in the Yorkshire Dales
Cycling the Pennine Bridleway
Mountain Biking in the Lake District
Mountain Biking in the Yorkshire Dales
Mountain Biking on the North Downs
Mountain Biking on the South Downs
The C2C Cycle Route
The End to End Cycle Route
The Lancashire Cycleway

SCOTLAND

Backpacker's Britain
  Central and Southern Scottish Highlands
  Northern Scotland
Ben Nevis and Glen Coe
Great Mountain Days in Scotland
Not the West Highland Way
Scotland's Best Small Mountains
Scotland's Far West
Scotland's Mountain Ridges
Scrambles in Lochaber
The Ayrshire and Arran Coastal Paths
The Border Country
The Cape Wrath Trail
The Great Glen Way
The Isle of Mull
The Isle of Skye
The Pentland Hills

The Scottish Glens 2 – The Atholl Glens
The Southern Upland Way
The Speyside Way
The West Highland Way
Walking Highland Perthshire
Walking in Scotland's Far North
Walking in the Angus Glens
Walking in the Cairngorms
Walking in the Ochils, Campsie Fells and Lomond Hills
Walking in Torridon
Walking Loch Lomond and the Trossachs
Walking on Harris and Lewis
Walking on Jura, Islay and Colonsay
Walking on Rum and the Small Isles
Walking on the Isle of Arran
Walking on the Orkney and Shetland Isles
Walking on Uist and Barra
Walking the Corbetts
  1 South of the Great Glen
  2 North of the Great Glen
Walking the Galloway Hills
Walking the Lowther Hills
Walking the Munros
  1 Southern, Central and Western Highlands
  2 Northern Highlands and the Cairngorms
Winter Climbs Ben Nevis and Glen Coe
Winter Climbs in the Cairngorms
World Mountain Ranges: Scotland

NORTHERN ENGLAND TRAILS

A Northern Coast to Coast Walk
Backpacker's Britain Northern England
Hadrian's Wall Path
The Dales Way
The Pennine Way

NORTH EAST ENGLAND, YORKSHIRE DALES AND PENNINES

Great Mountain Days in the Pennines
Historic Walks in North Yorkshire
South Pennine Walks

St Oswald's Way and St Cuthbert's Way
The Cleveland Way and the Yorkshire Wolds Way
The North York Moors
The Reivers Way
The Teesdale Way
The Yorkshire Dales
  North and East
  South and West
Walking in County Durham
Walking in Northumberland
Walking in the North Pennines
Walks in Dales Country
Walks in the Yorkshire Dales
Walks on the North York Moors – Books 1 & 2

NORTH WEST ENGLAND AND THE ISLE OF MAN

Historic Walks in Cheshire
Isle of Man Coastal Path
The Isle of Man
The Lune Valley and Howgills
The Ribble Way
Walking in Cumbria's Eden Valley
Walking in Lancashire
Walking in the Forest of Bowland and Pendle
Walking on the West Pennine Moors
Walks in Lancashire Witch Country
Walks in Ribble Country
Walks in Silverdale and Arnside
Walks in the Forest of Bowland

LAKE DISTRICT

Coniston Copper Mines
Great Mountain Days in the Lake District
Lake District Winter Climbs
Lakeland Fellranger
  The Central Fells
  The Far-Eastern Fells
  The Mid-Western Fells
  The Near Eastern Fells
  The Northern Fells
  The North-Western Fells
  The Southern Fells
  The Western Fells
Roads and Tracks of the Lake District

Rocky Rambler's Wild Walks
Scrambles in the Lake District
    North & South
Short Walks in Lakeland
    1 South Lakeland
    2 North Lakeland
    3 West Lakeland
The Cumbria Coastal Way
The Cumbria Way and the
    Allerdale Ramble
Tour of the Lake District

**DERBYSHIRE, PEAK DISTRICT
AND MIDLANDS**

High Peak Walks
Scrambles in the Dark Peak
The Star Family Walks
Walking in Derbyshire
White Peak Walks
    The Northern Dales
    The Southern Dales

SOUTHERN ENGLAND

Suffolk Coast & Heaths Walks
The Cotswold Way
The North Downs Way
The Peddars Way and Norfolk
    Coast Path
The Ridgeway National Trail
The South Downs Way
The South West Coast Path
The Thames Path
Walking in Berkshire
Walking in Essex
Walking in Kent
Walking in Norfolk
Walking in Sussex
Walking in the Isles of Scilly
Walking in the New Forest
Walking in the Thames Valley
Walking on Dartmoor
Walking on Guernsey
Walking on Jersey
Walking on the Isle of Wight
Walks in the South Downs
    National Park

WALES AND WELSH BORDERS

Backpacker's Britain – Wales
Glyndwr's Way
Great Mountain Days
    in Snowdonia
Hillwalking in Snowdonia
Hillwalking in Wales: 1&2
Offa's Dyke Path
Ridges of Snowdonia

Scrambles in Snowdonia
The Ascent of Snowdon
Lleyn Peninsula Coastal Path
Pembrokeshire Coastal Path
The Shropshire Hills
The Wye Valley Walk
Walking in Pembrokeshire
Walking in the Forest of Dean
Walking in the South
    Wales Valleys
Walking on Gower
Walking on the Brecon Beacons
Welsh Winter Climbs

**INTERNATIONAL
CHALLENGES, COLLECTIONS
AND ACTIVITIES**

Canyoning
Europe's High Points
The Via Francigena
    (Canterbury to Rome): 1&2

EUROPEAN CYCLING

Cycle Touring in France
Cycle Touring in Ireland
Cycle Touring in Spain
Cycle Touring in Switzerland
Cycling in the French Alps
Cycling the Canal du Midi
Cycling the River Loire
The Danube Cycleway
The Grand Traverse of the
    Massif Central
The Rhine Cycle Route
The Way of St James

AFRICA

Climbing in the Moroccan
    Anti-Atlas
Kilimanjaro
Mountaineering in the Moroccan
    High Atlas
The High Atlas
Trekking in the Atlas Mountains
Walking in the Drakensberg

**ALPS – CROSS-BORDER
ROUTES**

100 Hut Walks in the Alps
Across the Eastern Alps: E5
Alpine Points of View
Alpine Ski Mountaineering
    1 Western Alps
    2 Central and Eastern Alps
Chamonix to Zermatt
Snowshoeing

Tour of Mont Blanc
Tour of Monte Rosa
Tour of the Matterhorn
Trekking in the Alps
Walking in the Alps
Walks and Treks in the
    Maritime Alps

**PYRENEES AND FRANCE/
SPAIN CROSS-BORDER
ROUTES**

Rock Climbs in the Pyrenees
The GR10 Trail
The Mountains of Andorra
The Pyrenean Haute Route
The Pyrenees
The Way of St James
    France & Spain
Through the Spanish Pyrenees:
    GR11
Walks and Climbs in the Pyrenees

AUSTRIA

The Adlerweg
Trekking in Austria's
    Hohe Tauern
Trekking in the Stubai Alps
Trekking in the Zillertal Alps
Walking in Austria

EASTERN EUROPE

The High Tatras
The Mountains of Romania
Walking in Bulgaria's
    National Parks
Walking in Hungary

FRANCE

Chamonix Mountain Adventures
Ecrins National Park
GR20: Corsica
Mont Blanc Walks
Mountain Adventures in
    the Maurienne
The Cathar Way
The GR5 Trail
The Robert Louis Stevenson Trail
Tour of the Oisans: The GR54
Tour of the Queyras
Tour of the Vanoise
Trekking in the Vosges and Jura
Vanoise Ski Touring
Via Ferratas of the French Alps
Walking in the Auvergne
Walking in the Cathar Region
Walking in the Cevennes

Walking in the Dordogne
Walking in the Haute Savoie
    North & South
Walking in the Languedoc
Walking in the Tarentaise and
    Beaufortain Alps
Walking on Corsica

GERMANY
Germany's Romantic Road
Hiking and Biking in the
    Black Forest
Walking in the Bavarian Alps
Walking the River Rhine Trail

HIMALAYA
Annapurna
Bhutan
Everest: A Trekker's Guide
Garhwal and Kumaon:
    A Trekker's and Visitor's Guide
Kangchenjunga:
    A Trekker's Guide
Langtang with Gosainkund
    and Helambu:
    A Trekker's Guide
Manaslu: A Trekker's Guide
The Mount Kailash Trek
Trekking in Ladakh
Trekking in the Himalaya

ICELAND & GREENLAND
Trekking in Greenland
Walking and Trekking in Iceland

IRELAND
Irish Coastal Walks
The Irish Coast to Coast Walk
The Mountains of Ireland

ITALY
Gran Paradiso
Sibillini National Park
Štelvio National Park
Shorter Walks in the Dolomites
Through the Italian Alps
Trekking in the Apennines
Trekking in the Dolomites
Via Ferratas of the Italian
    Dolomites: Vols 1 & 2
Walking in Abruzzo
Walking in Sardinia
Walking in Sicily
Walking in the Central
    Italian Alps

Walking in the Dolomites
Walking in Tuscany
Walking on the Amalfi Coast
Walking the Italian Lakes

MEDITERRANEAN
Jordan – Walks, Treks, Caves,
    Climbs and Canyons
The Ala Dag
The High Mountains of Crete
The Mountains of Greece
Treks and Climbs in Wadi Rum,
    Jordan
Walking in Malta
Western Crete

NORTH AMERICA
British Columbia
The Grand Canyon
The John Muir Trail
The Pacific Crest Trail

SOUTH AMERICA
Aconcagua and the
    Southern Andes
Hiking and Biking Peru's
    Inca Trails
Torres del Paine

SCANDINAVIA
Walking in Norway

**SLOVENIA, CROATIA AND
MONTENEGRO**
The Julian Alps of Slovenia
The Mountains of Montenegro
Trekking in Slovenia
Walking in Croatia
Walking in Slovenia:
    The Karavanke

SPAIN AND PORTUGAL
Costa Blanca: West
Mountain Walking in
    Southern Catalunya
The Mountains of Central Spain
The Northern Caminos
Trekking through Mallorca
Walking in Madeira
Walking in Mallorca
Walking in Menorca
Walking in the Algarve
Walking in the Cordillera
    Cantabrica
Walking in the Sierra Nevada
Walking on Gran Canaria

Walking on La Gomera and
    El Hierro
Walking on La Palma
Walking on Tenerife
Walking the GR7 in Andalucia
Walks and Climbs in the
    Picos de Europa

SWITZERLAND
Alpine Pass Route
Canyoning in the Alps
Central Switzerland
The Bernese Alps
The Swiss Alps
Tour of the Jungfrau Region
Walking in the Valais
Walking in Ticino
Walks in the Engadine

TECHNIQUES
Geocaching in the UK
Indoor Climbing
Lightweight Camping
Map and Compass
Mountain Weather
Moveable Feasts
Outdoor Photography
Polar Exploration
Rock Climbing
Sport Climbing
The Book of the Bivvy
The Hillwalker's Guide to
    Mountaineering
The Hillwalker's Manual

MINI GUIDES
Alpine Flowers
Avalanche!
Navigating with a GPS
Navigation
Pocket First Aid and
    Wilderness Medicine
Snow

MOUNTAIN LITERATURE
8000m
A Walk in the Clouds
Unjustifiable Risk?

For full information on all our
guides, and to order books and
eBooks, visit our website:
www.cicerone.co.uk.

Walking – Trekking – Mountaineering – Climbing – Cycling

Over 40 years, Cicerone have built up an outstanding collection of 300 guides, inspiring all sorts of amazing adventures.

 Every guide comes from extensive exploration and research by our expert authors, all with a passion for their subjects. They are frequently praised, endorsed and used by clubs, instructors and outdoor organisations.

All our titles can now be bought as **e-books** and many as iPad and Kindle files and we will continue to make all our guides available for these and many other devices.

Our website shows any **new information** we've received since a book was published. Please do let us know if you find anything has changed, so that we can pass on the latest details. On our **website** you'll also find some great ideas and lots of information, including sample chapters, contents lists, reviews, articles and a photo gallery.

It's easy to keep in touch with what's going on at Cicerone, by getting our monthly **free e-newsletter**, which is full of offers, competitions, up-to-date information and topical articles. You can subscribe on our home page and also follow us on **Facebook** and **Twitter**, as well as our **blog**.

Cicerone – the very best guides for exploring the world.

CICERONE

2 Police Square Milnthorpe Cumbria LA7 7PY
Tel: 015395 62069 info@cicerone.co.uk
www.cicerone.co.uk